DATE DUE			
Mar 16 79			

Sociocultural Dimensions of Language Change

LANGUAGE, THOUGHT, AND CULTURE: *Advances in the Study of Cognition*

Under the Editorship of: E. A. HAMMEL

DEPARTMENT OF ANTHROPOLOGY
UNIVERSITY OF CALIFORNIA
BERKELEY

Michael Agar, Ripping and Running: A Formal Ethnography of Urban Heroin Addicts

Brent Berlin, Dennis E. Breedlove, and Peter H. Raven, Principles of Tzeltal Plant Classification: An Introduction to the Botanical Ethnography of a Mayan-Speaking People of Highland Chiapas

Mary Sanches and Ben Blount, Sociocultural Dimensions of Language Use

Daniel G. Bobrow and Allan Collins, Representation and Understanding: Studies in Cognitive Science

Domenico Parisi and Francesco Antinucci, Essentials of Grammar

Elizabeth Bates, Language and Context: The Acquisition of Pragmatics

Ben G. Blount and Mary Sanches, Sociocultural Dimensions of Language Change

Susan Ervin-Tripp and Claudia Mitchell-Kernan (Eds.), Child Discourse

In preparation

Eugene S. Hunn, Tzeltal Folk Zoology: The Classification of Discontinuities in Nature

James N. Schenkein (Ed.), Studies in the Organization of Conversational Interaction

Sociocultural Dimensions of Language Change

Edited by

BEN G. BLOUNT

MARY SANCHES

Department of Anthropology
University of Texas
Austin, Texas

With an introduction by John J. Gumperz

ACADEMIC PRESS   *New York San Francisco London*

A Subsidiary of Harcourt Brace Jovanovich, Publishers

301.21

So 1

103610

Jan. 1978

ACADEMIC PRESS, INC.
111 Fifth Avenue, New York, New York 10003

United Kingdom Edition published by
ACADEMIC PRESS, INC. (LONDON) LTD.
24/28 Oval Road, London NW1

Library of Congress Cataloging in Publication Data

Main entry under title:

Sociocultural dimensions of language change.

(Language, thought, and culture series)
Includes bibliographies and index.
1.   Linguistic change—Addresses, essays,
lectures.   2.   Sociolinguistics—Addresses, essays,
lectures.   3.   Anthropological linguistics—
Addresses, essays, lectures.   I.   Blount, Ben G.,
Date   II.   Sanches, Mary.
P142.S6   301.2'1   76-2943
ISBN 0–12–107450–1

Contents

List of Contributors

Numbers in parentheses indicate the pages on which the author's contributions begin.

Ned Anderson (227), Office of Arid Land Studies, University of Arizona, Tuscon, Arizona

Keith H. Basso (227), Department of Anthropology, University of Arizona, Tuscon, Arizona

Brent Berlin (63), Department of Anthropology, University of California, Berkeley, California

Ben G. Blount (1), Department of Anthropology, University of Texas, Austin, Texas

Lilyan A. Brudner (271), Department of Anthropology, University of Pittsburgh, Pittsburgh, Pennsylvania

Janet Wynne Dixon Dougherty (103), Department of Linguistics, Massachusetts Institute of Technology, Cambridge, Massachusetts, and Department of Anthropology, University of California, Berkeley, California

Robert French (35), Department of Anthropology, Harvard University, Cambridge, Massachusetts

Ian F. Hancock (161), Department of English, University of Texas, Austin, Texas

Nicholas A. Hopkins (185), Centro de Investigaciones Superiores del Instituto Nacional de Antropología Historia, Mexico

Frances Karttunen (173), Department of Linguistics, University of Texas, Austin, Texas

Paul Kay (21), Department of Anthropology, University of California, Berkeley, California

Keith T. Kernan (35), Neuropsychiatric Insitute, Mental Retardation Center, University of California, Los Angeles, California

ix

Carol H. Molony (131), Universität Essen, Gesamthochschule Anglistik, Essen, Germany

Joan Rubin (253), East-West Center, University of Hawaii, Honolulu, Hawaii

Mary Sanches (1, 51), Department of Anthropology, University of Texas, Austin, Texas

Gillian Sankoff (119), Department of Anthropology, University of Montreal, Montreal, Quebec, Canada

John Sodergren (35), Department of Anthropology, Harvard University, Cambridge, Massachusetts

Preface

Each of the articles in this collection deals with the topic of language change. In that respect, they continue a long fruitful area of scholarship. The study of changes in the forms of languages has been a rich field of inquiry, but considerably less attention has been devoted to changes in sociocultural terms. The articles here raise questions about language as a social phenomenon functioning in cultural contexts. While building on the solid foundations of earlier research in linguistic structure and linguistic change, they suggest a new, broader perspective. Language is treated in terms of a social and cultural world. Changes in language form must require not only a linguistic accounting but a social description and explanation. Changes of form may often involve differences in communication, though a particular change in form may be linguistically minimal. What is significant is the interpretation given to the change, and that significance must be described in sociocultural terms and dimensions.

These dimensions are theoretically diverse in scope and number, and include factors such as age, sex, generation and status differences, ritual, community contact and boundaries, urbanization, religious affiliation, and political organization. The particular social factors and cultural bases that operate to produce change also vary from situation to situation, and a major objective of research is to determine precisely what complex of sociocultural dimensions are present and activated in a given language change situation. It is to that objective that the articles in this collection are mainly addressed, and the authors illustrate clearly that the appropriate perspective is sociological/anthropological and that the necessary research methodology is ethnographic.

An anthropological perspective is an asset, if not a necessity, in a sociocultural approach to language change, since changes in language structure are related to and often dependent on social action and interaction in a speech community. An investigator of change must consider the uses of language and the diverse functions of language within the daily social intercourse of a community. A detailed, sensitive ethnographic record of the routines is the first priority of research, and it is in this regard that sociology and anthropology are in strong position to make timely contributions. We hope that this collection will stimulate further social research on the dynamics of language change.

Acknowledgments

We would like to express our gratitude to the contributors, first for their cooperation, and second, for their patience throughout the inevitable delays in producing the volume. Also, some liberties were taken in the interpretation of the articles in the Introduction. As case studies, the articles are individual units and stand on their own. Several were not written specifically to document language change, although they all contain discussions of change. We stressed in the Introduction the implications of the case studies for language, and we wish to emphasize that our selective interpretation did not always do justice to the articles in terms of content or focus.

We are grateful to John Gumperz for his encouragement and support during the preparation of this collection. Helpful suggestions and comments were also provided by Jan Brukman, Keith and Claudia Kernan, Brian Stross, and Dorothy Wills. We also thank Holly Hayataka and Janice Edmiston for assistance with the typing of the manuscripts. Our deepest debt of gratitude is to Elise Padgug for her editorial assistance and for her good-humored patience and support throughout the project.

Foreword: Sociocultural Dimensions of Language Change

JOHN J. GUMPERZ

In dealing with the interrelationship of linguistic and social processes of change, this volume takes up a familiar theme. Modern linguistics, as the editors point out in their introduction, developed out of a concern with history and evolution. Throughout the nineteenth and for much of the present century, the study of language was seen as an integral part of the wider search into the cultural origins of modern societies. This inquiry was motivated in part by abstract scientific interest, but in part also by the desire to provide a historical basis for and thus legitimize the national ideologies of the newly formed nation states.

Because of the lack of direct documentary sources and the great gaps in the published literature, scholars began to seek new ways of recovering what the German Romantics had called Versunkenes Volksgut, the "sunken treasures" of the past. Along with the quest for new unpublished folk manuscripts, the search for historical evidence also stimulated direct ethnographic investigation of tribal languages and peasant dialects throughout the world. The need to commit spoken words to paper led to the rediscovery of the ancient Indian science of phonetics and ultimately to modern grammatical theory.

Since the turn of the century, comparative analysis of both written and hitherto unrecorded languages has become established as a major tool of culture history. Among other things, it has clarified the role that folk traditions play in the growth of modern nation states, so that it is now generally recognized, for example, that the classical cultures to which we trace so many of our modern institutions are not the only sources of civilization. They are themselves descended from earlier preliterate cultures similar to the folk societies that existed alongside them and that continue to exist in many parts of the world. It follows that literary traditions and written codes of law are not a prerequisite for the existence of historically stable forms of social life. A common language provides the essential antecedents from which more complex forms of social sharing can evolve.

Although initially unintended, from the point of view of social science, perhaps the most important consequence of the efforts to account for the multivariate patterns of language uncovered by the early historical studies was the development of the construct of grammar as the underlying explanatory dynamic of all language behavior. Grammatical rules can be regarded as reflecting abstract, functionally related symbolic processes that constrain and channel our perception of environmental and behavioral cues. These rules are learned indirectly through early informal childhood socialization and subsequent interactive experience and thus reflect the conventions and values of interacting groups. They operate automatically as motor habits and are for the most part not immediately accessible to conscious recall. Yet although sharedness of grammatical rules is not usually overtly discussed, it is nevertheless taken for granted in everyday communication and in fact is a precondition of successful interaction. In other words, the mere fact that human populations live together successfully, cooperate in the pursuit of their daily affairs, and interact using a particular set of speech varieties is in itself prima facie evidence for the existence of stable systems of values and functionally related rules, which are subject to the same laws of change as those of the better known classical literary societies.

Although all human groups have language, and at the highest, most general level of abstraction all grammatical processes are similar, the actual form that language usage takes in any one population is a function of the history and the culture of that population. The way individuals express what they want to communicate, apart from the content it conveys, also provides information about speakers' social background and about the relationship to others. Potentially at least, therefore, language study could become an important source of information about otherwise unverbalized and relatively inaccessible social processes. So far, however, in spite of many insightful statements by nineteenth century pioneers of anthropology such as Humboldt, as well as Sapir, Whorf, and many others since them in this century, the value of linguistics to the study of social relations and social change has not been worked through theoretically.

The disciplines of linguistics and social relations studies have developed independently of each other, despite attempts to bring about intellectual collaboration. The linguist's concern with culture has remained limited to long-term prehistoric change, no systematic attempts have been made to use language data in the study of ongoing social processes. In fact, during the last decades, as our knowledge of languages increased and awareness of the real complexity of grammatical processes grew, attention has increasingly turned away from the sociocultural implications of verbal behavior to concentrate on the formal aspects of grammatical rules themselves. The shift in interest began with the structural linguists of the nineteen forties and fifties and, paradoxically, received its greatest impetus from the generative grammar of Noam Chomsky. Chomsky's use of data from English syntax to demonstrate the claim that stimulus response theories of behavior cannot account for the real complexity of human cognitive processes has opened up new areas of research in a wide range of disciplines. But the thrust of these developments has been in the direction of seeking explanations in terms of universal, individual psychological processes, rather than in the direction of a sociological concern with the recognition of social difference and social change. Furthermore, since it was the abstract structural relationships in terms of which the rules are couched that were seen to reflect the connection between language and human behavior, priority was assigned to increasing the logical consistency and explanatory power of formalizations as such. As so often happens, this also meant a narrowing of the data base. Only those verbal abilities that could be accounted for in terms of the existing research paradigms, such as the most widely shared core features of phonology, morphology, and syntax were recognized as grammatical. Others were set aside as part of performance, i.e., not part of grammatical competence and thus perhaps not subject to systematization. Thus, formal linguistic analysis became an exercize in abstraction divorced from the study of everyday verbal abilities.

The articles in this book, by contrast, take a different perspective and concentrate directly on those levels of language that most clearly reflect and signal social differences and are thus most readily affected by change. By demonstrating that the linguistic phenomena in question can be accounted for in terms of underlying rules, which, while perhaps less widely shared, are directly related in form and function to those governing the more commonly studied grammatical phenomena, these articles attempt to restore a historical and social perspective to the study of language change.

Contributions fall into three main thematic areas: lexical semantics, speech variation and language contact, and incipient processes of language change. The first two of these fields have already begun to receive increasing attention. Following the pioneering writings of Sapir and Whorf, linguistic anthropologists during the last two decades have embarked on in-depth analyses of terminological systems in domains such as kinship, color terms, and ethnobotany, to name just a few, in a number of folk societies and have provided empirical verification on the effect that language has on speakers' perception of behavioral cues. Several papers in this volume add a new comparative dimension to this work by showing that the structure of lexical systems changes with changes in the socioeconomic complexity of the social systems in which it is embedded and that the acquisition of lexical rules in childhood follows stages that are similar to the stages revealed in the learning of grammatical rules. Other papers, for the first time, explore the transition between terminological conventions and grammatical rules, concentrating on pidgin and creole language areas, where innovations arising at the level of lexicon gradually become incorporated into grammar as the functions of speech and the activities it reflects change.

Language variation and contact studies have become well known recently through the sociolinguistic surveys of phonological and syntactic variability in urban centers. The systematic analysis of spoken texts reflecting such variations in statistically significant samples of populations shows that macrosociological variables as class, education, sex, and ethnic origin directly affect language usage. Variable rules of grammar can be written that incorporate the social factors, and such rules both serve as linguistic indicators of group identity and as predictors of ongoing trends of change. Several studies here examine variation in Central American Indian and creole-speaking societies. It is shown that speakers' selection among such variables at the level of interpersonal relations signals both social background and cultural values. Innovations tend to diffuse along the networks of social relationships that underlie locally relevant sub-groupings.

The third theme, that of the initiation of innovation, significant as it is for understanding the social causes of change, has so far received relatively little attention on the part of modern scholars. Three major sources of change are considered here: (1) lexical borrowings resulting from worldwide processes of urbanization and integration of local societies into supralocal and international marketing and communication systems; (2) intentionally created change such as arise when new writing systems are created or when language planning requires the coinage of new words or the standardization of variants to comply with the communicative requirements of modern bureaucratic systems; (3) informal innovations that arise in the course of repetitive activities in task-oriented settings such as psychiatric sessions. Since the success of such sessions depenends on the interactants' ability to develop agreed ways of perceiving and verbally categorizing events, the study of such activities provides a good illustration that shared specific tasks in time lead to shared linguistic practices.

As is the case with much anthropological work on language, the papers in this volume point to new problems for investigation and suggest new sources of data and concern. On the surface, the questions raised seem quite similar to those discussed in earlier work on language and culture. What is specific about the contributions here is that they go beyond the mere listing of structural similarities between grammatical and cultural systems to isolate specific levels of language where interrelationships can most fruitfully be studied. By concentrating on ongoing processes of change, one begins to see how the communicative requirements of new types of situations and the conventions governing successful cooperation in these situations lead to linguistic innovation. Change can then be traced from its source in language usage and lexical semantics, and the processes both social and linguistic that lead to incorporation of change into grammar can be examined.

Introduction: Sociocultural Dimensions of Language Change

BEN G. BLOUNT
MARY SANCHES

Background

The phenomena of language change have long served as foci for varied research interests in linguistics and anthropology. The emergence, in fact, of linguistics as a scholarly concern stems largely from questions about the history of language, the changes languages manifest, and the origins of language. Evidence of interest in language change is present in the thought of the ancient Greeks and Hindus, but it was in eighteenth and nineteenth century Europe that one of the most important aspects of historical linguistics developed. That development was the comparative method. At least two centuries in developing, the comparative method was established as the cornerstone of historical linguistics by the middle of the nineteenth century, and certainly by the publication of Schleicher's "Die Darwinsche Theorie und Sprachwissenschaft" (1863). This development signified a crystallization in the thinking about the nature of language and relationships among languages, and it also provided a methodology that enabled linguists and, later, anthropologists to trace historically changes in languages and to reconstruct protolanguages.

Schleicher proposed that languages be viewed as objective, historical units subject to scientific analysis. Languages could, in effect, be viewed as autonomous systems independent of their users. Elements of language could be analyzed as purely linguistic facts, extracted from contexts of usage and functions. By isolating aspects of language, especially phonetics, and analyzing them diachronically, regularities in language change were discovered, and general processes and laws of change were identified. Schleicher and his followers, the neogrammarians, advanced the techniques of the comparative method in the latter part of the nineteenth century (see Ardener, 1971; Lehmann, 1968, for reviews), and their work established the comparative method as the proper set of questions to ask about language change, embodying the set of concepts as to what constitutes the data of language change.

1

The comparative method has been immensely useful, allowing linguists to make considerable progress in language reconstructions and discovering regularities in phonetic change, especially in the Indoeuropean languages. Early anthropological research in language change was also heavily indebted to the methodology and techniques of the comparative method. John Wesley Powell (1891) and Franz Boas (1911) produced a classification of families of American Indian languages, and Leonard Bloomfield (1933) applied the comparative method to American Indian languages to determine the genetic relationships among the Algonquian tribes. In addition many of Edward Sapir's contributions to linguistic anthropology were derived from his studies of language change phenomena, including some often cited work on genetic drift (Sapir, 1921).

A development unique to anthropology and built on the discoveries of the comparative method was Morris Swadesh's concept of basic vocabulary and the methodology of lexicostatistics. Shared retentions of basic vocabulary items among related languages could be used, under certain circumstances, to determine the approximate genetic relatedness of the languages (Swadesh, 1951).

While the comparative method continues to be a mainstay of historical linguistics and to be useful in linguistic anthropology, in recent years, new questions have been raised, especially by linguistic anthropologists, about the nature, motivations, and processes of language change. In the tradition of the comparative method, changes were viewed in terms of form (particularly phonetic form) and as self motivating. That is, formal changes in phonetic elements or rules were always seen as motivated by other phonetic rules, processes, or by grammatical segments of the system, but not by elements or units of meaning. The new questions about language change have both emerged from and necessitated the development of new concepts and perspectives on the nature of language and the processes of change. Four major shifts have been isolated that underlie the new approach to the study of language change, and all of them are reflected in the studies in this volume. Two of the changes are conceptual—(1) the extension of the linguistic system beyond classic definitions and (2) a reevaluation of the importance of language variation—and two are topical—(3) renewed interests in the study of contact phenomena and (4) the evolution of language.

Extension of the Concept of Language

The most important of the four developments, in terms of its far-reaching effects in redirecting research and reformulating questions, is a growing recognition that the concept of language must extend far beyond what was traditionally considered to constitute the purely linguistic system. While there has long been a recognition of the special dual nature of language, i.e., the relation of sound and meaning, meaning has been considered to exist outside the structures of the system that produce the relations. The investigation of meaning, and especially social meaning, was at one time considered to be in the province of philosophy or psychology rather than linguistics (see Bloomfield, 1933). Even as interest in the relationship between social aspects of language and language change proceeded, social meaning was considered to be only a correlate of linguistic form. A classic expression of this point of view was given in a statement about the aims of a "sociology of language":

> Since *languages* normally function in a social matrix and since *societies* depend heavily on language as a medium (if not as a symbol) of interaction, it is certainly appropriate to expect that their observable manifestations, language behavior and social behavior, will be appreciably related in many lawful ways . . . Although particular studies in this field of inquiry may more appropriately view either language behavior *or* social behavior as the independent or the dependent variable for their immediate purposes, it is my fundamental bias to view society as being broader than language and, therefore, as providing the context in which all language behavior must ultimately be viewed. (Fishman, 1968, p. 6)

While we agree that language behavior must be viewed within the larger dimensions of society, we do not accept a uniformly sharp cleavage between language and society. Language is fundamentally social behavior, and what were previously discussed as social correlates of language are conceptual distinctions and usually culturally specific.

Two developments beginning in the late 1950s led to those insights and reversed thinking about the order of importance of language features: (1) the role of meaning has become central and is a necessary component of a language model, and (2) linguistic features are now considered primarily in terms of their social aspects and importance. This reordering of priorities and reconceptualization is derived from several sources, but in particular from anthropological concerns with lexicography, cognition, kinship systems and terminology, and systems of nomenclature and taxonomy (see Romney and D'Andrade, 1964; Hammel, 1965; Tyler, 1968). The concern of research was primarily with lexical meaning, but the reopening of the study of meaning as a worthwhile and legitimate endeavor soon prompted more extensive inquiry. For example, semantic analysis of kinship terms led to interest in pronominal and other address and reference systems an area in which the criterial differences in the meanings of forms was expressible only in terms of social concepts (Brown and Gilman, 1960; Brown and Ford, 1961; Friedrich, 1966). The study of meaning was further expanded to include social meaning as expressed in terms of speech functions (Jakobson, 1960; Hymes, 1962), and social interaction variables such as form, message, topic, context, and interactants (Gumperz and Hymes, 1964, 1972). Also, studies of class-differentiated dialects began to see phonetic form as a basis for assignment of social class membership (Wcinreich, Labov, and Herzog, 1968).

The recognition that language is social behavior and that social meaning is a proper subject of study has required a crisp distinction between referential elements of meaning and social meaning. A further distinction is also required between elements internal to a sociolinguistic system and social pressures external to the communication but that have the potential for promoting certain kinds of changes. External social forces that may bring about change are numerous and include such phenomena as invasions, conquests, contact, trade, migrations, institutional changes and restructuring, social movements, and revolutions. Essentially any radical social change, especially where contact between different cultures is involved, brings about a restructuring of the communication system(s), thereby producing language change. The ecology of language is changed in such a way that elements of social meaning change in association with elements of forms.

Language as a social phenomenon has received considerable attention during the past decade. Sociolinguistics has come to enjoy a wide respectability, and its horizons have been expanded to include a variety of topics such as language planning, bilingualism, socialization, and aspects of extra-verbal communication. Social meaning and language change has also been subject to renewed interest and research. Uriel Weinreich, a pioneer in the study of languages in contact, raised questions of sources and motivations of change. He insisted that language be viewed as a system sensitive to social forces and modified, sometimes extensively, by those forces. In "Languages in Contact," Weinreich (1953) outlined sociocultural factors such as ethnicity, religion, sex, language attitudes, and cultural contact as potential forces affecting the types and degrees of linguistic interference for members of a language community. He defined as an ultimate goal of linguistic interference, the ability to predict typical forms of interference, given the sociolinguistic description of a bilingual community and a structural description of its languages (1966 [1953], p. 86). Weinreich's primary interest was in the linguistic system or systems of a language community, and although his treatment of social and linguistic factors was largely correlational, he did make an important advance in the study of language change by insisting that sociocultural factors be considered.

The question of how sociocultural factors influence and modify linguistic systems has come to be one of the principal research topics in the new approach to language change. Weinreich, Labov, and Herzog (1968) addressed themselves to the problem of mechanisms of change and how they operate. Utilizing a sociolinguistic approach to the study of change, they proposed that social assessment of the linguistic variation, inherent in language, is a potential base for change. Variation that becomes meaningfully marked by members of a speech community is regularized and serves to distinguish social differences. The more regular and distinctive the variation becomes, the more effective in demarcating social boundaries it is within the speech community. Changes once initiated may result in restructuring of a formal linguistic system, but the sources of initial change are viewed as sociocultural, i.e., emanating from the social resources of the speech community.

The papers in this volume are all concerned with the issue of social sources and mechanisms of change in languages. For instance, Paul Kay discusses the role of increasing complexity and diversity in producing a more autonomous, context-free language within a speech community. Nicholas Hopkins investigates the relative independence and isolation of Mayan communities in a regional network as the major variable in diffusion of linguistic features and dialect differentiation. On an individual level, to take another example, changes in languages may result from an increased awareness of the code itself, as Lilyan Brudner reports in an analysis of linguistic techniques employed in psychotherapy.

Language Variation

The second fundamental notion in the current redefinition of language change and a second theme in the papers is the inherent variability of language. Language is no longer viewed as a monolith whose structure can be stated in only one expression for a whole community or society. Rather, the perspective is on speech communities, groups of people who share or have overlapping codes, and on speech repertoires, including the societal and individual variation they manifest. Variation is in fact essential for language change, since it provides the material upon which social processes operate to produce significant social dimensions and categories, such as ethnic identification, stratification, group membership, and individual identification. Documentation of variation has become an essential research task in sociolinguistically based accounts of language change.

Individual variation exists at all levels of language and is related to differential sociocultural background. This holds true even in seemingly uniform areas such as semantic domains. For instance, Janet Dougherty demonstrates the considerable variation of West Futunese (New Hebrides) terminology for basic color terms, showing that various stages of development in color classification are represented by different individuals within the same speech community. Sanches's paper presents an account of variation across generations in the number and use of semantic numeral classifiers among Japanese speakers, and Frances Karttunen gives evidence for striking changes in American Finnish within a single generation. In an immigrant Finnish family, the parents spoke Finnish and American Finnish, the eldest children spoke American Finnish and American English, while the youngest children spoke only American English.

Language Contact Phenomena

Languages in contact provide dramatic instances of changes in language structure and use. Within one generation, contact situations can lead to extensive rearrangement of language structure, as in the American Finnish case. Some contact situations can also bring about the appearance of new languages. For example, when indigenous populations need to communicate regularly with speakers of languages representing economically and politically dominant societies, a pidgin language may result. Variation in the pidgin-forming process is extensive, since there are contributions to the pidgin from several donor languages and since there are no well-developed norms as to what the acceptable code is. As norms definining the code emerge, the variation is reduced (see Hymes, 1971, pp. 77–80). In such cases, it is clear that the linguistic system is not changed merely by the initiation of a specific feature or features but by underlying social bases that motivate and define the characteristics of the language system. Here one must examine the influence of social functions on the emergence of a linguistic system. Such an approach contrasts sharply with the approach in the comparative method in which one views change in linguistic structure as independent of social factors, or at most, of serving as a base upon which social differences may be mapped.

The study of pidgins and creoles has been instrumental in fostering a sociolinguistic approach to language change. The effects of social factors are most pronounced in periods of rapid social and linguistic change as is found in occurrences of pidginization and creolization. Since pidgins and creoles do not constitute the only codes in the speech communities where they are spoken, their structures (and the variation these structures exhibit) can be seen more readily in relation to social factors such as age, generation, origin, status, and education than would be the case for codes in monolingual societies. Supportive evidence can be found in the papers by Carol Molony and Ian Hancock.

Molony documents the contributions from the source languages to Philippine Creole Spanish, noting such features as dialect and generation differences, and spatial contiguity and social interaction. Hancock discusses the processes of lexical expension in Sierra Leone Krio as a result of contact with English, the dominant source language. There are, however, varieties of Krio, which can be recognized by differences in structure and content and conditioned by such factors as intensity of contact with English (as opposed to African languages), age of speakers, ethnicity, education, and (related to all of these) language attitudes.

In pidgins and creoles, functions of speech can also be readily investigated, since codes tend to be specialized, i.e., situationally or contextually restricted. A consequence of the specialization is differentiation of speech styles. Kernan, Sodergren, and French are able to show that in Belize City, Belize, for example, there is an elaborated metalanguage for the identification and discussion of numerous speech styles. An individual's status and personality are closely related to his ability to use a wide variety of these styles effectively and artistically. Pressures to communicate effectively serve also to introduce changes in the structure of the code. Gillian Sankoff identifies changes in the grammar of Tok Pisin (New Guinea) resulting from creolization with attendant pressures placed on the language as it assumes the communicative functions of a first (rather than an auxiliary) language.

Evolution of Language

The fourth development contributing to the new directions in language change is the renascence of interest in the evolution of language. Although the study of language evolution has a long history, only in recent years has there been a serious attempt in linguistic anthropology to explore the topic. The study of language change as adaptation to sociohistorical pressures has been neglected, except for Dell Hymes' (1961, p. 55) appeals for an evolutionary approach to language based on relativity of speech functions and societal organization of speech variation: "I want to maintain that the role of speech is not the same in every society, and that the differences can best be understood from an evolutionary point of view; that we must understand speech habits as functionally varying in their adaptation to particular social and natural environments, and recognize that there are ways in which some languages are evolutionarily more advanced than others."

It is not clear what constitutes evidence as to the ways in which some languages are more evolutionarily advanced than others, but it does seem clear that languages are subject to social pressures and that selection in response to those pressures occurs among competing aspects of language. The formation of pidgin languages, where there is selection among marked variants at a linguistic level and a consequent crystallization of structure as social norms emerge, is a case in point. Moreover, when pidgin languages become subject to the demands of a first language, the adaptive response is creolization, an expansion of linguistic structure and an extension of language functions.

In general, sociocultural complexity entails language complexity of that society, particularly in terms of social stratification. The more stratified a society, the more variation will appear in language (see Gumperz, 1962). Nomenclatural systems also reflect complexity of society. Brent Berlin traces the growth of ethnobotanical nomenclature as a response to linguistic recognition of the plant world. Although the mechanisms for this growth are not entirely clear, the development of plant vocabulary is related to the growth of technological and social complexity and specialization. Still another area potentially significant for studying evolution of language is language planning. As Joan Rubin points out, the language resources of a community may become subject to governmental manipulation, i.e., to economic and political issues and pressures, leading to differential selection of the language resources and affecting changes in language structure and use.

Another dimension on which languages may differ evolutionarily is autonomy of linguistic function and speech styles. We consider this dimension to be an important and promising concept for the study of language change, since it includes the three components essential to a new perspective in language change: sociocultural bases of language, inherent variability of language, and selective pressures operating on aspects of the variation. The concept of autonomy is introduced in the lead article in this volume, Paul Kay's "Language Evolution and Speech Style." Autonomy in speech style is defined as (1) confining messages to the linguistic channel (as in reading or a telephone call to a stranger), and (2) "communication minimally dependent on the contribution of background information on the part of the hearer." The important issue here for language change is the question of what constitutes background information. There appear to be two kinds:

1. Social information such that a speaker's message could not be appropriate or perhaps even understood without some knowledge of the receiver's social characteristics. Socially appropriate messages cannot be

formulated without some minimal knowledge about the dimensions of social categories and organization and their relation to ways of speaking.

2. Mutually shared information that allows speakers to use ellipsis or private reference.

Kay presents two hypotheses: (a) " . . . language evolves in the direction of autonomous, context-free systems of symbols"; and (b) that this overall change—an increasing set of styles, including an autonomous one, is motivated by " . . . adaptation to an increasingly complex and diversified speech community whose members collectively control a body of knowledge beyond that which any one speaker can control." According to Kay's first hypothesis—that languages become more autonomous—we would expect that background information would change from the ellipsis-type as in (2) to the abstract social type as in (1). The change would not be complete, of course, but the overall direction of change would be an increase in (1) and a decrease in (2). That pattern is evident in the speech communities discussed in the papers here.

Autonomy of Code and Style

In "Speech and Social Prestige in the Belizean Speech Community," Kernan, Sodergren, and French provide a sociolinguistic illustration of the relationship between sociocultural complexity and language complexity. Belize is a multiethnic society, populated by people of Creole or Afrocaribbean descent, Spanish descent, several Mayan groups, Caribs, and numerous smaller groups such as Germans and Lebanese. There are numerous languages and varieties: English (four categories along an English–Broad Creole continuum), Spanish, Mayan, Carib, and a number of lesser languages. As the authors note, there is an emphasis on the mastery of several codes of high value placed on verbal artistry, on code-switching, and on innovative and creative speech. Belize is clearly a diversified speech community, one in which no one speaker controls the entire range of codes. Is language there evolving toward a more autonomous code? The authors present evidence that such a change is occurring.

First, there is an increase in the autonomy as represented in the changes in the English–Creole continuum. Broad Creole is the language of the rural areas and contrasts with City Creole, which occupies an intermediate position in the continuum. Recent immigrants to the city begin to move from Broad Creole to City Creole, while native residents of the city are more apt to control a range of the continuum from City Creole to Standard Belizean English. The latter is the language of education, prestige, and government and the language in which the ellipsis type of background information is minimized. Although the premium placed on breadth of verbal repertoire slows the rate of change, an increase in level of education, literacy, and urbanization brings about a shift toward the Standard English end of the continuum and an increase in autonomy.

In "Language Acquisition and Language Change: Japanese Numeral Classifiers," Sanches offers another example of a speech community whose code is undergoing rapid change toward a more autonomous style. In this case, an increase in autonomy is reflected by the loss of numeral classifiers, a feature that requires agreement in the surface realization of a sentence between a quantifier and some semantic feature of the concept being quantified. Acquisition of numeral classifiers requires internalization of features to be used productively rather than suppletively.

The mastery of a large repertoire of numeral classifiers and their innovative use has always had the positive connotation of "scholarly, learned" within a traditional Japanese system of speech styles. As a result of extensive contact with English, there has been a devaluation of traditional speech, thus reducing the frequency of numeral classifiers in speech to a point where children no longer internalize a model to generate appropriate forms. It should be pointed out that the grammatical structure that previously required a classifier accompanying a numeral has not been lost, but rather the features of agreement between classifiers and nouns are no longer encoded. We could predict that in time the dummy-marker classifier (-ko) will tend to drop entirely, possibly allowing the development of plurals. This means that the degree of autonomy of two structural segments of the sentence has been increased. No longer do quantification expressions have to manifest features in agreement with the nouns they quantify.

An increase in autonomy occurs in the development of semantic systems of classification, as shown by Brent Berlin in "Speculations on the Growth of Ethnological Nomenclature." Using comparative linguistic data, Berlin establishes six major linguistic categories, constituting the necessary levels for names of classes of plants. These categories are ordered in terms of their appearances in the history of any language, and the ordering reflects a process of lexical marking in which there is a movement from lexically unmarked to lexically marked status. This means that comparatively more information is given in the surface realizations of forms as they become lexically marked. They become more specific, more context-free, and more autonomous. To illustrate, the developmental sequence for one of the six categories, life forms, is proposed as a series of steps. First, a newly encoded life form category is labeled according to the genetic level. In time, the life form becomes optionally marked with the attributive "genuine," which in the next step becomes obligatory. In the final stage, polysemy is totally obscured by changes in the original expressions (life form and/or generic). Thus the role of context and background information in the use of the term(s) becomes less necessary as the terminological system changes.

In "Color Categorization in West Futunese: Variability and Change," Janet Dougherty presents the findings of her research on color classification, one finding being that considerable individual variation exists for some of the color categories. That is particularly true for the blue and green areas of the color spectrum. Approximately 50% of her respondents demonstrated a blue-green category (GRUE in the revised Berlin–Kay terminology), whereas the other 50% had distinct categories for blue and green. Some of the respondents with the blue-green category distinguished blues and greens with the aid of attributives, so that in the community there were several terms for the blue-green focal area: *uiui* for blue-green; *uiui rounemahmata* for green, *uiui plu* for blue; and *uiui* for green and *plu* for blue. A change in the terminology seems to be underway. The term *uiui* is polysemous in current usage, but the appearance of the new term *plu* reduces the problem of ambiguity by rendering the terminological system more specific and, in usage, more autonomous.

A different aspect of autonomy is made explicit by Gillian Sankoff in "Creolization and Syntactic Change in New Guinea Tok Pisin." She documents the shift of forms from the status of lexeme to that of grammatical marker, characteristic of a shift from a pidgin to a creole language. She discusses two elements, *bai* (future tense marker, from *by and by*) and *ia* (adverbial, from *here*), which have undergone phonological simplification (*baimbai > bai; hia > ia*) and have " . . . become systematized as part of the obligatory grammatical machinery. . . ." How is increasing autonomy involved here? The referential semantic function of *bai* is dropped with its incorporation into the verb phrase. Concomitant with the loss of its adverbial function, *bai* is reanalyzed with *bihain* (later) and *klostu* (soon) in a set of tense markers that must occur in conjunction with every verb in the sentence. Since *bai* is no longer an optional adverb occurring at the beginning of the sentence, the hearer need not interpret which verb it was intended to modify on the basis of extrasentential context—Kay's background information—to decode the meaning.

The development of *ia* as a marker of relative clauses is analogous to the reanalysis of *bai* as a tense marker. The hearer can employ the *ia* bracketing of phrases to determine the structural relations among component parts of the sentence. Moreover, the status of the information in a relative clause is revealed by a marker developed for signaling that "the information contained in these *ia* brackets refers to background, contextual information." The marker therefore simplifies the task of deciding how background information is to be applied to interpret the sentence.

Two of the papers in this volume, "Recent Relexification Processes in

Philippine Creole Spanish" by Carol Molony and "Lexical Expansion within a Closed System" by Ian Hancock, deal almost exclusively with lexical changes in established creoles. Similar processes appear to be underway in the creoles in both the Philippines and West Africa. Contact languages heavily influence the lexicon, bringing about lexical replacement and reorganization. These processes illustrate factors common to many language change situations, such as prestige languages, types of speakers (differentiated along social dimensions), divergences in meaning between the source and recipient languages, frequencies of occurrence, and semantic domains.

Direct evidence for diminishing polysemy and standardization of languages is not given by Molony or Hancock, but it is likely that increases in autonomy as described by Kernan et al. and by Berlin are taking place in the Philippine and African creoles. Some indirect evidence is available. Molony notes, for example, that an important source of new terms in Ternateño is formal education, in English. The younger, more educated individuals are the chief innovators here, and we see an incipient standardization at work. As noted, the impact of English on Sierra Leone Krio has produced a more anglicized variety of creole "Talkee-Talkee," and English as a prestige language exerts considerable influence toward standardization. The fact that the lexicons of the creoles are increasing is an indication that the high degree of polysemy characteristic of creoles is being reduced.

In language contact situations such as Creoles in the Philippines and West Africa, language change is accelerated, and the extreme degree of variation among individuals in the speech communities makes documentation of differences a difficult research task. The same can be said of immigrant communities that rapidly lose their native language and adopt that of the host country. Frances Karttunen describes that process for Finnish immigrant communities in the United States, where the impact of English on Finnish produced American Finnish. The radical replacement of one language by another attests to the strong social pressures that the Finnish communities faced, and the harsh reaction to American Finnish by visitors from Finland indicates that the adoption of the new language may have been made despite strong language loyalty to Finnish. The strong negative reaction of the native Finns suggests that communication with the Finnish Americans may have been impaired and that loss of autonomy was involved. Karttunen notes that in American Finnish the grammar and phonology of Finnish changed only slightly in comparison with the extensive borrowing of vocabulary. The indignant reactions were to loan words, and interestingly, Karttunen remarks that borrowing included even basic vocabulary such as words for 'house', 'lake', 'to talk', and 'to run'. It is plausible that autonomy as ellipsis and private reference was affected by the replacement of basic vocabulary, and the Finns reacted to that aspect of language change.

In speech communities where extensive cultural contact has brought about marked changes, social factors motivating language changes may be discernible without particular difficulty. In relatively small and homogeneous speech communities, however, how do social factors affect language change? Hopkins addresses that question in his study of linguistic variants in Tzeltal and Tzotzil speech communities in Chiapas, Mexico. In studies of Indo-european languages, dialect surveys have been made to determine isogloss distributions reflecting social, political, and economic factors in the histories of the communities. Hopkins employs similar procedures to generate hypotheses about patterns of social interaction between indigeneous Indian communities in Mexico.

The results of the Tzeltal and Tzotzil surveys showed that linguistic variants are patterned in two interesting ways. There are dialect areas sharing a large number of linguistic features, while some lexical items and phonological developments are limited to single communities. Hopkins notes that the lack of strong isogloss bundles indicates that neighboring communities have not had rigid or longstanding barriers to spread of innovations. Communities have had considerable linguistic interaction, but not uniformly nor to the same degree. A pattern of relative independence has developed in each community—accounting for community-specific phonology and lexicon—within a network of regional affiliation. In Chiapas, dialect diversity reflects the social, economic, and political realities of community organization and history, and the pattern of interaction appears to be the critical variable.

Writing systems and their effects of language change have been relatively neglected topics of study, especially in anthropology. Keith Basso and Ned Anderson's "A Western Apache Writing System: The Symbols of Silas John" is a welcome and innovative addition to the literature. Basso and Anderson report on a writing system developed by Silas John Edwards, a Western Apache shaman, who devised the system to record aspects of Apache rituals and prayers. Although there is as yet no method for measuring the historically stabilizing influence of a notational or writing system on a code, the potential for maintenance of the code is clearly present. The stabilization fosters code specialization, and that in turn serves to differentiate codes within a speech community, starting perhaps on the basis of a formal–informal distinction and standardizing aspects of the former such that divisions appear within formal codes. An extreme example might be "Biblical" English as opposed to modern standard English, the former limited essentially to religious writings. It appears that the development of a writing system establishes conditions that are important for the eventual development of styles from nonautonomous to autonomous. In fact, an interesting question to raise is to what extent language communities develop autonomous styles without the presence of a writing system.

The historical context in which Silas John created his writing system provides an example of conditions that can foster changes in language. First, there are incipient class differences in Apache society—Silas John is a specialist, a shaman. Also, as a result of decades of massive contact with Anglos, there is increasing social and technological complexity. Silas John was, at an early period of his life, associated with Lutheran missionaries on the Fort Apache reservation, and he acquired an ability to read and write English. Although the script was Silas John's own invention and conceived of in a "dream from God," Basso and Anderson note that it contains considerable Christian symbolism and that the idea of writing undoubtedly is related to his earlier experience with English. Silas John also recognized the possibility that without preservation of the rituals in script form, they might be entirely forgotten. These elements—incipient class structure, disappearance of traditional culture, entrepreneurship, and infusions from a dominant contact culture—provide conditions conducive to the creation of the writing system and thus an incipient language variety.

An interesting aspect of the Apache writing system is the inclusion of kinetic information in some written symbols. Basso and Anderson propose the term "kinetic sign" for symbols that denote sequences of nonverbal behavior. Although the kinetic signs and the more standard phonetic signs are discussed largely in the context of etic–emic distinctions in writing systems, it seems relevant to consider their function as elements for storing purely verbal information, i.e., the autonomy of the graphic system. Kinetic signs in the Apache system signal not merely physical acts, but rather semantic ones, and degree of autonomy of sign is therefore diminished. In effect, the symbols are more contextualized than purely kinetic or phonetic ones would be. A phonetic/kinetic–semantic system, then, would be less autonomous than either an alphabet or syllabary, and one might expect changes in the direction of greater autonomy, a hypothesis supported by known historical developments in scripts originating in the Middle East and Far East. Those early writing systems were originally designed for religious (and commercial) functions, and we might speculate whether graphic autonomy can develop within a parent culture or whether external adoption (in a more permissive context) is a requisite to innovation.

The possible effects of conscious and deliberate efforts to introduce language change is an intriguing question. In language planning at a national level by an official agency, sources and types of change are made explicitly, but the likelihood that an innovation will be permanent may depend on the degree to which members of a speech community view their language as a malleable resource. Joan Rubin raises that issue in "Language Planning Offers New Insights into the Nature of Language." Rubin considers the acceptability and positive evaluation of language entrepreneurship as one dimension of a community's attitudes toward language as a resource. Language management may operate at several levels of sociocultural integration, and language planning at the national level may be one instance of a more general language treatment. Of course, language planning may be motivated and effected at the national level by factors other than attitudes of the speech community. Evaluation of a speech community's responses to planning must be empirically based in each case.

Noting that language treatment may operate at various societal levels, Rubin examines several cases of national language planning to document change and to search for patterns and processes. She concludes that all aspects of language may be subject to change, and motivations for change can be classified as linguistic, semilinguistic, and extralinguistic. The latter two categories include social and political factors responsible for the social pressures that produce language change.

It is worthwhile to consider the pressure toward code autonomy brought about by language planning. We would like to suggest two processes (though there are undoubtedly more):

1. Morphophonemic variation among the substandard varieties will be reduced in the standard. This entails restructuring of the underlying phonological representations or simplification of the rules for deriving the phonetic output from the underlying forms.

2. Background information peculiar to any nonstandard variety must be overtly marked in the discourse of the standard language. This seems to happen naturally in the process of creolization from subdialectal and idiolectal pidgins.

Language planning is one way to effect language change at a community level. Changes may be initiated, however, in more subtle ways at an individual level, as Lilyan Brudner suggests in "Language Creativity and the Psychotherapy Relationship." Brudner notes the importance of conventionalized aspects of language use and presents the view underlying the psychotherapy tradition that individuals must be socialized so that communication of personal feelings and intentions conforms to social conventions. To the extent that an individual does not know or cannot effectively utilize those conventions, he will experience difficulty in social interactions. In some cases, failure to manipulate codes appropriately may result in what our society deems "personal problems."

Brudner reports on some linguistic devices used by psychotherapists to inculcate new communicative patterns in their patients. A fundamental part of therapy is to train the patient to subordinate expressive behavior to the linguistic code and thus provide a basis for considering alternative patterns of communication. As the patient focuses increasing attention on the code itself, an interactional climate is established in which the patient can recognize that expected and appropriate interpretations of the code depend on what is assumed and conventionalized. Whether the initial communicative difficulties stem from erroneous or lack of common expectations implicit in the codes of interacting individuals, the result of successful psychotherapy is a more autonomous linguistic system. Thus, recognition of the conventionalized aspects of communication is recognition of code autonomy, and the learned changes lead to an autonomy of use.

The model on which these verbal conventions are based may itself be a novel cultural metaphor of social reality. The metaphor in this case was promulgated by Freudian psychiatry. During the last century, a large part of the western world has been socialized into accepting, defining, or redefining their social world in terms of Freudian assumptions, directly, by encounters with psychiatric practicioners, or indirectly, by the popularization of ideas based on this model. Thus, implicitly understood "folk" beliefs become crystallized into a social metaphor and reintroduced into the communication system to influence the interaction patterns.

Future Perspectives

The papers contained in this volume represent empirical studies of language change from sociolinguistic perspectives. They reflect the new directions emerging in the study of language change—topically, in the form of questions about language contact phenomena and evolution of the language, and conceptually, in a redefinition of linguistic systems and inherent variability in language. Autonomy of code and speech as a dimension of language evolution figures prominently in the discussions and can be seen to operate at lexical, grammatical, and stylistic levels of language.

Those developments constitute advances in our understanding of language change, although additional empirical studies are clearly desirable. It would be interesting to know, for instance, if other languages with numeral classifier systems are beginning to show changes similar to Japanese. Information on the Thai language (Palakornkul, n.d.) shows parallels with the Japanese situation and suggests that long-range contact with other societies and in the context of strong urbanization processes leads to the same structural reorganization of language loss of some numeral classifiers and incipient markers for plurals. No reports have been forthcoming about similar changes for languages in areas where urbanization is absent or minimal, as among the Tzeltal of Mexico (see Berlin and Romney, 1964), despite a long history of contact with Spanish. This raises questions about what kinds of pressures motivate speakers to adopt new aspects and patterns of language in the context of urban life (and perhaps the converse, why there is maintenance in other contact situations).

Ambiguity is one source for pressures leading to change. Inadequate distinctions and precision in nomenclature lead to development of new terms and reorganization of lexical systems. The increasing demands on communication resulting from increasing technological and social complexity set conditions for ambiguity and also for its dissolution. Since social pressures of those sorts are operating on many small-scale societies that are undergoing modernization, lexical and nomenclatural systems should show signs of change and reorganization, and we expect that this will be a highly productive area for research.

Another source for change-inducing pressures is to be found in creolization of languages. As pidgin languages undergo creolization and assume the functions of first languages, communication pressures lead to resolution of ambiguity through lexical, semantic, and grammatical expansion. Creolization affords a particularly rich area for research on mechanisms of language change, since changes are accelerated, concentrated, and pervasive in the language. Bickerton, for instance, suggests that " . . . creoles are, quite literally, invented, or reinvented, each time that they appear . . ." and that " . . . what distinguishes a creole language from a pidgin on one hand and a developed standard language on the other is simply that a creole is much closer than either to linguistic universals, in particular, to natural semantax" (1975, p. 6). Although those claims are not fully established, creoles do share remarkable structural similarities and thus afford unusual opportunities for studying conditions that helped produce the similarities.

Creolization of languages occurs in societies that are undergoing rapid social change. For a child to acquire a language that is not the first language of either parent and for that to occur regularly and consistently is a strong indication of the flux in social relations and alignments in those societies. Under conditions of rapid change, especially those resulting from contact situations, language change is apt to be more extensive and rapid.

At least, the external or ecological conditions are conducive to change, and within those favorable contexts, social factors such as position, prestige, and self-identity and processes such as socialization and social mobility can operate to change languages in structure and use. The system that changes is social, language as a social phenomenon, and goals for future research are the identification of the mechanisms, processes, and consequences of change as they pertain to social theory.

A social theory of language change has yet to be proposed, but some of the concepts that must be considered for a theory are contained in the papers in this volume. In addition to those mentioned above, we should add ideologies at individual and supra-individual levels; prestige, derived from personal skills and/or through acquisition of varieties, dialects, or languages valued as prestigious; social position, as related to prestige, power, and their differential distribution within societies and speech communities; boundary maintenance with attendant code prestige and emphasis (e.g., Black English, Jamaican Creole); and urbanization, with related language standardization, social anonymity, and code autonomy. Undoubtedly other concepts are required, and the issue must be addressed more fully as to how the concepts are translated from a social force level into social meaning incorporated into the code. In that respect, Labov's (1972) proposals concerning phonological change are helpful. Phonological variants become subject to differential perception, assessment, and evaluation as they become more socially significant, and individual adoption of variants in relation to those evaluations are indicators of self-identity and social group membership. Paul Kay's paper (this volume) identifies societal complexity as a force that induces change and increasing autonomy of style as a major type of change. More fine-grained analyses are needed, however, for advances in our understanding of how individuals conceptualize and operationalize the features of social meaning that are responsible for change. Issues raised in this volume point in that direction for future research.

References

Ardener, Edwin
    1971   Social anthropology and the historicity of historical linguistics. In *Social anthropology and language* edited by E. Ardener. London: Tavistock.
Berlin, Brent and A. Kimball Romney
    1964   Descriptive semantics of Tzeltal numeral classifiers, *American Anthropologist* **66** (pt. 2), 79–98.
Bickerton, Derek
    1975   *Creolization, linguistic universals, natural semantax and the brain.* Paper presented at the International Conference on Pidgins and Creoles, University of Hawaii, January 1975.

Bloomfield, Leonard
1933 *Language.* New York: Holt.
Boas, Franz
1911 Introduction to the handbook of American Indian languages. *BAE Bulletin 40.*
Washington, D.C.: Smithsonian Institution.
Brown, Roger and Marguerite Ford
1961 Address in American English, *Journal of Abnormal and Social Psychology* **62,**
375–385.
Brown, Roger, and Albert Gilman
1960 The pronouns of power and solidarity. In *Style in language* edited by Thomas A.
Sebeok. Cambridge, Massachusetts: MIT Press.
Fishman, Joshua
1968 Introduction. In *Readings in the sociology of language* edited by J. Fishman. The
Hague: Mouton.
Friedrich, Paul.
1966 Structural implications of Russian pronominal usage. In *Sociolinguistics* edited by
William Bright. The Hague: Mouton.
Gumperz, John
1962 Types of Linguistic Communities, *Anthropological Linguistics* **4** (1), 28–40.
Gumperz, John, and Dell Hymes (eds.)
1964 The Ethnography of Communication. *American Anthropologist* **66** (6) (pt. 2), 1–34.
1972 *Directions in sociolinguistics: The ethnography of communication.* New York:
Holt.
Hammel, Eugene A. (ed.)
1965 Formal semantic analysis. *American Anthropologist* **67** (5) (pt. 2).
Hymes, Dell
1961 Functions of speech: An evolutionary approach. In *Anthropology and education*
edited by F. C. Gruber. Philadelphia: University of Pennsylvania Press.
1962 The ethnography of speaking. In *Anthropology and human behavior* edited by T.
Gladwin and W. C. Sturtevant. Washington, D. C.: Anthropological Society of
Washington.
1971 Introduction. In *Pidginization and creolization of languages* edited by D. Hymes.
Cambridge, England: University of Cambridge Press.
Jakobson, Roman
1960 Linguistics and poetics. In *Style in language* edited by T. Sebeok. Cambridge,
Massachusetts: MIT Press.
Labov, William
1972 On the mechanism of linguistic change. In *Directions in sociolinguistics: The eth-
nography of communication* edited by J. Gumperz and D. Hymes. New York:
Holt.
Lehmann, Winfred
1968 Saussure's dichotomy between descriptive and historical linguistics. In *Directions
for historical linguistics* edited by W. Lehmann and Y. Malkiel. Austin, Texas:
University of Texas Press.
Palakornkul, Angkab
n.d. *Changes in Thai numeral classifiers.* Seminar paper, University of Texas, 1973.
Powell, John Wesley
1891 Indian linguistic families of American North of Mexico. In Seventh Annual Report,
Bureau of American Ethnology. Washington, D. C.
Romney, A. K., and Roy G. D'Andrade (eds.)
1964 Transcultural Studies in Cognition. *American Anthropologist* **66** (3).

Sapir, Edward
    1921 *Language: An introduction to the study of speech.* New York: Harcourt.
Schleicher, August
    1863 *Die Darwinsche Theorie und die Sprachwissenschaft.* Weimar.
Swadesh, Morris
    1951 Diffusional Cumulation and Archaic Residue as Historical Explanations, *Southwestern Journal of Anthropology* **7**, 1–21.
Tyler, Stephen (ed.)
    1968 *Cognitive anthropology.* New York: Holt.
Weinreich, Uriel
    1953 *Languages in contact.* Linguistic Circle of New York. (1966, The Hague: Mouton.)
Weinreich, Uriel, William Labov, and Marvin Herzog
    1968 Empirical foundations for a theory of language change. In *Directions for historical linguistics* edited by W. Lehmann and Y. Malkiel. Austin, Texas: University of Texas Press.

Language Evolution and Speech Style

PAUL KAY

"Elaborated" versus "Restricted" Speech Style

Two contrasting types of speaking style have been described by Basil Bernstein, who has called them "elaborated code" and "restricted code" (Bernstein, 1961, 1964). Although Bernstein uses the term "code," the phenomena he describes are ordinarily called speech styles, levels, or varieties (Hymes, 1964, p. 338). The basic empirical studies motivating Bernstein's distinction compared the speech of middle class and working class English youths under comparable conditions of prearranged, semi-formal group discussion. Although valid methodological objections have been raised to these studies, Bernstein has nevertheless succeeded in revealing an important phenomenon. The speech style Bernstein calls "elaborated," which characterized the middle class discussion groups, contains longer sentences with a vocabulary that is more varied and more explicit, especially with respect to logical connections, which are often left implicit in "restricted" speech. The syntax of elaborated speech is more complex and the delivery is usually more paused, more edited, and generally less fluent. Restricted speech tends to contain formulaic expressions such as *Don't you know* and *Isn't it so,* which are, in effect, appeals to the hearer to fill in from background knowledge those parts of the message the speaker has not made explicit. Subsequent studies have counted the ratio of nouns to pronouns, of types to tokens, of modifying adjectives, and so on. Without further detailed structural comparison, I think the distinction in question can be easily enough recognized. It is, for example, that which exists between the speech of an educated speaker in a formal academic context, such as a lecture or seminar, and speech of the same person when playing baseball, making love, or quarreling. (See Note 1 at the end of the chapter.)

Functionally, the style of speech that Bernstein calls elaborate may be characterized as "autonomous"; that is, it is minimally dependent upon simultaneous transmission over other channels, such as the paralinguistic, postural, and gestural, and it is minimally dependent on the contribution of background information on the part of the hearer. Characteristically, autonomous speech packs all the information into the strictly linguistic channel and places minimal reliance on the ability of the hearer to supply items of content necessary either to flesh out the body of the message or to place it in the correct interpretive context. Autonomous speech is suited to the communication of unfamiliar or novel content to someone with whom one has little in common. It is ideal for technical and abstract communication among strangers and inappropriate for the communication of immediate and emotionally laden content between intimates.

In their comprehensive treatise on cognitive development, Werner and Kaplan speak of a very general process of cognitive development, which they call the "autonomization of symbols." This, in their words, is "the development toward a system of vehicles which enables a person to communicate adequately with an audience psychologically quite distant from the addressor. In other words, the greater the interpersonal distance between individuals involved in a communication situation, the more autonomous must be the symbolic vehicles in order to be understood, that is, the *more communal* and the less egocentric, idiosyncratic, and contextualized must the vehicles become" (Werner and Kaplan, 1963, p. 49; italics in the original). (I am indebted to John Enrico for calling this passage to my attention.) Following Werner and Kaplan, I shall henceforth use the expression "autonomous speech" to designate what we have hitherto been calling "elaborated speech." The reason for the terminological change is that it puts the emphasis where I believe the emphasis belongs, namely, on the important functional aspects of autonomous speech. What is functionally important about the richer speech style is that it is precise and logically explicit; it conveys the speaker's intent without reliance on tone of voice, facial expression, gesture, or posture and makes minimal appeal to prior understandings between the addressor and addressee. As I have suggested, autonomous speech is suited to the communication of novel, exact, emotionally neutral information to an unfamiliar addressee. A prototypic situation for the use of autonomous speech would exist when one person had to explain to another how to disarm a complex bomb by one-way radio (see Note 2).

Language Evolution—Linguistic Evidence

It is now time to consider the topic suggested in the first half of the title, language evolution. We must first, however, dispose of an objection that is so firmly entrenched in anthropological linguistics that mere reference to it is sometimes sufficient to disbar any discussion of the topic. (See Note 3.)

This frequently heard argument goes: Whether or not there may have taken place in the past any process that might reasonably be considered linguistic evolution, scientific consideration of the question is now impossible, as there is no possibility of obtaining objective data relevant to the issue. In particular, while one may perhaps speak sensibly of primitive cultures (or simple, or preliterate, or traditional cultures), there are no such things as primitive languages. To be sure, the language associated with complex modern civilizations have larger vocabularies than those of the classic civilizations, which in turn exceed those of local, tribal languages, but, the argument runs, this is a linguistically trivial difference as there are no "structural" differences in languages that correlate with the complexity of the society in which the languages are spoken.

I would argue that while formerly such an argument was at least not directly controverted by our knowledge of language structure, recent developments render it no longer a coherent doctrine.

In 1965, Noam Chomsky concluded his discussion of the boundaries of syntax and semantics: "the syntactic and semantic structure of natural languages evidently offers many mysteries, both of fact and of principle, and . . . any attempt to delimit the boundaries of these domains must certainly be quite tentative" (1965, p. 163). Since then, much of the linguistic scene has been dominated by discussion and controversy regarding such issues as the lexicalist hypothesis, whether or not transformations always preserve meaning (and, if so, what theoretical status should be accorded this observation), whether semantics is generative or interpretive, and so on. It seems fair to say that whatever contemporary linguists can be said to believe as a group, any clear notion dividing lexicon from "structure" is not part of this consensus.

It would probably not be exaggerated to say that in one prominent modern view of grammatical structure the chief structural differences that exist between languages consist in the different lexicalizations they contain. One might argue that languages are fundamentally alike with regard to the deep semantic relations they express and that structural differences derive from differing patterns of lexicalization, i.e., different styles of putting together complex lexical items out of a roster of semantic primes that is largely shared across languages. I am aware that this hypothesis is hardly more than a vague suggestion. But the fact that such an hypothesis may now be advanced, however tentatively, illustrates that our view of the structural importance of lexical items has shifted markedly since the publication of Chomsky's "Aspects" in 1965. It is no longer possible to contrast lexical variation and structural variation as if lexical items were unrelated units that are simply plugged into a grammatical structure. Sapir said, "When it comes to linguistic form, Plato walks with the Macedonian Swineherd, Confucius with the head-hunting savage of Assam," and Hymes, in citing the passage, adds the trenchant comment, "What was in mind, presumably, were the formal morphological features of nineteenth century typology, but the statement was taken to stand for whatever one might mean by linguistic form" (Foreword to Swadesh, 1971, p. vii). In the same essay, Hymes says "The tabu against an evolutionary perspective on languages seems about to be broken" (1971, p. v).

The essay just cited is in fact the introduction to the recently published posthumous work of Morris Swadesh, "The Origin and Diversification of Language." I will not review that work here other than to note that as the title suggests, Swadesh is concerned with introducing an evolutionary perspective into the study of language. Swadesh speaks of world languages (e.g., Chinese, Russian, English), classical languages (Latin, Sanskrit, Aztec), and local languages (e.g., most of the unwritten languages studied by anthropological linguists).

While Swadesh's major tool is comparative historical reconstruction, other recent studies have considered the languages of contemporary preliterate societies. These studies are just beginning and the results to date are highly tentative to say the least. Still, there does seem to be emerging from studies of contemporary local languages a suggestive hypothesis regarding the evolution of language, which is that **the direction of linguistic evolution is from a nonautonomous to an autonomous system of communication.** Among these studies are Berlin's and my work "Basic Color Terms" and Berlin's "Speculations on the Growth of Ethnobotanical Nomenclature" (1971). The latter paper demonstrates that botanical lexicons grow in a way that has implications for the growth of vocabulary generally. Berlin has found that, while at the earliest stages vocabulary growth doubtless consists in adding names for more and more things, at later stages vocabularies grow by inventing or adopting new names that designate both subclasses and superclasses of the categories already named. The general result is that advanced languages tend to have more abstract words and more concrete words than local languages. World and classical languages thus provide richer resources for communicative subtlety than do local languages in that the former frequently offer a larger variety of names for a given thing, depending on the level of abstraction at which the speaker wishes to place his description and the features of the denotatum or denotata to which he wishes to draw attention. The larger implication of this finding, should it be corroborated generally, is that with respect to their nominal systems, world languages provide the means for more precise and explicit (i.e., more autonomous) communication at whatever level of abstraction is desired by the addresser.

The data on verbal systems are less well understood, but nevertheless there are clues to be found here. In goal attainment verbs, semantic incorporation of the object into the verb is a common, though not universal, feature of local languages. This may take place through a stem formation process from a relatively abstract transitive verb root, as appears to be the case in the famous example of Cherokee verbs for 'washing' (A. Hill, 1952). (See Note 4.) The morphs for the objects of the action are often phonologically unrelated or weakly related to the normal allomorphs. A second way in which semantic object incorporation may be achieved is by simply having a number of morphologically distinct roots that have the semantic effect of incorporating the object of the action, as is the case with Tzeltal verbs for 'washing' (Berlin, 1968). Comparison of the superficial Cherokee and Tzeltal transitive verb stems for 'washing' (Table I) shows greater reflection of the semantic object-incorporation process in the surface morphology of the former language.

There are probably other morphosyntactic processes that achieve the same or similar semantic results with goal attainment verbs in other local languages. The logical forms of such predicates is a binary relation whose domain or converse domain is restricted to the members of a set. Such predicates are alike in form to the basic English kin terms (which happen only incidently to be surface nouns); for example, as Russell says, "brother and sister express the same relation (that of a common parentage) with the domain limited in the first case to males, in the second to females" ("*Principia*," Summary of *35). It may be a characteristic of local languages to contain surface verbs that have this underlying semantic form. This is a highly speculative suggestion, and others, equally speculative, could be made. There does seem to exist sufficient evidence to warrant examination of the ways in which different languages combine logical types of predicates into surface verbs (cf. Langacker, 1973; J. Hill, 1971). For example, it is possible that speakers of world languages have greater resources for focusing on any chosen aspect of a reported event by varying the surface lexical items that together account for the same deep semantic structure of embedded predication. Suppose that it is true that the sentence *John killed Bill* has an underlying structure that is more visibly represented in the sentence *John caused that Bill became nonliving*. In English, we can combine the various underlying predicates *cause, become, not,* and *live* in a variety of ways to produce, in addition to the two sentences already considered, *John caused Bill's demise* and *John terminated Bill's life,* where *demise* incorporates *become, not,* and *live; terminate* incorporates *become* and *not;* and so on. It is at least a hypothesis worthy of investigation that not all languages have this richness of structural alternatives.

In the domain of syntax, Hale (1971) has shown suggestive evidence

TABLE I

Comparison of Cherokee and Tzeltal Transitive Verb Stems for 'Washing'[a]

Cherokee	Tzeltal
1. k-ata-wo 'I-reflexive-bathe (in a stream)'	1. -sap 'wash individuated objects, immersed in water'
2. k-ali-sdul-e 'I-reflexive-head-wash'	
3. tsi-sdule-e 'I-head-wash (whose head unspecified)'	
4. k-a-gɔ̄sk-wo 'I-him (or "it")-face-wash'	2. -pok 'wash surfaces'
5. tsi-gɔ̄sk-wo 'I-face-wash (whose face unspecified)'	
6. de-k-asul-e 'plural object-I-extremely-wash'	3. -saʔ 'wash hair'
7. de-tsi-ya-(a)-sul-e 'plural object-I-him-extremely-wash'	
8,9. Identical with (6,7).	4. -sak' 'wash clothing, fabric'
10. de-g-ɔ̄gil-e 'plural object-I-him-clothing-wash'	
11. de-tsi-y(a)-ɔ̄gil-e 'plural object-I-him-clothing-wash'	5 -suk' 'wash interior of an object'
12. de-k-atiy-e 'plural object-I-dish (or spoon)-wash'	
13. tsi-yɔ̄w(i)-e 'I-person (ʔ)-wash'	
14. g-owil-e 'I-meat-wash'	

[a] Because Hill emphasizes that his analysis is incomplete, I list the forms he analyzes exactly as he does, leaving for the reader to decide which segments represent the roots and which the derived stems.

that languages may not be all the same in their resources for embedding sentences. In particular, he has argued that certain Australian languages (including Walbiri specifically) do not have embedded relative clauses but rather adjoined relatives. Hale suggests, following a proposal of Thompson (1971), that in universal deep structure all relatives may be adjoined, but that relative-embedding languages such as English, Navajo, and Pitjantjatjara (a close relative of Walbiri) possess a rule that embeds relatives. (See Note 5.) In Hale's words,

One might describe the typological variety among relative clause structures in terms of a common deep structure of the adjoined type:

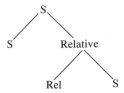

together with optional application, obligatory application, or no application at all, of an "attraction" rule by means of which a relative clause is drawn into the main clause to "modify" a noun phrase which is identical to a noun phrase appearing in the relative clause itself:

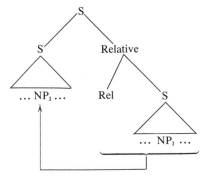

In a language like Walbiri, this rule does not apply, while in Kaititj it applies optionally [and in Pitjantjatjara it applies obligatorily] (1971, p. 13–14).

Hale points out further that if a language lacks the rule that embeds relatives, the number of NPs in a main clause that can be modified by a relative is thereby limited to one. In such a language, a sentence like *The woman who lives next door brought the flowers on the table,* would be unsayable. One would have a choice something like that between *The woman who lives next door brought the flowers. They are on the table,* and *A woman brought the flowers on the table. She lives next door.* Moreover, languages that embed relatives can attach one or more relatives to nouns in a main clause that has a conditional adjoined to it; for example, *The woman who lives next door will bring the flowers you asked for unless it rains.* The inability to embed relatives may be a communicational limitation, especially so if a wide variety of modifying expressions are to be derived from underlying relatives, as appears to be the trend in grammatical theory.

Hale draws an interesting parallel between these data in the transformational component of Walbiri grammar and certain lexical "gaps." Pointing out that Walbiri has a Stage I color terminology system (see Berlin and Kay, 1969), he notes that, like other speakers of languages that do not encode all eleven basic color categories in a basic color term, the Walbiri give every indication of perceiving the color categories in the same way we do and show evidence of this in their use of a wide variety of linguistic expressions for the communication of colorimetric information. Hale points out further that Walbiri is a language that lacks higher numerals; in fact, it may well be said to lack any numerals at all. However, in this as in the other Australian languages, "conventionalized counting systems, i.e., numerals are for the most part lacking, but *counting itself is not lacking*" (Hale, 1971, p. 2. italics in original). That is, the Walbiri can count and, when need be, can designate the natural numbers precisely by combination of the indefinite determiners *tjinta* 'singular' and *tjirama* 'dual'. For example, when necessary 'five' can be designated *tjiramakari-tjiramakari-tjinta*. "One might look upon the Walbiri lack of conventionalized numerals as a gap in the inventory of cultural items—since the principle which underlies counting is present, filling the gap is a rather trivial matter. This view is entirely compatible with the observation that the English counting system is almost instantaneously mastered by Walbiris who enter into situations where the use of money is important (quite independently of Western-style education, incidentally)" (Hale, 1971, p. 2–3).

Hale's analysis of these three distinct phenomena in Walbiri, two lexical and one syntactic, suggests a very general hypothesis about language evolution, namely, that the progress of linguistic evolution may be traced in terms of the appearance of lexical and syntactic devices that permit or require the explicit expression of certain universal semantic categories and the relations that are present implicitly (at least) in all languages and cultures.

Relation of Speech Style and Language Evolution

Having described a basic functional contrast in speech styles in contemporary complex societies and having suggested that languages of contemporary primitives may differ from world languages along this same dimension of autonomy of the linguistic medium, I would like now to sketch a hypothesis regarding the evolution of languages from less autonomous to more autonomous vehicles of communication.

We have noted that autonomous speech is called for when an addressor needs to communicate to an addressee with whom he shares a minimum of common experience precise information on an unfamiliar topic of an affectively neutral kind. We noted also that when autonomous speech is required, the fact of the information's being successfully transmitted may be of great emotional importance; what counts in determining the autonomous style of speech is the emotional neutrality of the content of the information, not the fact of its transmission; e.g., *Disconnect the automatic trip-hammer before moving the fuse*. I would hypothesize that the major mechanism underlying the process of language evolution is that social evolution produces speech communities in which situations calling for autonomous speech occur with increasing frequency. In the typical face-to-face local community, there are no people with whom one shares little common experience, and there are few topics about which one person is a specialist and the other not or about which neither participant is sufficiently expert. Increasing complexity of the division of labor produces specialists. Specialists produce finer lexical distinctions, and they also produce more abstract terms with which they can communicate their specialized knowledge to people outside their specialty. In a community of specialists, the shared vocabulary is pushed upward in generality. The development of occupational, regional, and other sorts of subcultures increases the frequency of occasions in which people are required to communicate information of the kind calling for autonomous speech to people with whom they have little in common. The division of labor and the increase in size of the political and economic unit require people to communicate increasingly often with strangers. Complexification of the division of labor is accompanied by the growth of elites. The usual process comprises a gradual growth of the size of kin group with an increasing differentiation of status within the group, beyond the primate universals of age and sex, and a general shift from genealogical to territorial definition of the group. Increasingly, leaders of kin groups identify themselves as leaders rather than as kin group members, as their chiefly role calls upon them to communicate with the leaders of other groups rather more than with their own kin. The same is true of craft specialists.

The evolutionary process of social differentiation, cultural complexification, and political stratification appears to reach a dead end unless writing is developed or adopted. If and when writing appears, the effect upon the sociocultural evolutionary process is dramatic, and it would be surprising indeed if writing were not to affect the direction of language change as well. Writing is language unsupported by all the vocal and visual signals and the process involving immediate feedback from the addressee that all primates, including humans, share when engaged in ordinary vocal communication. Writing is culture as far as possible divorced from our primate nature. Molière's *bourgeois gentilhomme* notwithstanding, we do not ordinarily speak prose, but to the extent that it is influenced by written language, our speech tends to approximate prose. Like a complex culture, a written language is known completely by none of its speakers; yet has an undoubted social reality.

Conclusion

I have advanced here two hypotheses, neither of which is entirely new. The first is that languages evolve in the direction of autonomous, context-free systems as symbols. The second hypothesis concerns the proposed evolutionary mechanism, which is adaptation to an increasingly complex and diversified speech community whose members collectively control a body of knowledge beyond that which any one speaker can control. The notion of autonomous use of language is exemplified in the contrast of the speech style of complex speech communities that has been called "elaborated" versus "restricted." Some evidence has been sketched suggesting that contemporary unwritten languages may differ from written languages along a dimension of autonomous communicational capacity that is directly analogous to the major functional dimension of contrast between autonomous and nonautonomous speech styles. I have also suggested that the speech communities corresponding to world languages differ as sociolinguistic entities from those in which local languages are spoken just in the respect that they present speaker and hearer with the increasing necessity to use language as an autonomous vehicle of communication.

The direction of linguistic evolution is toward the precise and explicit speech of the analytic philosopher, the scientist, and the bureaucrat. To know this is not necessarily to love it, and perhaps there is something to be said for the view expressed in the quip (Note 6): "Progress was a good thing, but it went on too long."

Notes

1. Bernstein's conclusion that the early socialization of lower-class children renders them incapable of elaborated speech and hence ensures their failure in school is open to serious debate. There is no question, however, that an uninformed application of a doctrine of this kind can lead to fundamentally misconceived research with disastrous implications for educational policy. An example is the well-known study of Bereiter and Englemann (1966), which demonstrates thoroughgoing ignorance of Black English as a linguistic phenomenon but which nevertheless is frequently cited by way of absolving the educational system of all blame for its failures in educating black children.

Labov (1969) discusses the shortcomings of the work of Bereiter and Engelmann in some detail and also draws attention to another misuse of the concept verbal elaboration. Arbitrary shibboleths of class or race are often taken as signs of elaborated or proper speech. To say *I ain't, he don't, don't nobody got* as against *I'm not, he doesn't, no one has* is, of course, irrelevant to the effective communication of the speaker's message—though through his choice, conscious or not, of a socially marked variant, the speaker may communicate a great deal about himself (see Gumperz, 1964, 1968, 1970). Nevertheless, the terms "elaborated code" and "verbal elaboration" are often used ambiguously between the meanings 'explicit speech' and 'socially approved speech'. Labov points to particular features of American black English that are systematic dialect variants but that have been mistakenly interpreted as "errors," and even worse as indications that black children lack logical concepts. Labov has shown that black English optionally deletes the copula in just those environments (or very nearly those) in which Standard English optionally contracts the copula. Thus, to the Standard *he's there* and disallowed **there he's* correspond the Black *he there* and disallowed **there he*. In general, copula deletion in Black English is governed by the same rules as those governing contraction of the copula in Standard English. Nevertheless Bereiter and Englemann, among others, interpret absence of the copula as evidence of "illogical" thought on the part of Black speakers.

In my view, the sort of error into which Bereiter and Englemann fall, and of which many of Bernstein's interpreters are also guilty, is part of a traditional confusion as old, probably, as writing. When a society develops writing and differentiates into social classes, literate persons will usually have more occasion to speak explicitly and will tend to develop a speech style more attuned to explicit, technical, context-independent messages. But the development of class dialects also involves a great many divergences, probably a majority, which are arbitrary from the point of view of communicative efficacy, and which serve merely to signal group membership and other metamessages regarding the social positions and attitudes of the participants in a speech act. The confusion is between speech that is "better" only in the silly snobbish sense and speech that is in some real sense more effective, which communicates the speaker's message more explicitly and economically. Labov points out with convincing examples from natural texts that speech can sound quite "educated" and lack logical tightness, while speech fraught with socially stigmatized forms may be logically incisive. Malapropisms, hypercorrections, and bureaucratese (e.g., excessive use of nominalization and passive transformations) are all symptoms of misguided attempts to achieve a "high-sounding" style based to a greater or lesser degree on the common confusion between those aspects of educated speech that represent a genuine expansion of linguistic resources and those features that have semantically irrelevant although socially crucial class and caste associations.

2. Note that in the example the content of the communication is affectively neutral although the fact of its accurate transmission would ordinarily be a matter of concern.

3. The situation is reminiscent of the way the doctrine of extreme linguistic relativity for so long prevented research into the subject of semantic universals, despite the fact that anthropological linguists were all the while using their intuitive feelings about semantic universals as heuristics in their elicitation and analysis of grammatical data.

4. However, Cherokee does contain at least two distinct roots for 'wash' according to Hill. Hill presents his analysis as a corrective to what he feels is a hasty conclusion of Jespersen's that the Cherokee forms listed represent a highly concrete way of encoding the domain. Hill suggests that Jespersen thought the forms listed were each distinct, unanalyzable roots and that he based his conclusion of extreme concreteness on the erroneous analysis. In fact, Jespersen may well have understood the object-incorporation process in just the way Hill does and considered it nevertheless to be an indication of context determination of linguistic expression.

5. Hale might disagree with my exact wording. In any case, he puts forth his proposal very cautiously: "I have serious questions about the correctness of such an analysis for the synchronic grammars of embedded relative languages like English, Navajo, Maori, etc., but the proposal is extremely suggestive and will probably turn out to have historical if not synchronic validity" (1971, p. 13).

6. I should very much appreciate hearing from any reader who knows the source of this line.

Acknowledgment

I would like to thank Brent Berlin, Derek Bickerton, Ben Blount, John Enrico, William Geoghegan, Kenneth Hale, Gregory Lee, Mary Sanches, Dan Slobin, and Wick Miller for comments on this paper, not all of which I have been wise enough to accept.

References

Bereiter, Carl, and S. Engelmann
    1966   *Teaching disadvantaged children in the pre-school.* Englewood Cliffs, New Jersey: Prentice-Hall.
Berlin, Brent
    1968   *Tzeltal numeral classifiers: A study in ethnographic semantics.* Janua Linguarum (series practica) 70. The Hague: Mouton.
    1971   *Speculations on the growth of ethnobotanical nomenclature.* Language-Behavior Research Laboratory Working Paper No. 39. University of California, Berkeley.
Berlin, Brent, and Paul Kay
    1969   *Basic color terms: Their universality and evolution.* Berkeley: University of California.
Bernstein, Basil
    1961   Aspects of language learning in the genesis of social process. *Journal of Child Psychology and Psychiatry.* **1,** 313–324. Reprinted in Hymes (1964).
    1964   Elaborated and restricted codes: Their social origins and some consequences, *American Anthropologist* **66**(6), part 2.
Chomsky, Noam
    1965   *Aspects of the theory of syntax.* Cambridge, Massachusetts: M.I.T.
Gumperz, John J.
    1964   Linguistic and Social Interaction in Two Communities. *American Anthropologist* **66**(6), part 2.
    1968   Speech communities. *Encyclopedia of the social sciences,* edited by D. L. Sills. New York: Crowell Collier.
    1970   *Verbal strategies in multilingual communication.* Language-Behavior Research Laboratory Working Paper No. 36. University of California, Berkeley.
Hale, Kenneth
    1971   *Gaps in languages and cultures.* Paper presented in ms. and read by title only. American Anthropologists Assoc. Meetings. New York.
Hill, Archibald A.
    1952   A note on primitive languages. *IJAL* **18,** 172–177. Reprinted in Hymes (1964).
Hill, Jane A.
    1971   *To cause to die in Cupeno.* Paper read at the Annual Meetings of the American Anthropological Assoc. New York.
Hymes, Dell (ed.)
    1964   *Language in culture and society.* New York: Harper and Row.
    1971   Foreword to Morris Swadesh, *The Origin and Diversification of Language.* Edited by Joel Sherzer. Chicago. Aldine-Atherton.

Labov, William
  1969 The logic and non-standard English. In *Georgetown Monograph Series on Language and Linguistics,* No. 22.
Langacker, Ronald
  1973 Predicate raising: Some Uto-Aztecan evidence. In *Issues in linguistics: papers in honor of Henry and Renée Kahane,* edited by B. Kachru *et al.* Urbana, Illinois: University of Illinois Press.
Swadesh, Morris
  1971 *The Origin and Diversification of Language.* Edited by Joel Sherzer; Foreword by Dell Hymes. Chicago: Aldine-Atherton.
Thompson, Sandra Annear
  1971 The Deep Structure of Relative Clauses. In *Studies in Linguistic Semantics,* edited by Charles J. Fillmore and D. Terence Langendoen. New York: Holt.
Werner, H. and B. Kaplan
  1963 *Symbol Formation.* New York: Wiley.
Whitehead, A. N., and Bertrand Russell
  1910 *Principia Mathematica.* Cambridge, England: Cambridge University.

Speech and Social Prestige in the Belizian Speech Community

KEITH T. KERNAN
JOHN SODERGREN
ROBERT FRENCH

Introduction

It is probably true that in all societies the social status of an individual depends to some extent upon his linguistic abilities. One's intelligence, one's personality, one's position in the social hierarchy, indeed, one's worth as a human being, may all be judged, to a greater or a lesser degree, by the way one speaks.

In our own culture, there is a prestige dialect—Standard English—and speakers are judged in many regards by how closely their particular idiolect approximates the Standard English form. Certain dialects that differ from Standard English in their phonology, grammar, or lexicon are devalued, and persons who speak them are considered to be ignorant, unschooled, unintelligent, or provincial. We send our children to "grammar" school so that they may escape such stigmas. Our notion of language, as it functions in the determination of social status, is one of correctness of linguistic form. Though a good raconteur is appreciated, he is rare, and the prestige his verbal ability brings him is confined to a limited sphere. The values that pervade middle class American culture have to do with the ability to use the standard well in its referential function. Breadth of verbal repertoire (see Gumperz, 1964) and verbal artistry are not devalued, but neither are they highly valued. The poetic function of language and language as performance are consigned to specialists and are not considered to be necessary aspects of the linguistic competence of ordinary members of our culture. Though all functions of speech are represented and recognized, they receive differential evaluative weighing. A hierarchy of the functions of speech acts (see Hymes, 1961) descriptive of either saliency or prestige in the minds of members of the United States speech community would have the referential use of an elaborated standard code at the very top.

As Hymes (1961, 1962, 1964a,b, 1972) has suggested and as a number of empirical studies have illustrated, speech communities may differ in the relative importance assigned to the various functions of speech and in the relative prestige that accrues to skill in the execution of those functions. Among the Burundi of Central Africa, for example, Albert (1972, p. 75) has found that "esthetic–emotive values are higher in the hierarchy than moral or logical principles in speech and other behavior." Speech among the Burundi is explicitly recognized as an important aspect of social life, and eloquence is highly valued in all types of discourse. "Elegance of composition and delivery, figures of speech, and the interpolation of stories and proverbs are expected and employed" (Albert, 1972, p. 93). In speech behavior, as in all aspects of life, Burundi believe that "success is beautiful and good, and the beautiful is more likely to succeed than the inelegant" (p. 87).

In the black American speech community, though ability in the use of Standard English in its appropriate context is valued, so, too, is ability in Black American English (see Mitchell-Kernan, 1971, 1972a). The clever use of speech is appreciated, and verbal artistry is more highly valued and more often exhibited than in white American culture. The proliferation of metalinguistic terms (Mitchell-Kernan, 1971, 1972a; Kochman, 1969; Labov et al., 1968) for types of speech acts is indicative of the cultural emphasis of speech and cultural appreciation of talented and elegant speech behavior. Labov (1969, p. 64) points out that among young, urban, male blacks there exist "many speech events which depend upon the competitive exhibition of verbal skills: singing, sounding toasts, rifting, louding—a whole range of activities in which the individual gains status through his use of language."

Cultures differ, then, in terms of their valuation of the importance of speech, in and of itself and as it relates to other cultural values; in terms of the evaluative hierarchy of speech functions; and in terms of the dimensions of speech behavior that help to determine the social status and relative prestige of speakers. Among young, male speakers of City Creole in Belize City, Belize, speech behavior is an important and highly salient component of all aspects of life. There is an elaborated metalanguage for the identification and discussion of a wide variety of speech acts and styles, the artistic performance of which is highly valued. One's personality may be judged by one's linguistic habits, and social status and prestige among one's peers depends upon breadth of verbal repertoire, knowledge of sociolinguistic rules, and artistry of performance.

The Language Situation

Belize is a colony of Great Britain, and the official language is English. English is the language of government, education, and the mass media. A form of English is the lingua franca of the country, and learning English is a prerequisite for access to high occupational status. Standard English is, however, the native or first learned language of very few citizens of Belize. The linguistic situation for the country as a whole is quite complex with Creole, Spanish, Black Carib, German, and Mayan languages being spoken as native languages and with a high incidence of multilingualism among the population.[1] Within the Belizian speech community itself, the first-learned language of most speakers is some form of an English-based Creole. Elsewhere (French, Kernan, and Sodergren, 1972), we have distinguished four categories along the English–Broad Creole language continuum that exist in Belize City. Briefly, they are: Standard Belizian English, which may be considered to be a dialect of Standard English and an instance of standard Caribbean English; Nonstandard Belizian English, which represents an imperfectly learned standard and which is highly variable in form from speaker to speaker and situation to situation; City Creole, which is a form of Creole with many lexical and a few grammatical borrowings from Standard English; and Broad Creole, which is the form of Creole most different from the standard and which closely resembles the English-based Creole of Jamaica as described by Bailey (1966). Of these four varieties, Standard and Nonstandard English are the native languages of practically no native born members of the speech community. Broad Creole is spoken by recent immigrants to the city from the surrounding countryside and by their children. The native speech of most of the residents of Belize City, however, is City Creole, and among the young urban males who were our informants, City Creole is far and away the predominant native language.

The linguistic competencies of individual speakers in the speech community do not occupy single points along the English–Broad Creole continuum, however. Rather, any speaker has at his command a span along that continuum and may shift his speaking style in response to the demands of the sociolinguistic situation. Speakers whose native language is City Creole, for example, as a result of their educational and social contacts, are able to speak Nonstandard or even Standard Belizian English when conversing with a monolingual speaker of English or when trans-

[1] See Le Page (1972) for a linguistic survey of Cayo District, British Honduras.

acting business with a government official. Conversely, they are able to use a form that is closer to the Broad Creole pole of the continuum than is their everyday style when the occasion demands it.

The Salience of Speech

Like black American culture (e.g., Mitchell-Kernan, 1971; Kochman, 1969; Labov et al., 1968), Belizian Creole is a highly verbal one. Each day of one's life is filled with words; the clever use of language is greatly appreciated; there is a highly developed metalanguage for types of speech acts and speech events; classification of an individual as to personality and character is based, in part, on the speech behavior of that individual; and one's status depends partially on one's ability to perform verbally.

In Belize, one knows another person and characterizes his personality by his speech behavior, both what he says and the way he says it. The "window to one's soul" is not his eyes, but his mouth, and people who don't expose their souls are neither liked nor trusted. Though a person may say disagreeable things, at least his hearers feel that they know him. They may not like him, but they will feel more comfortable with him than with the man who says little or nothing.

A "bósé" person, for example, is one who boasts and always has more to say than his interlocutors. Such a person is likely to be at least mildly disliked. One of our informants would not patronize a particular bar because he considered the owner to be *bósé*. He said the man was boastful and always tried to top others. If a customer told him that he had just bought a new pair of shoes for ten dollars, for example, the owner would claim to have bought a pair for seventeen dollars: *He always tries to **crow you down**, to **over talk you**. That's why I don't like him. The place I go to is a better place. The owner is cool and treats you right. He **talks straight**, man.*

So this person who is *bósé* is not only boastful, but he *crows you down* and *over talks you*. "He wants all the attention and always feels like he knows everything." He is not regarded as highly as a person who *talks straight*. Yet such a person is regarded more highly than one who is *braigin;* that is, one who shows off his possessions but does not boast about them. *If you are a **braigin** man and don't talk much, people will hate you for that.* Even a *braigin* man, however, is, informants explain, better than a *personal* man who keeps to himself and doesn't say much. Such a person is regarded as selfish and is accused of thinking he is better than others. *A **personal** man is worse that a **bósé** or **braigin** man because you don't know how he thinks. He don't talk. He don't mess with the community. How you going to know how he thinks?*

As people may be disliked for their speech behavior or lack of it, they may also be respected and admired for the way they can speak. A man who has a large repertoire of Bre'r Anancie[2] stories and the ability to tell them well is admired, appreciated, and considered to be gifted. A minor culture hero among the young, urban men is an older man who is particularly adept at *throwing a phrase*. Not only is he good at it, but he paints signs of his messages and displays them for all the world to see. He is, in the idiom of American Black English (Mitchell-Kernan, 1971; Mitchell-Kernan and Kernan, 1971), both *signifying* and graphically *loud talking*. Like *signifying, throwing a phrase* is conveying a message through indirection. To understand a speaker when he *throws a phrase*, one must share a psychological context (see Mitchell-Kernan and Kernan, 1971) with that speaker. The message is delivered in allegorical fashion and only those in the know can properly interpret it.

Throwing a phrase has some negative connotations attached to it. It is regarded as an indirect and diplomatic use of language in order to slander. Again, like *signifying, throwing a phrase* may depend for its indirection on ambiguity of addressee as well as on ambiguity of lexicon and syntax. Saying *Like deh ga deh own sash window, but deh brok fo yu one, an deh no realize deh ga one do don broke home* ('People talk about your business without realizing that similar things could be said of them') to an interlocutor in a loud enough fashion so that it can be overheard by a third party who has been gossiping about you is to *throw a phrase* in which both message and addressee are ambiguous. It is doubly indirect. Such clever use of language, though it might be regarded as slandering, is nevertheless appreciated for its artistic merit. While throwing a slanderous phrase is appreciated for the skill involved, *ceitfulling* 'talking about someone behind his back' is not. *Ceitfulling* involves no skill. It lacks artistic merit. Both *throwing a phrase* and *ceitfulling* are slightly negatively regarded, however; a feeling illustrated by the fact that our young male informants (who exhibit a high degree of sexual antagonism) feel that such use of speech is primarily a woman's habit, and that women are primarily recipients of the sign painter's messages.

Yerri so 'gossip', is regarded as the occupation of everyone, although, again, men accuse women of gossiping more than their fair share. *The biggest problem here in Belize is gossip. Women gossip everyday. Instead of being home cooking for her husband, they are out gossiping.* Perhaps the culture's attitude toward gossip is best illustrated by the following poem written by a young Belizian woman (Yorke, 1970, with permission of the author):

---

[2] Bre'r Anancie is the trickster-hero in a number of traditional Creole folktales.

Yerri So

by Joy Gwyneth Yorke

'Da yerri so dis, yerri so dat ah' yerri so tarrah;
Da only yerri so enna dis place. Warrah!
Mabel tell Gloria an' she tell y cuz'n, ah' y cuz'n tell di adda
      wan, right so.
Soon de whole town gat di yerri so.

Yo yer how lee Janey Smith fi gat wah' baby fi
Alan weh di work da New Capital.
How Mary di play wid y cuz'n bwoy,
She nuh gat no shame at all.
Ah' how Gwen bredda gyalfren sista gahn de States tru di
      back;
Y ma nehli gat haht attack.
Yo yer how Clive ma ded;
Y me fahl down Tuesday enna di shed.
Da Warrah! Now you yer seh de Vera sen y husband da
      Seaview;
Y ketch a wid y bes' fren' da Bayview.
Gyal, yo yer weh Elaine dehndi seh bout yo?
If yo mes wid deh' yo da woh cunnumunnu.
Yo yer how Liza come back frah States,
Now y di bruck y tongue wid lone American, yo heah.
Di jackass gyal even bleach y heah.

Da yerri so dis, yerri so dat, ah' yerri so tarrah.
Da only yerri so enna dis place. Warrah!

Gossip

Gossip this and gossip that and gossip all the time;
There's only gossip in this place. Warrah!
Mabel tells Gloria, and she tells her cousin and her
Cousin tells the other one, right so.
Soon the whole town has the gossip.

Did you hear how little Janey Smith had a baby by
Alan who works at the New Capital.
How Mary is playing around with her cousin's boy,
She doesn't have any shame at all.
And how Gwen's brother's girlfriend's sister has entered the United States
      illegally.
Her mother nearly had a heart attack.
Did you hear that Clive's mother is dead;

She fell down Tuesday in the shed.
Da Warrah! Now you hear it said that
Vera sent her husband to Seaview [mental institution];
She caught him with her best friend at the Bayview nightclub.
Girl, have you heard what Elaine and they are saying about you?
If you mess with them, it'll be over for you.
Have you heard how Liza came back from the United States,
Now she breaks her tongue speaking only American, you hear
The jackass girl even bleaches her hair.

Gossip this, and gossip that, and gossip all the time.
There's only gossip in this place. Warrah!

So gossip is regarded as permeating the culture. Everyone gossips and does it frequently. Everyone is, or should be, highly verbal. If not engaged in *yerri so,* then one is probably engaged in simply *chatting* 'talking', or in *wapping,* which is similar to Black English *rapping* (Kochman, 1969). Or perhaps, one is *gabbing off* 'talking a lot' or *humbugging* 'making promises with no intention of keeping them' or *knocking his ting* 'displaying his talents' or *back chatting* 'talking back, being saucy' or *playing hard* 'purposely not taking a hint'. Perhaps one is being *wási* 'contrary' and is engaged in *bad talking,* which may be *ceitfulling, throwing a phrase, humbugging,* swearing, interrupting, or the inappropriate use of a code, such a speaking Raw Creole to someone who doesn't understand it. But regardless of the particular speech act being performed, one is usually talking. In fact, it is only when a social relationship has completely broken down that one treats another with silence, and even that silence is not likely to last for long but will be ended by one of the quarreling parties saying *Bret da no fi me,* i.e., 'the breath of life (speech) is not controlled by me but by God. We may as well give in to the laws of nature and begin speaking to one another again'.

The power of speech as a mechanism of social control is also evident in the following text which is excerpted from an extensive argument in which two of our informants were not only attempting to convince one another of the validity of their respective positions, but were also attempting to best one another in a verbal dueling sense by decisively winning the exchange.

A: Boy, you boy, I will take something and wap your head, man.[3]
B: Do it, man.
A: I'm telling you . . .
C: Watch how you'll make this thing to violence.

[3] This exchange has been translated into English from the more creolized version in which it occurred.

B: See, he was getting angry, man. You were getting vexed.
A: Because I was trying to tell you: he was trying to say that I was telling a lie in front of his face, man.
B: Why were you getting mad?
A: You can't say . . .
C: The best way is for you to keep cool.
B: I never mentioned "lie." I never mentioned "lie." You can't say that.
C: **Who gets vexed first loses.**
B: You see, you want to put words . . .
A: No, I wasn't getting vexed, but it's the lie this guy was telling me, man.
C: It's vexed you're getting.

In this way, C short-circuited the possibility of physical confrontation. By edict, he introduced the cultural norm that violent behavior in such a context is to be avoided, being reckoned as an admission of verbal defeat.

The high salience of speech behavior and the cultural value for filling each moment of social interaction with talking is constantly brought home to us; not only in our research per se, but also in our attempts to act as social participants in the Belizian speech community. Periods of silence of any length at all on our part are regarded as clear evidence of our lack of any sort of linguistic competency or social grace (as indeed they are). We were questioned about the verbal habits of Americans and our lack of knowledge of entertaining stories. The few jokes we were able to dredge up from our limited repertoires on such occasions were treated with a mixture of disdain and pity. Our interlocutors would fill the awkward silence with an Anancie story learned as a child during lengthy evening story telling sessions in their homes or with an elaborate and protracted account of some personal incident, thereby relieving our embarrassment while, at the same time and not entirely coincidentally, establishing their own verbal superiority as verbal artists.

Prestige, Social Success, and Language

In the Belizian speech community, social success and prestige as a speaker are not dependent, as they are in the United States, upon mastery of the standard code. A native speaker of City Creole who has mastered Standard Belizian English but who ignores the sociolinguistic rules that govern the choice of style would not be greatly admired; neither would the speaker whose verbal performances lack artistry nor the man with a limited verbal repertoire enjoy prestige and social success as a speaker.

This is not to say, however, that knowledge of Standard Belizian English is not admired nor that the standard docs not enjoy a certain inherent prestige.

In terms of Weinreich's (1953, p. 79) rather narrow definition of linguistic prestige as "the value of a language in social advance," English is indeed prestigious. It is, after all, the standard, the language of government and education. A knowledge of Standard Belizian English is a prerequisite for a good job; members of the elite speak it. Belizians recognize that a knowledge of English helps to pave the way to much that is desirable and to facilitate contact with the rest of the world. If one were to poll a sample of Belizians as to which language in their speech community is the "best" language, the consensus would undoubtedly be English. The pollster would, however, frequently encounter the questions, "best for what?" and "best in what context?" for though English is necessary for some kinds of economic and social success and is spoken by the elite, the other end of the linguistic continuum, Belizian Creole, also enjoys a certain inherent prestige.

As is the case in many Caribbean cultures, nationalism and cultural pride is growing in Belize. This is reflected in dance, music, art, politics, and, of course, attitudes toward the native language, Belizian Creole. Literary works are beginning to appear in Creole, as exemplified by the poem quoted above. An increasing number of newspaper articles are written in Creole and demands are heard for more Creole programs on the national radio station. Though this emerging pride in the native language is apparent on all social levels in the society and is actively encouraged and promoted by the intellectual elite, it is perhaps most strongly felt among the young adults we worked with. Comments such as *Dat de fe wi culture—dat de fe wi dialect*, 'That (Creole) is our culture—that is our language' are made frequently and with pride.

Both Belizian Creole and Standard Belizian English, then, enjoy a certain inherent prestige based on their associations with socioeconomic success and cultural pride. A speaker, however, who controlled one or the other code, or even both, would not automatically enjoy the prestige that attaches to them. Considerations of artistic performance aside, what is admired in Belize is not solely the ability to use the phonology, grammar, and lexicon of one particular code correctly, but rather the breadth of one's verbal repertoire in terms of number of languages known and the sociolinguistic knowledge and sensitivity that results in the use of the proper code at the proper time.

An individual limited by his knowledge or by his personal style to a single code in all verbal interaction is not only not admired, but he is criticized and censured. Generally, City Creole is the native language of our informants and is used colloquially for most informal conversation. The unregulated, almost pathological use of English—to the point of even denying a knowledge of Creole—on the part of one of our informants was received with ardent criticism by his peers. Such use of English was not prestigious because the speaker did not attempt to adapt his speech to the style deemed appropriate by his interlocutors, not even creolizing his speech in heated argument with other native Creole speakers. His speech was regarded as artificial and snobbish. Indeed, his use of careful English in formal and informal situations alike generated hostility by threatening the coherence and integration of the specialization of functions of English and Creole. [See Mitchell-Kernan (1972b) on determinants of language choice among Black English speakers.]

As the use of English is appropriate only in certain contexts, so, too, is the use of Broad Creole. Since English is not only taught in the schools but is the medium of instruction and the language of the school room setting, departures from the standard in the classroom typically provoke ridicule, punctuated by taunts such as *You come from the bush* on the part of the other pupils. One native Broad Creole speaker recounted an incident that occurred during his first day of school. "During the roll call, I forgot to say *present* and I said *a di ya* and the whole class took it funny and laughed at me; but it is the same thing, only *present* is English and *a di ya* is Creole." It is not that, in itself, Creole was revolting or funny to the students, since they, after all, were native speakers of Creole themselves. Rather, the circumstances made the Creole form inappropriate according to the sociolinguistic dictates of the culture.

The term *bad talking,* in the Belizian speech community, refers to breaches of the etiquette of speaking, such as cursing or rudely interrupting a speaker. However, *bad talking* may also refer to the utilization of a linguistic variety that is inappropriate to the occasion. During the first part of our research, talking to the investigators in Creole was regarded as *bad talking* inasmuch as we were non-Creole speakers, and the use of such Broad Creole forms as *unu* 'you (plural)' was met with verbal rebuke.

As a knowledge of the proper situational use of linguistic code is necessary for social success and prestige as a speaker, so, too, is breadth of verbal repertoire—both in terms of number of languages and varieties known and in terms of the ability to adequately perform the numerous and differentiated speech acts that exist in the Belizian speech community.

Though Standard Belizian English and Belizian Creole carry a certain amount of inherent prestige, there are also some negative values attached to them. Speakers of Creole regard English, in the abstract, as snobbish, unnecessary, and a manifestation of colonialism. Broad Creole, on the other hand, is considered to be rustic and provincial. Though these negative attitudes are not as strongly felt as the more positive ones, they do militate against the unqualified acceptances of either code as greatly prestigious in and of itself.

What is primarily valued in the Belizian speech community is not one language or another but the knowledge on the part of a speaker of a number of languages and his ability to use each in its proper context. The value is on speech rather than on language; on verbal performance rather than on a particular code. Thus an individual who can say of American English, "it enlightens the tongue," and of Belizian Creole, "it's too broad," can at the same time be proud of his knowledge of more Broad Creole forms than any of his friends. His pride is in his command of both American English and Broad Creole and at times he emphasizes the positive qualities of one language and at other times the positive qualities of the other. His choice of code is determined by other components of the speech act in question, such as topic, interlocutor, setting, message form and genre, and so forth (see Hymes, 1962). A native speaker of City Creole who uses City Creole for most unmarked colloquial purposes will speak English to monolingual speakers of English on formal occasions, for topics such as those related to education, for impression management when he wishes to appear well informed and expert, and so forth. He will employ his broadest form of Creole, however, when speaking of his Creole heritage, when playing the rustic, when performing Creole genres such as Anancie tales or proverbs, when wishing to emphasize folk values or wisdom as opposed to those that are viewed as coming from outside the culture, and on other similar occasions.

Individual abilities in English and Broad Creole vary with social background and education, of course, and the speaker who has spent some time in the United States or who has attended the local junior college is able to more closely approximate the standard than someone with a more limited background. Similarly, a recent immigrant to the city is able to speak a broader form of the Creole than a third-generation urbanite. Such ability in the command of the poles of the linguistic continuum is recognized as a skill and appreciated as such. A high degree of competency in both Standard Belizian English and Broad Creole is rare, however, and no one among the group we studied is recognized by his peers as being one of the better speakers of Broad Creole. In other words, an individual's competency, if it includes one pole of the linguistic continuum, does not extend all the way to the other extreme. Everyone, however, is competent in that span of the continuum that we have identified as City Creole, and many also have some knowledge of Spanish. These two languages, like Standard Belizian English and Broad Creole, perform certain functions, have inherent values, are appropriate to certain situations, and add to the prestige of those who speak them well.

City Creole, as pointed out above, is the native language of most of our informants. As such, it performs most of the functions that the stylistically and situationally unmarked variety performs in any speech community. It is the language of the home, of work, and of casual conversations between friends. Its use is also appropriate to stylistic genres such as personal narrative and the verbal dueling that occupy so much time and serve to establish status among the young male peer groups that constitute our sample. Like the first learned languages in other speech communities, City Creole is also the language of strong emotion and argument.

Since City Creole is the colloquial language of the speech community and since most verbal performances are done in the colloquial style, the skillful and entertaining use of City Creole is appreciated. Unlike Standard Belizian English and Broad Creole, however, City Creole carries little inherent prestige as a language. Though it does have the status of a separate language in the sense that it is named and is sometimes claimed by its speakers to be mutually unintelligible with both Broad Creole and Standard Belizian English, it is nevertheless recognized and defined as a mixture of Creole and English. Our informants sometimes refer to City Creole as a dialect and define it as both "broken English" and "broken Creole," which they contrast to "real Creole" as spoken in the rural areas of the country. Moreover, they not infrequently express the wish that Broad Creole were taught in the schools so that they would be more proficient in what they regard as the language of their cultural heritage.

On the other hand, the use of City Creole, because of the admixture of English forms, is seen as a mark of broad experience, which in itself is highly valued in Belizian culture. It represents a sophistication and knowledge of the world that is not implied by the use of Broad Creole with its rustic connotations. City Creole, for this reason and because it is the language that is appropriate to most speech situations in the life of a member of the Belizian speech community, is a necessary part of everyone's verbal repertoire. One is not a full-fledged member of the speech community without a knowledge of it, and linguistic success depends upon its appropriate use. Moreover, City Creole is naturally regarded as being easier to speak and more expressive of emotion and affect.

A form of City Creole known as American Creole, which is spoken almost exclusively by young males, has a special status of its own. Among the peer group, American Creole is regarded as both an indication of worldliness and the sine qua non of the clever use of language. It is an argot of the young and differs from the rest of City Creole in that it contains many slang words and expressions. Like slang anywhere, the forms are constantly changing and one must be an active participant in the speech community of the young in order to remain current and avoid becoming dated. The forms themselves are, in large part, borrowed from American English in general and Black American English in particular.[4]

The primary personal contact that most young Belizian Creoles have with the outside world is with Black America. Some Black American tourists do visit British Honduras, but the main sources of exposure to Black American English are visits to the United States. Belizian Creoles are of African ancestry, and partly because of that and partly because the Black American lifestyle and stylistic use of language so closely resembles their own, young Belizians associate primarily with blacks during their visits to the United States. As a result, the direction of the acculturation of young Belizians in terms of language, dress, and attitude is toward black America. The most popular music in Belize is the soul music of the United States. Popular dances are imported almost as soon as they are invented. Afro hairstyles are popular, as is the latest in American fashion. The popular personalities of black American culture are admired and serve as sources for the prevalent habit of "taking names" among the young men we studied. We are personally acquainted with three James Browns, two Ray Charleses, a Wilson Pickett, and two Cassius Clays.

Perhaps the most admired aspect of black American culture, however, is its language, from which American Creole borrows extensively. *Dig it, dude, check it out, motherfucker, hip, say what?* and many other similar expressions are used with a high degree of frequency. Much of the slang is, of course, of local invention. A particular section of town in which two popular bars are located is referred to variously as *yonder, the bottom,* and *down South.*

The slang of American Creole changes rapidly, and therefore, serves as a marker of "hipness" for those who know the latest version; that is, it serves as a marker of group membership, as well as a measure of one's status within the group. Moreover, the very latest versions serve as a limited secret language for conversing in the presence of individuals who are not part of the group at all.

American Creole is a highly valued part of the verbal repertoire among the young men who speak it and is part and parcel of the verbal dueling that is so important in establishing relative status within the peer group. Those who speak it well and know all the latest slang have an immediate advantage in any argument or verbal performance.

[4] The speech of the investigators, which contained a certain amount of slang including some Black American English idioms, constituted another source of lexical borrowing for the informants.

According to the 1946 census, a little over twenty-two percent of the population of British Honduras speaks Spanish as a native language. Although none of our informants is a native Spanish speaker, a number of them are able to speak some Spanish as the result of having lived or worked for a time in one of the Spanish speaking districts of the country. Degree of competency, of course, varies considerably, but since even a minimal knowledge adds to the breadth of one's verbal repertoire and, therefore, to one's status as a speaker, Spanish forms are not infrequently used by the members of the speech community we studied. Greater competency, of course, brought greater prestige, and speakers competed with one another for the status that comes with linguistic ability.

An example of the fierce competition that takes place occurred one evening during the early stages of our research. An informant answered one of our questions in Spanish. His knowledge of Spanish was limited and the grammatical form of his response was slightly incorrect. Another informant, who had a better command of the language as the result of having worked for a time in a sugar processing plant in one of the Spanish-speaking districts, immediately pointed out the grammatical errors of the sentence and supplied the correct form. He then fired a series of questions in rapid Spanish at the first informant, none of which were understood or answered. The victory was obvious but not yet complete, and as the loser, who had lapsed into embarrassed silence, took his leave later in the evening, he was disdainfully wished a *buenas noches*.

Summary and Conclusion

In Belize, then, to be a competent member of the linguistic community—to be a good speaker—one must do more than simply speak the standard flawlessly. The standard, with its own rules of logic, evidence, and argumentation, is admired as it is in our own culture. However, in Belize the standard is appropriate to only a few of the contexts in which the speaker's abilities are judged. Its use in all contexts and for all purposes in regarded as evidence of linguistic deprivation rather than linguistic skill. The talented speaker, the person with true verbal ability, is the individual whose linguistic competency covers a large span of the language continuum. He has a broad verbal repertoire and uses the proper style in the proper context. Moreover, he is a performer, an artist. His repertoire includes not only a broad range of languages and varieties, but a broad range of genres as well. He is entertaining, clever, and amusing, as well as convincing and erudite. His social success depends upon the performance of a number of speech functions in a number of speech styles and not simply upon the performance of the referential function in the standard style.

The Belizian speech community is neither unique nor unusual in its lack of total emphasis on the referential function, the standard language, and the elaborated code. Overall verbal ability is an even more important aspect of social success and prestige than it is in our own culture, and yet the members of our Belizian sample would undoubtably do quite poorly on any of the tasks our behavioral sciences have devised that purport to measure verbal ability. The metaphorically highly elaborated performance of the verbal artist would surely qualify as an instance of a restricted code in Bernstein's (e.g., 1964) scheme of linguistic ability. Our syntacticists, with their limited notion of what constitutes language, would consider culturally significant linguistic variation in the speech of Belizians to be only minimally rule governed (simply optional rules in a referential code), rather than recognizing that from a broader functional perspective quite the contrary is the case. Our linguistic theory reflects our cultural values in its emphasis on the analysis of the standard code as it is used to perform the referential function. As Hymes (1972, p. 2) and Jakobson (1960) have pointed out, questions of function are fundamental to sociolinguistic research. We have attempted to show here that in one area of sociolinguistic research, that of the relationship between speech behavior and social prestige, the differential functions of speech and their relationship to choice of code must be considered.

Acknowledgments

Thanks are due to Claudia Mitchell-Kernan, Catherine Macklin, Vernon Leslie, Gilroy Moore, James Brown, and Charles Golsen for their advice and many helpful comments at various stages of this work. Support for the field work upon which this paper is based was provided by the Harvard University Clark Fund, the Harvard Comparative International Program, and National Institute of Mental Health Training Grant 5T01 MH2487-01.

References

Albert, Ethel M.
    1972   Culture patterning of speech behavior in Burundi. In *Directions in Sociolinguistics; The ethnography of communication* edited by John J. Gumperz and Dell Hymes, pp. 72–105. New York: Holt.
Bailey, Beryl Loftman
    1966   *Jamaican Creole Syntax: A transformational approach.* Cambridge, England: Cambridge University Press.
Bernstein, Basil
    1964   Elaborated and restricted codes: Their social origins and some consequences. *American Anthropologist* **66**(6) (Part 2), 55–69.
French, Robert, Keith T. Kernan, and John Sodergren
    1972   Manuscript.

Gumperz, John J.
  1964   Linguistic and social interaction in two communities. *American Anthropologist*
         66(6) (Part 2), 137–153.
Hymes, Dell
  1961   Functions of speech: An evolutionary approach. In *Anthropology and Education*
         edited by Frederick C. Gruber, pp. 55–83 Philadelphia: University of Pennsylvania
         Press.
  1962   The ethnography of speaking. In *Anthropology and Human Behavior* edited by
         Thomas Gladwin and William C. Sturtevant, pp. 13–53. Washington, D.C.:
         Anthropological Society of Washington.
  1964a Directions in (ethno-) linguistic theory. *American Anthropologist* **66**(3) (Part 3),
         6–56.
  1964b *Language in culture and society; A reader in linguistics and anthropology.* New
         York: Harper and Row.
  1972   Editorial introduction to *Language in Society. Language in Society* **1**(1), 1–14.
Jakobson, Roman
  1960   Concluding statement: Linguistics and poetics. In *Style In Language* edited by
         Thomas Sebeok Cambridge, Massachusetts: The M.I.T. Press.
Kochman, Thomas
  1969   "Rapping" in the black ghetto. *Trans-action* **6** (February 1969), 26–34.
Labov, William
  1969   The logic of non-standard English. In *Report on the Twentieth Annual Round Table
         Meeting on Linguistics and Language Studies* edited by James Alatis. Washington,
         D.C.: School of Language and Linguistics, Georgetown University.
Labov, William, Paul Cohen, Clarence Robins, and John Lewis
  1968   *A Study of the Non-standard English of Negro and Puerto Rican Speakers in New
         York City.* (Cooperative Research Report No. 3288) V. II. New York: Columbia
         University.
Le Page, R. B.
  1972   Preliminary report on the sociolinguistic survey of multilingual communities, part
         I: Survey of Cayo District, British Honduras. *Language in Society,* **1**(1), 155–172.
Mitchell-Kernan, Claudia
  1971   Language Behavior in a Black Urban Community. *Monographs of the Language
         Behavior Research Laboratory. University of California, Berkeley.* No. 2.
  1972a Signifying and marking: Two Afro-American speech acts. In *Directions in So-
         ciolinguistics; The ethnography of communication* edited by John J. Gumperz and
         Dell Hymes, pp. 161–179. New York: Holt.
  1972b On the status of Black English for native speakers: An assessment of values. In
         The Functions of Language in the Class room, edited by Courtney B. Cazden,
         Vera P. John and Dell Hymes, pp. 195–210. New York: Teachers College Press.
Mitchell-Kernan, Claudia, and Keith T. Kernan
  1971   *Language behavior: A sociolinguistic approach to the relations between language,
         society and the individual.* Paper presented at NIMH Conference on Anthropology
         and Mental Health. October 1971, Palo Alto, California.
Weinreich, Uriel
  1953   *Language in Contact, Findings and Problems.* New York: Publications of the
         Linguistic Circle of New York, No. 1.
Yorke, Joy Gwyneth
  1970   Yerri So. *Open Paki,* **1**(2), 17. Belize City, British Honduras.

Language Acquisition and Language Change: Japanese Numeral Classifiers[1]

MARY SANCHES

> . . . invoking children's incomplete language learning as an explanation of language change is vacuous unless it suggests at the same time a *pattern* of learning failures
>
> —Weinreich, Labov and Herzog, "A Theory of Language Change," p. 109

Japanese shares with a number of East Asian, American Indian, and Oceanic languages the usually obligatory use of a linguistic form known as numeral classifiers.[2] In these languages, when counting something, one generally cannot use cardinal numbers alone as, for example, we do in English. Quantification usually requires the selection of one of a set of special morphemes, usually bound to a numeral form, that designates certain semantic features of whatever is being enumerated.

There have been reports that for some numeral classifier languages (e.g., Chinese, Thai, Tzeltal, and Japanese) a reduction in the number of numeral classifier forms in the system is taking place. The study of pos-

[1] The research on which this paper is based was supported by National Science Foundation Science Development Grant, GU-1598-26-3320 administered by the University of Texas. This paper is part of a longer monograph on Japanese numeral classifiers soon to be completed that will describe in detail the data and theoretical points raised here in addition to the methodology involved. A previous version of this paper was presented at a symposium on the acquisition of culture at the annual meeting of the American Anthropological Association, 1970, San Diego, California.

[2] The numeral classifier system in Japanese is morphophonemically quite complex because of the existence of two sets of canonical shapes for number morphs (and even some classifier morphs): indigenous Japanese, and Sino-Japanese. This is reflected in the examples here in the differences between the representations for "one": *hito-*, "one (indigenous Japanese canonical shape morph)" and *ichi-*, "one (Sino-Japanese canonical shape morph)". Currently a third set is being developed: *yan-, tsu:-, suri:-*, based on borrowings from English. These variant representations and their implications is more fully described in the forthcoming monograph.

sible changes in such a linguistic form is interesting for a number of reasons. First of all, numeral classifiers function semantically much like lexical paradigms. That is, they are formally describable in terms of criterial attributes. However, unlike lexical items, they usually are grammatically obligatory and part of morphologically complex constructions. This means that in working out the process of change in numeral classifier systems, we would be gaining insights about principles of change in semantic systems generally. In addition, looking at changes in classifiers is interesting because it provides us with an occasion for investigating an idea of traditional concern in linguistics—the relationship between language learning and language change.

I hold with the view of the three authors quoted above, that a theory of language change must be empirically founded, that it must take into account individual variation, and that "structuredness" does not presuppose homogeneity (Weinreich et al., 1968, pp. 100–101). In their words, what a theory of language change must take into account is, "How are the observed changes embedded in the matrix of linguistic and extralinguistic concomitants of the forms in question?"

In this paper, I will outline (1) demonstrable differences in the numeral classifier models of individual native Japanese speakers of different generations, (2) how these changes are related to the way in which children learn the numeral classifier system, and (3) how they are related to a context of social meanings.

Quantification expressions in Japanese can be formed by one of the following syntactic expressions:

1. number morph + noun, as with *ichigun* 'one county' (*ichi-* 'one' + *-gun* 'county') or *hitokawa, "one river"* (*hito-*, "one" + *-kawa*, "river")[2]

2. noun (+ case marker) + number morph and $\begin{cases} \text{numeral} \\ \text{cardinal} \end{cases}$

classifier (2a) $\left.\begin{array}{l} \\ \\ \end{array}\right\}$
number marker (2b)

That is, in example 2a, follow the noun being quantified with a word composed of a number morph and a numeral classifier, for example, *ju:tan (-ŋa) sanmai* 'three carpets' (*ju:tan* 'carpet', *san-* 'three', + *-mai* 'broad, flat things') or *inu(-ŋa) nihiki* 'two dogs' (*inu* 'dog', *ni-* 'two', *-hiki* 'nonhuman animal'). In example 2b, the syntactic form is the same, but instead of a numeral classifier the cardinal number marker is used. For example, *ikikata(-ŋa) hitotsu* 'one route' (*ikikata* 'route', *hito-* 'one', *-tsu* 'cardinal number marker'). In other words, this particular alternative specifies nothing at all about the semantic properties of the "thing" being enumerated. This last is an alternative which may not be available in some other numeral classifier languages.

Which of these expressions is chosen by a speaker is ideally determined by the kind of thing being counted. For example, items that are quantified by simply prefixing a number morph to a noun seem to include inseparable natural features and concepts with no material referents. The cardinal number forms seem to function primarily, though not exclusively, for abstract counting. However, these determinants are not hard and fast rules at the present time, whatever they were in the past, and it is in the use of these alternatives, and others that individual competencies differ and lead to change over time.

The numeral classifier morphemes possible in syntactic form 2a belong to four semantically defined subcategories.[3] These are: (1) containers; (2) taxonomy-specific classifiers (i.e., forms that correspond to the basic taxonomic category of the thing being counted); (3) shape classifiers; (4) process classifiers (i.e., classifiers that specify something about the process by which the enumerable item was made, or achieved its present shape). Table I shows an analysis of domains (2), (3), and (4). We will not be concerned with domain (1) "containers," which, functioning syntactically like "true" classifiers, do not specify semantic features of the enumerated.

As is evident from an examination of Table I, in addition to the choices mentioned above, a speaker must decide, if using a numeral classifier form, which of the classifier domains he will select one from and what level of specificity he will designate. One could just as well use shape or process classifiers for most of the things that have their own taxonomy-specific classifiers. In addition, within a given classifier domain, for example, (2.2) "living things," there is a general classifier, in this case -*hiki* 'head', for all animals, and more specific ones depending, in this instance on whether they are birds, fish, etc. In counting fish, one has a choice of whether to use the classifier for animals generally or the one for fish, -*bi* 'tail', specifically.

We can conceptualize these differences in terms of degrees or levels of marking—the more general terms are less marked, and the more specific are more marked—corresponding to the features of the head noun of the

---

[3] There is another set of forms that also can be considered classifiers and that will not be considered here; they modify verbs rather than, as these do, nouns. They are part of expressions that specify the number of times an action is performed.

TABLE I

Numeral Classifier Domains in Japanese (nonliterary, by single units)

1	Containers (not considered here)	2.1.6.2.1	smaller (pistols) -*chō*	3.	Shape specifiers, by predominant dimension
2	Taxonomy-specific classifiers	2.1.6.2.2	larger (cannon) -*mon*	3.1	One-dimensional -*hon*
2.1	Inanimate human artifacts	2.1.6.2.3	Ammunition	3.2	Two-dimensional
2.1.1	relatively smaller -*ko*	2.1.6.2.3.1	small -*tama*	3.2.1	length predominating -*suji*
2.1.2	relatively larger -*dai*	2.1.6.2.3.2	large -*hatsu*	3.2.2	length and breadth equally important -*mai*
2.1.3	Vehicles -*dai*	2.1.7	Printed and written works	3.2.3	height and breadth equally important -*men*
2.1.3.1	Wheeled vehicles -*dai*	2.1.7.1	bound -*satsu*	3.3	Three-dimensional -*ko*
2.1.3.1.1	on tracks -*ryo:*	2.1.7.1.1	relatively thick (volume) -*kan*	3.3.1	length and breadth predominating -*hen*
2.1.3.1.2	not on tracks -*dai*	2.1.7.1.2	relatively thin (copy) -*bu*	3.3.2	Cubic -*chō*
2.1.3.2	Winged flying vehicles -*ki*	2.1.7.2	unbound -*tsu*	3.3.3	Irregularly shaped -*kai*
2.1.3.3	Ships	2.1.7.3	Literary works -*hen*	3.3.4	Spherical -*ko*
2.1.3.3.1	relatively smaller -*so:*	2.1.7.3.1	nonpoetry -*hen*	3.3.4.1	Relatively larger -*kyū/-tama*
2.1.3.3.2	relatively larger -*seki*	2.1.7.3.2	poetry	3.3.4.2	Relatively smaller
2.1.3.3.3	Warships -:*an*	2.1.7.3.2.1	shorter -*ku*	3.3.4.2.1	Solid -*tsubu*
2.1.4	Furniture and implements	2.1.7.3.2.2	longer -*shu*	3.3.4.2.2	Liquid -*teki*
2.1.4.1	legged -*kyaku*	2.2	Living things	4.	Process classifiers
2.1.4.2	nonlegged -*sao* (with drawers, chests)	2.2.1	Animal	4.1	Strung -*ren*
2.1.4.3	Fire receptacles -*sue*	2.2.1.1	Human -*nin*	4.2	Lumped -*katamari*
2.1.4.4	Hanging scrolls -*fuku*	2.2.1.2	Nonhuman -*hiki*	4.3	Stretched over a frame -*hari*
2.1.4.5	Eating implements -*zen*	2.2.1.2.1	Mammals -*hiki*	4.4	Grasped -*nigiri*
2.1.4.6	Saleable -*hin*	2.2.1.2.1.1	Deer -*tē*	4.5	Cut -*kire*
2.1.4.7	Work of art -*ten*	2.2.1.2.2	Fish -*bi*	4.6	Pinched -*tsumami*
2.1.4.8	Framed, nonhanging calligraphy -*ka*	2.2.1.2.3	Birds -*wa*		
2.1.4.9	Metal implements -*cho*	2.2.1.2.5	Large domestic mammals -*to:*		
2.1.5	Clothing -*chaku*	2.2.1.2.6	Dead animals -*tai*		
2.1.6	Weapons	2.2.2	Nonanimal = vegetable -*kabu*		
2.1.6.1	Swords -*furi*	2.2.2.1	Leaf -*yō*		
2.1.6.2	Guns	2.2.2.2	Flower -*rin*		

phrase they modify. Thus, for the domain corresponding to 2.2.1.2 of Table I "nonhuman living things":

The choices a speaker has to make in producing a quantification phrase form a set of alternatives to which we can look for directions of change in the numeral classifier system as a whole. We can pose these directions in the following question:

1. Is there more use of cardinal numbers for counting items by the younger generation than by the older? This would be equivalent to our use of cardinal numbers in English and would signify, if widespread, that

agreement between number and enumerated is dropping out of Japanese.

2. Could younger people be giving priority to shape-specific and/or process classifiers versus taxonomy-specific forms?

3. Is it happening that within each classifier domain forms that are more marked are being discarded in favor of forms that are less marked?

It is possible, of course, that change in all three of these directions is taking place; the problem is to specify how much and in which direction. To be able to answer these kinds of questions it is necessary to tap the competence of native speakers of different generations[4] and of children at various stages in the process of learning the language. Accordingly, after a preliminary formal analysis of the numeral classifier system based on intensive work with a small number of informants and surveys of classifier usage in magazine texts and recordings from radio and television, a questionnaire of "frames" based on this ideal model was designed to elicit the total number of distinctions native speakers had encoded in their individual classifier systems. The "frames" were a series of questions requiring people to specify a particular quantity of something. For example, in English we might have the frame: "Today I bought three _____ of cattle," and an informant would have to provide an appropriate form with which to fill in the blank. This kind of elicitation procedure has been standard in ethnographic semantics for a number of years; one of the aims of this research was to expand the methodology to take into account individual variation in a monolingual population.[5] The elicitation test was administered to 212 male and female adults ranging in age from 18 to 73 and to about 100 children ages 9 to 12. Additional data was gathered from other children ages 2 through 9 using a verbal version of the test and two other tasks.

The data that resulted from these tests provides two kinds of evidence that can be used to answer the questions about change posed above: (1) the number of classifier forms in the repertoires of individuals and (2) the range of application of the numeral classifier forms being used. A summary answer to the question of whether there is a difference in the number of classifiers in the models of older and younger individuals is indicated by the fact that the mean number of forms in the repertoires of people over 30 is 36, while those under 30 have an average of only 28

---

[4] In addition, data were gathered on various social characteristics of the sample population in order to relate the changes that are occurring to factors like occupation, education, dialect. These points are discussed fully in Sanches (in preparation).

[5] For references on methodology in ethnographic semantics serving as models for this research, see: Berlin and Romney, 1964; Berlin and Kay, 1968; Frake, 1961, 1964.

forms each. That is, older people have an average of 8 more forms than do younger people.

Furthermore, if we look at the individual domains of classifiers, the structural changes taking place are even clearer. Two representative domains are: "living things" (2.2), which seems to be holding up fairly well across generations and, "furniture and implements" (2.1.4) in which we can see far more structural change. Informants' responses to the questions in the "living things" domain indicate that two forms included in our test have for all practical purposes, dropped out of their individual repertoires. These are -*bi* 'tail', the classifier for fish, and -*tē*, the classifier for deer. While it was possible to encode these distinctions in response to questions on the test, no one in either age group did so. The form that was used in their place were -*hiki* 'general animal classifier'. This means that the unmarked classifier is being used in place of the more specific, marked forms. This generalization is also true in situations where there are intergenerational differences in use of forms in this domain. While the mean number of classifier forms in the repertoires of both younger and older informants is approximately the same, 4.8 forms for the younger and 5.7 for the older, there are differences in how well we can predict, given individuals from both generations having the same number of forms, just what those forms will be.

That is, everyone in both groups has three basic forms:

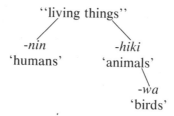

Of those individuals in the older group who have four forms, 90% of them can be predicted to have -*tai* 'dead animals' and only 10% to have added -*tō:* 'large, domestic mammal'. In the younger group, however, only 50% of the people having four forms had added -*tai* to their repertoires, while 30% added -*rin* 'flower', and 20% added -*tō*.

Another exemplary domain, where intergenerational differences in individual repertoires show up even more clearly is "furniture and implements." The older group used an average number of 6.1 classifier forms, almost two and a half more than the average 3.8 of the younger group. In attempting to predict which forms people will have, given a certain number, it is quite clear that different classifiers are basic to the two age groups.

TABLE II

Classification of Three Items in -*kyaku* Range

		"Legged furniture" -*kyaku*	Cardinal number	-*dai*	-*ko*	"Long shape" -*hon*
		A. By individuals over 30 years old				
isu	'chair'	70.0%	11.5%	1.9%	15.4%	—
te:buru	'table'	9.1%	36.1%	18.2%	21.1%	—
hashigo	'ladder'	9.1%	44.4%	9.1%	3.0%	17.3%
		B. By individuals under 30 years old				
isu	'chair'	29.0%	49.0%	3.0%	18.6%	—
te:buru	'table'	3.0%	54.4%	32.2%	10.1%	—
hashigo	'ladder'	5.0%	47.4%	11.8%	8.4%	25.4%

Even more revealing of change is the range of application of the classifiers in individual repertoires. One illustrative example is seen in the use of -*kyaku*, the classifier for "legged furniture," in relation to its range. Informants had the opportunity to apply this classifier to three items in the test as representatives of "legged furniture": *isu* 'chair', *te:buru* 'table', and *hashigo* 'ladder'. Responses indicate that the focus of the classifier -*kyaku* is *isu* 'chair' for both age groups and that it is considered applicable to *te:buru* 'table' and *hashigo* 'ladder' by only a few people. Intergenerational differences in usage are revealed in the alternatives to the ideally correct form -*kyaku*, as shown by Table II. Most striking is that while for *isu* 70% of the older group used -*kyaku*, only 20% of the younger group did so, and while only 11.5% of the older group used the cardinal number, 49% of the younger group did so. In addition, the use of the unmarked forms in this domain, -*dai* and -*ko*, and of the shape classifier -*hon* are seen as alternatives far less than are semantically unmarked cardinal numbers.

Although there are differences among the classifier domains, these examples illustrate the kinds of changes taking place in the system as a whole:

1. Classifier forms are being dropped in favor of use of the cardinal numbers.

2. There is slight but probably nonsignificant increase in the use of shape classifiers at the expense of taxonomy-specific forms, but none in the use of process classifiers.

3. Within the taxonomy-specific classifier domains, forms that are

most likely to remain are the unmarked, most general ones, usually found at the head of the domain.

Let us look now at the process of acquiring numeral classifier forms by children, asking what relationship it might have to what is happening to adult competence models. What we would especially like to know is whether classifier forms are being learned randomly or whether there is a scale of forms according to which some classifiers are learned prior to others.

The first quantification forms children learn in Japanese, usually starting at about 2½ years, are the cardinal numbers. There is good reason why numeral classifier forms are not among the earliest part of the language mastered; they depend not only on the mastery of number concepts, but also on having a set of lexemes representing concepts to which they can be applied. That is, one could not have the classifier for large, domestic animals if one has no lexical items for or concept of horse, cow, etc.

After the cardinal number forms appear, there seem to be two paths to the acquisition of classifiers:

1. Some children go on to learn to count in the abstract and master the quantification concepts involved and then start to incorporate classifier forms.

2. Other children, however, start to incorporate into their counting forms that encode semantic features, while still not being able to count above two or three. This process is usually quite imperfect, as, for example, with the little boy who was counting the arms and legs of his doll for me: *ippon*, 'one long-shape item', *futatsu* 'two (cardinal number)'. In other words, at first, classifier forms will be applied to lower numbers and higher quantities will be expressed simply with cardinal numbers.

In addition to the priority of cardinal numbers, the data reveal that there is an order in which classifier forms are learned that is related to the structure of the forms surviving in adult models. There is a "basic" set of six numeral classifier forms that are mastered first by children. By the age of 5 or 6, all of these forms (and possibly a couple of others) had been learned by most of the children in the sample. Below this age, children may have anywhere from two to six forms from this set in any combination. The set is shown in Table III.

From this point on, elaboration is accomplished by the addition of forms at the lower levels of these domains and by selection of forms from other domains. The two forms most likely to become added to this basic six are -*satu* 'volume' and -*wa* 'wing (bird classifier)'. Next are -*so* 'ships' and -*ken* 'houses'. Beyond this there is very little predictability as to which forms will be added; 6-year-olds have an average of 7 classifiers, 7-

TABLE III
Basic Set of Numeral Classifier Forms as Acquired by Children

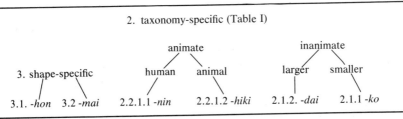

year-olds an average of 9, 8-year-olds an average of 12; by 12 years, children have an average of 22.3, only slightly below that of the young adult group's 28 forms.

While we can see from these examples that the order in which classifiers are learned parallels the disposition of forms that are retained and those that are dropped from adult usage, this does not serve as an explanation as to why change is taking place in just this pattern. In other words, just because children learn -*hiki* 'nonhuman animal' and -*wa* 'bird' first and -*rin* 'flower' later and less predictably does not explain why -*rin* should be less stable in the repertoires of adults. What does give us a hint as to why change should be proceeding in just this way is data on the range of application of particular classifiers. As we saw for adults in the example of the range of application of -*kyaku,* while some people could generalize the form to apply to all "legged furniture," in this case "table" and "ladder," most could not. This is because as far as our evidence is indicative, children are learning that taxonomy-specific classifiers and even some shape classifiers are applicable to a class of referents corresponding to one lexeme, e.g., -*kyaku*—criterial attributes of *isu* 'chair' rather than to a class defined by its own criterial attributes that would potentially be applicable to an infinite set of lexemes.

This is most clearly illustrated by one of the questions included on the test to determine if people could extend to new instances the concepts encoded by classifiers, probably the best test of whether or not a concept has been attained (see, e.g., Bruner, Goodow, and Austin, 1956). The question involved counting a "new" kind of "living thing," *seibutsu,* discovered on the moon.[6] The "living thing" domain seems to be, of all domains, the most salient and least changing over generations, so this question was calculated to reveal the most conservative responses from subjects. The ideal response would have been to encode the attributes "living nonhuman animal" -*hiki* (2.2.1.2) or a possible shape alternative, "length predominant" -*hon* (3.1), because the "animals" were described and pre-

---

[6] Questions were included for the concepts represented by other classifier forms also.

TABLE IV

Classifications of Hypothetical "Living Things" Instance (%)

	No attribute encoded	Classified as animal	Classified as shape
Adults	25	66	9
Children (6–12 yrs)	22	68	10
Children (under 6 yrs)	50	40	10

sented in a picture as being "very long and thin." Table IV shows the percentage of individuals who gave each of the three kinds of responses possible. It is noteworthy that there seems to be no great difference between the responses of children and adults.[7] While large percentages of the subjects did respond with the ideally appropriate classifier, even in the case of this most salient form, almost a quarter of our sample responded in terms of the cardinal number, which indicates these people could not generalize any classifier in their repertoires to include this new example.

Imperfect learning of language has been suggested as a "cause" of language change for a long time (see, e.g., Paul, 1880). Recently this idea has been taken up anew with a view to explicating the mechanisms of such a theory. One of the people concerned with language change in relation to the process of acquisition has been King (see King, 1969, pp. 67–101, for a complete discussion). King has suggested, for example, that learning of "late" rules by adults accounts for intergenerational differences in language, especially with reference to phonology. I would like to augment this explanation to include what is happening in other areas of language by proposing that children can be learning two kinds of rules for language competence—generative and listings—and that it will be the conjunction of these with certain kinds of changes in the nonlinguistic sociocultural environment that will account for many of the changes we observe in lexical and morphological systems.

A number of scholars have suggested that certain kinds of language changes can only be understood in social context. Labov (e.g., 1966) has shown, for example, how the social referrents of phonetic features can motivate change in the phonological system.

Numeral classifiers differ from phonology, however, in several ways; classifiers appear infrequently in spontaneous conversation and are determined by a specific kind of comment—a need to express quantification. For this reason, unlike phonological features, they are poor indicators of

[7] There are differences between male and female, young and old adults that will be fully discussed in Sanches (in preparation).

social distinctions. Obviously people don't go about counting for each other as markers of social class or to signal power or intimacy. Accordingly, they are not subject to the same kind of pressures to change in as direct a relationship as are phonological structures. If they were, we would have individuals who are upwardly mobile striving to increase their repertoires of classifiers.

How then can social factors be influencing the direction of change in this language form? In the last hundred years, Japan has probably been the world's outstanding example of "modernization" and material culture change. This means that many things in the material cultural environment of Japanese speakers have disappeared, only to be replaced with new things, whose lexical motivation and function stem from foreign sources. I am convinced that what is responsible for the shrinking numeral classifier system, and, more importantly, for the pattern of shrinkage that occurs, is the interaction of the way in which they are learned in combination with the changes in material and social culture that are occurring. That is, we have seen that most of the numeral classifier forms in Japanese can be analyzed as classifying items that all belong to the same taxonomic domain. These forms are learned in relation to the items they classify, in lists, rather than as representative of categories of criterial attributes that are potentially generalizeable to an infinite variety of items. Shape classifiers, on the other hand, applicable as they are to a wide variety of items from a range of taxonomies, demand to a greater extent internalization of the semantic features to which they refer, rather than simple association with a limited set of lexical items. Given this listing rule by which forms are learned plus the shift in material objects and their lexical representation, we can only expect the system to atrophy.

This has already happened to classifiers of many traditional things that have disappeared from the scene and for which only a few members of the older generation know the "proper" classifier. The fact that when a new thing replaces an old—for example when *rēnji* '(western-style) cooking range' replaced *kamado*, '(traditional) hearth'—and the old classifier is not extended to it confirms our conclusion that the classifier was represented in the speakers competence, not by generative semantic rules, but by a listing procedure. In addition, it gives us a clue as to why a classifier domain like "living things" remains in effect to the extent it has—the semantic domain to which it refers is obviously quite stable.

This poses some new questions for us. We wonder why the production of such forms should rely on list storage rather than generative rules. Could it be because they are not among the earliest parts of the language learned by the child? Could it be related to the fact that they are not primary lexicon; that is, that they only reiterate features that are already encoded in other lexemes? What does determine whether children, and even adults, learn language structures in terms of lists or in terms of sets of rules that allow for the extension of a concept to a new situation? Finally, how and why do rules change from generative to listing and vice versa? In the answer to these questions would seem to lie an understanding to a great part of the kinds of changes that take place in semantic and grammatical systems.

References

Berlin, Brent
    1968 *Tzeltal numeral classifiers.* The Hague: Mouton.
Berlin, Brent, and Paul Kay
    1968 *Basic color terms.* The Hague: Mouton.
Berlin, Brent, and A. K. Romney
    1964 Descriptive semantics of Tzeltal numeral classifiers. *American Anthropologist,* **66** (3) (pt. 2), 79–98.
Bruner, Jerome, J. J. Goodnow, and G. A. Austin
    1956 *A study of thinking.* New York: Wiley.
Frake, Charles O.
    1961 The diagnosis of disease among the Subanun of Mindanao. Reprinted in *Language in Culture and Society* edited by Dell Hymes. New York: Harper and Row.
    1964 Notes on queries in ethnography. *American Anthropologist,* **66** (3) (pt. 2), 132–145.
King, Robert D.
    1969 *Historical linguistics and generative grammar.* Englewood Cliffs, New Jersey: Prentice-Hall.
Labov, William
    1966 *Social stratification of English in New York City.* Washington, D.C.: Center for Applied Linguistics.
Paul, Hermann
    1880 *Prinzipien der Sprachgeschichte.* Halle, E. Germany: Niemeyer. (Fourth edition, 1909; fifth edition, 1920.)
Stross, Brian
    1970 Tzeltal: Acquisition and componentiality. In *Papers from the Sixth Regional Meeting Chicago Linguistic Society,* pp. 120–128. Chicago: Chicago Linguistic Society.
Weinreich, Uriel, William Labov, and M. I. Herzog
    1968 Empirical foundations for a theory of language change. In *Directions for historical linguistics* edited by W. P. Lehman and Y. Malkiel, pp. 95–188. Austin, Texas: University of Texas Press.

Speculations on the Growth of Ethnobotanical Nomenclature[1]

BRENT BERLIN

It is impossible that men, even the most primeval and unlettered, manage their affairs with various denizens of the plant world without classifying them. Names of plants, generic and specific, and also other names more comprehensive, are part of the vernacular of every tribe of the uncivilized, as well as that of every rural province within the bounds of civilization to-day. The very names attest the fact of classification; for no name is that of an individual plant. It is that of a group of plants, always; a group specific, generic or more comprehensive than either.

Edward Lee Greene
LANDMARKS OF BOTANICAL HISTORY (1909, p. 39)

Introduction

A general observation about the vocabularies of most languages is that they tend to increase in size over time. This pattern is more readily seen when one thinks in broad evolutionary terms, comparing the development of the rudimentary lexicon of early *Homo sapiens* to the complex vocabularies of modern man. We know almost nothing about the causal mechanisms involved in this lexical expansion, but most anthropologists and linguists would not quibble about the fact that it most likely mirrors general cultural evolution.

That languages increase the size of their vocabularies through time is, of course, a trivial observation. The study of lexical growth becomes a topic of relevance only if it is possible to point out regularities that allow for useful generalizations and predictions about the broader problem of linguistic evolution.

In this essay, I hope to focus on the development of one area of vocabulary common to most, if not all, languages—names for categories of plants. I will assume that man's vocabulary for kinds of plants has devel-

[1] Reprinted with minor changes from *Language and Society* 1, 51–86 (1972). More recent advances in the study of ethnobiological classification will be published in the near future.

oped over time, an assumption that allows one to ask at least the following questions: Can one observe regularities in the ethnobotanical lexicons of past and present day languages that allow one to make plausible inferences as to the major patterns of nomenclatural growth? If such patterns can be described, are they related to other aspects of man's sociocultural development? And, finally, do such regularities appear to have productive implications for the evolution of vocabulary generally?

I would like to propose in this openly speculative paper that one can in fact recognize some rather general patterns in the development of ethnobotanical nomenclature that are not necessarily self evident. I can make no claims, however, that the ideas presented here are based on well-documented empirical studies. In fact, many of the examples I cite as evidence are drawn from incomplete descriptions of ethnobiological systems. Nonetheless, as further information becomes available, I have become more strongly convinced that the nomenclatural principles sketched here have widespread applicability. I also believe that their recognition may serve as a useful starting point for further research on the evolution of other lexical domains, specifically ethnozoological nomenclature and, more broadly, to vocabulary generally.

The Six Universal Categories of Ethnobotanical Nomenclature

It now appears that the ethnobotanical lexicons of all languages can ultimately be described given the recognition of six major ethnobotanical categories. These six basic categories will be labeled (1) generic, (2) specific, (3) major life form, (4) varietal, (5) intermediate, (6) unique beginner. The names of plant taxa occurring as members of these categories will be, accordingly, generic names, specific names, major life form names, and so on.

It is furthermore suggested that in the life histories of individual languages, the encoding of each of these nomenclatural categories occurs in a relatively fixed order. Generic names are considered fundamental and will appear first. These will be followed in time by major life form names and specific names. At yet a later period, intermediate taxa and varietal taxa will be labeled. Finally, the last category to be lexically designated in the development of any ethnobotanical lexicon will be the unique beginner. The suggested sequence can be seen diagrammatically as

$$\text{generic} \rightarrow \begin{Bmatrix} \text{life form} \\ \text{specific} \end{Bmatrix} \rightarrow \begin{Bmatrix} \text{intermediate} \\ \text{varietal} \end{Bmatrix} \rightarrow \text{unique beginner}$$

Several clarifications of the above sequence should be noted. The first is to indicate that each of the nomenclatural categories, with the exception of the unique beginner, is theoretically an open class. Thus, given the appearance of the generic category, a language may continue to encode generic taxa throughout its history. The same applies to the specific category. The major life form, intermediate, and varietal categories are likely to be few membered classes when compared with the generic and specific. This observation is probably a reflection of the nature of the recognizable discontinuities of the plant world as will be seen in more detail in the following sections.

It should also be observed that no temporal ordering is implied for some categories. Thus, no claim is made as to the priority, in time, of specific names over major life form names. On the other hand, a claim is made that a language must have encoded at least one major life form name and one specific name before the appearance of intermediate and varietal named taxa.

As well as noting a general progression in terms of an increase in the number of ethnobotanical nomenclatural categories in a particular language's history, one may also describe a regular sequence of lexical development for members within each category. Thus, given the appearance of the specific category, one may observe the further linguistic development of specific names from lexically unmarked to lexically marked expressions. The same observation holds for each category. This general feature suggests that languages may not only be rated in terms of the number of ethnobotanical nomenclatural categories encoded but can be ranked as well in terms of the extent to which members of particular categories have passed from an unmarked to a marked status.

Reality of Natural Groupings of Organisms

Man is by nature a classifying animal, and nowhere is this fact exemplified more clearly than in his classification of the biological universe. But unlike the sometimes capricious and apparently arbitrary classification of certain social phenomena, all men appear to be constrained in their conceptualization of the world of plants and animals. It now seems clear that certain naturally occurring groupings of organisms are recognized as discrete classes in societies that maintain a direct and intimate contact with nature. While several ethnographers have long assumed this to be true (see especially Lévi-Strauss, 1966), the recent work of Ralph Bulmer presents the most explicit statement to this effect. In a series of perceptive papers on the ethnoscience of the Karam of New Guinea (Bulmer,

1967, 1968, 1970; Bulmer and Tyler, 1968), Bulmer convincingly demonstrates the psychological reality of such natural groupings. He generalizes to all folk systems of ethnobiological classification and states that ". . . in any total classification of plants and animals there are important lower order categories which are seen as 'objective' by the users of the classification and which are the smallest *logically* natural units defined by multiple criteria . . ." (Bulmer 1970, p. 1072).

These minimal, naturally occurring units may or may not correspond in a one-to-one fashion to modern biologically defined taxa, although they generally do (Bulmer and Tyler, 1968; Bulmer, 1970; Berlin, Breedlove, and Raven, 1966; Diamond, 1966). They are logically comparable, however, in that in numerous instances such groupings are formed on the basis of ". . . objective regularities and discontinuities in nature" (Bulmer, 1970, p. 1072).

The essence of Bulmer's generalizations are clearly in accord with recent research in Tzeltal botanical ethnography (Berlin, Breedlove, and Raven, 1974), as well as with the work of Conklin (1954), Lévi-Strauss (1966), and others who have worked closely with ethnobiological materials.

Primacy of Generic Names

In the ethnobiological lexicons of all languages, one is immediately struck by the structural uniformity of expressions that linguistically characterize man's recognition of the basic objective discontinuities of his biological world. These expressions are, for the most part, unique "single words" that can be said to be semantically unitary and linguistically distinct. Examples of such semantically unitary names in English folk biology would be *oak, pine,* and *maple.* Primary terms of this sort appear to represent the most commonly referred to concepts of the botanical world and can be referred to as "generic names." There may or may not be expressions of greater generality (e.g., *tree, vine*) or specificity (e.g., *black oak, sugar maple*), a fact that later will be shown to have important evolutionary implications.

An explicit recognition of these psychologically basic ethnobotanical generic terms can be traced ultimately to Theophrastus, the father of Western systematic botany (see Greene, 1909). A more recent exploration of the subject has been provided by the ethnobotanist, Harley Harris Bartlett in his important paper "History of the Generic Concept in Botany" (1940). Bartlett, a good field biologist with considerable ethnobotanical experience on several Malayan tribes, noted that a well-defined idea of genera could be found in all of these languages. For Bartlett, the ". . . concept of genus must be as old as folk science itself" (1940, p. 341). He defined the concept as any class ". . . which is more or less consciously thought of as the **smallest** grouping requiring a **distinctive** name" (1940, p. 356, emphasis added). While somewhat vague as a definition, Bartlett's idea concerning the fundamental nature of generic taxa and their corresponding distinctive labels is essentially correct. In fact, generic names can be seen to exhibit a readily identifiable linguistic structure that allows, in most cases, for their immediate recognition (Berlin, 1969; Berlin, Breedlove, and Raven, 1973; Conklin, 1962, p. 122; Bulmer and Tyler, 1968; Friedrich, 1970).

The centrality of named generic taxa as "semantic primitives" (Friedrich 1970, p. 156) in ethnobotanical classification has important evolutionary significance as concerns the growth of ethnobotanical nomenclature. The most obvious one is that generic names are the first to become encoded in the ethnobotanical lexicons of all languages. Thus, one may postulate a period in the development of the plant lexicon of any language whereby one finds a series of plant classes, each labeled by generic names, that partially partition a yet unlabeled taxon best glossed as 'plant'. (It will be shown that 'plant' is the last taxon to be uniquely labeled in any plant lexicon.)

It should be reiterated that the partition of the unlabeled category, 'plant', is not exhaustive at this time and that numerous, potentially namable classes remain unlabeled by generic forms and are linguistically ignored. I would also emphasize the fact that folk generic taxa are likely to correspond to botanical genera only in those cases where the scientific classification reflects obvious morphological characteristics of plant groupings that are readily observable by simple visual inspection. Thus, some folk generics will match almost perfectly standard botanical genera, e.g., oaks, pines, etc., while others will be more inclusive, e.g., cacti, ferns.

HORIZONTAL EXPANSION OF GENERIC NAMES

It is supposed, then, that at some point in the development of a language's ethnobotanical nomenclature one finds a single-leveled taxonomy comprised solely of generic taxa labeled by generic names. Through time, groupings of organisms earlier not recognized linguistically are named. If one attempts to speculate on how this hypothetical early plant taxonomy expands the most plausible argument at the moment is that the direction is at first "horizontal." By horizontal growth, I mean the formation of new generic names. The linguistic process of analogy, i.e., when some new category is seen to be conceptually related to an already existing category and named accordingly, is an extremely common form of name formation in contemporary languages. One can assume it to have been productive at an earlier time as well. Heinz Werner has discussed this process from a psychological viewpoint and has referred to it as "concrete transposition." This process ". . . can frequently be observed in every-day speech. It occurs whenever one uses the expression 'something like' or the suffix '-like' or '-ish', for the description of an object. Concrete transposition is at the basis of many creations of words and changes of meanings. . . ." (Werner, 1954, p. 204).

Concrete transposition forms an important part of the naming of behavior of the Tzeltal and Tzotzil Mayan Indians of Southern Mexico. When presented with a plant that is conceived to be "related" to a known plant class, the typical Tzeltal informant will respond that it is *kol pahaluk sok x*, i.e., 'it is likened to/related to' some already named class, x. The same semantic information is indicated by the Tzotzil expression *k'os x 'like x'*. In both languages, the process is a very common one, allowing for the classification of the vast majority of all plants in the environment, inasmuch as most plants are seen to be related to some named class. An identical situation has been reported by Bright and Bright (1965) for the Tolowa speaking Smith River Indians of California and by French (1960) for the Sahaptin Indians of Oregon.

The most thoroughgoing example of this kind of naming that I have found, however, is reported for a group of Arawak speakers of Surinam. Stahel (1944) notes that "Arawak Indians in Surinam, when they are naming plants and animals, make liberal use of the suffix BALLI to reduce the number of primary or 'generic' names of the hundreds maybe thousands of kinds they have to distinguish. For this purpose they have still two other words—DJAMARO and OJOTO. The first means the same as BALLI, the second 'related to'" (1944, p. 268). As an example, one may note the following set of Arawak plant names, using Stahel's orthography.

TÁTABU	*Diplotropis guianensis* Benth.
TÁTABUBALLI	*Coutarea hexandra* K. Schum.
TÁTABU DJAMARO	*Copaifera epunctata* Amsh.
TÁTABU OJOTO	*Ormosiopsis flava* Ducke

Stahel states that "All four are high jungle trees. The first, 'zwarte kabbes', is a well known Surinam timber, the others are less important but all resemble TÁTABU" (1944, p. 269).

There is some doubt that most linguistic anthropologists would treat the examples mentioned above as legitimate plant names. In a real sense, concrete transposition is a method of making new labels by the use of descriptive phrases. The principle, however, is a productive one, and it may become so prevalent in horizontal expansion of generic names that descriptive phrases are eventually replaced by genuine lexical expressions.

Such an advance may be illustrated in certain of the Mayan languages, whereby one notes the use of a generic name plus an animal name to refer to a plant class seen to be related to one indicated by the generic name alone. In Tzeltal one finds numerous sets like the following:

č'omate?	'chayote'	*Sechium edule* (Jacq.) Sw.
č'omate?č'o	'rat's chayote!	*Cyclanthera bourgeana* Naud. ex Char.
?isim	'corn'	*Zea mays* L.
?isim ?ahaw	'snake's corn'	*Anthurium* spp.
k'eweš	'custard apple'	*Annona cherimola* Miller
k'eweš maš	'monkey's custard apple'	*A. reticulata* L.

In Yucatec Maya, the process is also typical, as can be seen in this example from Roys (1931, p. 223):

Cat	'tree cucumber'	*Parmentiera edulis* DC.
Cat-cuuc	'squirrel's tree cucumber'	*P. aculeata* HBK.

An identical process in naming generic classes that are seen to be related in some form or other is also found in Hanunóo (Conklin, 1954) and Subanun (Frake, personal communication), both languages of the Philippines, and Nahuatl of Central Mexico (Paso y Trancoso, 1886). The use of the adjectives *false* and *mock* in American English folk botany may lead to the formation of generic names in an analogous fashion, e.g., *lilac:false lilac; cypress:false cypress; orange:mock orange.*

It is important to note that names formed by analogy of the sort just described are legitimate generic forms and are not conceptually seen as subordinate taxa. Thus, *mock orange* is not a kind of orange, it is simply like orange in some respect. This point is illustrated nicely by reference to the writings of Theophrastus as discussed by Edward Lee Greene in his little-read "Landmarks of Botanical History" (1909). Greene notes that about half of Theophrastus' generic names are complex expressions including a noun and an adjective. Several appear to be derived from generic names of a single constituent, e.g., *Calamos* 'reed grass' (*Arundo* spp.) and *Calamos Euosomos* 'sweet flag' (*Acornus calamus*). But Greene has no doubts about Theophrastus' classification of *Calamos* and *Calamos Euosomos* as distinct genera. He writes:

It is not imaginable that a botanist of Theophrastus' ripe experience and great attain-
ments should think those large grass-plants and the sweet-flag to be of the same genus.
Beyond doubt, however, the name Calamos Euosomos did originate in the notion that
arundo and acornus are next of kin; for, however, unlike they are as to size, foliage, and
other particulars, there is a remarkably close similarity in their rootstocks, these being
of almost the same size, form and color in the two. The gatherers of roots and herbs, as
we know, looked first of all to the "roots" of things, and these were their first criteria of
plant relationships. To these it should be perfectly natural to place the sweet-flag alongside arundo, the true [Calamos] by its closely imitative "root", and then on account of
the aromatic properties of the root to call the plant [Calamos Euosomos].   (Greene,
1909, p. 123)

Finally, it should be observed that the conceptually central name in a
pair consisting of a generic name and one formed by semantic analogy is
lexically unmarked, i.e., it occurs in an unmodified form, while the non-
central and historically secondary expression is distinguished by a modi-
fier of some sort. As will be seen a little further on, this process of lexical
marking is a most productive form of name formation in the overall development of ethnobotanical nomenclature.

In summary, I have suggested that the original ethnobotanical vocabulary of any language (and, by implication, the vocabulary of early man) is
at first comprised solely of semantically unitary linguistic expressions that
mark the smallest conceptually relevant groupings of plants in man's environment. These expressions are known as generic names.

At the outset, the expansion of generic names is seen to be accomplished via the process of concrete transposition. It is expressed first in
the form of descriptive or descriptive-like phrases or expressions that at a
later period in the history of a language may be more formally codified by
the formation of definite lexical forms. This form of expansion is to be
joined by the processes of generalization and differentiation as nomenclature develops over time. Concrete transposition is to remain, however, as
a potentially productive process throughout the history of a language's
development.

Differentiation and Generalization: The Appearance of
Specific and Major Life Form Names

I had at one time hoped to show that specific names become encoded in
a language's ethnobotanical lexicon before the appearance of major life
forms such as *tree, vine, grass.* The data that I have been able to gather at
this time do not allow for a definitive answer as to which ethnobotanical
category may be prior. I know of no language that lacks at least some specific plant names, although there may have been languages, such as that

spoken by the Tasmanians, that lacked general life form terms. The evidence on this point, however, is scanty and probably unreliable. Consequently, a weaker hypothesis is presented here that posits no temporal distinction as to the rise of specific and suprageneric categories, although further research may well require a modification of this view.

Differentiation and the Formation of Specific Names

In Bartlett's paper on the genus concept, he also noted that "With enlarging experience, people make finer distinctions and need different names for newly distinguished entities which have previously been called by the same original name. The original name becomes generic in its application; variously qualified it provides the basis of specific names" (1940, p. 349).

I would take issue only with Bartlett's phrase ". . . The original name becomes generic in its application . . . ." It had originally been generic and, with enlarging experience, is merely partitioned into subclasses.

There appears to be some psychological evidence to support such a position. Werner notes ". . . that the predominant developmental trend is in the direction of differentiation rather than of synthesis. [Likewise], the formation of general concepts from specific terms is of lesser importance in non-scientific communication though it is rather a characteristic of scientific endeavor. In other words, language in every-day life is directed toward the concrete and specific rather than toward the abstract and general. Because of this trend toward the concrete, semantic generalization develops slowly and by intermediate steps" (Werner, 1954, p. 203).

If differentiation is to occur and be lexically encoded, there appears to be a fairly concise way in which one can imagine it happening. First, the division of a generic name is most probably binary, at least at the outset. This observation is borne out in fact in present-day folk taxonomic systems that have been well studied. By far, the greatest number of contrast sets comprised of specific taxa in folk biotaxonomies are comprised solely of two specific names (Berlin, Breedlove, and Raven, 1974; Conklin, 1954, p. 128).

TYPE-SPECIFIC NOMENCLATURE

A highly regular labeling process can be described for the encoding of specific taxa, given the primarily binary partition of a generic taxon. In general, one specific category, because it is most widespread, larger, best known, or the like, will always be recognized as the best representation of the set. This taxon can be referred to as the "type-specific," the archtype, or to use Platonic terms, the ideal type. "Type-species" have long been recognized in systematic biology. The notion, codified by Linnaeus, can be seen to have its origin in folk biosystematics since earliest times and has been reported by many anthropologists working with societies intimately involved with nature. Dentan, who has worked extensively with the primitive Semai of Southeast Asia, notes, "My impression is that the Semai think that some species are more 'typical' of their categories than other species are. For example, *naga* (snakelike dragons) seem to represent the quintessence of 'they beneath the earth'. Giant monitors, in turn, are the prime representatives of 'lizard', and regal python of 'snake'" (Dentan, 1968, p. 35).

A strikingly general nomenclatural regularity can also be suggested as regards the relationship of the type specific, its contrasting nontypical specific, and the superordinate generic name. In the early stages of the division of a generic taxon into two specific categories, the **type specific will invariably be polysemous with its superordinate generic in characteristic usage.** Stated in other terms, the type specific taxon will be lexically unmarked in normal speech, being referred to by the identical linguistic expression as its superordinate generic. Such polysemous labeling of taxa at differing levels of generalization has been discussed by Frake (1962) and Conklin (1962) in reference to folk biosystematics and by Greenberg (1966) in reference to lexicon in general. Several examples will illustrate this nomenclatural principle. As Wyman and Harris have said in referring to Navaho ethnobotany, "The situation is as if in our binomial system the generic name were used alone for the best known species of a genus, while binomial terms were used for all other members of the genus" (1941, p. 120).

Washington Matthews (1886) was the first to recognize explicitly type-specific nomenclature in Navaho. In an especially careful piece of research for its time, Matthews notes that ". . . there are three species of juniper growing in the Zuni mountains; each has its own appropriate name, yet the generic name for juniper . . . appears in all" (1886, p. 767). Diagrammatically,

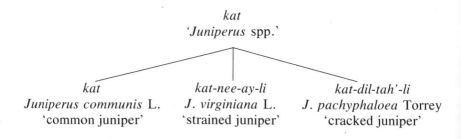

	kat 'Juniperus spp.'	
kat	*kat-nee-ay-li*	*kat-dil-tah'-li*
Juniperus communis L.	*J. virginiana* L.	*J. pachyphaloea* Torrey
'common juniper'	'strained juniper'	'cracked juniper'

Several other examples found in Matthews show the same principle at work:

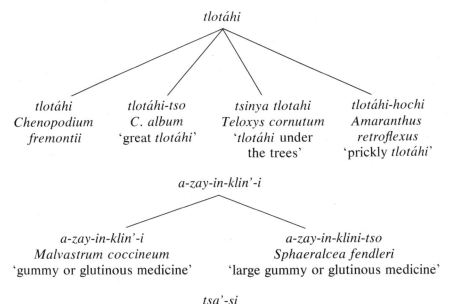

tlotáhi

tlotáhi	*tlotáhi-tso*	*tsinya tlotahi*	*tlotáhi-hochi*
Chenopodium	*C. album*	*Teloxys cornutum*	*Amaranthus*
fremontii	'great *tlotáhi*'	'*tlotáhi* under	*retroflexus*
		the trees'	'prickly *tlotáhi*'

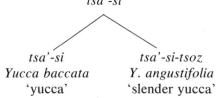

a-zay-in-klin'-i

a-zay-in-klin'-i	*a-zay-in-klini-tso*
Malvastrum coccineum	*Sphaeralcea fendleri*
'gummy or glutinous medicine'	'large gummy or glutinous medicine'

tsa'-si

tsa'-si	*tsa'-si-tsoz*
Yucca baccata	*Y. angustifolia*
'yucca'	'slender yucca'

Classical Nahuatl also exhibits this nomenclatural regularity in that the most common specific form included in a particular generic class is labeled polysemously by the generic name. Thus, one observes that in the Nahuatl classification of sedges, *tollin* included a ". . . type-species [sic] that carried simply the name *Tollin* and that [also] referred to the sedge family, various other related species of it having been grouped under the same name, each with a different determination" (Paso y Troncoso, 1886, p. 218).

A final example of polysemous generic and type-specific plant names can be seen again in the early work of Theophrastus, who, as a plant nomenclator, took great pains to preserve the essential structure of the names discovered to be in common usage in his day. As Greene says, Theophrastus ". . . left plant nomenclature as he found it" (1909, p. 123). Greene captures the essence of the early botanist's view aptly:

The Theophrastan nomenclature of plants is as simply natural as can be imagined. Not only are monotypic genera called by a single name; where the species are known to be several, the type-species of the genus—that is, that which is most historic—is without a specific name, at least very commonly, and only the others have each its specific adjective superadded to the generic appelation.   (Greene, 1909, p. 120)

The following examples attest to this fact:

Theophrastus' names	Modern equivalents
Peuce	*Pinus picea*
Peuce Idaia	*P. maritima*
Peuce conophoros	*P. pinea*
Peuce paralios	*P. halepensis*
Mespilos	*Mespilos cotoneaster*
Mespilos anthedon	*Crataegus tominalis*

LEXICAL MARKING OF TYPE-SPECIFIC NAMES

While many languages find no need to linguistically mark the focal type-specific within a particular grouping of specific names, a situation that I suggest is characteristic of the process employed in the earliest specific name formation, situations of social intercourse may arise whereby one must be able to linguistically differentiate the type-specific category from its contrasting neighbor(s). The linguistic process by which this contrast comes to be indicated is also quite general. **Invariably, the type-specific will be modified with an attributivelike expression best glossed as 'genuine', 'real', or 'ideal-type'.** Such a situation is found characteristically in many languages, of which Tzeltal and Hanunóo may be cited as examples.

In Tzeltal, *?ič* is the generic name for 'chili pepper' (*Capsicum* spp.). In most contexts, *?ič* can be used alone to refer to the most prominent specific class. However, when greater precision of designation is required, the attributive *bac'il* 'genuine' is readily applied to distinguish this specific class, *bac'il ?ič* 'genuine chili pepper', from its contrasting coordinate specific classes. Thus, one finds:

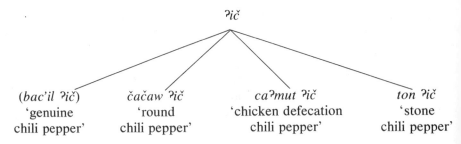

An identical nomenclatural principle has been described for Hanunóo. Conklin, in an as yet unpublished ethnobotany of this people, notes that ". . . a shared term [i.e., a generic plant name partitioned by two or more specific names] when not followed by an attribute, may be read as that term plus *ʔurūŋan* 'real'. The resulting name is a preferred synonym, required where the designated plant name is distinguished from others in the same set" (Conklin, 1954, p. 259). An example can be seen in the classification of Job's tears.

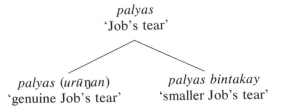

palyas
'Job's tear'

palyas (urūŋan)
'genuine Job's tear'

palyas bintakay
'smaller Job's tear'

While the type specific remains unmarked, or marked only in contexts where ambiguity might arise, the nontypical specific(s) will obligatorily be marked. The linguistic structure of such nontypical (or secondary) specifics appears to be of a specifiable form. **Such names will be comprised of the generic names** (in which they are included) **plus a modifying attributive-like expression. In all cases, such nontypical specific expressions will be binomial in structure.**

The feature(s) focused on by the modifying attributivelike expression is generally some obvious perceptual dimension such as color, size, growth habit, habitat, or the like. Such a situation may be diagrammatically indicated in the following hypothetical specific contrast sets.

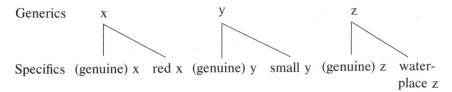

Generics   x   y   z

Specifics   (genuine) x   red x   (genuine) y   small y   (genuine) z   water-
                                                                    place z

FOSSILIZATION OF THE TYPE-SPECIFIC ATTRIBUTIVE

In some languages, especially the Mayan language, Tzeltal, "pattern pressure" appears to be working so as to make the presence of the type-specific attributive (i.e., 'genuine') obligatory or independent of context. As an example, the type-specific *bac'il ʔalčaš* 'genuine orange' is almost universally the preferred usage (versus the simple unmarked *ʔalčaš*) in contexts where it contrasts with forms such as *pahal ʔalčaš* 'sour orange', *ʔelemoneš ʔalčaš* 'lemon orange'. This tendency, I think, represents a later development that follows quite logically from the prior, unmarked usage.

An even further logical sequence can be seen at work in Tzeltal that may or may not have general validity as a subsequent development in all systems. This is seen in few membered contrast sets (i.e., of two or three members) whereby one notes the tendency for the type-specific to assume a value on the semantic dimension indicated in the name(s) of its contrasting member(s). Thus, while a contrast set might have at one time included members labeled as:

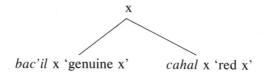

bac'il x 'genuine x'   *cahal* x 'red x'

where the semantic dimension of color appears indicated in the marked nontypical specific, it now becomes habitually labeled as:

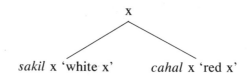

sakil x 'white x'   *cahal* x 'red x'

As concerns specific examples where the dimension of color is involved, I think it of no mean theoretical significance that the attributive replacing 'genuine' in the type-specific member is *sakil* 'white', a rather "typical color" in flower pigmentation (flower color being a major semantic dimension used to differentiate many closely related specifics) and almost neutral, as it were, in terms of its marking potential.

DEVELOPMENT OF LEXICAL MARKINGS IN SPECIFIC NOMENCLATURE

I now want to summarize the theoretical developmental sequence for the lexical marking of specific plant names.

(a)   First, the generic taxon is partitioned into a type-specific and one (or more) nontypical specific(s). The type-specific is lexically unmarked and polysemous with its superordinate generic. The nontypical specific(s) is lexically marked, a feature leading to a binomial expression

Diagrammatically,

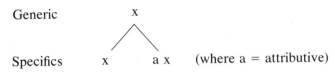

Generic   x

Specifics   x   a x   (where a = attributive)

(b)　Over time, the type-specific must be linguistically distinguished in certain contexts of semantic contrast from the nontypical specific(s). An optional "type-marking" attributive is applied to the type-specific. Invariably it will best be glossed as 'genuine', 'real', or 'most typical'. Diagrammatically:

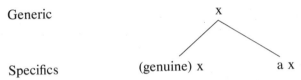

Generic   x

Specifics   (genuine) x   a x

(c)　In the penultimate stage, time, usage and binomial pattern pressure of specific nomenclature will force the type-marking attributive 'genuine' to become obligatory. Once obligatory, its semantic marking function is radically reduced, and ultimately it becomes completely neutralized. Diagrammatically:

Generic   x

Specifics   genuine x   a x

(d)　In the ultimate stage, pattern pressure will force the neutralized type-marking attributive to be replaced by an attributive from the same semantic dimension as the attributive indicated in the contrasting nontypical specific(s). Thus, a set of forms that were formally:

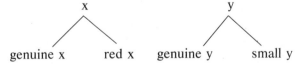

      x   y

genuine x   red x   genuine y   small y

will become:

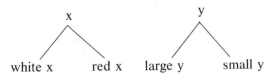

      x   y

white x   red x   large y   small y

Rise of Major Life-Form Names

While generic and specific names account for the vast majority of names for plants in natural ethnobotanical vocabularies, a smaller number of forms occur that are of greater inclusiveness than generics and specifics. These expressions may be referred to as life form names. At some point in man's classification of the plant world, the concrete differences marked by generic names could be dispensed with in some contexts and higher-order abstract names were developed that marked such major life forms as 'tree', 'vine', 'herb', and so on. This is not to say that such categories had not been conceptually recognized by man since earliest times. I find it difficult to conceive that such was not in fact the case. It is highly likely, however, that these higher-order categories lacked simple, monolexemic designations. The development of life form names is most certainly subsequent to the appearance of generic names in the evolution of ethnobotanical nomenclature.

While very little is known concerning the processes involved in the formation of life form names, it is clear that in many languages the labels for life form categories are drawn directly from the existing inventory of generic names. Furthermore, the labeling of major life-form taxa can be seen to follow identical marking principles as those described for generic and specific names. Applying the principles we have seen to be at work in the case of generics and specifics, one can make fairly good guesses as to which names get elevated to major class status—precisely those generic names that, because of their distribution and cultural importance, are most salient culturally. In many of these instances, the life form name and its subordinate generic are polysemous.

Buck's massive compilation of synonyms for the major Indoeuropean languages provides data on the rise of the major life form name 'tree' that bears on this hypothesis: "A widespread group of words for 'tree', many of them meaning also 'wood', go back to an IE [Indoeuropean] word which probably denoted a particular kind of tree, namely the oak" (Buck 1949, p. 48). And again, "Noteworthy is the primacy of the oak, as shown in mythology and in the recurring use of 'oak' as the tree par excellence, for 'tree' " (1949, p. 528). Finally, Buck notes the reconstruction " 'Oak'. 1. IE*derwo-, dru-, etc. in words for 'oak', and for 'tree', 'wood', the former, specific use being probably the earlier" (1949, p. 528).

The most recent and authoritative statement on the proto Indoeuropean arboreal system is that of Paul Friedrich (1970). Friedrich rejects the generally accepted alternative hypothesis that *derwo originally meant 'tree' rather than 'oak'. His conclusions are especially interesting:

> . . . it seems probable that the primitive, arboreally oriented PIE distinguished several species of oak by distinct morphs, and that *ayg-, *perk^w- and *dorw- served in this

way. As the oak and mixed-oak forests were reduced and contracted, and as the speakers of the PIE dialects migrated into their new homeland—two simultaneous processes
during the third and second millennia—the denotations of the *dorw-* reflexes shifted to
'wood, tree, hardness,' and yet other referents; this would hold especially for the shift
to 'fir, tar, pinewood' and the like in the Baltic and North Germanic dialects, since the
speakers are thought to have migrated into northern coniferous zones during the centuries when the oaks were receding. It is also quite possible that even in PIE times the
main name for the oak—a sort of *Urbaum*—was occasionally or dialectically applied to
'tree' in general. Within pre-Homeric Greek δρῦσ and δρυόσ could denote either 'oak'
or 'tree' with disambiguation through social or literary context. By Classical Greek
times the meaning had narrowed to the original PIE 'tree'. In more recent centuries the
identical process has been documented in Germanic, where *eik* shifted from 'oak' to
'tree' in Icelandic—oaks being virtually absent in that country.   (Friedrich, 1970, p.
146)

While the polysemous origins of life form names in nomenclaturally advanced languages have become obscure, their etymologies determinable
only by historical reconstruction, such is not the case with numerous less
advanced societies yet in the early stages of their nomenclatural life histories. In fact, some of these data suggest that one is observing in some
languages the actual accension of some suprageneric taxa, suggesting that
such languages have only recently moved from the prior stage of ethnobotanical nomenclature of generic names only. Furthermore, it is not surprising to find polysemous generic and life form plant names in languages
spoken by societies that are rather simple in their cultural–technological
development.

The best reported cases now available to me are found in the Great
Basin and the Southwestern areas of the United States, although there are
doubtless other examples in other parts of the world. Trager (apparently
unaware of an earlier paper by Albert Gatschet who reports the same
data) noted that in several Southwestern Indian groups, the word for
'tree' was polysemous with the word for 'cottonwood', the only deciduous tree that grows with abundance outside the major forests. Thus, he
notes in Taos Pueblo that ". . . the ordinary word for 'tree' . . . *tŭłöna*
is also the word for 'cottonwood' " (Trager, 1939, p. 117). Furthermore,
"In Isleta and Sandia (southern Tiwa dialects not very different from the
northern Taos and Picuris) the word *tŭła* means 'tree, cottonwood'
. . ." (1939, p. 117). Finally, in Hopi, ". . . we find the same word,
söhövi, used for both" (1939, p. 117).

A more recent study by Fowler and Leland on Northern Paiute ethno-
systematics verifies Trager's observations for this Great Basin people.
They state that ". . . the terms for cottonwood tree [*siŋábi*] can include
the willow tree at one level and can also be used in popular speech for any
deciduous tree" (Fowler and Leland, 1967, p. 387).

In a paper recently brought to my attention by Barbara Demory, Almstedt (1968) reports generic name–life form name polysemy for Diegueño,

a Yuman speaking group of Southern California. Here, however, the term for 'tree', *isnyaaw,* is polysemous with another ecologically important tree, the California life oak, *Quercus agrifolia.* This species of oak has the widest distribution and is the most generally available source of edible acorns in the area inhabited by these people. For Almstedt, ". . . it seems logical that this name *isnyaaw* should be used for tree when the need arose" (1968, p. 13).

Demory (in press) surveyed additional languages in the Hokan family and found numerous other examples of life form–generic polysemy. In each case, the generic of major cultural significance in that particular geographic area appears to have assumed life form status. Thus in Karok, *ʔipahA* 'juniper, tree'; Achumawi, *aswō* 'sugar pine, tree'; Atsugewi, *ajwi* 'kind of pine, tree'; Yana *baaculʔi* 'broad leaf maple, tree'; Salinan, *hat'* 'oak, tree'; Chumash, *ku-wu* 'live oak, tree'.

Earlier work by Bright and Bright (1965, pp. 253–254) reports the term *tepo* as polysemously meaning both 'fir' and 'tree' and Gatschet notes Kalmath *k'osh* as both 'pine' and 'tree', (1890, Chapter I, p. 146).

A final example of this nomenclatural regularity is found in Western Apache as described by Keith Basso. It is made even more important because Basso's data bear both on the rise of major life form names as well as the formation of specific names. Basso writes:

> The situation among the Western Apaches is much the same as that you describe for the Great Basin and other portions of the Southwest. The term for cottonwood (*tíís*) is also used for 'tree'; in addition, however—and this is what makes it interesting—*tíís* may also designate a 'real cottonwood'—namely, those which are tall, heavily foliaged, and situated near the banks of flowing streams and creeks. A few cottonwoods, much more stunted and less green frow in dry washes and arroyos. These are called *títs daiską́ą́ne* ('cottonwoods underfed'). *Tíís* in the sense of 'genuine cottonwood' is sometimes labeled *tíís da'bííhi* 'cottonwood true'/'cottonwood correct'.   (Basso, personal communication)

Basso diagrams the taxonomic structure of these lexical items as follows:

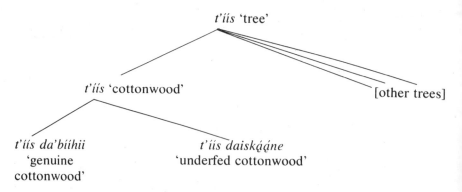

A linguistic expression does not become a major class form overnight, however. Presumably, the process is a relatively slow one. Data from Shoshone, another language of the Great Basin, may be relevant at this point. Wick Miller, who has been involved in an extensive study of the Shoshone, notes the common use of *sohopi* for tree, cottonwood, willow, aspen, stick, and log, but is uncertain as to whether the term can be applied to any tree, e.g., "What I do not know, and what would be of particular importance to you, is whether or not these terms [*sohopi*] can be used generically [i.e., inclusively]; that is, can I say, for example, 'an oak tree is a *sohopi*' ('cottonwood tree')?" (Miller, personal communication).

Fowler (personal communication), on further consideration, also questions the use of Northern Paiute *siŋábi* for all deciduous trees, suggesting that the term might be restricted to aspen, cottonwood, and willow. Ash, alder and mountain mahogony, potential candidates for *siŋábi,* grow outside the Northern Paiute range.

Miller's and Fowler's comments bring up an interesting point concerning the assumption of suprageneric status by a particular generic taxon. We have no reason to assume that a recently elevated suprageneric should have, at the outset, an extension radically different from that of the generic from which it has arisen. Thus, a term that may eventually come to refer to all 'hard, single-stemmed, erect plants attaining a specified height' (i.e., 'trees') might originally be restricted to a small subset of 'trees'. In the case of the Shoshone term *sohopi,* it might be restricted to 'cottonwoodlike deciduous trees' (e.g., cottonwood, willow, aspen) and later come to refer to deciduous trees generally. An even later development might force the extension of the general term to include the obviously abberant conifers (e.g., pines, firs). This surely must have been the case with the general use of Indoeuropean **derwo* from 'oak' to 'tree' in general. A comparable situation is illustrated in Tzeltal where 'tree' is seen to include only truly woody stemmed organisms attaining a specified height, excluding such "obvious" trees (from the folk western point of view) as *palms,* these latter forms being considered as unique generic classes.

The ultimate extension of the major class suprageneric 'tree' can perhaps best be illustrated in modern American English folk botany where any single-stemmed upright plant with leaves at the top is admitted to the class, allowing for the botanically unlikely assortment of such diverse organisms as oaks, pines, palms, banana (trees), and even certain treelike bamboos.

MARKING OF "TYPE GENERICS"

The examples I have thus far cited have all referred to languages where the culturally central generic term that gives rise to major life form names remains unmarked in common usage, being polysemous with its superordinate suprageneric. Reviewing examples of generic-specific polysemy, might one not also expect to find systems whereby the generic name becomes marked, at least in certain contexts? And might not these instances be seen as a subsequent development, just as was the case in generic-specific polysemy? In fact, such examples are found, though in the fossilized state of development, in Tzeltal and Tzotzil, although there is also evidence of a similar situation in Kiowa Apache of Oklahoma.

The marking processes distinguishing what now might be called the "type-generic" are identical to those described earlier for type-specifics. Thus, if modified, the polysemous form comes to be qualified linguistically with an expression best glossed as 'genuine'.

To illustrate, in Kiowa Apache, the term for 'tree' is ʔádw while that for 'cottonwood', the most prominent deciduous form, is a-hi, a form literally translated as 'tree-real', i.e., 'genuine tree' (see Trager, 1939, p. 118). For some speakers of Tzeltal, the term bac'il ʔak' 'genuine vine' (< ʔak' 'vine') occurs as a generic for the most important vine utilized in house construction binding, Smilax subpubescens A. DC. One also finds, for some speakers, the generic bac'il ʔak 'genuine grass' (< ʔak 'grass') for the most common and important grass employed as a major thatching in house roofing, Muhlenbergia macroura (HBK). Hitchc. Finally, in Zinacantan Tzotzil, the most important tree, both in house construction and as a firewood, is bac'i-teʔ 'genuine tree' (< teʔ 'tree), a form that refers to the prominent oak species of the area, Quercus peduncularis Née.

These terms in the Mayan languages just cited are not metaphorical or synonymous expressions for the informants who have them as terms in their respective nomenclatural systems, although synonymous expressions do exist. The fact that the attributive constituent bac'il 'genuine' has become frozen in each case, its presence being obligatory, is quite analogous to the situations whereby the type-marking attributive fossilizes and becomes obligatory in specific names.

Finally, Gatschet (1899) reports a similar body of data from Nipissing, a dialect of Ojibwa. Here andak means 'evergreen tree' and inin andak 'real evergreen tree' or 'pine'. Likewise, ātik 'deciduous tree' includes the generic name inin ātik 'real deciduous tree', i.e., 'maple'. One can see how a culturally central generic name in each case has become obligatorily marked linguistically by the form 'genuine'.

SUMMARY OF THE DEVELOPMENT OF LIFE-FORM NAMES

The theoretical development sequence for the appearance of major life-form taxa may now be summarized as a series of at least four steps.

(a) At the outset, the newly encoded life form category is labeled polysemously with the most common generic form from which it was derived. Its extension is, at first, rather limited, perhaps only to those generics that are seen to be quite similar to the type-generic. Diagrammatically,

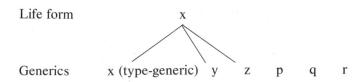

(b) Over time, the type-generic comes to be optionally marked, linguistically, with the type-marking attributive, 'genuine'.

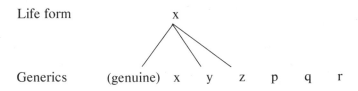

(c) Further development leads to the fossilization (neutralization) of the type-marking attributive, 'genuine', and it becomes obligatory. Meanwhile, the life form is expanding its referential extension, including taxa originally excluded.

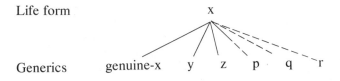

(d) Final stages of growth are indicated when polysemy is totally obscured in the current forms, the original expressions having been replaced or otherwise changed.

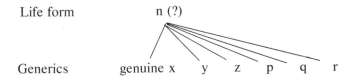

Appearance of Varietal Names

It would appear that the naming of varietal taxa will, in general, follow the appearance of the major life form taxa. This is not a contradiction, as it might at first seem, of the tendency for abstract terms to occur later in a language's history than highly specific ones. It is a reflection of the greater control over the processes of domestication that man has acquired only through long millenia of trial and error methods. All of the information available to me at the moment shows that legitimate varietal names occur almost exclusively in the classification of important cultivars. I would imagine that the same holds true for animals. The control over nature that is required in selecting and maintaining a particular race of corn, beans, rice, chili pepper, squash, or what have you morphologically distinctive enough to merit habitual lexical designation can be accomplished only by relatively advanced horticulturalists. Accordingly, one should not expect to find varietal ethnobotanical nomenclature in the languages of societies that do not practice rather refined methods of cultivation. Even in these languages, varietal names will be restricted to highly important groups of plants.

Given the appearance of varietal taxa, however, it appears relatively simple to specify the linguistic structure of names used to refer to such taxa. In all cases, the specific name (logically of the form attributive, generic, order being irrelevant) will be formed by the addition of another attributive. And, as one might expect, the processes of lexical marking described earlier apply equally well in varietal name formation.

The general principles seen to be at work can be illustrated in Tzeltal. In this language, the generic taxon *lo?bal* 'banana' includes at least twelve distinct specific classes, e.g., *bac'il lo?bal* 'genuine banana', *sakil lo?bal* 'white banana', *sera lo?bal* 'wax banana', *cahal lo?bal* 'red banana', etc. One of these specific forms includes two varietals labeled in the expected manner, i.e., the type-varietal occurring unmarked in typical usage but marked with the type-marking attributive, 'genuine', if ambiguity occurs, and the nontypical varietal being obligatorily marked. Thus, one notes the forms:

(bac'il) cahal lo?bal	'(genuine) red banana'
sakil cahal lo?bal	'white red banana'

It is rare that varietal names include more than two modifying expressions, i.e., indicate classes of greater specificity than "first-order" varietals. In Hanunóo, of the 1094 terminal taxa that are specific or varietal names, 961 are specific taxa and 97 are varietals. Of these 97 varietals, 87 are first-order forms, i.e., marked only by two attributives.

Only two generic names include "subvarietals" comprised of more than two attributives, and these occur in the highly important cultivars, corn and chili peppers (Conklin, 1954).

In actual speech, it is also rare that a varietal be referred to by its "full name." There is a strong tendency for such forms to participate in what Conklin has called "abbreviation" (Conklin, 1962, p. 122), i.e., when a part of the name may be used to stand for the varietal class as a whole. In such cases, abbreviation will lead the primary, i.e., specific, attributive to function as a head of the expression, the resulting form in most cases being, then, binomial in form. As an example, note the English varietals *butter lima(s) bean, baby lima(s) bean,* where *butter lima(s)* and *baby lima(s)* may occur as complete expressions. The same can be noted in Tzeltal, also for beans, where one notes the forms:

> *cahal šlumil čenek'*   'red ground beans'
> *ʔihk'al šlumil čenek*   'black ground beans'

where *cahal šlumil* 'red ground [ones]' and *ʔihk'al šlumil* 'black ground [ones]' can occur alone.

The Problem of Intermediate Taxa

In examining the ethnobiological lexicon of numerous languages, I have noticed a strong tendency for the hierarchical depth of biotaxonomies to be uniformly shallow. Superordinate taxa of greater inclusiveness than the folk genus, the life form names, are invariably few in number and are inclusive of the majority of all named taxa. Subordinate taxa of lesser inclusiveness than folk genera, i.e., specific names, are likewise few in number and occur predominantly in those taxa with critical cultural importance (e.g., cultivated plants or domesticated animals). One may generalize and claim that **most folk biotaxonomies are comprised primarily of named generic, major life form, and specific taxa, with generic classes being by far the most numerous and psychologically significant.**

Covert "midlevel" categories of greater inclusiveness than folk generic but not yet life form categories may be seen to exist in many taxonomies, and their recognition is of crucial importance to a full understanding of the complete classificatory structure (see Berlin, Breedlove, and Raven, 1968). However, the fact that these midlevel categories have not been labeled suggests that the need to distinguish such classes is as yet relatively unimportant in most cultural contexts.

Nonetheless, the question remains, why are named intermediate taxa almost totally absent in natural ethnobiological taxonomies? The conclusion that I have tentatively come to is that such taxa are rare because they are basically unstable categories, a point that will be developed below.

How are named intermediate taxa likely to arise? At one point, it was suggested that the already present covert categories of this taxonomic rank would be the most probable candidates for labeling (see Berlin, Breedlove, and Raven, 1968, p. 297). As research continues, this hypothesis appears not to be verified in fact. What has been discovered, however, is that named taxa of less inclusiveness than major life forms yet more inclusive than folk generics appear primarily as a response to situations whereby native polytypic generics must be distinguished from newly encountered generics (see Berlin, Breedlove, and Raven, 1974, for a detailed discussion).

Thus far, two distinct processes—or better, paths—have been observed that account for the rise of named intermediate taxa. The first occurs in culture-contact situations where certain introduced organisms must be incorporated into the native taxonomy. If the introduced plants are conceived to be similar—in the native view of the world—to a named polytypic native generic class and yet not similar enough to be included as a legitimate specific of that generic, a named higher order taxon will arise that will include both the native and introduced forms.

The second process, not as clearly understood as the first, occurs when some specific taxa become "conceptually" distinct from their neighboring specific taxa. When this occurs, the conceptually distinctive taxon **will assume the status of a generic, will cease to be labeled by a binomial expression, and in so doing, will force the original generic to assume a superordinate taxonomic status.**

The first process can be illustrated with examples from Tzeltal. At the time of the Hispanic conquest, the highland Mayan groups were introduced to two similar and yet quite distinct grain crops, wheat and sorghum. These grain-bearing crops were considered to be similar by the Tzeltal population to their own polytypic generic class of native corn, *ʔišim*. Logically enough, the two introduced classes were linguistically designated as *kašlan ʔišim* 'Castillian corn' (i.e., wheat) and *móro ʔišim* 'Moor's corn' (i.e., sorghum). Their conceptual affiliation with corn is verified in that both names occur as responses to the query, *bitik sbil huhuten ʔišim* "What are the names of each kind of corn?" Further questioning, however, clearly demonstrates that these two introduced plants are not kinds of "genuine" corn, or, as the Tzeltal would say, not *bac'il ʔišim*.

The new taxonomic structure, then, is seen as one where a superordinate class of greater inclusiveness than those that have been considered as generic groupings, has arisen. Diagrammatically,

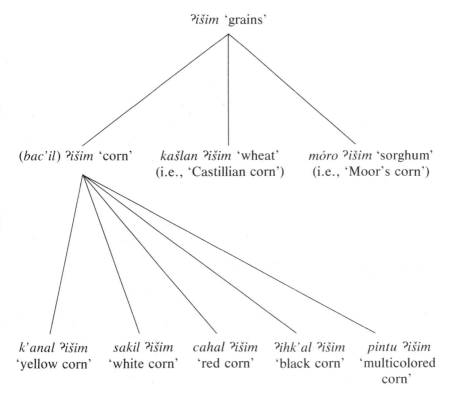

ʔišim 'grains'

(*bac'il*) ʔišim 'corn'   *kašlan* ʔišim 'wheat'   *móro* ʔišim 'sorghum'
                          (i.e., 'Castillian corn')   (i.e., 'Moor's corn')

k'anal ʔišim   *sakil* ʔišim   *cahal* ʔišim   ʔihk'al ʔišim   *pintu* ʔišim
'yellow corn'   'white corn'   'red corn'   'black corn'   'multicolored
                                                                          corn'

The newly formed superordinate taxon ʔišim may best be glossed as 'grains', at least for the moment. And, in precise accord with the processes of lexical marking described earlier, the type-generic 'corn' is marked optionally by the attributive *bac'il* 'genuine', distinguishing it in situations of ambiguity from wheat and sorghum. Otherwise, it is polysemous with the newly formed superordinate intermediate taxon, 'grain'.

Nomenclaturally, the recently introduced generic names are binomial in structure and in this respect do not conform to the otherwise linguistically unitary structure of other generic names. Time and usage, however, will tend to neutralize the marking properties of the attributive forms *kašlan* and *móro,* and the expressions will come to be conceived of as single semantic units. Geoghegan has aptly characterized the process as follows:

> Either because of frequency of perception, need to communicate or what-have-you, a single pattern can be established . . . i.e., rather than identification proceeding from the use of two patterns, as in the first stage, a single unsegmented pattern recognition routine comes into use. At this point, the [complex] nature of the coding no longer has support (since only one feature rather than two is being used), and the complex term

will have a tendency to decay, [becoming] a lexeme with a unitary cognitive representation." (Geoghegan, personal communication)

A strikingly similar situation to that described for the Tzeltal data can be seen in the classificatory treatment of the introduced New World sweet potato (*Ipomea batatas*) among the primitive peoples residing in the vicinity of Mt. Hagen in the Central New Guinea Highlands. The Mt. Hagen material illustrates, furthermore, the interplay of lexical marking and cultural significance in an interesting and important way.

In Hagen ethnoscience, *oka* refers to the sweet potato, *I. batatas*. *Oka mapumb*, a contrasting generic, refers to the indigenous edible tuber, *Pueraria lobata*. A third name, *oka koeka*, refers to a wild, inedible tuberous vine, and *oka kombkla* to a wild tuberless vine with leaves similar to *oka*.

Marilyn Strathern reports that all of the four above names are considered conceptually similar to one another in terms of a variety of characters. On the other hand, it is clear from Strathern's paper that each form refers to a distinctive generic class. Thus, *oka mapumb* 'Pueraria' is not a kind of *oka*.

> *Oka mapumb* (Pueraria) may be contrasted with *oka ingk* (true [ingk] *oka*, i.e., sweet potato) or with *oka* alone, which, when unqualified, always refers to sweet potato [sic]. Only if modified by *mapumb, koeka,* etc. does oka mean something other than sweet potato. Conversely, Pueraria can only be referred to by employing a special suffix such as *mapumb;* it is never just *oka.*   (Strathern, 1969, p. 193).

Furthermore, additional evidence shows that *oka* is partitioned into various specific names, none of which includes the forms *oka mapumb, oka kombkla,* etc. In Strathern's words:

> *Oka* (sweet potato) may be divided into numerous secondary taxa. When collections of these names were made, only once did *mapumb* enter any list. In all the other cases the secondary taxa referred to divisions of *oka* = sweet potato, and excluded any mention of *oka mapumb. Mapumb* is thus not seen as a named type of sweet potato on a par with the other varieties (*konome, pora,* etc.).   (Strathern, 1969, p. 193).

The linguistic and ethnographic evidence suggests that one may characterize the Hageners classification of the plants involved as diagrammed on p. 89.

The Mt. Hagen example, then, can be said to be strikingly parallel to the Tzeltal treatment of grains. Here one sees the possibly covert recognition of an intermediate taxon, *oka* 'sweet potatolike vines' that includes not only sweet potato but as well *Pueraria* and related vines. Unlike the Tzeltal case, however, the introduced generic *oka* has come to assume unmarked status, being optionally marked only in contexts of ambiguity. While the details of this development are unclear, one may make several inferences that are fairly well supported on linguistic grounds.

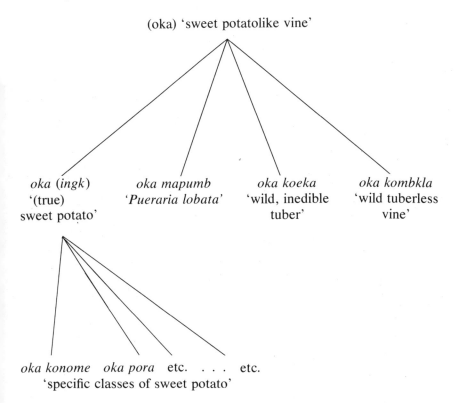

(oka) 'sweet potatolike vine'

oka (*ingk*)
'(true)
sweet potato'

oka mapumb
'*Pueraria lobata*'

oka koeka
'wild, inedible
tuber'

oka kombkla
'wild tuberless
vine'

oka konome   oka pora   etc.   . . .   etc.
'specific classes of sweet potato'

It is highly likely that at one point, before the introduction of the sweet potato, *oka* referred, in its unmarked form, to *Pueraria lobata*. The terms *oka koeka* 'wild inedible tuber' and *oka kombkla* can be seen simply as examples of generic name extension formed on the basis of analogy as discussed on p. 68 above. With the appearance of sweet potato, clearly morphologically similar to *P. lobata*, one can surmise a period whereby the class linguistically referred to as *oka x,* where *x* must have represented some unknown qualifying expression. Through time, the cultural importance of sweet potato increased dramatically, eventually exceeding that of *P. lobata*. At some point in this process, *oka* came to refer, in its unmarked form, to sweet potato and *P. lobata* became obligatorily indicated by the complex expression *oka mapumb*. In fact, a process identical to the one just supposed can be documented with some accuracy for certain Tzeltal animal names. (see p. 97 below).

   The second process whereby superordinate intermediate taxa are named does not necessarily result from the introduction of new organisms. This situation occurs when a native specific assumes the status of a generic category. There may be a period in the process when the distinctive (conceptually) specific taxon is labeled by a unitary lexeme and not the standard binomial expression characteristic of most specific taxa.

The process can be illustrated by an example from Tzeltal and concerns the classification of oaks. For most informants, the generic *hihte?* 'oak' includes four specific taxa—*ca?pat hihte?* 'excrement-barked oak', *sakyok hihte?* 'white-footed oak', *k'eweš hihte?* 'custard-apple oak', and *čikinib hihte?* 'armadillo-eared oak'. This last form may, for most informants, be cited in abbreviated form, i.e., simply *čikinib*. For some informants, the abbreviated form is, indeed, the preferred usage. Some Tzeltal speakers, however, recognize only the first three classes of oaks as (*bac'il*) *hihte?* '(genuine) oaks' and treat *čikinib* as being a closely related but distinct and coordinate taxon. One Tzeltal Indian for whom the above classification of oaks holds produced the following folk tree diagram:

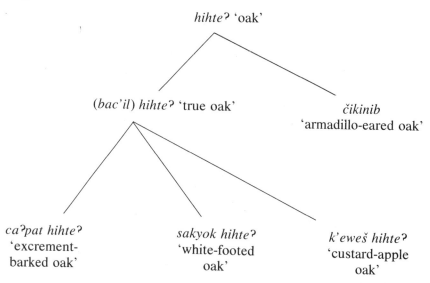

That such a situation could arise is partially explained by the fact that *čikinib* is by far the most divergent class of oaks referring to the native live oaks of the area (*Quercus acatenangensis, Q. sapotaefolia*). *čikinib* possesses scores of objective characters that readily distinguish it from the other three deciduous classes of "(true) oaks." I lack direct evidence that the higher-order taxon *hihte?* is at the present time a fully stabilized taxon, and, as will be pointed out below, it never may become so.

In each of the examples just described, it would appear that the intermediate taxa that have arisen are each unstable as the new generics continue to be used over time. In the case of the introduced grains, it was suggested that the new forms become conceptually "a single unsegmented pattern," to use Geoghegan's phrasing. In the case of *čikinib,* already a monolexemic form, the prior linguistic affiliation with *hihte*ʔ is eventually lost (neutralized?) and the optional marking of the type generic (*bac'il*) *hihte*ʔ will most likely be eliminated. One may predict that the same will occur with the type generic, (*bac'il*) ʔ*išim.* The final result will be the ultimate loss of the intermediate taxa as named categories, although conceptually they will clearly continue to remain.

SUMMARY OF THE DEVELOPMENT OF INTERMEDIATE NAMES

One may summarize in tabular form the sequential steps that lead to the formation and final loss of named intermediate categories in Table I.

Linguistic Recognition of 'Plant'

While man has no doubt tacitly recognized the world of plants as a conceptual category since earliest times, it does not appear to have been essential to provide the concept with a distinctive label until quite recently. In contemporary languages of primitive peoples, a single, unique expression for 'plant' is notably lacking, and there is no reason to assume that such was not the case in prehistoric times. Interestingly enough, when the notion of 'plant' is expressed, it is done via circumlocution or by the use of a form that is polysemous with some lower-order major life form term. We might surmise an identical situation in Theophrastus' time, where it does not appear that a single common expression for the full category of the plant kingdom existed. The term Theophrastus chose for the domain as a whole, φυτόν, was in every day usage the word for cultivated plant or 'herbaceous plant of cultivation', with the sometimes restricted meaning of '(cultivated) tree' (Greene, 1909, p. 110).

In Kirwinia and Hanunóo, the term for "tree" can be used in some contexts to refer to plants in general (Malinowski, 1933; Conklin, 1954). Likewise, in Ilongot, *ra*ʔ*ek* is polysemously 'herbaceous plant' (i.e., not 'vine' or 'tree') and 'plant' (M. Rosaldo, personal communication). Furthermore, in Spanish, *planta* appears polysemously as 'herbaceous plant, plant'; in Latin, note *herba* 'grass, plant', and Russian *trava* 'grass, plant'. These data, while not conclusive, seem to validate the suspicion that the label for the unique beginner in plant taxonomies is often drawn from one of the major class taxa, replicating a nomenclatural process that we have seen to be quite general in other areas of ethnobotanical nomenclature.

TABLE I

Hypothetical Stages Involved in the Formation and Subsequent Loss of Intermediate Taxa

Path I	Path II

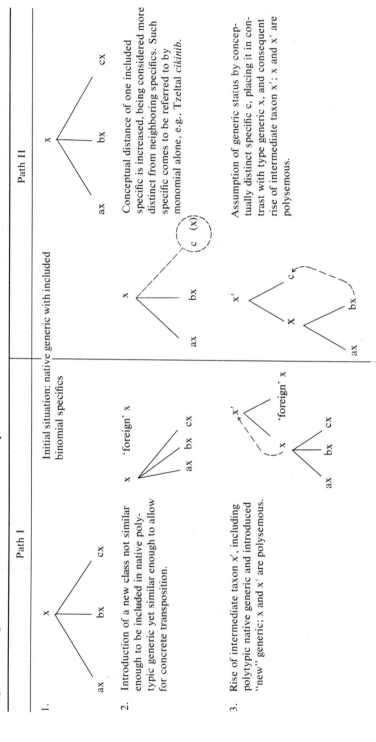

1. Initial situation: native generic with included binomial specifics

2. **Path I:** Introduction of a new class not similar enough to be included in native poly-typic generic yet similar enough to allow for concrete transposition.

   Path II: Conceptual distance of one included specific is increased, being considered more distinct from neighboring specifics. Such specific comes to be referred to by monomial alone, e.g., Tzeltal *cikinib*.

3. **Path I:** Rise of intermediate taxon x', including polytypic native generic and introduced "new" generic; x and x' are polysemous.

   Path II: Assumption of generic status by concep-tually distinct specific c, placing it in con-trast with type generic x, and consequent rise of intermediate taxon x'; x and x' are polysemous.

4.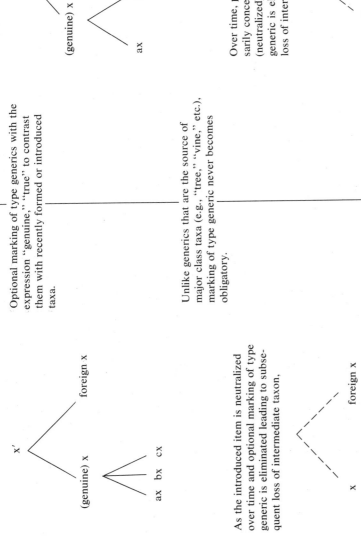

Optional marking of type generics with the expression "genuine," "true" to contrast them with recently formed or introduced taxa.

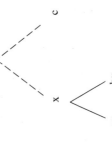

Unlike generics that are the source of major class taxa (e.g., "tree," "vine," etc.), marking of type generic never becomes obligatory.

5.

As the introduced item is neutralized over time and optional marking of type generic is eliminated leading to subsequent loss of intermediate taxon.

Over time, prior linguistic (but not necessarily conceptual) affiliation with x is lost (neutralized) and optional marking of type generic is eliminated leading to subsequent loss of intermediate taxon.

On the other hand, there is some evidence that the term for the unique beginner might in some languages derive as a compound. In ancient Sumerian, the concept "plant" was apparently designated by the conjunction of three lower-order terms that translated approximately as 'tree', 'grass', and 'vegetable' (Robert McC. Adams, personal communication). This corresponds quite well with what we know of ancient Latin, where the expression of 'tree', 'herb' (*arbor et herba*) was used to designate the more general concept. In this regard, Ullmann notes:

> There was in Latin no generic term for "plant" in the modern sense: *arbor* and *herba* were the most comprehensive classconcepts in the botanical field. According to a recent enquiry, the modern meaning of "plant" is first found in Albertus Magnus in the 13th century, whereas the French *plante* did not acquire this wider sense until 300 years later." (Ullmann, 1963, p. 181)

Finally, while there is no commonly recognized term for 'plant' in Tzeltal, there are instances where something like the notion can be expressed by the compound *teʔ-ʔak'*, literally, 'tree-vine'. It might be suggested that we see something like this going on in English folk biology, when we attempt to refer to the concept "living things" often by the phrase "plants-and-animals."

Ethnozoological Parallels

While I have restricted my survey of the development of ethnobiological nomenclature to categories of plants, it should not be surprising to find rather close parallels in ethnozoological nomenclature. The data in this area are far from complete, but those I have seen suggest that identical nomenclatural processes are at work. Type-specific–generic name polysemy can be found in animal names as well as in plant names. Thus, in the Chinese of Hong Kong Harbor, the Karam of New Guinea, and in Guarani of Argentina, one notes examples such as seen below (Anderson, 1967, p. 71; Dennler, 1939, p. 233; Bulmer, 1968, p. 622).

Chinese   *ling ʒhal* 'lobster'

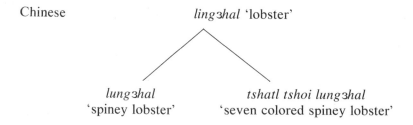

lung ʒhal   *tshatl tshoi lung ʒhal*
'spiney lobster'   'seven colored spiney lobster'

Karam

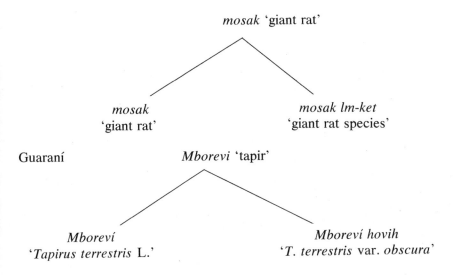

mosak 'giant rat'

mosak
'giant rat'

mosak lm-ket
'giant rat species'

Guaraní   Mborevi 'tapir'

Mborevi
'*Tapirus terrestris* L.'

Mborevi hovih
'*T. terrestris* var. *obscura*'

Furthermore, the optional marking of the otherwise polysemous type-specific with an attributive glossed as 'genuine' is also found in animal nomenclature. Some selected examples are seen from Karam and Tonkawa (Bulmer, 1968, p. 624; Gatschet, 1899, p. 160):

Karam   yabol 'worms'

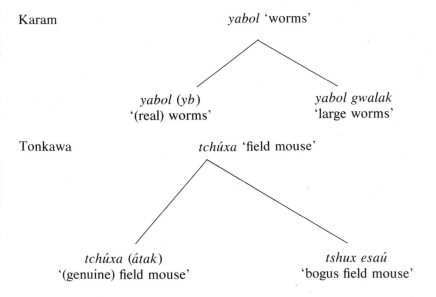

yabol (yb)
'(real) worms'

yabol gwalak
'large worms'

Tonkawa   tchúxa 'field mouse'

tchúxa (átak)
'(genuine) field mouse'

tshux esaú
'bogus field mouse'

Apparently, generic name–life form name polysemy is also a process observed in the development of ethnozoological nomenclature. Gatschet, in his large Klamath grammar notes that the Klamath ". . . often use . . . *wíshink* 'garter snake' for 'snake', the Modocs *wáměnigh* (black snake) for the same order of reptiles, these species being the most frequent of their kind in their respective countries" (1890, p. 145). In Pomo, notes collected by the zoologist A. Hart Merriam (n.d.) show the form *shah* as meaning polysemously 'salmon' and 'fish', while in Shoshoni of the Snake River drainage, we find *ʔakai* 'salmon, fish' (Wick Miller, personal communication). From Karam, Bulmer (1968) reports *kmn* as generically 'small edible mammals' but as well a life form name indicating all 'game animals'.

As concerns evidence indicating type-generic lexical marking analogous to that found for plant names, Gatschet cites *gúato* 'bird' and guató-hi 'real bird, i.e., eagle'; likewise, *sane* is 'snake', while *sanehi* refers to 'rattlesnake, i.e., real snake' (Gatschet, 1890, p. 145).

I have only one example of life form–unique beginner polysemy in ethnozoological nomenclature. In Orok of Sakhalin Island, Austerlitz (1959, p. 211) notes *buju* as meaning both 'bear' and 'animal'. It is not unlikely, however, that polysemy of this type will also be found widely as more information becomes available.

Finally, data from Tzeltal ethnozoology seem to replicate in important ways some of the problems suggested in the discussion of the formation of intermediate taxa, especially as concerns the classificatory treatment of introduced organisms in the case of the New Guinea Mt. Hagen materials. At the conquest, the Spanish introduced to the Tzeltal three domestic animals that were to assume critical cultural importance: chickens, sheep, and pigs. For each of these introduced organisms, there existed native classes for which the foreign animals could be seen as similar, namely, birds, deer, and wild pigs. On historical linguistic grounds, we know that the preconquest Tzeltal terms for these native forms were *mut* 'bird', *čih* 'deer', and *čitam* wild pig. The situation at the present time is, however, as follows:

mut 'chicken'	versus	*teʔtikil mut* 'bird' (lit. 'forest chicken')
čih 'sheep'	versus	*teʔtikil čih* 'deer' (lit. 'forest sheep')
čitam 'pig'	versus	*wamal čitam* 'wild pig' (lit. 'brush pig')

In each case, the unmarked form has become restricted to the introduced animals, while the aboriginal organisms have become linguistically marked. Full information is lacking on the complete historical cycle leading to this outcome, but there are sufficient data to suggest that the situation is very close to that seen in the Mt. Hagen treatment of *oka.*

One may note the developmental sequence tabulated below for one item of the set *čih* 'deer'. In both the Tzeltal and Mt. Hagen data, it

Preconquest	*čih* 'deer'		
Conquest	*čih* 'deer'	*tunim čih*	'sheep'[a]
Early postconquest	(*te?tikil*) *čih* 'forest deer' (optional marking of native form)	*tunim čih*	'cotton deer'
Late postconquest	*te?tikil čih* (obligatory marking)	(*tunim*) *čih*	(optional marking)
Present	*te?tikil čih* 'deer'	*čih*	(optional marking of introduced form has become unnecessary)

[a] Literally, 'cotton deer', attested in some contemporary dialects of Tzeltal.

seems clear that similar processes have been followed leading names for introduced organisms from a lexically marked to lexically unmarked status and that this process is directly related to the high cultural significance of the organisms involved.

An Aside Concerning Nomenclatural Devolution

At the beginning, I noted that vocabularies of languages tend to increase in size over time. This is, of course, generally true when total vocabulary is considered. Specific lexical domains, however, undergo not only growth but decay as well. As with lexical expansion, the likely underlying causal mechanisms must be ultimately related to cultural evolution. Wholesale vocabulary loss in some specific area must be due in part, at least, to the lessening of cultural importance associated with that particular area of human concern. Examples of such nomenclatural devolution can be found in almost any area of vocabulary, terms for agricultural implements or carriage lexicon being obvious examples in English.

As concerns ethnobotanical nomenclature particularly, it now seems likely that the direction of vocabulary loss will be from the particular to the general. To use the terminology of my colleagues Kay and Geoghegan, loss will occur "from the bottom up." With little introspection, speakers of English who have been reared in an urban setting will recognize at once that they know virtually no specific names for kinds of plants, that many generic names are recognizable linguistically only as "names" of plants, the organisms referred to being totally unfamiliar. Nonetheless, abstract life form names, such as "tree" or "grass" apparently remain as useful terms for referring to an ever shrinking (both literally and figuratively) portion of one's natural environment. The topic is an intriguing one deserving further study, and English would be as good a language as any on which to begin research.

Conclusions

Assuming a uniformitarian view for the growth of ethnobotanical vocabulary, I have attempted to outline a plausible sequence of development of nomenclatural categories characteristic of man's linguistic recognition of the plant world. I have argued for the primacy of generic taxa as the first ethnobiological categories to become encoded in a language's plant lexicon. Expansion appears to be horizontal at first, and with enlarging experience, develops both by differentiation and generalization. A similar argument has been made by Brown in reference to vocabulary as acquired by the child (Brown, 1958), so one might suspect the process discussed here to have wider ontogenetic applicability as well.

Six major linguistic categories have been posited as sufficient for describing the names for classes of plants in all languages. It appears highly likely that these categories become encoded in the history of any language in the following order:

$$\text{Generic} \rightarrow \left\{ \begin{array}{l} \text{life form} \\ \text{specific} \end{array} \right\} \rightarrow \left\{ \begin{array}{l} \text{intermediate} \\ \text{varietal} \end{array} \right\} \rightarrow \text{unique beginner}$$

An additional claim has been made that states that with the encoding of each category, a specifiable process of lexical marking is operable, leading plant names from a lexically unmarked to a lexically marked status.

If the principles I have discussed prove to be general, they could allow for a plausible typological classification of the various types of ethnobotanical nomenclature seen in the languages of the world. It is also likely that a similar classification may be appropriate for ethnozoological nomenclature. I would speculate that the typological classification can best be interpreted as indicative of how plant nomenclature becomes encoded diachronically.

But a classification is not a theory. It is one thing to describe typological regularities and to suggest that their interpretation is best understood historically. It is quite a different task to outline the developmental processes involved in the change of one system into another.

On the other hand, one usually searches for causal explanations only after one has observed something that might be interesting to explain. Until recently, studies into the nature of the growth of vocabulary have been accorded little importance in linguistics and anthropology. I believe that as detailed descriptive reports reveal conclusively that aspects of man's lexicon develop in a regularly patterned fashion, efforts toward providing theoretical explanations of the processes involved will be increased. While I cannot predict what mechanisms will be finally suggested as causal explanations as future work proceeds, it seems likely that the details underlying the development of vocabulary must eventually be encompassed within some more general, technologically based theory of cultural evolution.

Acknowledgments

An earlier draft of this paper was prepared with the fellowship support of the Center for Advanced Study in the Behavioral Sciences and the National Science Foundation, Grant GS-2280. Essentially, this version has been distributed as Working Paper No. 39, Language-Behavior Research Laboratory (March 1971). Many individuals have provided encouragement in developing these ideas further. I am especially appreciative of the continued collaboration of Paul Kay and William H. Geoghegan of the Language-Behavior Research Laboratory. As much of the data relevant to issues discussed here are unpublished, I am grateful for ethnographic information provided by colleagues from their own field notes. I would like to thank the following persons for their criticism, data, and helpful comments: Barry Alpher, Eugene Anderson, Robert Austerlitz, Donald Bahr, Keith Basso, Katherine Branstetter, Dennis E. Breedlove, Jan Brukman, Ralph H. Bulmer, Robbins Burling, Wallace Chafe, Harold C. Conklin, Lincoln Constance, Christopher Day, Barbara Demory, Robert M. W. Dixon, Mary LeCron Foster, Catherine S. Fowler, Charles O. Frake, Paul Friedrich, William H. Geoghegan, Robert F. Heizer, Nicholas A. Hopkins, Eugene Hunn, Dell Hymes, Paul Kay, Robert M. Laughlin, Yakov Malkiel, Robert McC. Adams, David Price, Robert Randall, Peter H. Raven, Michelle Rosaldo, David Schneider, Brian Stross, Oswald Werner, and Michael Wilson.

References

Almstedt, Ruth L.
  1968 Diegueño *Tree:* an ecological approach to a linguistic problem. *International Journal of American Linguistics* **34,** 9–15.
Anderson, Eugene N.
  1967 *The ethnoichthyology of the Hong Kong boat people.* Unpublished Ph. D. dissertation in Anthropology. University of California, Berkeley.
Austerlitz, Robert
  1959 Gilyak religious terminology in the light of linguistic analysis. *Transactions of the Asiatic Society of Japan,* Ser. 3, **7.**
Bartlett, Harley Harris
  1940 History of the generic concept in botany. *Bulletin of the Torrey Botanical Club* **67,** 349–362.
Berlin, Brent
  1969 *Universal nomenclatural principles in folk science.* Paper presented at the 1968 annual meeting of the American Anthropological Association, New Orleans.

Berlin, Brent, Dennis E. Breedlove, and Peter H. Raven
 1966   Folk taxonomies and biological classification. *Science* **154**, 273–275. (Reprinted in Steven Tyler (ed.) *Cognitive Anthropology.* New York: Holt, Rinehart and Winston; 1968.)
 1968   Covert categories and folk taxonomies. *American Anthropologist* **70**, 290–299.
 1974   *Principles of Tzeltal plant classification.* New York: Academic Press n.d. *Universal principles of nomenclature and classification in folk science*
Bright, William, and Jane Bright
 1965   Semantic structures in Northwestern California and the Sapir–Whorf hypothesis. *American Anthropologist* **67** (part 2).
Brown, Roger
 1958   How shall a thing be called? *Psychological Review* **65**, 14–21.
Buck, Carl Darling
 1949   *A dictionary of selected synonyms in the principal Indo-European languages.* Chicago: University of Chicago Press.
Bulmer, Ralph
 1967   Why is the cassowary not a bird? A problem of zoological taxonomy among the Karam of the New Guinea Highlands. *Man* **2**, 1–25.
 1968   Worms that croak and other mysteries of Karam natural science. *Mankind* **6**, 621–639.
 1970   Which came first, the chicken or the egghead. In *Échanges et Communications, Mélanges offerts à Claude Levi-Strauss à l'occasion de son 60ème anniversaire,* edited by Jean Pouillon et Pierre Maranda.
Bulmer, Ralph, and Michael Tyler
 1968   Karam classification of frogs. *Journal of the Polynesian Society* **77**, 333–385.
Conklin, H. C.
 1954   *The relation of Hanunóo culture to the plant world.* Unpublished Ph. D. dissertation in anthropology, Yale University; New Haven.
 1962   Lexicographical treatment of folk taxonomies. In *Problems in Lexicography,* edited by F. W. Householder and Sol Saporta. Indiana University Research Center in Anthropology, Folklore and Linguistic Publication 21 [and] *International Journal of American Linguistics* **28** (part 4).
Demory, Barbara
 1971   The word for 'tree' in the Hokan language family. *Informant* Department of Anthropology, California State College at Long Beach.
Dennler, J. G.
 1939   Los nombres indígenas en guaraní de los mamíferso de la Argentina y países limítrofes y su importancia para la systemática. *Physis* **16**, 225–244.
Dentan
 1968   The Semai: a nonviolent people of Malaya. In *Case Studies in Cultural Anthropology,* edited by G. Spindler and L. Spindler, New York: Holt.
Diamond, J. M.
 1966   Classification system of a primitive people. *Science* **151**, 1102–1104.
Fowler, Catherine S., and Joy Leland
 1967   Some northern Paiute native categories. *Ethnology* **6**, 381–404.
Frake, Charles O.
 1962   The ethnographic study of cognitive systems. In *Anthropology and Human Behavior,* edited by T. Gladwin and W. C. Sturtevant. Washington, D.C.: Anthropological Society of Washington.

French, David
1960 *Types of native taxonomic process.* Paper presented at the Fifty-ninth Annual Meeting of the American Anthropological Association, Minneapolis.
Friedrich, Paul
1970 *Proto-Indo-European trees.* Chicago: University of Chicago Press.
Gatschet, Albert Samuel
1890 *The Klamath Indians of Southwestern Oregon.* Contributions to North American Ethnology Vol. II, Part II. Washington, D.C.: Department of Interior, U.S. Geographical and Geological Survey of the Rocky Mountain Region.
1899 "Real", "true", or "genuine" in Indian languages. In *American Anthropologist,* **1,** 155–161.
Greenberg, Joseph H.
1966 Language Universals. In *Current trends in linguistics,* Vol. 3, *Theoretical foundations,* edited by T. A. Sebeok, pp. 61–112. The Hague: Mouton.
Greene, Edward L.
1909 *Landmarks of botanical history.* Smithsonian Miscellaneous Collections Vol. 54. Washington, D.C.
Lévi-Strauss, Claude
1966 *The savage mind.* Chicago: University of Chicago Press.
Malinowski, Bronislaw
1935 *Coral gardens and their magic,* Vol. II. New York: American Book.
Matthews, W.
1886 Navajo names for plants. *American Naturalist* **20,** 767–777.
Merriam, A. Hart
n.d. *Field checklists, Pacific Coast Region.* U.S. Department of Agriculture biological survey. [Notes in the library of the Archaeological Research Facility, Department of Anthropology, University of California, Berkeley].
Paso y Trancoso, F. del
1886 La botanica entre los Nahuas. *Anales del Museo Nacional de México* III. Mexico.
Roys, Ralph L.
1931 *The ethno-botany of the Maya.* Middle American Research Series, Number 2. Department of Middle American Research, Tulane University, New Orleans.
Stahel, Gerold
1944 Notes on the Arawak Indian names of plants in Surinam. *Journal of the New York Botanical Garden* **45,** 268–279.
Strathern, Marilyn
1969 Why is the Pueraria a sweet potato? *Ethnology* **8,** 189–198.
Trager, George
1939 "Cottonwood" = "Tree": a Southwestern linguistic trait. *International Journal of American Linguistics* **9,** 117–118.
Werner, Heinz
1954 Change of meaning: A study of semantic processes through the experimental method. *Journal of General Psychology* **50,** 181–208.
Wyman, Leland C., and S. K. Harris
1941 *Navajo Indian medical ethnobotany.* University of New Mexico Bulletin 366, Anthropological Series 3.5.

Color Categorization in West Futunese: Variability and Change

JANET WYNNE DIXON DOUGHERTY

This paper describes the system of color classification for West Futuna, a Polynesian outlier in the New Hebrides, and considers the dimensions of variation within the system and the theoretical implications of the classification. The system of color categorization on West Futuna, in terms of the sequence (see Table VII) predicted by Berlin and Kay (1969) is variable, including adult representatives of the contiguous stages IIIa, IV, and V. Data is presented to illustrate the processes by which a given informant is concluded to have a particular color system. In addition, it is shown that LIGHT and DARK rather than WHITE and BLACK categories are in evidence for speakers of West Futunese. A revision of the Berlin and Kay developmental sequence is suggested by the West Futunese data. Incorporating this revision, the sequence accurately predicts the current synchronic situation and the diachronic implications of variation within the domain of color for the West Futunese.

Throughout this paper, color terms in small capital letters will be used to represent color categories. Bold-faced lower case letters will represent color foci, and italic phonetic orthography will represent actual color terms as used by individual speakers of West Futunese.

Of the forty-five adults who participated in the research, 5 or 11% use a traditional system, Stage IIIa, with basic color terms for: WHITE, BLACK, RED, and GRUE (the region including both the greens and blues). This system is considered traditional because none of the basic labels are foreign loans as is the case for later stages. Eighteen adults, 40% of the sample, are at Stage IV, having added the basic category YELLOW to the IIIa system. Twenty-one individuals, 46%, are at Stage V, with terms for the categories WHITE, BLACK, RED, YELLOW, GREEN, and BLUE. One of the forty-five adults was unclassifiable. In addition, many of the children sampled who have been exposed to the recently established British and French schools on the island have Stage VI systems with all the categories noted above for Stage V plus BROWN. One child has encoded both

TABLE I

Test Objects for Naming Task

1.	Gray metal slide box	0Grey 4,5		21.	Dried leaf, (underside)	not coded
2.	Black chap stick tube	0Grey1		22.	Red Fuji box	7.5R4,3
3.	White chap stick cap	0Grey10		23.	Dark blue pen cap	2.5BP2,3
4.	Pink talcum powder tin[a]	5R7,6 10RP6		24.	Light yellow flower	2.5Y8 5Y9
5.	Gold box	2.5Y5,4		25.	Dark red center of 24	5R2,3
6.	Creamy white cowrie	5Y9		26.	Nautilus shell, cream	10YR9
7.	Brown dotted shell	5YR2 2.5YR3		27.	Nautilus shell, black	0Grey1
8.	Brown cowrie	7.5,5YR2		28.	Nautilus shell, brown-purple[a]	7.5RP4 10R2
9.	Cloudy brown cowrie	2.5,5YR2		29.	Wooden table	5YR2
10.	Orange Agfa film box	10R5		30.	Brownish stapler[a]	2.5Y3
11.	Yellow Kodak film box	10YR7 10YR8		31.	Light blue GAZ can	10,5B5
12.	Dark red pin cushion	7.5R3		32.	Light green-blue typewriter[a]	5BG3
13.	Blue-green felt[a]	2.5BG6 10BG4		33.	Blue-purple flower	2.5BP3 7.5BP2
14.	Silver battery	not coded		34.	Leaf of 33	2.5,5GY3,4
15.	Green notebook	10GY6		35.	Researcher's hair	not coded
16.	Ripe lime	7.5,10Y8		36.	Red flower	7.5R5,4
17.	Ripe pineapple	10YR8 7.5YR7 5YR6		37.	Purple flower	7.5RP2 7.5P3[b]
18.	Frosty green leaf[a]	7.5GY5,7		38.	Tan paws of dog	5YR6
19.	Yellow leaf	2.5Y8		39.	Green handiwrap box	5.7,5G4
20.	Dried leaf	2.5YR2 5YR3		40.	Green glass bottle	10GY3 2.5G3

[a] Indicates low-saturation test item, poor object–chart match.

[b] When more than one set of co-ordinates is given for a single test item, the first indicated is the match used in recording naming responses on a code sheet.

ORANGE and PURPLE in addition to BROWN, making her the single representative of Stage VII.

The forty-five adults participated in two research tasks conducted exclusively in West Futunese. They were first asked to respond with a color term to each of a series of forty objects representing the eleven basic color categories at least twice each. The objects and their approximate Munsell co-ordinates are given in Table I. Test objects were matched to the Berlin–Kay Munsell color array so that one chip represented one object for purposes of coding naming responses. The Berlin–Kay Munsell color array is a standardized display of 410 chips. 320 chips vary in 8 degrees of brightness on the vertical dimension and 40 hue distinctions on the horizontal dimension. 40 chips each of white and black border the array on the bright and dark edges, respectively. At one side, set off from the main array, is a nonchromatic set of chips arranged vertically in 10 degrees of brightness from black to white, the intermediate chips representing grays. In the second task, informants were asked to indicate the focus and range of every color term they had volunteered plus any of a set of common color terms not volunteered. This was done with the Berlin–Kay Munsell color array.

In addition to the adult subjects, fifty-two children participated in the research. Twenty-four of the oldest, ranging in age from 9 to 15, who demonstrated relatively stable color systems will be considered here. They participated in the two adult tasks plus two additional tasks involving the adult stimulus materials just described. Following the initial naming task, children were asked to select from the group of forty objects a representative of each of a series of color terms listed in Table II. The list includes both basic and secondary terms in West Futunese and the basic terms of English. It was necessary to include the English terms, as some children are learning these labels before they master their native ones. Following this, the children were asked to map as adults did. Subsequently, they were asked to identify each of the eleven basic focal areas. The researcher would indicate one or two chips in the focal region of a basic category on the color array and ask the child to name the color being indicated. Table III gives the specifications of the chips indicated as focal in this task. Yellow-green was added to the list of indicated foci midway through the task in the hopes of identifying a focus for *rounemahmata,* a common secondary color term.

Results of this research revealed variation in the lexicosemantic organization of the domain of color for speakers of West Futunese. The categories WHITE, BLACK, RED, YELLOW, GRUE, GREEN, and BLUE are named by different groups of adult speakers who are classifiable as having either Stage IIIa, Stage IV, or Stage V systems. The basic West Futunese terms

TABLE II

Common Color Terms

	Color Terms Used in Adult Mapping
hkeŋo	WHITE
uri	BLACK
hmea	RED
uiui	GRUE or GREEN
iela	YELLOW
hleu	YELLOW, ripe
plu	BLUE
krin	GREEN
praon	BROWN
rounemahmata	GREEN, living, green leaf
sekaumkufatu	BLUE-PURPLE, flower of the kaumkufatu
fero fero	YELLOW, multicolored, patterned
kanuhkanu	multicolored, patterned, striped
sekafika	PINK, flower of the Malay apple
hkosi	GRAY, BROWN, pastel, low saturation

Color Terms Used in Children's Identification

pipul	PURPLE	*plak*	BLACK
pink	PINK	*uait*	WHITE
aranc	ORANGE		
krei	GRAY		
eret	RED		

designating these categories are as follows: LIGHT is designated by *hkeŋo*, DARK by *uri*, RED by *hmea;* GRUE is designated by *uiui* for those speakers who have a GRUE category. For other speakers *uiui* designates GREEN. YELLOW is designated by *iela* and BLUE is designated by *plu*.

Consider the categories labeled by *hkeŋo* and *uri* first. They designate categories similar to the English categories LIGHT and DARK. Maps 1a and 1b illustrate Stage IIIa speakers' mappings of *hkeŋo* and *uri*. The boundary lines on the map represent contour lines at maximum extension, 30% and 70%. Dots represent foci; The heavy dot is the most commonly se-

TABLE III

Foci and Coordinates for Children's Identification Task 4

White	0Grey10	Brown	5YR2
Black	0Grey1	Pink	2.5R6,7
Red	2.5,5,7.5R3,4	Purple	10BP2
Yellow	7.5YR7 10YR8	Orange	10R5
Green	2.5G4	Gray	0Grey5
Blue	5BP3	Yellow-green	7.5YG6,7

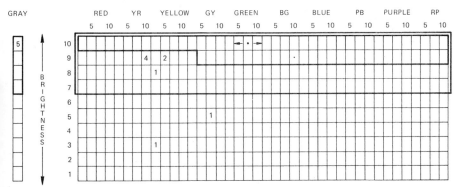

Map 1a. Stage IIIa: *hkeŋo* (WHITE)—5 informants. Contour lines represent range mappings for 70% agreement and maximum extension. Dots represent foci. Predominant foci are indicated by heavy dots. Integers represent naming responses and indicate the number of times an object matched to the chip in which the integer is written was named with the color term concerned.

lected focus. Numbers represent naming responses and indicate the number of times an object of the color of the chip in which it is written was named by the color term concerned. Notice that the terms are not restricted to pure whites and blacks, but extend into the light and dark areas of the color array. Naming responses to the test objects and usage in natural conversation support this observation. Items we would refer to as blond, tan, yellow, or pastel are commonly labeled *hkeŋo* while most dark colors may be referred to as *uri*.

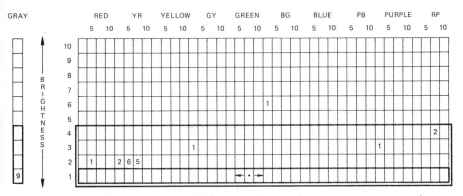

Map 1b. Stage IIIa: *uri* (BLACK)—5 informants. Contour lines represent range mappings for 70% agreement and maximum extension. Dots represent foci. Predominant foci are indicated by heavy dots. Integers represent naming responses and indicate the number of times an object matched to the chip in which the integer is written was named with the color term concerned.

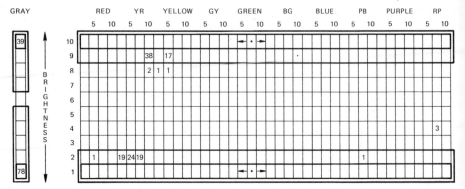

Map 2. Stages IV and V: *hkeŋo* (WHITE) and *uri* (BLACK)—39 informants. Contour lines represent range mappings for 70% agreement and maximum extension. Dots represent foci. Predominant foci are indicated by heavy dots. Integers represent naming responses and indicate the number of times an object matched to the chip in which the integer is written was named with the color term concerned.

If we examine the mappings for *hkeŋo* and *uri* as shown in Map 2, illustrating responses for non-IIIa speakers, we find that range indications are polarized and indicate pure white or black more closely than is the case for speakers found to have IIIa systems. Naming responses also include fewer nonwhite or nonblack test items as referents of *hkeŋo* and *uri* for these individuals, but *hkeŋo* and *uri* are not exclusively restricted to pure white and pure black. Some yellow objects are frequently named *hkeŋo*, and several brown objects are named *uri*. Speakers at Stages IV and V appear to use *hkeŋo* and *uri* to designate LIGHT and DARK categories as do speakers at Stage IIIa, but those individuals with Stage IV and V systems are restricting the ranges of *hkeŋo* and *uri* as they define and name new color categories.

hmea is the universally shared basic term focusing in **red** for the West Futunese. Map 3 indicates the range and foci of *hmea*. The results of the mapping tasks for speakers at all stages were similar with the exception of the three naming responses noted on Map 3 outside the maximum range. *hmea* is a RED category focusing in **red** and including browns, oranges, pinks, and purples consistently in its range. Color naming responses to the test items, however, indicate that the range of *hmea* is not accurately depicted for every informant by his mapping response. Informants may name brown, pink, or purple test items as *hmea*, even though they may fall outside their own range mapping. Two individuals extended the label *hmea* to yellow objects. These are the individuals responsible for the naming responses in yellows shown on Map 3. The naming responses indicate that *hmea* includes YELLOW for these two individuals, even though their own range indications are more restricted.

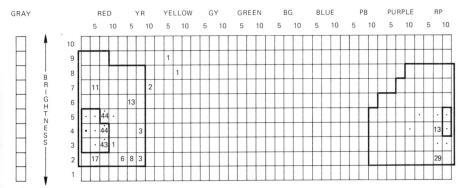

Map 3. Stages IIIa, IV and V: *hmea* (RED)—44 informants. Contour lines represent range mappings for 70% agreement and maximum extension. Dots represent foci. Predominant foci are indicated by heavy dots. Integers represent naming responses and indicate the number of times an object matched to the chip in which the integer is written was named with the color term concerned.

This kind of result (i.e., restricted range mappings) may be due to the order in which individuals were asked to map the color categories. Foci were located before range indications were made, an ordering of tasks that may have set informants to respond in terms of focal boundaries rather than boundaries for complete categories. It was found that supplementing the data on range indications with naming responses gave a more faithful indication of category boundaries as they were observed to be used in natural conversation.

Continuing an examination of the color categories, the problem posed by YELLOW is encountered. It has been said that five West Futunese are at Stage IIIa with respect to color classification and do not recognize YELLOW as a basic category. This determination was based on the fact that two of these individuals included YELLOW in *hmea* as was just described. The same two volunteered *iela* a loan from pidgin English *iela* meaning 'yellow' infrequently and only for objects other than the best yellow examples. They mapped *iela* outside the focal **yellow** area of the array as illustrated on Map 4. The same two informants restricted *hleu* 'ripe' a term that is basic for some informants at later stages to naming examples of ripe fruits.

Although the three other informants reported to have Stage IIIa systems did not explicitly indicate that YELLOW was included in *hmea,* they also failed to demonstrate a well-defined YELLOW category. They volunteered *iela* infrequently and used it inconsistently in both naming and mapping responses—notice the range extensions and the inconsistent naming responses illustrated on Map 4. These three individuals refer-

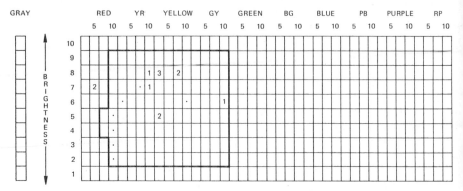

Map 4. Stage IIIa: emerging *iela* (nonbasic YELLOW)—5 informants. Contour lines represent the maximum extension of informants' range mappings. There is no area that was included within the range of *iela* by 70% of informants. Dots represent foci. No focal area was predominantly selected. Integers represent naming responses and indicate the number of times an object matched to the chip in which the integer is written was named with the color term concerned.

red to YELLOW test items as *krin* and *hkeŋo,* among other responses. *hleu* 'ripe' was restricted in its application by them to ripe fruits.

In contrast to these results other adult speakers did indicate a well-defined YELLOW category, although their basic label for this category varied. These are individuals reported to have Stage IV and V systems of classification. The recentness of the YELLOW category is attested by the broad focal spread and by the lack of agreement on one basic term. *iela* (from pidgin English), *hleu* 'ripe', and *fero fero* (a YELLOW term from

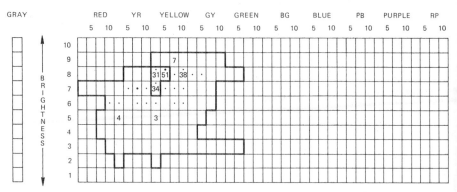

Map 5. Stages IV and V: *iela, hleu,* and *fero fero* (YELLOW)—39 informants. Contour lines represent range mappings for 70% agreement and maximum extension. Dots represent foci. Predominant foci are indicated by heavy dots. Integers represent naming responses and indicate the number of times an object matched to the chip in which the integer is written was named with the color term concerned.

Aniwa, a neighboring island) are all used in reference to the YELLOW category. Twenty of the thirty-nine adults at Stages IV and V used *iela* consistently to designate YELLOW in both naming and mapping responses. Nine individuals use both *hleu* and *iela* to designate YELLOW. The terms appear to be competing for these individuals for the position as the basic label. Five individuals have generalized *hleu* to refer to yellow items whether or not they are ripe. They use *hleu* consistently in reference to YELLOW and do not volunteer *iela* or map it consistently toward focal YELLOW. For three of these informants, this represents a conscious denial of a foreign loan. They recognize *iela* and could use it, but have chosen to exclude it from their idiolects, preferring to use a native term especially in the testing situation. The final speaker recognizes *iela* and can use it to designate YELLOW but prefers to use *fero fero*. *fero fero* is the basic YELLOW term used on Aniwa, a neighboring island where a closely related dialect is spoken. It is not commonly used on West Futuna, and those who do recognize the term indicate that it means multicolored or patterned.

So far, the basic categories LIGHT (WHITE) and DARK (BLACK), RED and YELLOW have been presented. With these four categories, it has been possible to distinguish a small group of five individuals as distinct from the other adults by virtue of the inclusiveness of their categories LIGHT, DARK and RED and by their lack of a YELLOW category. The following discussion will explore another difference in speakers with regard to color categories. The discussion concerns the categories GRUE, GREEN, and BLUE and the labels *uiui, rounemahmata,* and *plu.*

Twenty-three informants, including the five who do not have a basic YELLOW category, indicate that *uiui* is a GRUE category with variable foci, as Map 6 shows. Half of the informants focus *uiui* in *blue,* and six more, an additional 26%, focus *uiui* in both **blue** and **green**. The remaining five individuals focus *uiui* in **green** alone. When asked to indicate the range of *uiui,* eight informants included both BLUE and GREEN. The remaining fifteen informants restricted the range of *uiui* to the region of their indicated focus. However, as was the case for some informants for *hmea,* naming responses indicate a more inclusive category range for *uiui* than do boundaries drawn on the array. Notice the naming responses enumerated on Map 6, where each numeral represents the number of times an object of the color of the chip in which it is written was named *uiui.* Each individual named at least one of five green objects and one of two blue objects *uiui.* Frequently, three or four of the green objects and both blue objects were designated as *uiui* by a single informant. These naming responses suggest that those individuals who do not demonstrate a complete GRUE category range in the mapping task should still be classified as having a GRUE category.

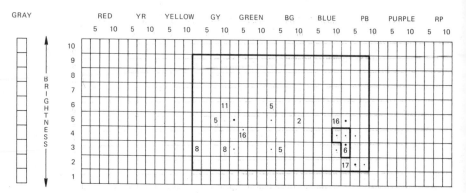

Map 6   Stages IIIa and IV: *uiui* (GRUE)—23 informants. Contour lines represent range mappings for 70% agreement and maximum extension. Dots represent foci. Predominant foci are indicated by heavy dots. Integers represent naming responses and indicate the number of times an object matched to the chip in which the integer is written was named with the color term concerned.

Several secondary terms are also used for colors in the blue and green regions of the spectrum. *rounemahmata,* referring to green leaves, was volunteered as a secondary term for GREEN. *plu,* a Pidgin English loan meaning GRUE; *tai* meaning 'ocean'; and *sekaumkufatu,* a 'dark blue-purple flower' were all volunteered as secondary terms for BLUE. The secondary nature of these terms is evident from naming and mapping responses. Mappings of these terms most frequently outlined regions of the array either synonymous with or included in *uiui*. When this was not the case, naming responses indicated the more inclusive nature of *uiui*. For example, if an informant could name both blue and green objects *uiui* even though his map restricted *uiui* to BLUE, And if he also referred to some green objects as *rounemahmata* and restricted his mapping of *rounemahmata* to GREEN, it was concluded that he had a basic GRUE category that he called *uiui* and that included at least the secondary category referred to as *rounemahmata*.

As is implicit in this data, and as two informants explicitly stated, "we have two kinds of *uiui, uiui rounemahmata* and *uiui plu,*" which designate GREEN and BLUE, respectively. *uiui* as it is currently used by the Stage IIIa and Stage IV individuals is polysemous and possibly in the process of change. It may be used to refer to the region selected as focal GRUE or to indicate the complete GRUE category.

In contrast to these twenty-three speakers who demonstrate a GRUE category, twenty-one other speakers do not have a GRUE category, but label BLUE and GREEN distinctly as separate basic color categories. These individuals are the ones reported to have Stage V systems. The original

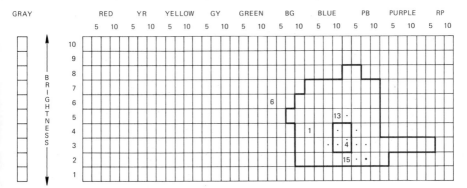

Map 7. Stage V: *plu* (BLUE)—21 informants. Contour lines represent range mappings for 70% agreement and maximum extension. Dots represent foci. Predominant foci are indicated by heavy dots. Integers represent naming responses and indicate the number of times an object matched to the chip in which the integer is written was named with the color term concerned.

GRUE term, *uiui* is restricted by these adults to refer to GREEN. *plu*, borrowed from pidgin English, has been adopted as the basic term for BLUE, focused and bounded as indicated on Map 7.

Map 8 shows the *uiui* naming responses for the twenty-one Stage V individuals. In general they are restricted to GREEN. Three individuals, however, designate a light BLUE object as *uiui*. This object does not represent focal **blue** for the West Futunese, and darker focal **blue** objects were specifically excluded from *uiui* by these same three informants; observa-

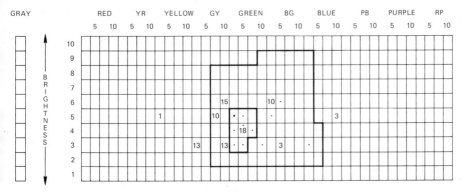

Map 8. Stage V: uiui (GREEN)—21 informants. Contour lines represent range mappings for 70% agreement and maximum extension. Dots represent foci. Predominant foci are indicated by heavy dots. Integers represent naming responses and indicate the number of times an object matched to the chip in which the integer is written was named with the color term concerned.

tions that led the researcher to conclude that these naming responses do not indicate a GRUE category, but rather include a broad range for *uiui*–GREEN. The responses may, in fact, indicate that these individuals have only recently divided their GRUE category and still include some nonfocal BLUES in the new category, *uiui*–GREEN.

We have seen that twenty-three speakers have GRUE and twenty-one speakers do not, but rather treat BLUE and GREEN as distinct color categories. All of the twenty-three speakers who demonstrate a GRUE category also have basic categories and basic terms for LIGHT and DARK and RED. Five individuals stop there. These are the Stage IIIa informants with basic categories for LIGHT, DARK, RED, and GRUE. The remaining eighteen adults who have a GRUE category have acquired YELLOW in addition to LIGHT, DARK, and RED, making them Stage IV. The twenty-one speakers who have established BLUE and GREEN as separate basic categories also have basic categories LIGHT, DARK, RED, and YELLOW. These individuals are at Stage V.

In addition to adult variability, children show a tendency to acquire color categories beyond those encoded by adults. As the Berlin and Kay evolutionary sequence would predict (see Table VII), the category BROWN is the universal addition to Stage V for children who have acquired a basic category in addition to those noted for Stage V. Thirteen of the twenty-four children have a basic BROWN category consistently labeled, *praon* (as Map 9 illustrates). Although they have been exposed to all of the basic English categories but GRAY in school, BROWN is the first new category they have encoded. The other children who participated have not established BROWN as a basic category. They are familiar with the term *praon*, although they are unsure of its referent, and may acquire the basic category at some later time. Compare the responses of basic BROWN (Map 9) with the mapping responses for *praon* (Map 10) by children who were not included as representatives of Stage VI. In addition to BROWN, one child has acquired two additional basic categories, ORANGE and PURPLE, which she labels *aranĉ* and *vaiolet*.

A number of theoretical considerations arise from these data. First of all, *hkeŋo* and *uri,* the terms for LIGHT and DARK, suggest the persistence of a LIGHT–DARK dichotomy through Stage V. A finding that complements Heider's description (1972) of a dark–cool, light–warm division of the spectrum for the Stage I Dani of New Guinea.

Second, this work indicates that variable stages of color categorization may be found within a single small population speaking one native language. These results and comparable data from Berlin and Berlin (1975) and Hage and Hawkes (n.d.) indicate that vocabulary does not change in a pattern of steps and plateaus, but gradually and predictably through ex-

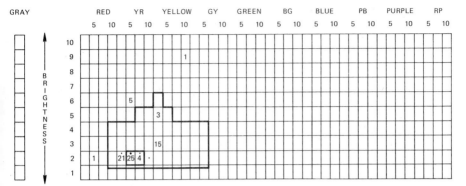

Map 9. Stage VI (children): *praon* (BROWN)—13 informants. Contour lines represent range mappings for 70% agreement and maximum extension. Dots represent foci. Predominant foci are indicated by heavy dots. Integers represent naming responses and indicate the number of times an object matched to the chip in which the integer is written was named with the color term concerned.

tended periods of synchronic heterogeneity with respect to a given domain.

The data from West Futuna show that schooling, experience off West Futuna, and proficiency in pidgin English as reported on Table IV, account for the relevant differences between the individuals at Stages IIIa and IV, Stage IIIa individuals being the more conservative. Both youth and schooling appear to account for the post Stage V children.

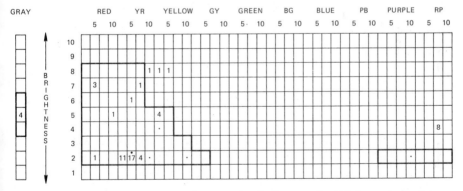

Map 10. Stage V (children): emerging *praon* (nonbasic BROWN)—11 informants. Contour lines represent the maximum extension of informants' range mappings. There is no area that was included within the range of *praon* by 70% of informants. Dots represent foci. Predominant foci are indicated by heavy dots. Integers represent naming responses and indicate the number of times an object matched to the chip in which the integer is written was named with the color term concerned.

TABLE IV

Association of Variables Motivating Development and Developmental Stage

Stage	Age (years)	Sex	Foreign languages schooling (years)	Experience off West Futuna (years)	Pidgin English/ English
IIIa	45.0	4m 1f	None	2.58	fair-PE
IV	48.3	15m 3f	1.67	7.18	good-PE + 2-E
V	35.1	2m 19f	1.38	2.69	fair-PE
VI	11.0	10m 14f	3.96	1.43	fair-PE fair-E
VII	10.0	1f	3.00	1.00	fair-PE

    Two separate groups as shown in Table V are seen to have Stage V systems. Five individuals, all the Stage V adults under age 25, have developed basic categories for BLUE and GREEN for the same reasons—youth and schooling—that children are developing in Stage VI and VII systems. These adults have an average age of 20 and an average of 8 years in school, both values significantly different than the comparable values for Stage IV individuals. They were the first generation of West Futunese to attend school. They appear to have learned *plu* through the English school system and adopted it into their own color classification, simultaneously restricting *uiui* to GREEN.

    The remaining sixteen Stage V adults can not be accounted for in exactly the same way. Their average age is 40, few have been to school in a foreign language, and none demonstrate proficiency in pidgin English. A plausible explanation of this second group results from the correlation of developmental stage with sex shown in Table VI. Seventeen percent of

TABLE V

Division of Stage V Informants Showing Difference in Factors Motivating Change

Stage	Age (years)	Sex	Foreign language schooling (years)	Experience off West Futuna (years)	Pidgin English/ English
V_1	20	1m 4f	8.00	3.20	good-PE fair-E
V_2	39.69	1m 15f	0.125	1.92	poor-PE

TABLE VI

Correlation of Stage, Sex, and Foci of *uiui*

Stage	Sex	Foci	
IIIa and IV	19m/4f	12	blue
		6	dual
		5	green
V	2m/19f	21	green

the informants at Stages IIIa and IV are women, while 90% of the Stage V informants are women. Men, predominantly Stage II and IV, are proficient in pidgin English and have learned *plu*, which designates a *blue*-focused GRUE category in pidgin English, as synonymous with their own *uiui*. Women, on the other hand, do not know pidgin English well. It is likely that their borrowing *plu* was learned from their own children, who for the past decade have been learning English in the recently established British schools. *plu*, as it is used in English and taught in the schools, is a BLUE term not a GRUE term as it is in pidgin English. It appears that women have adopted *plu* through their children to refer to BLUE and simultaneously restricted the reference of *uiui* to GREEN.

The observed variability for *uiui* and *plu* is interesting from a second point of view. The occurrence of variable foci for *uiui*–GRUE implies a revision of the Berlin and Kay predicted sequence for development. West Futunese data show that a GRUE term encoded at Stage IIIa or Stage IV may focus either in **blue** or **green** or both. It need not be consistently or exclusively focused in **green** as Berlin and Kay (1969) suggested. Data collected by Berlin (Berlin and Kay, 1969) on Tzeltal, by Berlin and Berlin (1975) on Aguaruna, and by Hage and Hawkes (n.d.) on Binumarien corroborate the West Futunese evidence for revision.

In the original sequence shown in Table VII, **white** and **black** preceded **red,** which preceded **green** and **yellow,** which preceded **blue,** and so on. The recent data show that it is actually a GRUE category that is labeled at Stage IIIa or IV and that this category may be focused in **blue** or **green** or both. At Stage V, **blue** is not added to the classificatory scheme, but GRUE is divided, and both BLUE and GREEN are labeled.

In summary, the major findings of this research are four. (1) That a light–dark distinction may persist in languages at least through Stage V to the exclusion of pure white and pure black categories. (2) That individuals within a single speech community may be found to represent various stages of development with regard to color classification, which will be correlated with nonlinguistic factors such as age, sex, and education, and

TABLE VII

Developmental Sequence Predicted by Berlin and Kay

I	II	III	IV	V	VI	VII
white	→ red	a. green → yellow		→ blue	→ brown →	pink purple orange
black		b. yellow → green				gray

Revised Sequence

						PINK
LIGHT–WARM	→ RED	a. GRUE → YELLOW		→ BLUE and → BROWN →		PURPLE ORANGE
DARK–COOL		b. YELLOW → GRUE		GREEN		GRAY

that the linguistic variables will be contiguous developmental stages as is the West Futunese range from Stage IIIa to VII. (3) That a revision of the Berlin and Kay developmental sequence recognizing the categoric GRUE light–warm and dark–cool is required. (4) That incorporating this revision, the Berlin and Kay sequence predicts the development and change noted for the West Futunese system of color categorization.

References

Berlin, Brent and Eloise Ann Berlin
  1975   Aguaruna color categories. *The American Ethnologist,* **2**(1), 61–88.
Berlin, Brent and Paul Kay
  1969   *Basic color terms. Their universality and evolution.* Berkeley and Los Angeles: University of California Press.
Camden, W.G.
  n.d.   *Dictionary—English to Bislama.* Unpublished manuscript.
Hage, Per and Kristin Hawkes.
  n.d.   *Binumarien color categories.* University of Utah monograph.
Heider, Eleanor Rosch
  1972   Probabilities, sampling and ethnographic method: The case of Dani colour names. *Man* **7**, 448–66.

Creolization and Syntactic Change
in New Guinea Tok Pisin

GILLIAN SANKOFF

Background

Tok Pisin, also known as Neo-Melanesian, New Guinea Pidgin, and Melanesian Pidgin, has existed for about a hundred years as a second language lingua franca in New Guinea. (See Note 1 at the end of the chapter.) The vocabulary is between 75% and 80% English based (see Salisbury, 1967, p. 46; Laycock, 1970a, p. 115), the second most important lexical contributor being Kuanua, the language spoken by the Tolai people in the area of Rabaul, the German colonial capital at the time Tok Pisin became established in New Guinea. In many ways, particularly in terms of semantics, Tok Pisin's structures parallel those of the Austronesian languages of the area. (See Note 2.)

The 1966 census indicates that some 532,000 of the 1.5 million Papua New Guineans age 10 and over speak Tok Pisin, that is, approximately 36%, a higher percentage than that speaking any other language (Bureau of Statistics, 1969, p. 31; see also Sankoff, in press.) What the census does not indicate is that a growing number of children and adolescents have Tok Pisin as their first language. Laycock (1970a, p. 102, no. 2) estimates that this population may now number "perhaps 10,000 or more speakers, mainly on Manus and New Britain." Manus and the two New Britain districts are indeed among those having the highest proportion of Tok Pisin speakers, and it is true that these are districts where Tok Pisin has been spoken over a longer period than in most other areas of Papua New Guinea. Given the lack of census data or other demographic work on first-language Tok Pisin speakers, however, the location of such people is problematic. In a study designed to examine syntactic change in progress in Tok Pisin, Laberge and I decided to work in one of the growing urban centers (Note 3) where the intermarriage of people whose only common language is Tok Pisin has produced a generation of first-language Tok Pisin speakers. We chose the Morobe District town of Lae, the second largest urban center in Papua New Guinea and the port for the busy Highlands Highway. In 1966, the population of Lae was 16,500; in 1971, the year in which we carried out the study, it had grown to approximately 35,000 (Note 4). Rather than attempt any systematic sample of the whole town, we decided to do an intensive study of a relatively small number of people. The bulk of our recordings are of the parents and children in approximately a dozen families (Note 5), though these are supplemented by other data. The parents came from districts as widely separated as Bougainville, West New Britain, Madang, Chimbu, and the Eastern Highlands; the children grew up away from their parents' home areas.

Before examining some of the features of grammatical change as they are being carried on by this new generation of first-language Tok Pisin speakers, it will be useful to consider some of the reasons why the study of syntactic change in a creolizing pidgin should be of theoretical interest.

Theoretical Issues in Depidginization

Pidgin languages have generally been defined more in social terms than in terms of their structural characteristics. That is, they are not natural languages in that they have no native speakers. The literature on pidgin languages abounds with suggestions that they are somehow reduced, even minimal languages, with few or no grammatical categories and syntactic rules and little or no morphonemics. The recent literature on pidgins, however, has gone beyond a narrow or strict Whorfianism in rejecting the notion that the reduction in grammatical machinery implies anything about the thought patterns or mental capacity of those who speak such languages. Rather, it has focused on the nature of the social and communicative contexts in which pidgin languages are spoken and on how such contexts come to constrain the grammatical machinery available for communicating ideas, experiences, etc. A language universals perspective leads us to assume that information, ideas, or concepts can be transmitted with virtually any grammatical machinery. The question then becomes essentially a functional one, asking why particular devices become systematized as part of the obligatory grammatical machinery of a language.

The broader functional perspective is most clearly set forth in Hymes (1969). This perspective is applied to pidgins and creoles in Hymes' introduction to Part 3 of his volume, "Pidginization and Creolization of languages" (1971). It is also the framework underlying Labov's (n.d.) important paper "On the adequacy of natural languages," Ferguson's work on simplified registers (1971), Traugott's approach to parallels in historical linguistics, language acquisition and pidgins and creoles (1973; n.d.), and my own previous work with Suzanne Laberge (Sankoff and Laberge, 1973) and with Paul Kay (Kay and Sankoff, 1974).

The argument as applied to a contact situation, where people need to communicate but have limited means of learning one another's language (because of minimal exposure whether due to the constraints of time or of social roles), is that the codes that emerge resemble some of the "parent" languages but without at least a surface marking of many of their grammatical categories and many of their syntactic and morphophonemic rules. This can be viewed as an extension of the second-language acquisition situation in which adults learning a language tend both to overgeneralize rules and not to learn some of the later rules in the new language. In the pidgin situation, all speakers are subject to such processes. The most detailed analysis of any actual case of which I am aware (Note 6) involves not a pidgin per se, but rather the general process of convergence. This is the situation described by Gumperz and Wilson (1971) for the northern Indian community of Kupwar, where pervasive bilingualism has existed for several centuries and where the languages involved have come to resemble each other more closely, in that they have regularized some of their grammatical categories, dropping distinctions that do not conform to those present in the others. Comparisons made with the standard languages as spoken elsewhere put this convergence in relief. Pidgin languages are more difficult to handle in this comparative perspective, because the parent languages are more difficult to identify, given the great linguistic diversity in most areas where pidgins have developed and because there have generally been no linguists on the spot to scrutinize them during their crucial formative stages.

There are certainly other problems of great linguistic interest raised by pidgins, particularly the question of the locus of linguistic rules in a language that is native to no one. The heterogeneity of the speech community is therefore at least theoretically greater than that of most other communities. That is, pidgin speakers do not share as great a linguistic competence as do those who share a native language, since they all exhibit varying degrees of "interference" from their different native languages. This point is somewhat peripheral to my main argument here, but I mention it to illustrate the importance of the social processes underlying the very definition of a language.

As has been pointed out in the literature, there are a number of possible outcomes for pidgin languages, all dependent on the social, i.e., material conditions of their existence. They can "lose their usefulness" and die out, whether because the contact situation that produced them no longer exists (i.e., all the speakers go home and speak their own native language again), or because everyone is forced, or enabled, to learn the native language of one of the groups involved (though note that in this case the pidgin may survive as appropriate to particular situations). Another possibility is the continued existence of the pidgin as a second-language lingua franca over a long period of time, whether restricted to particular communicative contexts or extended to a wide variety of usage situations. A third possibility is that it may pass to the status of a natural language, at which point it is called a creole, through the acquisition of native speakers. This is generally the result of dramatic social changes in which people's native languages fall into disuse on the part of their speakers, or at least are not transmitted to succeeding generations. It can result, for example, from intermarriage of people who have no language but the pidgin in common, as is the case with Tok Pisin (Note 7).

Theoretically, this third alternative would be the crucial case to examine from the point of view of the universals of natural languages—the question being what features are basic to a natural language and therefore would be created at this stage. I think, however, that in the light of the literature cited above, one would have to regard this view as being vastly oversimplified. There may indeed be linguistic features that are characteristic only of languages having a community of native speakers, but this is probably only a special case of the general functional question. A language used in a multiplicity of social and communicative contexts, and which carries much of the "communicative load" for numbers of speakers will develop grammatical machinery appropriate to its needs. This grammatical machinery will probably be more extensive than that found in a language restricted to a very few communicative contexts that form a small part of any speaker's repertoire of communication situations and that is therefore marginal in terms of usage for all its speakers. It is important to stress that this does not mean that the pidgin is incapable of expressing ideas, experiences, and relationships which are readily expressible in any natural language. The question is rather under what circumstances devices for expressing certain relationships (cognitive, logical, interactional, or whatever) are regularized as part of the grammar. The two features to be examined here involve tense marking and embedding mechanisms, both of which can be seen to be "useful," in some sense. Another area, which I will not broach in this paper, might involve the circumstances under which relatively "informationless" features (such as gender systems) become established.

To summarize the theoretical implications of the line of enquiry pursued in this paper, I am trying to understand the way surface forms are constrained in fundamental ways by the purposes for which and the ways in which language is used as a vehicle of human (i.e., social) communication. In particular, I am examining the changes occurring in the syntax of a creolizing (depidginizing) language in an attempt to see whether, and how, these might shed light on the general problem.

Two Syntactic Changes in Progress

Tok Pisin's roots are in a language called Beach-La-Mar, a western Pacific trade pidgin of the nineteenth century. An early and rather cursory description of Beach-La-Mar is provided by Churchill (1911), the bulk of whose data comes, however, from New Guinea, culled from a dozen or so publications dating from the turn of the century. Churchill's general view of Beach-La-Mar is that it is a joke ("Beach La Mar is an amusing speech," p. 31), a poor excuse for a language, with no grammar to speak of, and in which is found evidence of the illogic and primitiveness of its speakers. A quotation shows that this judgment was also made about the native languages of the majority of Beach-La-Mar's speakers:

> In the vocabularies proper to the several Melanesian languages, the paradeictic words are very few in number and correspondingly general in their employment . . . in the Melanesian languages, indeed throughout the speech of the Pacific, the specific need of conjunctives has been little felt, and of disjunctives still less. . . . The conditional particle . . . is scarcely necessary to Melanesian thought and is forced upon the jargon from European needs.   (Churchill 1911, p. 25)

Despite this view, however, Churchill provides a large number of sentences and phrases from which it is possible to deduce many of the features of the language. For example, he warns the reader to interpret positive responses to yes–no questions in a way opposite to that which they are used to, e.g.,

Q: "Don't we have any bananas?"
A: "Yes."   i.e., 'yes we have no bananas'

thereby revealing a pattern shared by many of the Melanesian languages. This is an areal discourse feature, which crosses language-family boundaries and is clearly the result of communicative interaction. Further examples given by Churchill illustrate other widespread areal features, principally semantic. The following sentence illustrates the supposedly unnecessary conditional, the use of the suffix *-im* (represented by Churchill as *'m*) to mark transitive verbs, and the dual, another pervasive areal feature (Note 8).

(1) *S'pose you look'm these two fellow Adam Eve, you shoot'm plenty too much.*   (Churchill, p. 32, originally from London, 1909.) (Note 9.)

'If you see Adam and Eve, really shoot them.'

We see that already at the beginning of the twentieth century, the language shared a number of syntactic, semantic, and discourse features with the Austronesian languages spoken as first languages by its speakers. There were, however, areas where the grammar of Tok Pisin did not possess structures analogous to those of such languages or of other natural languages. Two broad areas of grammar that we looked at in this regard in Tok Pisin are tense and aspect and the structures available for generating complex sentences. The two features I will discuss here are the future marker *bai* and the *ia* marker for embedding relative clauses. Both of them have progressively taken on more specialized grammatical functions, having originally had other, less specifically grammatical, functions in the language. Both of these features are discussed elsewhere in greater detail—*bai* in Sankoff and Laberge (1973) and *ia* in Sankoff and Brown (1976). Here I will briefly sketch the arguments for change in each one, and then point out the important parallels in the two processes.

(i) *Bai.* *Bai* appears to be derived from English *by and by* (Mihalic, 1971, p. 63), and its original form in Tok Pisin was indeed *baimbai*. It is cited as early as 1893 (Wawn, 1893, p. 207; see also Grimshaw, 1907, p. 198). Though the reduced form *bai* does not appear in early sources, recent dictionaries list both forms, giving a range of meaning such as:

1) will, shall; 2) in order to; 3) after a while, somewhat later, later on; 4) it also indicates the stress of certainty. (Mihalic, 1971, p. 63)

Speakers we recorded exhibit the following range of forms: [baimbai] (with approximately equal stress on each syllable), [bə'mbai], [bə'bai], [mbai], [bai], [ba], and [bə], the most commonly used forms currently being [bai] and [ba].

Traditionally, *baimbai* functioned as an optional adverb, usually in sentence initial position, indicating a general notion of futurity. Today the unreduced form is extremely rare, forming a very small percentage of the surface representations of *bai* for any speaker, and not appearing at all in the speech of the native speakers (under age 18) we recorded. In addition, the position of *bai* within the sentence has changed. Typically, *bai* now either immediately precedes the verb or is separated from the verb only by a pronoun, cases where *bai* is separated from the verb phrase by more than a pronoun forming only 6% of the sentences we examined.

That *bai* has almost completed its transition to becoming a fully grammatical particle, a future marker, is also supported by two further facts. First, it has become highly redundant, appearing many times (with virtually all verbs) in a single sentence. It is also redundantly used in conjunction with several other adverbs indicating futurity, e.g., *bihain* 'later' and *klostu* 'soon'. Last, native speakers show reduced stress on *bai*, in comparison with current second-language speakers, indicating that the process of transition to a future marker already in progress in the language is being carried further by this new generation of native speakers.

(ii) *Ia.* As with futurity in the early stages of Tok Pisin, relative clauses seem to have been largely a matter of inference from context, involving no markers in the matrix sentence, and only an equi-NP deletion rule in the embedded sentence. Churchill (1911) contains only four sentences containing relative clauses, all of which are of this type. Two of these are:

(2) *He look out all man [stop this place].*   (Churchill, p. 50; originally from Wawn 1893, p. 386)
     'He looked for the people who were there.'

(3) *Some place [me go] man he no good.*   (Churchill, p. 48; originally from London, 1909, p. 361)
     'Some places I went the people were bad.'

Hearers probably deduced the embeddedness from word order and juxtaposition of elements alone, with perhaps some help from prosodic features like stress and intonation. The absence of a relative marker, with the one "relativizing" transformation being equi-NP deletion, seems to have persisted throughout most of Tok Pisin's history, as the relatives observable in citations and texts collected by Wurm (1971), Laycock (1970b), and Mihalic (1971) show nothing but this pattern (Note 10).

This is in great contrast to what we observed when we began looking at the relatives appearing in the 1971 recordings made by Laberge and myself. The majority of relatives appeared to be bracketed off from the matrix sentence by the particle *ia.* The basic relativization transformation, operating on very simple phrase structure rules, can be sketched as follows.

Phrase structure rules:

$$S \rightarrow NP - VP$$
$$NP \rightarrow N(S)$$

$$T_{rel}: \quad NP_i - \underset{s}{[X - NP_i - Y]}$$

$$\underset{1}{} \quad \underset{2}{} \quad \underset{3}{} \quad \underset{4}{\overset{s}{}} \Rightarrow 1 - (ia) - 2 - 3 - (ia) - 4$$

Examples (4) through (7) illustrate the relativization transformation. Equi-NP deletion is optional, as can be seen from comparing sentences (6) and (7), uttered by the same speaker a few minutes apart. The equi-NP deletion rule is not presented here, as it is related to other aspects of the grammar in addition to relativization.

(4) Na pik *ia* [ol ikilim bipo *ia*] bai ikamap olsem draipela ston.   (Elena Z.)
'And this pig they had killed before would turn into a huge stone.'

(5) Nogat, em wantok *ia* [putim long maunten *ia*] na nau tasol senesim givim mi.   (Tim D.)
'No, it was my friend who was wearing it on the mountain and only now did he exchange it with me.'

(6) E, yupela lukim meri *ia* [bipo em istap *ia*]?   (Noemi S.)
'Hey, did you see the woman who used to live (there)?'

(7) Em yupela lukim meri *ia* [bipo igo istap *ia*]?   (Noemi S.)
'Did you see the woman who used to live (there)?'

There are two classes of relative clauses in our data to which the *ia* bracketing does not always apply, both of which are discussed in more detail in Sankoff and Brown (1976). The first class, relative modifiers of locatives containing *long,* need not concern us here. The second class, however, is of some importance. Within this second class, equi-NP deletion always applies (as noted in relation to sentence (6) above, this latter is not an obligatory rule for *ia*-bracketed relatives). In other words, these sentences are similar to the early examples from Churchill. Two of them are cited as (8) and (9).

(8) Yu no ken painim ol man [isave Tok Pisin].   (Jack W.)
'You won't be able to find anybody who knows Tok Pisin.'

(9) Ol pikinini [igo long Sande skul] ol isave yusim Pisin.   (Emma M.)
'The children who go to Sunday school use Tok Pisin.'

Nevertheless, the fact that there are a number of sentences where equi-NP deletion applies, and where *ia* bracketing is used, as in (5) and (7) above, forces us to seek other distinctive characteristics for this class. As shown in Sankoff and Brown (1976), *ia*-bracketing applies to both restrictive and nonrestrictive relatives, so this distinction is not useful as a possible defining characteristic of the class. Rather, its most pertinent defining feature has to do with the information structure of the discourse. *Ia*-bracketing does not apply in the case of noun phrases whose referents are indefinite, but only to noun phrases with definite, specific referents.

Looking at the previous discussions of *ia,* none of which mentions its role as a bracketing device for relative clauses, we note that it has been treated as a place adverbial (Laycock, 1970b, p. xxviii; Hall, 1943, p. 100) and as a demonstrative (Mihalic, 1971, pp. 16, 22; Wurm, 1971, p. 12) when co-occurring with *tispela* or *em*. Etymologically, it is derived from English *here* (indeed the sources quoted above spell it *hia*). Our data indicate that although *ia* is still used for these functions, it is more widely used as a generalized deictic marker and is employed interactionally in discourse sequencing, as discussed in detail in Sankoff and Brown (1976). Use of *ia* after a noun phrase introduces a possible slot for the speaker (or someone else, interrupting) to provide an additional description of the noun phrase in question. This additional description is generally followed by a second *ia*, which acts as a right-hand bracket. Thus *ia* brackets provide a regular, easily recognizeable surface marking of information that hearers are to interpret as subordinate, information that is there to help disambiguate referents in the matrix sequence. That embedded sentences can easily be heard as such can be readily seen to be a useful feature in the structuring of discourse in general.

Parallels and Generalizations

The most important parallel between the two cases discussed in the previous section is that both involve the evolution of the surface marking of a grammatical category that was completely unmarked at an earlier stage in the language. As such, both are innovations, innovations that have used lexical resources available in the language and have specialized them to fill a grammatical function. That they are innovations is quite clear; it is possible to locate earlier descriptions and texts in which (*bai*)*mbai* and (*h*)*ia* do not seem to be used at all for the grammatical functions described in the previous section. It is difficult, however, to locate precisely when either of the changes began. Certainly, both of them are well established in the speech of current, fluent, adult, second-language speakers of Tok Pisin, though at least with *bai*, the new generation of native speakers has carried the change process further (in terms of reduction of stress). Both features are probably quite widespread, since the adults we observed using them, though residing at the time in Lae, were from many parts of Papua New Guinea.

Transition toward the status of grammatical particles has not completely eradicated the earlier lexical force of *bai* and *ia;* however, this is not surprising (compare English *will* and *that*). It is also quite clear that their present grammatical function is semantically related to the earlier lexical meanings and that both would figure in any set of possible candidates for a language seeking to regularly mark categories that have previously gone unmarked or for a speaker seeking to make explicit relationships that otherwise might have to be guessed at. No Tok Pisin speaker of a previous era would have had trouble interpreting the usages of *bai* and *ia* described above when encountering them for the first time, given a knowledge of their previous usages, and it is no doubt this naturalness that makes them easy to learn, even easy to invent. "Invention" in this case involves the creative transfer of usage of a known and previously used form to do certain kinds of grammatical work that is naturally, semantically, and logically related to the previous usage.

Notes

1. Papua New Guinea is a newly independent nation of some 2½ million people. New Guinea was a former German colony that came under Australian rule in 1914; Papua was a former British colony that came under Australian rule in 1906. They were jointly administered by Australia as a United Nations trust territory from 1946 to 1974. As Tok Pisin was the lingua franca of New Guinea, I refer only to New Guinea when discussing the early period of development of Tok Pisin.

2. Discussing subject-marking particles in New Guinea Austronesian languages, Capell (1960, p. 49) states, "Every verb, even if it has a noun subject expressed, must be preceded by such a marker. The pattern is reproduced in Pidgin, where one says, e.g., *man i kam,* 'a/the man comes/came', not just *man kam.* . . . In this as in so many regards, Pidgin reproduces with largely English lexemes, Austronesian forms and modes of expression."

3. Census figures for 1966 for the seven major towns in Papua New Guinea indicate that in each case, the proportion of Tok Pisin speakers is much higher than that of the district in which the town is situated. Five of the towns show at least 90% of their Papua New Guinean residents to be Tok Pisin speakers, and even Port Moresby, the lowest of the seven at 55%, is much higher than the 28% for the Central District as a whole. Language data are not yet available for the 1971 census, but a preliminary bulletin (Papua New Guinea Population Census, July 1971, Preliminary Bulletin #1, January 1972) indicates a doubling in the urban population between 1966 and 1971. That is, whereas in 1966 approximately 100,000 Papua New Guineans lived in towns, in 1971 this figure had reached 200,000. It is highly probable that at least 75% of them were Tok Pisin speakers.

4. Figures taken from the 1966 Census Preliminary Bulletin #33, and from the 1971 Preliminary Bulletin #1.

5. My very great thanks are expressed to the many kind people who welcomed us into their homes and who permitted us to record them and their children. I also wish to thank Col. Harrington of the Pacific Islands Regiment, who granted us access to Igam Barracks, where a number of the recordings were made, and Suzanne Laberge, whose help throughout the study was invaluable. All the people quoted in this paper are referred to by pseudonyms. For the reader who may wish to know a little more about them, all are fluent speakers of Tok Pisin: Elena Z. is a 17 year old for whom Tok Pisin is her most fluent language, although she also speaks her parents' language (a Morobe District Austronesian language) and English; Tim D. is a Chimbu (a Papuan language) from the Kerowagi area and is about 35 years old; Noemi S., in her early twenties, is a native speaker of Labu (Austronesian) from south of Lae; Jack W., approximately 40–45 years old, is from the Cape Hoskins area of West New

Britain (and thus probably speaks an Austronesian language); Emma M., in her late twenties, is a native speaker of Bukawa (Austronesian) from near Lae.

6. Bickerton (1975, pp. 170 ff) also discusses pidgin formation in the context of adult second-language learning.

7. This does not mean that the native languages of Tok Pisin's second-language speakers are dying out; most of these languages continue to be spoken in their *ples,* or home areas.

8. This applies particularly to the geographically most widespread group of New Guinea Austronesian languages according to Capell (1971), who refers to it as AN_1, but not to his AN_2 group.

9. As Laycock (1970a, pp. 110–111) rightly points out, such early citations are often unreliable and should therefore be used with discretion.

10. With the exception of time and place relatives, which are special cases outside of the scope of the present discussion. In addition, Hall (1943) provides several sentences in which, as in our materials, *ia* appears to be used as a relativizer. These are, however, a small minority of the relatives in Hall's texts, as discussed in Sankoff and Brown (1976).

References

Bickerton, Derek
   1975 *Dynamics of a Creole System.* London: Cambridge University Press.
Bureau of Statistics, Territory of Papua and New Guinea
   1969 *Population Census, 1966. Preliminary Bulletin No. 1.*
Capell, A.
   1969 *A survey of New Guinea languages.* Sydney: Sydney University Press.
   1971 The Austronesian languages of Australian New Guinea. In *Current Trends in Linguistics 8* edited by T. A. Sebeok, pp. 240–340. The Hague: Mouton.
Churchill, W.
   1911 *Beach-La-Mar.* Publication No. 154, Carnegie Institution of Washington.
Ferguson, C. A.
   1971 Absence of copula and the notion of simplicity: a study of normal speech, baby talk, foreigner talk, and pidgins. In *Pidginization and creolization of languages* edited by D. Hymes, pp. 141–150. London: Cambridge University Press.
Grimshaw, Beatrice
   1907 *Fiji and its possibilities (from Fiji to the Cannibal Islands).* New York: Doubleday.
Gumperz, J. J., and R. Wilson
   1971 Convergence and creolization: a case from the Indo-Aryan/Dravidian border. In *Pidginization and creolization of languages* edited by D. Hymes, pp. 151–167. London: Cambridge University Press.
Hall, Robert A., Jr.
   1943 *Melanesian pidgin English: grammar, texts, vocabulary.* Baltimore: Linguistic Society of America.
Hymes, D.
   1969 *Functions of speech and linguistic theory.* International Days of Sociolinguistics, Istituto Luigi Sturzo, Rome, pp. 111–144.
   1971 Introduction to Part III, *Pidginization and creolization of languages* edited by D. Hymes, pp. 65–90. London: Cambridge University Press.

Kay, Paul, and Gillian Sankoff
   1974   A language-universals approach to pidgins and creoles. In *Pidgins and creoles: Current trends and prospects* edited by D. DeCamp and I. Hancock pp. 61–72. Washington, D.C.: Georgetown University Press.
Labov, W.
   n.d.   *On the adequacy of natural languages.* Manuscript.
Laycock, D.
   1970a   Pidgin English in New Guinea. In *English transported* edited by W. S. Ramson, pp. 102–122. Canberra: Australian National University Press.
   1970b   Materials in New Guinea Pidgin (coastal and lowlands). *Pacific Linguistics, Series D, No. 5.*
London, John
   1909   Beche de Mer English. *Contemporary Review,* No. 525, London.
Mihalic, Rev. F.
   1971   *The Jacaranda dictionary and grammar of Melanesian Pidgin.* Port Moresby, New Guinea: Jacaranda Press.
Salisbury, R. F.
   1967   Pidgin's respectable past. *New Guinea* 2(2), 44–48.
Sankoff, G.
   In press   Multilingualism in Papua, New Guinea. In *New Guinea area languages and language study* edited by S. A. Wurm. Volume 3. *Language, culture, society, and the modern world.* Pacific Linguistics C40. Canberra: Australian National University Press.
Sankoff, G., and P. Brown
   1976   On the origins of syntax in discourse: a case study of Tok Pisin relatives. *Language,* **52**(3), in press.
Sankoff, G., and S. Laberge
   1973   On the acquisition of native speakers by a language. *Kivung* **6,** 32–47.
Traugott, E. C.
   1973   Some thoughts on natural syntactic processes. In *New ways of analyzing variation in English* edited by C.-J. Bailey and R. Shuy, pp. 313–322. Washington, D.C.: Georgetown University Press.
   n.d.   *Historical linguistics and its relation to studies of language acquisition and of pidgins and creoles.* Manuscript.
Wawn, W.
   1893   *The South Sea islanders and the Queensland labour trade: A record of voyages and experiences in the West Pacific, from 1875 to 1891.* London: Swan Sonnenschein.
Wurm, S. A.
   1971   New Guinea Highlands Pidgin: course materials. *Pacific Linguistics,* Series D, No. 3.

Recent Relexification Processes in Philippine Creole Spanish

CAROL H. MOLONY

Introduction

Word adoptions taking place in Philippine Creole Spanish give one focus for examining the history of the language and its speakers. Field work on Ternateño has shown it to be the dialect of the Philippine Creole Spanish language (or Chabacano) most closely related to the parent language transmitted in the seventeenth century from Ternate, Moluccas, to the Philippines. Evidence for relexification changes includes reports by native speakers, analysis of texts gathered by the author, and historical documents. Words are sorted according to source, by semantic domain, by frequency of occurrence, by category of speakers, and by divergences in meaning from the source languages and by divergences in meaning that have developed between the various dialects of the language. Word adoptions taking place currently and in the recent past give insights into movements of Philippine Creole Spanish speakers and their contacts with other peoples in the Philippines. Word adoptions also give evidence for changes of other linguistic features and into linguistic change in general.

Creoles

Creole languages are a dramatic result of languages in contact, and therefore are rich sources for the study of linguistic change, since a number of features of change are so readily apparent. Semantic changes, for instance, stand out clearly where there is heavy borrowing from one or more languages and divergences in meaning from these source languages. The most rapid changes presumably take place when a creole language is in the process of formation, although even for established creoles, lexical and semantic changes are often not subtle, especially when there is continued language contact. Relexification processes in an established creole, Philippine Creole Spanish, will be the focus of this paper.

Creoles are a class of languages that share certain features, for in-

stance, grammar "simplification" such as no tense, aspect, or sex inflection, and absence of copula. Many grammatical markers sound similar
from one creole language to another. The grammatical features do not appear to be unique to creoles, but are found with much greater frequency in
this class of language. The vocabulary is largely borrowed from another
known language, but with noticeable changes in meaning, and there is historical evidence that two or more languages have been in contact during
the formation of the language. There has been agreement among creolists,
with some historical evidence, that creoles develop when pidgin languages become first languages by a group of speakers. The combinations
of these features characterize the creole phenomenon.

Creoles have attracted the interest of linguists in attempting, first, to
explain the apparently divergent sources of lexicon and grammar, second,
to learn how such languages came about, and third, to examine whether
they are qualitatively different from "normal" languages. By examining
the fundamental problem of creoles, that of accounting for the apparently
divergent sources of lexicon and grammar, linguists have hoped to gain
new insights into genetic origin and linguistic change. In addition, that
creoles appear to display structural and lexical similarities in different
places in the world has led to the search for evidence of universals of language evolution and acquisition. Accounting for the creole combination of
features and the startling similarities among all acknowledged creoles has
led to theories of origin. The three main theories have been based on (1)
simplicity, or "baby talk"; (2) common origin, e.g., Portuguese or African substratum, with possibly rapid relexification; and (3) universal underlying deep structure of human languages.

Linguists stress that there are no linguistic features unique to creoles,
and therefore the normal linguistic tools of analysis can be used with
them. However, implied in the definition of the class of languages is that
they behave differently from other languages. First, they have life cycles,
with discernible starting points. Genetic classification of creoles has been
questioned. Should they be considered (1) a continuation of either the
source language or the contact language(s) or (2) discontinuous with their
base languages? There is some question that they may give evidence of
language mixing. They may display rapid relexification, although the
mechanisms for starting or stopping this process have not been demonstrated. They may have simplified some features found in other languages. And finally, for some reason, the deep structure common to all
human languages may come to the surface in creoles. The contradiction in
present-day linguistic treatments of creoles, however, remains; they are
considered to behave on the one hand differently from other languages,
since they probably have had a different kind of origin, while on the other,

the usual tools of analysis can be applied to them, and insights into their nature should contribute to the understanding of human language in general. For the established creole under consideration, I would like to stress that the changes taking place are in no way unique to creoles; they also occur in other noncreole Philippine languages. There is no evidence for the "different" behavior that presumably caused this language to develop in the first place. Since the changes taking place are "normal," standard linguistic methodology should therefore be appropriate, e.g., etymological analysis, including examination by specific semantic domains; sound shift analysis (see Molony, 1973b); and contrastive analysis of regional and generational dialects. Examining current changes in this language does not appear to be a profitable way to gain insights into the origin of this creole, or of creoles in general. Such research would best be undertaken with emerging creoles and/or with the collaborative evidence of historical documents. The main purpose of this project is the documentation of changes in this established creole, both past and current, using direct and indirect evidence, both historical and linguistic, reflecting the changing language behavior of these creole speakers.

The term "relexification" here refers to the substitution of vocabulary items by others, with or without changes in meaning. Whereas the term when used by some creolists implies that almost the entire vocabulary has, possibly suddenly, shifted from words of one source language to words of another source language in the process of formation of the pidgin or creole (even though we have as yet no documented evidence for such a phenomenon ever having occurred), I am using the term in a fourfold different way in referring to Chabacano:

1. The relexification is not sudden. It appears to be relatively rapid, as language changes in the world go, but then, other Philippine languages, which are not creoles, appear to be making similar rapid lexical changes.

2. The relexification is not complete, nor does it refer simply to substitution of words from one source by words of another source, but rather, the addition and loss of terms, with or without changes of meaning, and including the adoption of new words for new concepts. In other words, we find the same kinds of relexification processes that can be observed in so-called "natural" languages.

3. The new terms come not from a single source language, but from several; and the obsolescent terms are not exclusively of one source language.

4. The process is taking place not with a newly emerging creole, but rather, with a long-established one.

Left unanswered is the question of whether or not the types of relexification changes described here reflect on the one hand the way in which the lexicon was developed when this language emerged, or on the other, the ways in which total relexification would take place in the formation of any creole language from, say Portuguese.

In my opinion, the data I describe from this long-established creole language are inappropriate for tackling the notion of relexification as necessary for the "common origin" theory of creole language formation.

Philippine Creole Spanish

Five or six dialects of Philippine Creole Spanish exist today in two areas of the Philippines: Ternateño, Caviteño, and Ermiteño are spoken in or near Manila on the island of Luzon; and Zamboangueño, Cotabato Chabacano (which appears to be a variety of Zamboangueño), and possibly Davao Chabacano are spoken on the island of Mindanao, some 500 miles to the south.

Ternateño is spoken by the 8000 inhabitants of the town of Ternate, who gain their living mostly by fishing in the Manila Bay and the river that divides their town. Their income is supplemented by rice and sugar cane agriculture, fish pond cultivation, and the aid of relatives who have gone to seek their employment in Manila or the United States. Ternateño is the first language of almost all of the people of Ternate, though almost everyone is bilingual in Tagalog, an Austronesian language and one of the two official national languages of the Philippines (the other being English). The only outsiders who learn Ternateño are the few men and women who have married into the town. Two-thirds of the way toward Manila one comes to Cavite, site of the traditional naval base for Manila, a large city where some 5000 people, mostly over the age of 40, claim Chabacano as their first language. And in Manila itself, there are a few dozen people in their sixties or older who remember their mother tongue Ermiteño. These people have scattered to various places in Manila and beyond, and all communicate via Tagalog today. Nowhere between the Manila Bay area and southern Mindanao have there been verified reports of Chabacano speakers.

In Zamboanga City and Basilan Island there are more than 100,000 first-language speakers of Chabacano (Frake, 1968), by far the largest community of people speaking this language. In Davao and Cotabato, also on Mindanao, there are small numbers of people speaking Chabacano, which has derived from Zamboangueño. Since Ternateño is the dialect of Chabacano most closely linked with the language spoken in the Moluccas during the seventeenth century, this study of relexification processes in Philippine Creole Spanish focusses on Ternateño, with collaborative evidence from the other dialects found in the Philippines. Historical documents show that Philippine Creole Spanish (or Chabacano, a commonly-used cover term for all the dialects) was brought to the Philippines around 1662 by some 200 immigrants from the island of Ternate, most important of the Spice Islands in the Moluccas, Indonesia. During the sixteenth and seventeenth centuries, Portuguese, Spanish, and Dutch fought over the Moluccas in order to control the spice trade. About 1662, Spaniards withdrew their forces and mission from Ternate and other outlying areas back to Manila in order to fortify against the threatened attack by the Chinese warlord called Koxinga by Filipinos. The Spanish priest in Ternate brought with him some 200 Christians who settled for a short time in Ermita, a district of Manila, and by 1700 most of them had moved to the mouth of the Maragondon River, some 50 miles south of Manila and just opposite the island of Corregidor, which guards the entrance to the Manila Bay. They named their settlement Ternate after the homeland of most of them. There is some evidence of later movements by Ternateños to Cavite near Manila and later to Zamboanga and later movement of Zamboangueños to Cotabato and Davao.

Whether the Philippine creole language first developed in the Moluccas or was brought there from another place has not been established. Linguistic evidence for the transmission of Ternateño to the Philippines occurs in the form of a few Indopacific, Malay, and Portuguese terms used today, mostly in the dialect of Chabacano spoken in Ternate, Philippines. (See Note 1 at the end of this chapter).

Recent and Current Lexical Change

As examples of the possible kinds of change in an established creole language, I will present some current changes in lexicon in Philippine Creole Spanish. Four kinds of data will be used: (1) frequency of occurrence in speech of certain words, such as sorting out of new elements versus old elements in the speech of young people versus old people; (2) divergences in meaning from the source languages; (3) lexical divergences between dialects; and (4) the relative distribution of source language over semantic domains (see Note 2 at end of chapter). Speakers of Ternateño have been the judges of both frequency of occurrence in speech and whether the words are new or old in the language.

ANALYSIS BY FREQUENCY

Frequencies of occurrence of various words in speech have held some clues for changes taking place in the language. I have recognized frequencies by examining texts and by asking the opinions of the speakers.

Words of low frequency can signal either newly emerged forms in the language or obsolescence (as well as static words); these were sorted out by asking people which are new terms and which are old and by observing how their use sorts out by speakers, whether old or young people, educated or uneducated people, monolinguals or bilinguals, males or females (Note 3). Reports of people and observations in Ternate coincide generally as follows (the tendency demonstrated is not yet based on actual text counts):

	Relative frequency of occurrence in speech among:	
	Older speakers	Younger speakers
Recent loans	Low	High
Old, obsolescent words	High	Low

Words that are reported as obsolete or obsolescent are heard used mostly by older people. A large percentage of the obsolescent terms are Spanish or "Mardika":

banyus (<Sp., *baño* 'bath' and Tag. *banyos* 'sponge bath') 'folk medicine'. Medicinal liquids are applied to joints of the body as treatment for colds, fever, headaches, etc. The liquid is a mixture of vinegar, urine, salt, and coconut oil. Cav. X. Syn: *baynus,* also infrequent.
aunke (<Sp. aunque) 'even though'. Cav. Zbo. X. The more common synonym now in Ternate is *maske* (<Sp. *mas que*).

Spanish-oriented exclamations are much more common among old people:

asos, asus, sus (<Sp. *Jesus*) 'Jesus!', expression of surprise or disagreement. *Asos! No di pwedi kel, ya habla ya yo kuŋ bo.* 'Oh! That will not do, I have already told you.' (Text BB-4) Cav. X.
a la bwena di Dyos (<Sp. *a la buena de Dios*) 'By the grace of God'. (Text B-37). Cav. X.

Some "Mardika" terms apparently passing out include:

balansyá (<Sp. *balancear,* rock, swing) 'to become restless. A person who is sick after being visited and smelled by the *asuwan* (witch), or a sick person with high fever who mutters inaudible words and makes involuntary body movements.' (Text AA-26)
baleŋga (<Iberian ?) 'excessive swinging of arms while walking'. *No masyaw se baleŋga kel brasu si ta kamina.* 'Don't swing those arms too much while walking.'

bandilyeru (<Sp. *bandera*, 'flag'?) 'town crier' (obsolete). *Bandilyu, se* (<Sp. *bandera, se*, reflexive). 'to read aloud by the town crier, the new orders, laws or new information for the townspeople to know; also, to read new stories or new subjects in public.' (Text M-24)
alapár (<Sp. *a la par*, 'together, at the same time') 'arranged in rows'. Syn. *helera* (Sp. *hilera*.)
balistrokis (<Mar.) 'to cheat; to be a bad credit risk'; *se balistrokis* 'to cheat, defraud'. *No bo se balistrokis kumigu, ey demanda yo kung bo* 'Do not cheat me, or I will sue you.' (Text MM-11)

Not all obsolescent terms are Spanish or Mardika, however. Some Tagalog and English terms are on their way out, e.g.,

balikocha (<Tag. *balikotsa*) 'taffy, from cane sugar molasses.' Cav. X. Syn.: *harigi di kampanyaryu* (<Sp. ?); so-called because to make taffy one pulls the sugar or bangs it against something such as a post, and if one were to bang it against the church, the bells would ring.
bagúl (<Tag. *bagol*) five centavos, a five-centavo coin. *Bende kumigu uŋ* **bagul** *di sal* 'Sell me five centavos of salt.' (Text D-32) Syn. *siŋku sen* (<Sp. *cinco* 'five', *centavo* 'cent'?).
bab-heyr (<Engl. *bobbed hair*). Cav. X. *Kalu mira yo muher gora* **bab-heyr** 'These days I seldom see girls with bobbed hair.'

Some of these terms are used by outsiders, especially Caviteños, to characterize Ternateño speech, and to tease Ternateños, for example, *balistrokis, bagul*, and *balikocha*, above, and

sursi (<Sp. *ir y venir*) 'back and forth'. Here, it should be stressed, the local people say this is the etymology of *sursi*. Edgar Knowlton suggests Sp. *zurcir* 'to darn, patch, mend'.
chinkletas (<Sp. *chancleta*) 'sandals' (obsolescent). Syn: *swekos* (<Sp. *zueco*, clog, wooden shoe).

Of course, not all Spanish or English infrequently-used terms are on their way out. Some reflect education:

asma (<Engl. or Sp.) 'asthma'. *Muchacha pa eli kwandu ya tene* **asma** 'She was still a child when she had asthma.' (Text GG-1) Syn: *disneya* (<Sp. *disnea*) 'to have difficulty breathing' (also obsolescent); *hika* (<Tag.   ), the most commonly-used term; and *asmatiku* (<Sp. *asmático*).
admirá (<Sp. *admirar* 'to admire') (used by people educated in Spanish). *Anda bo mira, para* **admira** *bo* 'You go and see, to admire it.' Syn: *mahaŋa* (<Tag.); *admirabli* (<Sp. *admirable*) 'admirable, lovable'

(used by people educated in Spanish). Syn: *kahaŋahaŋa* (<Tag.) (more frequent).

aktwalmente (<Sp. *actualmente*) 'actually, really'. *Actwalmente no eli el dwenyu* 'Actually, she is not the owner.' Cav. Zbo. X. Syn: *kasalukuyan* (<Tag.) is more frequent. *Aktwalmente* even retains the final /e/ of Spanish, even though there appears to be taking place a general sound shift in Ternateño to final /i/.

Nor are all Mardika terms less frequent and by implication obsolescent. The following are in common use:

bakudali (<Sp. *va con dale?*) 'to fight back, attack; to attack foods by eating voraciously'. *Ya huga bakudali kel tropa di iskwela kontra kel maŋa awtsayder* 'That group of students had an encounter against those outsiders.' (Text LL-22, J-23) Syn: *labaŋ* (<Tag. labán). Cav. *iŋkwentro* (<Sp. *encuentro*).

balandráŋ (<Mar?) 'in the wrong place, misplaced, haphazard, carelessly placed'. *Komu ta balandraŋ esti mesa aki? Icha na urilya.* 'Why is this table in here? Set it in the corner.' *Balandraŋ esti buh trabahu; deseta esti.* 'You have done this improperly; untie it.'

andinanti (<Sp. *endenantes*, 'earlier') 'earlier; sometime between daybreak and now; awhile ago.' *Andinanti pa mihotru ki.* 'We have been here since awhile ago'. Syn: *inanti*. Cav. *andinante*. Cot. Chab., Zbo. *endenantes*.

aŋyaya (<Mal *anlaya* < Skr.) 'to harm; to inflict injury to the helpless'. *No yo di ase anyaya kuŋ ustedi.* 'I will not harm you.' (Text T-7, p-11).

bádju; bàdju-bádju (<Bahasa Ternate?) 'untidy; dirty; wearing baggy or inappropriate clothing.' *No bo di pwedi tene muher gwapa, buŋ badju bo.* 'You will not be able to have a pretty wife, you are very untidy.' Syn: *badji*.

baka-báka (<?) 'to crawl, as a baby'. *Mi iha ta se baka-báka ya.* 'My daughter is crawling already.' (Text W-18) Syn: *gatyá* (<   ).

bakera, -o (<Sp. *vaquero*?) 'careless; untidy; not very sanitary.' *Bakera kel maŋa muher ta kamina na kalyi susyu el pantuhrilya.* 'Untidy are those women walking around the streets with dirty legs.' Cav. *babuy* (<Tag. 'pig'), *porkada* (<Sp. *porcachon* 'filthy'). Syn: *porkada*.

Young people are the main innovators of new English and Tagalog terms, and most of the new terms entering this language are from these two sources. Many of these would be appropriately classed as slang and are more frequently used by young men than women:

kats (<Tag. < Engl. *cats*) 'girls' (slang). Cav. X. Syn: *bobits* (<Tag.?), *chiks* (Engl. *chicks*).

babeski (<Tag. *baboy* 'pig') 'pork meat' (slang).

katok, se (<Tag. *katok,* 'to knock, rap'; Sp. *se* reflexive) 'to steal' (slang). *Manda se katok galyina para tyeni para kome.* 'Let us go steal chickens in order to have something to eat.'

bahre kalyi (<Sp. *barrer calle* 'sweep the street') 'sweep the streets; by-standers, or idle young men who stand around on the streets'. Syn: *istambay* (<Engl. *standby* 'understudy'); *kanto boy* (<Tag. *kanto* 'corner'; Engl. *boy*); *amboy* (abbreviated to *ab* in graffiti) (<Tag. <Engl. *American boy,* abbreviation in Tagalog).

adre (<Tag. <Sp. *compadre* 'godfather; pal') 'friend, buddy'. *Adre, no bo ya mira basket bol?* 'You did not see the basketball game, friend?' (Text VV-4) Cav. X. Syn: *migo, migoy* (<Sp. *amigo* 'friend'); *boy* (<Engl.); *choy* (<Chi.?)

arbor (<Tag. ?) 'to ask for another's possession in a demanding rather than a begging way' (slang). *Ya se pa arbor kel su kamisa, kaya ya bolbe nway kamisa.* 'His shirt was still being asked for, so he went home without a shirt.' Syn: *pidi* (<Sp. *pedir* 'to ask for').

atik (<Tag., metathesis of *kita* < Sp. *quita* 'earnings') 'money'. Cav. X. Syn: *sen* (<Sp. *centavo* 'cent'?). ˙

baŋaw (<Tag. < Maranaw?) 'bot fly' (from T. Ramos), 'feast. (crude)' Cav. Zbo. X.

Not all slang terms are used mostly by young people, however, some are frequent in the speech of both old and young:

echos (<Sp. *hecho* 'genuine') homosexual. Syn: *bakla* (<Tag. *bakla* 'homosexual, transvestite'). *Muchu bakla ya sigi na prusisyon.* 'Several homosexuals went with the procession.' (Text T-4, p-23) Cav. X. *bakla-baklá,* to act like a homosexual, particularly the stereotypical manner of speech. *Buŋ bwenu eli se di bakla-baklá.* 'He is very good in acting like a homosexual'. (Text C-60) Cav. X. Another synonym is *binabai* (<Tag. 'homosexual, effeminate').

kasti; kastyá (<Prt. *castear* 'to reproduce') 'intercourse'. The verb seems to be more vulgar than the name, which means 'whore' for females. *kastyona* (f.), *kastyoŋ* (m.) 'A person with intense desire for sex.' The noun women often use to call names, even to young children or to a young girl in the presence of her fiance. (See Note 4.)

Young people are also more likely to use disguised, or *baliktad* (<Tag. *baligtad* 'backward, upside down, etc.') speech. Most of these terms are being borrowed from Tagalog:

bals wals (<Tag. *bali wala* < Tag. *wala* 'none'; Sp. *valer* 'to be worth')
'useless'. Syn. *nuay sirbi* (<Sp. *no (hay) servir).*
álaws (<Tag. *wala* 'none') 'broke, no money'. Cav. X.
atab (<Tag. *bata* 'child; girlfriend') 'girlfriend'. Cav. X. Syn: *shota*
 (<Sp.)

Some disguised speech terms are from English, e.g.,

tehots (<Engl. *hostess*) 'prostitute'.
bóyan (<Engl. *American boy*, see above) 'idle teenage boy; wearing the
 dress of an American, including long hair'.

I have noted the frequencies of some specific terms, and how their use
sorts out the population of Ternateño speakers. Now, the different languages that have loaned words can be sorted out by frequency of ap-
pearence in speech. At the top of the list, of course, would be Spanish,
providing some 90% of the vocabulary in Ternateño. Then, in descending
order, we find Tagalog and English, both with growing numbers of loan
words, then Chinese, Japanese, Malay, Portuguese, and other Philippine
and Indonesian languages. The Portuguese, Malay, and Indonesian terms
appear to be obsolescent.

DIVERGENCES FROM SOURCE LANGUAGES

Of the divergences of meaning from the source languages that can be
observed, some are obvious, others more subtle (see Note 5):

amiga (<Sp. 'friend (f.), girlfriend') is becoming specialized now to
 usually mean 'mistress'. Cav. Zbo. X. *Eli el **amiga** di buh manoŋ.*
 'She is the mistress of your brother.' Syn: *kaibigan* (<Tag.), *kerida*
 (<Sp. *querida,* 'sweetheart').
abilidad (<Sp. *habilidad* 'skill, cleverness'), 'tactics'. *No pwey pasa su*
 abilidad. 'He was not able to use his tactics.' (Text T-9, p-11). Cav.
 Zbo X. Syn: *para'aŋ* (<Tag.).
alborokyentu, burukyentu (<Sp. *alboroto*) 'talkative, noisy, loudmouth'.
 *Masyaw **borokyentu** henti esti.* 'This man is very talkative.' Cav. X.
 Zbo. *alborokyento.* Syn: *buŋ ruwidu* (<Port. *bon* 'very', Sp. *ruido*
 'noise') used more frequently by young people.
kuryosu (<Sp. *curioso,* 'curious') 'good'. *Akesti el **kuryosu** pehkaw.*
 'These are the good fish.' Cav. X.
abuhridu (<Sp. *aburrido,* 'boring, bothered, etc.') 'desperate; deprived;
 steals food for family.' ***Abuhridu** ya eli kaya ya pensa eli se di kel.* 'He
 is already desperate, so he thought of doing that.' Cav. X. Zbo.
 aburrido 'furious, as in a rape' (so the meaning has become stronger
 in Chabacano).

tamyeŋ (<Sp. *tambien* 'also') 'however, anyway, again, by the way.' *Pirmi tamyeŋ anda-anda buh nay aya.* 'Your mother used to go there anyway.' *Absent ya tamyeŋ eli.* 'He is absent again.' (Text O-11) (In Cav., the cognate is *tamyen* 'also', in Zbo. *tamen* 'also'. In Tern., 'also' is *ring* (<Tag.). Here we find an example of divergences of both meaning and sound from the source language and among the dialects of Chabacano.)[1]

andá (<Sp. *andar* 'to walk') 'to go'. Forms of Sp. *ir* 'to go' are not generally used. *No ma bu anda na Kabiti.* 'Do not go to Cavite anymore.' (Text A-7-64) Cav. X. Other forms are *andà-andá* used to go', *andada* 'trip, journey', *andandu* 'on going', but: *andar* 'to operate a machine'. *Se bo andar kel djip para sali ya mihotru.* 'You operate that jeep so that we can leave already.' (Text C-15) Cav. X. Syn: *maneha*, (<Sp. *manejar*, 'to operate'). Cot. Chab. also has *andada*. Ter. *Maŋ anda ya.* 'Let's go.' Syn: *bamos* (<Sp. *vamos*) Cav. X.

abla (<Sp. *hablar* 'to speak') 'idle talk, gossip'. *Buŋ muchu abla pa esti henti esti.* 'This man has too much idle gossip.' Cav. *daldal* (<Tag.) Syn: *platikada* (<Sp. *platicar* 'to chat') *daldal.*

The domain of kin terms (see Molony, 1973a, p. 13) shows many divergences from Spanish meaning. For instance, the Ternateño term *tay* (<Tag. *tay* < Sp. *tata* 'father') is used to name not only father, but also father-in-law, father's elder brother, mother's elder brother, father's elder cousin, mother's elder cousin, and sometimes grandfather and even great grandfather.

Divergences from contemporary American English (the major source of English) include, at least in frequency, the following (Dr. Teresita Ramos points out that all of these terms are also in Tagalog):

kaswál (<Engl. *casual*) 'temporary government employee'. *Ya pwedi ŋa eli trabahu, peru kaswal duma.* 'He was able to work really, but as a **casual** employee only.' Cav. Zbo. X.

kécher (<Engl. *catcher*) (1) 'catcher in baseball game' (2) 'a man who accepts a girl for his wife or girlfriend after being left for another man; one who "catches someone on the rebound"'. *Eli pala el maridu? ya keda eli kecher.* 'So he is the husband? then he has become a **catcher**.' Cav. X.

karoliŋ (<Engl. *caroling*) 'to go Christmas caroling'. What this means in practice is something closer to "trick-or-treat," where songs are

---

[1] Edgar Knowlton gives (from Vicente, 1967): *tamián* (p. 96) Old Leonese; *tamién* (p. 149) Popular Leonese (cf. Port. *tamién*); *tammién* (p. 276) Aragonese. Also note Sp. *tan bien* 'as well, so well' versus Sp. *tanbién*, and Port. *tão bem* 'as well, so well' and *tanbém* 'also, indeed, really'.

sung at doorsteps, and at the same time the group asks for money or food. *Nway eli aki, yanda se* **karoliŋ**. 'He's not here, he's gone caroling.' Cav. X.

badyet (<Engl. *budget*) 'budget, ready cash, funds'. *No pwedi manda kompone esti kasa, nway* **badyet**. 'This house cannot be repaired due to lack of funds.' Cav. X. Syn: *presupwestu* (<Sp. *presupuesto*, 'budget').

An important area where divergences from the source language can be observed is with grammatical markers. Some grammatical markers are borrowed from the source language, but only as unproductive artifacts:

alrebés (<Sp. *al reves*) 'opposite, inverted, wrong side out'. *Ya bisti bo kamiseta* **alrebes**. 'You wore your undershirt the wrong side out.' (Text T-4, p. 38). Cav. X. Zbo. *arebes, arabes*. Syn: *baliktad* (<Tag. *baligtad*).

Some Spanish words are adopted by Ternateño in the singular form, others in the plural form, but the number marking is dropped for meaning and remains only as artifact:

áhus (<Sp. *ajo, ajos*) 'garlic, garlics'. *ahus muda* (<Sp. *ajo*, Tag. *mura*, 'young') 'young garlic', or *ahus berdi* (<Sp. *ajo, verde*, 'green'). *tomátis* (<Sp. *tomate, tomates*) 'tomato, tomatoes'. *algunas, (gunas, alguna, algunas)* 'some'. **Algunas** *bes tyeni ta kohe, peru malimit nway*. 'Sometimes a catch is made, but often times there is none at all.' Cav. X. Syn: *tyeni bes* (<Sp. *tiene vez*).

But, we find *sili* (<Sp. *chili*) 'chili, chilis', to have the singular form, whether referring to one or more chilis. *Ahus* and *sili* have the same status in Ternateño, both being mass nouns.

Other Spanish artifacts include:

a, in *na aplaya* (<Tag. *na* 'at', *Port. < *em a* 'in the' (from E. Knowlton), Sp. *a playa* 'at the beach') 'at the beach'. The redundancy of 'at' is not evident because *a* is an unproductive artifact. The gender distinction of the definite article as: *el*, in *alas* (<Sp. *el*) 'the ace, of cards'. *el*, in *el amiga* (see *amiga* above).

Gender distinctions are usually retained, however, to signal sex distinctions, for people and animals, e.g., *iha, ihu*, 'daughter, son' (<Sp. *hija, hijo*). We could say that the gender markers in Spanish are approaching sex markers in Ternateño, though they are neither obligatory nor consistant.

Other Spanish markers are productive, even with non-Spanish words, for instance *uŋ*, which has become a nongender-marked indefinite marker (whereas indefinite is usually not marked at all):

uŋ bara di american bred, hustu ya kel. 'A loaf of white bread, that is enough already.' (<Sp. *barra* feminine, 'stick, bar').
uŋ aper kat pwerti na paŋa ki ya se durmi kuŋ su kalabaŋ. 'A strong upper cut to the jaw sent his opponent to the canvas for a full count.' Cav. X. (Engl. *upper cut*).

The forms of Ternateño *se* (from Spanish *hacer*, 'to make, do') do not appear to be productive, even though used frequently but rather become part of the word as artifacts. *Se, ase* or *hase* (Sp. *hacer*, 'to make, do') is found associated with Tagalog and English words:

se ani (<Sp. *hacer* Tag. *ani*) 'to harvest'. *Yanda se ani mi nay na kaiŋiŋ.* 'My mother went to harvest in the swidden.' Cav. X. Syn: *se pitas* (<Tag. 'to pick, pluck').
se áru (<Sp. *hacer*, Tag. *aro*) 'to match fighting cocks and see them fight'. Also applied to people, particularly boys or girls, who fight after having been incited by others. 'To match a young man to a young girl'. *No bo se áru kumigu kuŋ eli, no yo el ki ta buska eli.* 'Do not match me to her, I am not what she wants.' (Text GG-18).
se balut (<Sp. *hacer*, Tag. *balut*) 'to wrap; to enclose'. The process of installing the enclosures to the posts of fish corrals. *Di se ya lotru balut na Lunis.* 'They will install the enclosures of the fish corral on Monday.' (Text EE-11) Cav. X. Syn: *imbolbe* (<Sp. *involver*).
se bakay (<Sp. *hacer*, Tag. *bakay*) 'to wait in order to ambush'. *Aki mihotru hase bakay kuŋ kel galyina.* 'We wait here for that hen.' (Text NN-74) Syn: *bisya* (<?), *se haraŋ* (<Tag.), *ambus* (<Engl.), *ataha,* (<Sp. *atajar*) 'to hold up, to ambush, to make a blockade'. (Text L-8) Cav. Zbo. X.
se balita (<Sp. *hacer*, Tag. *balita* 'news') 'to give information'. *balita* is used alone as a noun: *Kosa balita di gehra na Byetnam?* 'What's news about the war in Vietnam?' *Balita di mi ta perde raw el Amerikanu.* 'I was informed that the Americans are losing the war.' (Text T-6, p. 4) Cav. X. Syn: *notisya* (<Sp. *noticia*). Also found are *balitaŋ barbero* (<Tag. *balita*, Sp. *barbero*) 'barber's news, unreliable hearsay' and *balitaŋ kuchero* (<Sp. *cochero*) 'rig driver's news, unreliable hearsay'. *No bo kre kel, balitaŋ kuchero numa kel.* 'Do not believe that, it's mere hearsay.' (Text JJ-28)
asi born (<Sp. *hacer*, Engl. *born*) 'to be born', passive. *El yir kwandu ya asi born* . . . 'The year that I was born . . . .'

Some grammatical markers are abbreviated, or have an abbreviated variant, in Ternateño: Sp. *de* > *y* after vowels:

< Spanish *de* 'from, of':

pwerkuy monti, pwerku y monti (< Sp. *puerco de monte*) 'wild pig'. Cav., Zbo., X. Syn: *baboy damo* (< Tag.)

< Spanish *de*, in:

esti bida y peskador, adbenturaw. 'The life of a fisherman is adventurous (risky).' (Text K-26)

agwa y bebe (< Sp. *agua de beber*) 'drinking water'. *Tapa bwenu kel balde de agwa y bebe.* 'Cover well that can of drinking water.' Cav. X.

< Sp. *el*, 'the' in >-*l* on previous word:

todul byernis (< Sp. *todo el viernes*) 'every Friday'. *Tyeni bahraka na Bahra todul Byernis.* 'Friday is the market day in Ternate.' (Text Z-48). Cav. 'market' is *paleŋke*.

Sp. *esta alli*, 'is there', >*tayi:*

tayi el habon na banyu. 'The soap is in the bathroom.' (Text A-10)

Tayi appears to be becoming a demonstrative, in which case the copula will be an artifact.

Tagalog has also loaned grammatical markers, some unproductive, others productive, including Tagalog markers for Spanish or English words:

< Tag. *ma-* verbal marker:

ya ma-hospital eli. 'He was confined to a hospital.' (< Engl. *hospital*).
ma-trapik (< Engl. *traffic*) *Ya keda eli pustrera na klasi, kasi ya ma-trapik.* 'He came late to class because of the traffic.' (Text T-2, p. 3) Cav. Zbo. X.
ma-arti (< Sp. *arte*) 'skill; overacting'. *Buŋ ma-arti pa no sali ya, si di bolbe?* 'You are overacting; why don't you leave, if you are on your way home?'

< Tag. *ika*, cardinal marker:

ika tres bes (< Sp. *tercero vez* 'third time', *tres veces* 'three times') 'for the third time'.

< Tag. *ka-:*

ka-rancho (< Sp. *rancho* 'ranch', *ka-* normalizer, 'companion') 'helpers, comrades'. *Ya se eli birtdey, taya todu su ka-rancho.* 'He celebrated his birthday and all his comrades were there.' Syn: *Alyadus* (< Sp. *aliados*), *tropa* (< Sp.) (Text H-4)

One of the frequently-observed features of creoles is reduplication of words. Many Spanish words have become reduplicated or have reduplicative variants, some possibly as an influence by Philippine languages, as reduplication is used in the same ways in other Philippine languages. It is difficult to say whether creolization may also have offered some incentive for reduplication.

poku-poku (<Sp. *poco, poco a poco*) slowly. Syn: *banayat* (<Tag. *banayad*). Cav. *despasyo*, Zbo. *banayad. banay-banay.* **Buŋ banay-banay** *tamyeŋ el kuhrida di esti djip esti, mudidiya ya.* 'This jeepney is moving very slowly; it is already late.' Another synonym is *hinay-hinay* (<Tag.)

ta rih-rih (<Sp. *risa*) 'continually laughing'.

todu-todu (<Sp. *todo*) total. *Bali beynti tiklis* **todu-todu** *ya pwedi kohe ayer.* 'The total catch yesterday was equivalent to twenty basketfuls of fish all in all.' (Text 1, p. 1) Cav. X.

bali-bali (<Sp. *valer* 'be worth') 'very good, special quality'. **Bali-bali** *kel kuhida di ayer.* 'Yesterday's catch was quite valuable.' (Text D-63) Cav. X. It should be emphasized that *bali* is even stronger, so *bali-bali* is a deintensifier, the reduplication serving the opposite function of the usual expectation of reduplication. Reduplication as deintensifier occurs commonly in Southeast Asian languages.

aseyti-aseyti (<Sp. *aceite* 'oil', *aceitoso* 'oily') 'oily, something with oil traces'. *Komu* **aseyti-aseyti** *esti agwa?* 'Why is this water oily?' *Siguru tyeni* **aseyti** *esti lata.* 'Maybe this can has oil.' Cav. X.

agwa-agwa (<Sp. *aguado*) 'watery'. *Komu* **agwa-agwa** *esti morisketa? siguru ya gutya agwa aki na olya.* 'Why is this rice watery? Maybe water was spilled into it.' Cav. X. Syn: *agwaw*.

English forms do not seem to take to reduplication so easily. (The Philippine English form *always* as in "always running" possibly could be a translation of reduplication in Tagalog and other Philippine languages.)

English grammatical forms that survive as artifacts include *bakwét* (<Engl. *evacuate*) 'evacuees'. The English verb form is used nominally in Ternateño. The verb form in Ternateño is distinguished, by addition of *e-* and stress change: *ebakwet*.

Many two-part words or phrases are found where part is from Spanish, part from Tagalog. These include:

kasiŋ-edad (<Tag. *kasiŋ*, Sp. *edad*) 'same age, born same year'. **Kasiŋ-edad** *eli di mi muher.* 'She is of the same age as my wife.' (Text L-6) Cav. X.

olor kambiŋ (<Sp. *olor* 'fragrance, smell', Tag. *kambiŋ* 'goat') 'body odor'. Syn: *aŋhit, ma-aŋhit* (<Tag.) Zbo. *aŋhit*.

alagay di kel (<Tag. *sa lagay* 'like that', Sp. *de aquel* 'of that') 'emphatic expression, just like that'. E. Knowlton suggests influence of Sp. *a* as in *a manera de, a modo de* 'in the manner of'.

Words borrowed into Ternateño do not have grammatical markers added, unlike, say, Tagalog or English; they become "Ternateñized" mostly by phonological changes (see Molony, 1973b, p. 45). It should be emphasized that Spanish and English words are often borrowed in via Tagalog, and changes may take place in that medium rather than by Ternateño speakers. Changes that do occur can be found at all levels, phonological to semantic.

DIVERGENCES BETWEEN THE DIALECTS

Another clue to lexical changes taking place is an examination of the divergences between the different dialects of Chabacano. The assumption I make in examining differences found between the various dialects is that they have diverged from a common source. Historical evidence indicates that Chabacano entered the Philippines in Manila, traveled via its speakers to Ternate, and spread from there. Another assumption that I make is that the bulk of the vocabulary at one time was made up of Iberian terms, whether Spanish or Portuguese, and that Philippine and English terms have been added to or replaced this base.

There are relatively fewer differences at all levels between Ternateño and Caviteño than between Ternateño and other dialects, Zamboangueño and Cotabato Chabacano. For most of the differences, we find that where Caviteño has a Spanish word, Ternateño has a Tagalog word, or uses a Tagalog word with greater frequency. Most Caviteño differences show up as less-frequently-used synonyms in Ternateño, including (Ternateño):

kayud, ase (<Tag. *kayod,* Sp. *hacer*) 'to grate, scrape, scrub'. *Ta se kayud esti bago ta icha ahus, tomatis.* 'This is grated when garlic and tomatoes are added.' (Text T-3, 33, SS-9) Cav. *raspá.* (<Sp. *raspar*). Syn: *raspá.*

kasaŋkapaŋ (<Tag.?) charm, amulet. *Akel el kasaŋkapaŋ ta sirbi yo na kel maŋa maŋgagaway.* 'This is the amulet I am using against those witches.' (Text Q-19) Cav. *galiŋ.* Syn: *galin.*

katunuyaŋ (<Tag. *katunayan*) 'proof'. *Dali mira bo katunayaŋ kuŋ eli para kre kuŋ bo.* 'You show him proof so that he will believe you. Cav. *prweba* (<Sp. *prueba*). Syn: *prweba.*

Caviteño, Sp.-based words that are not used in Ternateño include (in Ternateño):

kaynamaŋ (<Tag. *kaynaman*) 'sufficient, just enough; it fits'. *Kaynamaŋ*

ya esti di muchu; no ma di paltu. 'This quantity is just enough; it will not be short now.' Cav. *bastante* (Sp.)

kawayan (<Tag.) 'spiny bamboo'. Cav. *kanya* (<Sp. *caña*).

kasalukúyaŋ (<Tag.) 'incumbent; present'. *Kasalukuyaŋ meyor di mihotru bun plohu.* 'Our present mayor is very lazy.' (Text L-1). Cav. *aktwal* (<Sp. *actual*).

katála (<Tag.) (1) 'monkey wrench' (2) 'white parrot'. *Sirbi bo katala ayi para prestu keda hechu.* 'Use a monkey wrench to finish quickly.' *Ya iskapa kel katala na kuluŋaŋ.* 'That white parrot escaped from the cage.' Cav. (1) *lyabe* (<Sp. *llave*), (2) *loro* (<Sp.).

kása (<Sp. *casa* 'house') 'house, home; prostitution house; shop.'

kasá (<Sp. *casar*) 'to marry'.

kasá (<Tag. <Sp. *cazer* 'to cook') 'to set the bet in cockfight or other game'.

kasá (<Sp. *cazar*) 'to cock a gun'.

kasadór (<Tag.<Sp.) 'person who takes bets'.

kasál (<Tag.) 'wedding; taking of vows by a nun'. Cav. *kasamyento* (<Sp. *casamiento*).

ikakasal (<Tag. *i* verbalizing focus marker, *ka* incomplete action marker; Sp. *casar*) 'to marry'. Cav. *di kasá.*

kinasal (<Tag. *-in-* past tense marker, Sp. *casar*) 'married'. Cav. *ya kasá.*

nagkasal (<Tag. *nag-*) 'officiator of wedding'.

baŋyaŋ (Hil. ?) 'storage for *palay*, harvested rice'. Cav. *deposito de palay* (<Sp. *deposito de*, Tag. *palay*).

katiŋaŋ (<Tag. *katiŋan*) 'a large cooking earthen jar in which whole tuna fish are cooked and taken to market for sale'. Cav. *olya grande* (<Sp. *olla grande*). Syn: *grandi olya.*

Not all differences are Caviteño–Spanish, Ternateño–Tagalog, however:

katkat (<Tag.) 'to bring out a different subject in a conversation; to expose, to reveal something during a conversation'. *Komu ya se katkat pa kalya na kel platikada di lotru?* 'Why was the subject brought out in their conversation?' Cav. *bisa* (<Tag.) Syn: *uŋkat* (<Sp. *un*, Eng. *cut?*).

Cotabato Chabacano speakers have apparently come from Zamboanga in the recent past; the two dialects are so closely related, that Cotabato Chabacano should probably be considered a regional variation of Zamboagueño. Some semantic features which distinguish Cotabato Chabacano from Ternateño include (in Cotabato Chabacano):

Donde tu nase? 'Where were you born?' Whereas Ternateño has *Dondi asi pari?* 'Where were you born?' The Ternateño sentence to a Cotabato Chabacano speaker would mean something like 'Were you given birth?' since *pari* means 'to give birth'.

pronto-pronto (<Sp. *pronto*) 'quickly' in Cotabato Chabacano is *prehtu-prehtu* (<Sp. *presto*) in Ternateño.

la mitad (<Sp. 'half') 'to cut in half' in Cotabato Chabacano is *man mitad* (<Tag. *man* verb marker, Sp. *mitad*, 'half') in Ternateño.

platika in Cotabato Chabacano is used only for a priest's sermon. See p. 141 for meaning in Ternateño, 'to chat'.

bibiw in Ternateño (<Sp. *bebido*) is 'drunk'. ***Bibiw eli, kwandu ya kayi.*** 'He was already drunk when he fell down.' In Caviteño 'drunk' is *tomaw* (<Sp. *tomado*). Synonyms in Ternateño are *tomaw, buhrachu* (<Sp. *boracho*). In Cotabato Chabacano, *tomaw* is 'drunk', *buhracho* is 'drunkard'.

Cotabato Chabacano distinguishes between *aserka* (<Sp. *acerca*) 'about' and *serka* (<Sp. *acerca*) 'near'. Cotabato Chabacano class dialects sort *prikura* (<Sp. *precurar*) to 'try, attempt', as lower class vs. *propura* (<Sp.   ) as upper class.

Ternateño–Zamboangueño differences are also found at all levels (see Molony, 1973a,b), including color terms (see tabulation). Most color

	Ternateño	Zamboangueño	Spanish
'red'	*koloraw*	*koloraw*	*rojo, colorado*
'white'	*blankihka, blanko*	*blanko*	*blanco*
'black'	*prietu*	*negro*	*negro;* (*prieto* 'very dark'); Portuguese *preto*
'yellow'	*kuniŋ* (Malay)	*amarilyo*	*amarillo*

terms in both languages are Spanish. However, Ternateño has acquired the term for yellow from Malay and very likely the term for black from Portuguese, but it has assimilated to Spanish pronunciation. Both Ternateño and Zamboangueño use a secondary Spanish term for red, and Ternateño uses a secondary Spanish term for white. If my information of the history of movements of Chabacano speakers is correct, then Zamboangueño must have dropped the Malay and Portuguese terms. Indeed, most of the Mardika terms found in Ternateño appear in the other dialects of Chabacano.

Some different words for the same meaning have already been presented in the sections on frequency and divergences from language of origin. Some differences of meaning for the same word include *tamyeŋ* as shown on p. 141.

The various source languages of Ternateño are sorted out broadly by the relative distribution of source language words over semantic domains in Ternateño. Most noticeable are English loans, which predominate in the domains of education, "modern" technology, military, medicine, administration, government, and American sports. They also figure importantly in slang terms and cultural items brought in. The "signs of progress," the material inventory associated with English words, is somewhat dismal, filled with such words as:

baykant peryud (<Engl. *vacant period*) 'recess'. Cav. X.
ays krim (<Engl.) 'ice cream'. Syn: *sorbetis* (<Sp.).
bábol gam (<Engl.) 'bubble gum'. Syn: *pepsin*
adbertaysment (<Engl.) 'advertisement'. Cav. X. Syn: *patalastas* (<Tag.).
aspirin (<Engl.) 'aspirin'. Cav. X. Syn: *aspirina* (<Sp.).
awtopsi (<Engl.) 'autopsy'. Cav. X. Syn: *awtopsya* (<Sp. *autopsia*).
bos (<Engl.) 'boss'.
baŋkrap (<Engl.) 'bankrupt'. Syn: *desparkaw* (<Sp. *desparcado*).
karpyu (<Engl.) 'curfew'. *Karpyu awar*, 'curfew hour'. *Maŋ bolbe ya baka iŋkalsa **karpyu awar** kuŋ mihortru.* 'Let's go home; we may be caught up by the curfew hour.' Cav. X.
bam (<Engl.) 'bomb'. Syn. *bomba* (<Sp.).

Some of these above words appear to be replacing Spanish-based terms. American sport terms are largely English (*karteyn reyser* in boxing, *atlit*, 'athlete', etc.). But even the Chinese-originated domino-like game of mahjong has a couple of English terms:

bambu (<Engl.) '"bamboo," sticks used in mahjong, green painted'.
baktubak (<Engl. *back to back*) 'in mahjong game, two pairs.' Cav. X.

Mardika terms are Malay, Bahasa Ternate, and other Indo-Pacific, Spanish, and Portuguese in origin. They focus around manners of personal behavior, e.g., manner of walking, talking, personal cleanliness. Many of these have negative connotations. The Mardika terms that appear to be most resistant to disappearance from Ternateño are marine-related.

The few Portuguese-based words are a few high-frequency terms, such as *prietu* 'black', *buŋ* 'very', *agwelu* 'grandfather', *bunyeka* 'doll', *agora* 'now'.

Japanese terms are largely brand names of goods, e.g., *katol*, 'mosquito repellant coil'; *katorisenko; aji-no-moto*, 'monosodium glutamate'. The few Chinese terms focus around foods, with a second focus around terms of reference for friends.

Tagalog seems to be donating lexical items in all domains, even providing some replacements for basic terms, such as *anim* 'six', replacing *seys* <Sp. *seis* 'six'.

Synonyms appear to be very largely words of similar meaning from another source language. Ternateño has many synonyms where the one word is of Spanish origin, the other of Tagalog origin. With less frequency, we find English words associated with Spanish words and with Tagalog words as synonyms.

Another way to examine lexical change is to see how various semantic domains sort out the languages from which words have come. For example, in the domain of cooking, most methods of cooking and cooking-related terms are Spanish, such as:

aśa (<Sp. *asar*) 'to roast; to barbecue'. *Ya asa kel taloŋ, kaya sabrosu.*
    'That eggplant was toasted, that's why it is delicious.' Cav. Zbo. X.
asado (<Sp.) 'meat dish cooked or broiled in soy sauce and spices'. *Dali kumingu uŋ gayat di kel asado.* 'Give me a slice of that broiled meat.'
    Cav. X (*asada* in Zbo. is 'hoe'.)
asáw (<Sp. *asado*) 'meat or fish barbecued on grill or in embers'. *Asaw di pehkaw kuŋ kalamansi el ki ya se ulaŋ yo.* 'Grilled fish with lime juice was my viand.' (Text Z-48) Cav. Zbo. X.

But a few cooking-related terms are from Chinese, and a few are from Tagalog:

baŋgli (<Tag.) 'to scald'. Cav. X. Syn: *saŋkucha* (<Sp.).
atay-atay (<Tag.) 'to boil slowly, to simmer'.
katay, se (<Tag. *katay,* Sp. *se*) 'to slaughter for eating'. *Taya ta se lotru katay pwerku; pidi bo un pukitiŋ saŋgri.* 'They are slaughtering a pig; you ask for a little blood.' (Text I-3) Cav. X.

Names of fish are mostly Tagalog, but Tagalog descriptive terms are translated into Spanish. A great share of fruit and vegetable terms are from Tagalog. Most of these name tropical flora. A similar kind of relation holds for the sources of place names; whereas the names of places surrounding Ternate are largely Tagalog names, most of the names of places within Ternate are Spanish-based, some of them diverging from Spanish in form and meaning, including:

Bahra (<Sp. *barra* 'sand bank') 'the most commonly used name for the town, used to fellow townspeople.
Bukana (<*boca na rio* <Sp. *boca* 'mouth', *rio* 'river', Tag. *na* 'at' or Port. *na* 'in') 'a district in town toward the mouth of the Maragondon river, on a small delta in the Manila Bay.'

Aplaya (<Sp. *a playa* 'at the beach') 'the beach area of Ternate'.

Gordu Punta (<*punto gordo* 'fat point') 'one of the extensions into the Manila Bay along the cliffs that form part of Ternate'.

Agwada, Gwada (<Sp. *aguada*) 'the area of a spring in Ternate, the main source of water supply before the construction of an artesian well in 1916'.

Abahu, Bahu (<Sp. *abajo,* 'down, below') 'the section in Ternate along the bank of the Maragondon river'.

Kasuyaŋ, Kasuy (<Tag. *an* place marker) 'an area on the road to Maragondon, which formerly had a cashew grove'.

Some names of body parts and fluids, terms that are usually considered rather basic vocabulary, have been contributed by Tagalog, including:

baba (<Tag.) 'chin'. Syn. *uŋku* (<?).

bagán (<Tag.) 'molar' (infrequent). Zbo. X. Syn: *mwelas* (<Sp. *muelas,* plural).

babas (<Sp. *baba*) 'saliva'. *Sirbi baberu papa na muha el pechu kuŋ babas.* 'Use a bib so as not to wet the chest with saliva.' Cav. X. Syn: *laway* (<Tag.)

kasù-kasúaŋ (<Tag. *kasu-kasuan*) 'body joints'. *Ta dole mi maŋa kasu-kasuaŋ, siguru di teni traŋkasu.* 'I feel pain in my joints, perhaps I will have the flu.' Cav. S.

balikat (<Tag.) 'shoulders'. Cav. X. Syn: *ombru* (<Sp.) (Note singular from Spanish.)

atáy (<Tag.) 'liver'. Cav, Zbo. X. Syn: *higadu* (<Sp. *higado*)

balakán (<Tag.) 'lower back'. Cav. X. Syn: *kadera* (Sp. *cadera*)

Some of these might be considered secondary terms, e.g., lower, back, molar. One cover term has come from English:

bádi (<Engl.) 'body'. *Kel el badi, hustu na sukat.* 'That is the body, with good measurements.' (Text 0-7) Cav. X. Syn: *kwerpu* (<Sp. *cuerpo*).

While most marine terms, including boat names, are from Spanish, several of the Mardika terms in Ternateño are found, and many Tagalog terms. Not all source words are specifically nautical.

amora (<Mar <Sp. *amarra* 'mooring line') 'in sailing, a length of rope, a line'. Cav. X.

agwahit (<Mar.; Sp. *aguaje*) 'wake, of water'. (Sp. is *estela*).

balagbag, keda (<Tag., Sp. *quedar,* 'to stay, remain') 'to become parallel to waves'.

astay [<Tag. <Sp. <Engl. *stay* (from E. Knowlton)] 'halyard'. *Helpa pa*

*uŋ pukitiŋ kel **astay** para subi pa kel bela.* 'Pull that halyard some more to raise the sail some.' Cav. *adrisa. adrisa* (<Sp. *adriẓar* 'to right').

ánud (<Tag.) 'carried away by river current'. Cav. X. Syn: *yuba agwa* (<Sp.)

kátik, kátig (<Tag. *katig*) 'outrigger'. *Kuryoso kel **katig** di su baŋka.* 'His banca boat has nice outriggers.' (Text P-22) Cav, Zbo. X.

kawaŋ (<Tag. *kawan*) 'school of fish, herd, flock'. *Ya tira dinamita na kel **kawaŋ** di pehkaw.* 'Dynamite was thrown at the school of fish.' (Text T-11, p. 4) Cav. *kawan.*

kawaŋ (<Tag.) 'condition of gill net: A space developed between net and sea bottom caused by impact of fishes. The net is raised from the bottom but soon settles back to the bottom when the fishes finally settle in the net.'

kawit, kalawit (<Tag. *kawit*) 'fish hook; hooking device to pick up fish traps under the sea'. (The name of the town Cavite is from *kawit*.)

kawit palakól (<Tag.) '"skeleton with scythe," the period when fishermen cannot go out to fish due to foul weather; period of starvation'. (Text K-17)

Idioms and metaphorical expressions come largely from Spanish, but there are also sayings from Tagalog, and sayings may include words from more than one origin.

abri boka na byentu (<Sp. *abriboca en el viento*) '"open mouth in wind," to wait in vain'. *Kosa di esperansa bo kuŋ eli?* **abri boka bo na byentu.** 'What can you expect from him? You will wait in vain.'

anchu papél (<Sp. *ancho papel*) '"wide paper," good reputation; powerful politically'. **Anchu el papel** *di kalaya kuŋ presidenti Markus.* He has good connections with President Marcos.' Cav. X. Syn. *malakas.* (<Tag.)

ahriba y baho (<Sp. *arriba y baho*) '"above and below," food poisoning, with both diarrhea and vomiting'. *No eli di pwedi trahaha, ya dali **ahribay** baho kuŋ eli anochi.* 'He cannot report for work because he had the food poisoning last night.' Cav. X.

a la berde (<Sp. *a la verde* 'on the green') 'free, especially referring to the time during the last portion of a show or movie when the gates are opened so that some "standby's" can see the end without paying admission.'

amo kandela [<Mar. *amo* <Hil? 'like, as' (E. Knowlton says <Sp. *amodo de* 'in the manner of'), Sp. *candela* 'candle') '"like candles," attentive.' *Taya eli ta paraw **amo kandela** na harap del prinsipal.* 'There he is, standing like a candle in front of the principal.' (Text II-10)

If *amo* is really from Hiligagnon (as are many loan words into Zamboangueño), then we have evidence for Philippine input other than Tagalog into Ternateño. That Ternateños consider it Mardika is also interesting, suggesting there may have been two-way influence between Ternateño and Zamboagueño.

kasa puga-puga, bibi badju-badju (<Sp. *casar* 'to marry' *fugar* 'to flee, escape', *vivir* 'to live'. Mar. *badju-badju* 'dirty, poor, etc.') "Marry early and live miserably." A popular saying of adults, now being replaced by a new saying meaning the same thing: *hudi hudi, nway para kumi* 'Sex sex, there's nothing for us.'

awtsayd di kulambu (<Engl. *outside the,* Tag. *kulambu,* 'mosquito net') 'outside the mosquito net,' an expression used when a woman is mad at her husband, implying he cannot sleep with her inside the mosquito net, but outside. Cav. X. (Tag. also has *ande de saya* 'under the skirt, hen pecked', per Dr. T. Ramos.)

Summary

Examination of some specific words in Ternateño has shown that the use of words sorts out their speakers and gives clues to change. Reports by people in Ternate confirm the impression that older people are more conservative in their speech at all levels. They are more likely to retain terms that are not now being used by younger people, implying that the words are being phased out of the language. The bulk of these obsolescent terms are either Spanish or Mardika, terms considered to have been brought by the original settlers from Indonesia. The folk etymology Mardika does not appear to be dropping out. Some of these cluster around certain domains, such as exclamations.

And, we have seen, as would be expected, younger people are the main introducers of new terms. The bulk of these are from Tagalog and English, and many of them would be classed as slang, and many of these must have been consciously creative. Education has brought in many terms, too. Those older people educated under the Spaniards have tended to introduce Spanish terms; and in this century, English terms have been introduced, especially by the more educated people.

The languages from which words have been borrowed are sorted out in Ternateño according to the frequency of occurrence in speech. Tagalog and English terms both seem to be on the increase, especially those terms being introduced by young people. The words that the original settlers from Indonesia brought are disappearing, suggesting that we are now able to witness the very last of this trend and that quite possibly many more terms were brought from Indonesia during the seventeenth century and have long died out from Ternateño, as well, possibly, as from the other dialects of Chabacano.

Regarding divergences from the source languages of words in Ternateño, differences are found of several types. We find changes of meaning from Spanish by specialization in Ternateño (e.g., *abilidad*), by simply drift (e.g., *kuryoso*), and by changing frequency (e.g., *anda*). We have seen different meanings becoming distinguished by different forms of one source word (*anda* versus *andar*), and we have seen divergences among the dialects of Chabacano in the ways they have diverged semantically from the source language (e.g., *tamyeŋ*). And semantic changes have been demonstrated, some in response to cultural differences (e.g., kin terms).

Divergences from English may reflect current use in Ternateño of obsolescent or low-frequency words in American English (e.g., *kaswal*), specialization (e.g., *kecher*), and adaptation to cultural differences (e.g., *karoliŋ*).

Words borrowed into Ternateño usually are not equipped with new grammatical markers, unlike the situation of loan words in, say, English or Tagalog. Rather, they appear to be "Ternateñized" mostly by phonological changes at first, and sometimes, by changes in meaning.

Regarding grammatical markers, it has been shown that a good share of the borrowed grammatical markers survive only as unproductive artifacts, e.g., Spanish gender markers that survive for some use of definite and indefinite markers in Ternateño, where the gender distinction is usually not made. The exceptions are mostly words referring to people and animals, so we find that the gender markers of Spanish have moved in the direction of sex markers in Chabacano, though they are used infrequently and inconsistently in Chabacano. We also have seen that *se*, reflexive of Spanish, is unproductive in Ternateño, and *se* or *ase* or *hase* 'to make or do something' may also be on the road to unproductive artifact, though it is used in conjunction with a few Tagalog words. Some productive grammatical markers from Spanish include the sex markers of indefinite and definite articles, and *-o* versus *-a* endings. Some Spanish grammatical markers are regularly abbreviated or have an abbreviated variant, especially the *de* and *el* from Spanish. Tagalog has also loaned some productive grammatical markers, including *ma-* (verbal marker) and *ika* (cardinal marker).

Reduplication, which occurs frequently in Chabacano, mostly on words from Spanish, Tagalog, and Mardika sources, may for the Spanish words have had some influence by Tagalog and other Philippine languages, which use reduplication a lot. English appears to have been much more resistant to, or inappropriate for, reduplication.

Many two-or-more part phrases in Ternateño are found in which the words are from two or more sources, some Spanish–Tagalog, others English–Tagalog, etc. Since many words and phrases from English as well as possibly Spanish have been borrowed via Tagalog, the combining and the changes of meaning may have taken place in that medium rather than in Ternateño. It is difficult to sort out the medium.

Many other phenomena are found in this section on divergences from source languages, also, for instance, divergence between dialects of Chabacano, and of synonyms of words presented that have been borrowed from another source language.

Noting divergences between the dialects has been another way of examining changes that have taken place in the dialects, since we know historically that they came from a common source. Chabacano apparently entered the Philippines in the seventeenth century from Indonesia to the Manila Bay area and spread from there, southward again, to Zamboanga and later to Cotabato City. Differences in meanings between the dialects show the Manila Bay dialects to be more closely related to each other than to Zamboangueño; and Zamboangueño and Cotabato Chabacano are closely related. The Manila Bay dialects have more Spanish vocabulary, and Philippine terms have not entered so heavily into the basic vocabulary as they have in Zamboangueño. Whereas the Manila Bay dialects are continually influenced by Tagalog, Zamboangueño and Cotabato Chabacano show increasing influence by the Cebuano Bisayan language. Caviteño (and Ermiteño) have been most influenced continuously by Spanish, whereas Ternateño seems to have been mostly ignored by Spaniards after the initial importance of the town as a lookout site early in the eighteenth century.

We have seen that of the many bidialectal synonym sets having one word in Tagalog and the other in Spanish, Ternateño speakers usually use the Tagalog more frequently, or exclusively, while Caviteño speakers use the Spanish more frequently, or exclusively. That Caviteño has a somewhat greater number of Spanish terms used with greater frequency is probably the result of more contact with Spaniards throughout the Spanish occupation. Another difference between Ternateño and Caviteño speakers is found with Tagalog–Tagalog synonym sets, where Caviteño uses one Tagalog word, Ternateño another.

Cotabato Chabacano uses different Spanish words then Ternateño for similar meanings, uses different Philippine-based terms, and has somewhat different meanings for some Spanish-based words than does Ternateño. I have also noted that Cotabato Chabacano uses two forms of Spanish words to distinguish different meanings (*serka* versus *aserka*), and Cotabato Chabacano speakers distinguish social classes by the words the speakers choose from a set of synonyms.

Zamboangueño and Ternateño color terms differ in interesting ways.

Ternateño appears to have retained a couple of terms of Indonesian source, whereas Zamboangueño has Spanish-based terms.

Zamboangueño differences have been shown by different meanings for the same source word and different words for the same meaning. Zamboangueño also has much greater social style variation than does Ternateño, reflecting the history of the people in Zamboanga in contrast with those in Ternate. The divergences between the dialects can be seen as overlapping with changes noted by frequency.

Examination of Ternateño by certain semantic domains has been another way of revealing changes taking place in the language. The source languages are sorted out by the domains into which their words have been borrowed. English, for instance, has evidently been an important carrier of twentieth century culture, as shown by heavy loans in the domains of modern military, education, medicine, administration, government, sports, and young peoples' culture. Portuguese and Mardika terms are few in number and are probably obsolescent.

Synonym sets are very largely composed of one Tagalog word and one Spanish word. Clearly, the Tagalog word has been added, and in many cases has become the more frequently-used term.

Some source languages associated with certain domains include Spanish, Tagalog, and Chinese terms for cooking and food; Tagalog for fruits, vegetables and fish; Spanish, then Tagalog for local place names; and heavy influence by Tagalog for names of body parts. Marine terms are Spanish, with Tagalog and Mardika terms. Of the idioms and metaphorical expressions in Ternateño, some appear to be local idioms using words borrowed from another language (some possibly translations of Tagalog idioms), while for others it appears the idiom itself was borrowed.

I have described processes of relexification that are currently taking place or have recently taken place in an established creole language. The data suggests that the changes taking place are no different qualitatively from the types of change found in noncreole languages. As with noncreole languages, not all the vocabulary is being relexified; rather, the language appears more likely to retain the words from some languages than from others.

There appears to be pan-Philippine agreement on the types of borrowings as well as specific borrowing. Extent of continuing exposure to source languages and prestige of the source language and its speakers appear to be factors influencing the rates of adoption and loss of words. And, as in English and other "natural" languages, the words borrowed in are simultaneously coming from multidonor languages, and there appear to be no mechanisms to halt or change the situation.

The lexicon will probably continue to grow, with the current trend of many more words entering the language than dropping from it, and some words becoming specialized in meaning but very few generalizing. The different dialects of Chabacano have different sources from which to draw for new vocabulary. Ternateño is borrowing largely Tagalog and English words, while Zamboangueño is borrowing largely Cebuano Bisayan and English words. Even though the dialects continue to diverge, mutual intelligibility will probably remain high, because Cebuano Bisayan and Tagalog are closely related, with many easily recognizable cognates, and because so many people know a fair amount of English.

Acknowledgment

The project is supported by NIH MH-20102 from June 1, 1971 through September 30, 1973, and June 1, 1974 through May 31, 1975, and CRIS, Stanford University, from October 1, 1973 through March 1, 1974. Field work in the Philippines was conducted from June 1, 1971 through April 17, 1973 and in Spanish archives May–July 1973. I am especially grateful for the help and advice of Antero Icasiano of Ternate and Cavite City, Philippines, throughout the entire period of the project.

Notes

1. Three languages spoken in Ternate, Moluccas, during the seventeenth century were Malay, Bahasa Ternate (Indo–Pacific), and the language of the Mardikas, presumably the creole brought to the Philippines. The latter was recorded in manuscripts by an Agustinian priest about 1606 (cited by Perez, 1901, from Osario) and a Jesuit priest around 1660 (cited by Murillo Velarde, 1749). My search for the Jesuit document continues.

2. **Abbreviations used:** Cav. = Caviteño, Chi. = Chinese, Cot. Chab. = Cotabato Chabacano, Engl. = English, Hil. = Hiligaynon, Mal. = Malay, Mar. = Mardika (words that in the opinion of Ternateños were brought to the Philippines from the Molucca Islands in the seventeenth century), Prt. = Portuguese, Skr. = Sanskrit, Tag. = Tagalog, Tern. = Ternateño, Zbo. = Zamboangueño. Most of the words shown appear in a dictionary I am in the process of compiling. If data for each entry has been gathered for the other dialects of Chabacano, these have been included. An X marks identity with the Ternateño entry. Information on the other dialects was given by Antero Icasiano for Caviteño, S. Isabelita Riego de Dios for Cotabato Chabacano, and Charles Frake for Zamboangueño; I gratefully acknowledge their help. Ternateño synonyms for each entry are given whenever available. Some of these are from taped transcriptions gathered in the field; of these, the text code number appears to indicate the text is available for review.

Some notes on the designation of etymology are relevant here. First, the indication that a word is Mardika, rather than indicating that it can be found in a dictionary as one can with words from other languages, means that (1) local speakers say the word is Mardika, and usually (2) I have not yet found another etymological explanation for the term. This folk etymology is interesting in itself. The notion that there is a category of words that belong exclusively to this language is a notion not shared with speakers of other dialects of Chabacano. Even though a few of these words do survive in the dialects of Chabacano (e.g., *endenantes* in Zamboangueño), the folk etymology as coming from Mardika does not, suggesting that the etymological category "Mardika" emerged after the split of Zamboangueño from Ternateño. Second, sometimes the ultimate source indicated does not sort out the medium through which Ternateño speakers adopted the word. They were presumably never in contact with Sanskrit speakers, for instance, and have undoubtedly learned Sanskrit words through Tagalog. Whenever the evidence is clear that there has been another language as vehicle for adopting a word, I have tried to indicate so in my etymological notation. Similarly, many English and even Spanish adopted words may have come into Ternateño via Tagalog, so that the simple designation of English or Spanish as source is sometimes somewhat misleading for this examination of the history of lexical changes. Regarding folk etymology, however, it may also be that along with borrowing in a Spanish or English word from Tagalog, the knowledge of the source of the word may be borrowed also.

Some words are designated as of Spanish origin even though they could also be Portuguese. Some words are designated as of Tagalog origin even though many other Philippine words share the identical form. Not every "Tagalog" word can be found in a Tagalog dictionary; some are designated so by Tagalog informants.

The etymological analyses of the words presented are still under examination and are considered quite tentative. One of the fears of anyone doing etymological analysis is that it has been incomplete. In the case of many of these words presented, especially, the analysis has barely begun. Information will be welcomed by the author.

For the lexical entries in this paper, if the word of the source language is identical to that in Chabacano, the source word does not appear with the name of the source language. Similarly, if the English gloss of the source word is identical to the gloss of the Chabacano word, then the source gloss is omitted. Synonyms and texts in which they appear are sometimes indicated even if they are not relevant to the discussion in the section under which they are found. They will be found to be relevant to discussions in other sections of the paper. If frequency is not specified, then no relative frequency is implied.

3. A frequency count of the some 7000 words included in some 2500 pages of transcriptions of tapes would yield some insights into the changes taking place in the language. Such a count is being contemplated. Most of the words used in this paper are from some 15,000 entries gathered from the dictionary in progress, to be published by Australia National University.

4. One of the characteristics of all the dialects of Chabacano, possibly with the exception of Cotabato Chabacano, seems to be the frequent use of sex-related terms for expletives and name-calling, even by women and little girls—terms that would be considered inappropriately vulgar in Spanish, English, or other Philippine languages.

5. The language also has some artifacts of earlier stages of source languages. For instance, Iberian terms are sometimes difficult to sort into Spanish versus Portuguese, because they were closer to one another in the sixteenth and seventeenth centuries than they are today. Early twentieth century English terms are also found, such as *dear* referring to high prices.

References

Frake, Charles O.
    1968 *Semantic structure and lexical origins in Philippine Creole Spanish.* Seminar on
          Pidgin and Creole Languages, Jamaica. Printed as Lexical Origins and Semantic
          Structures in Philippine Creole Spanish. In *Pidginization and creolization of languages* edited by Hymes, pp. 223–242. Cambridge, England: Cambridge University Press, 1971.

Molony, Carol H.
  1973a *Lexical Changes in Philippine Creole Spanish*. Paper presented at the XI International Congress of Ethnological and Anthropological Sciences, Chicago. *To appear* in its proceedings by Mouton, The Hague, 1975: 22pp.
  1973b Sound Changes in Chabacano. In *Parangal Kay Cecilio Lopez: Essays in honor of Cecilio Lopez on his 75th birthday* edited by Andrew B. Gonzalez. *Philippine Journal of Linguistics Special Monograph Issue*, No. 4, 38–50. Quezon City: Linguistic Society of the Philippines.
Murillo Velarde, Pedro, S.J.
  1749 *Historia do la provincia de Philippinas de la Compania de Jesus*. Manila: Lib. III.
Perez, Fr. Elvira
  1901 *Catalogo bio-bibliografico de los Religioso Agustinos*. Manila: Santo Tomas University.
Vicente, Alonso Zamora
  1967 *Dialectologia española*. Madrid: Editorial Gredos.

Lexical Expansion within a Closed System

IAN F. HANCOCK

I discussed in an earlier article a possible sequence of events leading to the establishment of English on the West African coast (1972). This involved the retention of the nautical varieties of the English spoken by the British seamen who (it was suggested) formed permanent family communities with Africans on the Guinea Coast during the early seventeenth century and perhaps earlier. This situation lasted until the growing traffic in African slaves upset African–European relationships to the extent of making such communities impossible on the same basis of equality. These European settlers were known as Lançados (see Note 1 at end of chapter).

It was further suggested that many features of the West African creoles, as well as those elsewhere in the Atlantic area, constitute a core of direct retention demonstrably traceable to the early Lançado speech and that at the time of its acquisition by Africans, the social situation within the communities was an equable one.

During these years, a creole population of European and African parentage was coming into being and establishing itself as a privileged group on the coast. To the indigenous Africans, they were Europeanized in language, culture, and appearance and they received as middlemen special deference from visiting Europeans. Their language in particular had especial prestige; this was thought of as being the English of the first Lançado settlers, although with the passage of time, the proportion of actual British-born speakers to Africans in the settlements tilted heavily toward an African and Eurafrican majority, and what was still called English was in fact taking on more and more non-European features—in other words, creolizing.

As long as there were European-born members of the communities to expand the local speech by drawing upon their various English dialects to supplement it where the restricted nautical speech was inadequate, it could continue as a variety of English, in the sense of taking on lexical and structural accretions having their origins somewhere in the British Isles. This period of adoption from the home dialects probably accounts for the considerable regional vocabulary (of British origin) in modern Krio, much of which was unlikely to have existed in the original nautical lingua franca, where the reverse process of dialect leveling would have excluded from general use items not familiar to everybody.

Geert Koefoed (1976) is probably right when he suggests that creolization is not initially the nativization of a pidgin, but its becoming established as the first language of a community, and is thus an adult, rather than a child-initiated process, the children following the adult models. The establishment of any nonnative language in a community as its first language (cainoglossia) may or may not involve the retention of the ancestral tongue, although it usually does lead to its eventual replacement (as in many Amerindian or immigrant communities). The processes of the linguistic stabilization of a pidgin by adult speakers challenge the current claims made for the language acquisition device (see, e.g., Selinker, 1972).

With the decline of the domestic situation of the first period, however, and the growth of a more uniformly creole (mulatto) population propagating among itself, centered around the factories and slaving stations, the language was being transmitted less by Englishman to African and more by Eurafrican adults to their children. Indigenous tribal Africans resident in the areas around the settlements must also have acquired some knowledge of the language; those brought from further afield as slaves probably had less opportunity to learn from the creoles, and learned the language in rudimentary form only, as pidginized creole.

The prestige, plus sheer universality of English[1] was such, that even when the non-African varieties were no longer spoken locally, or sufficiently widely in the West African environment, and had become a closed system for contributing means of grammatical and lexical augmentation to the African varieties, rather than expand the creole by drawing upon the available African languages, English continued to be the preferred source. English-derived morphemes already part of the creole were employed whenever possible. This was made doubly necessary by the limited currency of the African languages themselves.

By processes of natural linguistic evolution, English-derived morphemes already available were remodeled, often undergoing semantic modification to yield accreted creolized forms having no English-language source, e.g., Krio *sweet piss* for 'diabetes'. Similarly, structural expansion made use of existing internal resources, such as combining the past tense marker *bin* with the infinitive marker *foh* to provide a conditional

---

[1] "English" here refers to a collection of related dialects. So-called "World English" had not yet come into being.

'should have'. These do not have locatable African models and may be regarded as examples of true, or noncalqued, creolization. The majority of such examples, however, are demonstrable calques. While lexicons differ considerably from language to language in West Africa, structure and idiom share much greater currency, and models for calques (such as *big eye* for 'greedy', or *take belly* for 'conceive') can be found very extensively throughout the area. Loan translations of this sort had a good chance of being widely intelligible, relying as they did upon Panafrican idiom and English-derived morphemes.

The language of the Lançados-turned-creoles must have reached a point of maximum difference in its pendulum swing from English, as indicated by, e.g., Sranan, which, having developed in a non-English-language environment has not decreolized, especially phonologically, as rapidly as Krio. For English sailors visiting creole communities in later years, when the period of very sporadic contact slowly gave way to large-scale commerce, the local inhabitants would have had to relearn a kind of English intelligible to the Europeans. Eldred Jones has remarked upon a more anglicized contact speech, Talkee-Talkee, being spoken alongside Krio (Note 2). Dillard, too, suggests that while many slaves in the United States spoke a pidginized yet intelligible English, some reportedly spoke a distinct, far "deeper" variety that has been referred to as "Guinea speech" and that Dillard goes as far as to call a creole that was " . . . closer to Saramaccan" than to Gullah (Dillard, 1975, p. 96). This Guinea speech, if it existed, was probably the same as the Lançado creole discussed in this paper. Africans being transported were likely to have heard more of, and learned more of, the Talkee-Talkee than of the home language of the creoles (discussed further in Hancock, 1975).

The examples below have been chosen from Krio in particular, but the processes discussed are equally applicable to related creoles in the Caribbean area and elsewhere, for which similar work is still in progress. Many of the examples given probably came into being during the African-to-African period of transmission during the nineteenth century, when recaptives were arriving in Freetown in concentrated numbers; some survive from the earlier period, e.g., "under-hand" for 'armpit' (Krio *onda-an,* Sranan *ondr'anu*) (Note 3), while the fact that the process is continuing in modern times is illustrated by examples such as Krio *wheel-pan* for 'hubcap', *presser-pin* for 'sewing-machine foot', *rubber-mint* for 'chewing gum', etc.

The processes of expanding the Krio lexicon while keeping it supposedly English related, include incoining, calquing, tonalizing, reduplication, and semantic extension. Each will be discussed in turn (Note 4).

Incoining

Incoining is the creation of new terms from morphemes already existing in the language (rather than a priori or totally "coined" creations, which appear to be minimal), e.g., having no apparent source in either English or any African language[2]: *anko* 'an accomplice or colleague' (*<and* +*co[mpany]*); *ai-savis* 'fawning or currying favor' (*<high* + *service*); *jakas-os* 'a glutton for hard work' (*< jackass* + *horse*); *man-kyan-tel* 'a dark horse, a mystery' (*< man* + *can't* + *tell*); *triminit* 'a very short-tempered person' (*< three* + *minutes*); *waiwoh* 'a casual or carefree person' (*< why* + *wo[rry]*); *bridin-mak* 'abdominal creases resulting from childbirth' (*< breeding* + *marks*); *kot-nek* 'skin creases around the neck (a sign of beauty)' (*< cut* + *neck*); *bak-swim* 'the backstroke' (*< back* + *swim*); *tai-wata* 'to tread water' (*< tie* + *water*); *cher-kov* 'to take a stroll' (*< tear* + *curve*); *doti-boi* 'pig's trotters' (*< dirty* + *boy*); *kis-ich-oda* 'a style of braiding the hair' (*< kiss* + *each* + *other*); *flan-ship* 'airplane' (*< flying* + *ship*); *flai-bowt* 'seaplane' (*< fly* + *boat*); *moto-rowla* 'steamroller' (*< motor* + *roller*); *owbey-di-win(d)* 'type of loose, flapping pants' (*<obey* + *the* + *wind*), *freyd-na-fam* 'scarecrow' (*<afraid* + *na* + farm); *wer-lef* 'hand-me-down clothes' (*<wear* + left).

A series of indigenous incoinings employing the enclitic suffix *-na* may also be listed here. This appears originally to have been either a regular syntactic function of prepositional *na* with subsequent abbreviation, for example, *growna* 'an urchin' (*< gro na trit* 'grew up in the streets'), or perhaps from Manding languages, in which postpositional *na* has a similar function: Mdg. *buŋ na* 'in the house', cf. Krio *tritna* 'street girl' (*< street* + *na*). This appears to have established a pattern for similar incoinings in which *-na* acts agentively: *wansaina* 'thing better left aside for the present' (*< one* + *side* + *na*); *draina* 'a thin person' (*< dry*, i.e., "skinny" + *na*); *abona* 'a waif' (*< I* + *born* + *na*) (Note 5); *krachna* 'a soccer shot barely scraping the goal post' (*< scratch* + *na*). Such morphological devices are rare in the creoles.

Calquing

Calquing, or adoption–translation, was probably not widely employed as a method of augmenting the lexicon during the early period; it results from insufficient acquaintance with the original vocabulary, and at that time, Lançados were present to supply new English lexicon as needed. It appears instead to have developed later, when, in the multilingual situa-

---

[2] There remains the possibility that some of these may be calqued forms whose models have not yet been traced.

tions of the slaving depots, African captives would have acquired the Eurafrican creole in pidginized form, as the Talkee-Talkee discussed above. They would not have remained long enough, nor have had adequate social contact with the creoles, to have learned their language. On arrival in the Americas, the situation made the continued use of this pidginized–anglicized creole, and its subsequent creolization there, inevitable.

Because the period of maximum calquing into Krio probably took place during the nineteenth century, when over 200 African languages were spoken in Freetown at one time, it is not easy to trace a calqued form in Krio to any particular language. Indeed, as noted above, the same idiom very frequently occurs in many African languages. Thus, the equivalents listed here are not necessarily the immediate sources for the calques, but are included by way of illustration (Note 6).

Practically all calques refer to nonbasic concepts. While a pidgin would need terms for, say, "eye" and "child," a more specific term for "pupil of the eye" would have been unnecessary. A mother tongue, however, as the means of expression for every experience its speakers may encounter, will at some time require a term for "pupil" specifically. Not having acquired the term from the Europeans or Eurafricans, speakers of indigenous languages could draw upon these, translating their component morphemes into the Creole. Thus, e.g., Yoruba ɔmɔ l'odzu meaning 'pupil', but literally 'child in the eye' yields the new, additional lexemes yai-pikin or beybi-yai in Krio. Likewise while "hand" and "stomach" are primary terms, "palm of the hand" is secondary. Jamaican calques upon the African idiom (such as Ewe asi-vome 'palm', (<asi 'hand" + vome 'stomach') and acquires the further term han-beli (beli-han in Trinidad) for this concept. The following may be listed as examples: bobi-mot 'nipple' (cf. Ngombe monoko wa libeli 'nipple', literally, 'mouth of the breast'); yeys-doti 'cerumen, earwax' (cf. Mende wɔli kpɔlii 'cerumen, earwax', literally 'ear dirt'); big-yai 'covetous' (cf. Igbo anya uku 'covetous', literally, 'big eyes'); get beleh 'to be(come) pregnant' (cf. Temne ba kor 'to be(come) pregnant', literally, 'have belly'); ron-beleh 'diarrhea' (cf. Fula dogu redu 'diarrhea', literally, 'run belly'); dia (i) 'expensive', (ii) 'scarce, of a person' (cf. Yoruba ɔwɔ 'expensive; scarce'); kot at 'to make angry' (cf. Mende ndi tee 'to make angry', literally 'cut heart'); swit mot 'flattery' (cf. Twi ano dɛdɛ 'flattery', literally, 'sweet mouth'); wan pot 'a kind of rice dish' (cf. Wolof bena tʃin 'a kind of rice dish', literally 'one pot'); mit mi na elbo 'stew diluted so as to serve more people' (cf. Yoruba kpade mi ni gbɔ̃wɔ 'diluted stew', literally, 'meet me at the elbow'); oni (i) honey (ii) bee (cf. Yoruba ɔyĩ, Mende kɔmi, 'honey; bee'); do klin 'daybreak' (cf. Wolof bər bu sɛt 'daybreak', literally, 'day clean'; Mandinka dugu jɛra

'daybreak', literally, 'the land is cleaned', etc.); *mami-wata* 'water sprite' (cf. Yoruba *iya olodo* 'water sprite', literally 'mother of the waters'); *tumos* (i) 'too much' (ii) 'very much' (cf. Twi *dodo,* Yoruba *kpukpɔ,* 'too much, very much'); *weytin du* 'why' (cf. Igbo *gɛnɛ mɛrɛ* 'why', literally, 'what (thing) does'); *god os* 'praying mantis' (cf. Mandinka *ala suwo* 'praying mantis', literally, 'God's horse'); *nows owl* 'nostril' (cf. Igbo *oyele imi* 'nostril', literally, 'nose hole'); *beleh wod* 'confidences, private thoughts' (cf. Mandinka *kɔrɔ ma kuma* 'confidences, private thoughts', literally, "belly (or inside) speech').

Sometimes what appear to be calques occur in more than one creole, but no African source is (so far) locatable, e.g., Krio *fit-yai* 'impudence; to be impudent' (as well as Gambian Krio *yai-fit* 'impudence' (<*eye* + *fit*), and Trinidad Creole French *furé dwɛ na zyé* 'to insult', literally, 'poke finger in eye').

Tonalizing

Tonalizing involves the creation of a new or specialized semantic concept, related to and having the same phonological shape as the source form, but being distinguished from it by tonal modification: *bróda* 'brother', *brodá* 'term of address to elder male'; *kóntri* 'country, countryside', *kontrí* 'a rural inhabitant'; *rubí* 'a ruby', *rúbi* 'the proper name Ruby'; *sísta* 'sister', *sistá* 'a nun; term of address to elder female'; *ténki* 'thank you', *tenkí* 'gratitude'; *trimbul* 'to tremble, shake', *trimbúl* 'a shaking, flapping thing such as a pair of baggy trousers'; *watá* 'water', *wáta* 'to sprinkle water on' (Note 7).

Reduplicating

Reduplicating (Note 8) appears to serve to limit the number of homophones, for example *was* 'wash', *waswas* 'wasp'; *san* 'sun', *sansan* 'sand'; *town* 'penis' (<'stone'), *towntown* 'stone', etc., although it may be argued that the concept of mass of quantity is shared by each of these reduplicated forms; further instances of semantic extension by reduplication include *af* 'half', *afaf* 'mediocre'; *kona* 'corner', *konakona* 'secret, illicit; a secret sweetheart'; *mas* 'crush, mash', *masmas* 'bribery', 'small change', etc.

Semantic Extension

Semantic extension without reduplication occurs where the primary gloss for an item has a source form parallel, but for which a further meaning exists with no traceable English origin. Examples of some of these, which may in fact prove to be calques themselves, include *jagwa* (i) 'Jaguar automobile' (ii) 'super, terrific, splendid'; *grani-frok* (i) 'old fashioned dress, a granny's frock', (ii) 'an old-time Coast penny' (from the robed figure of Britannia on one side; similar calques in Hausa and other languages); *wata* (i) 'water', (ii) 'any unspecified liquid'; *kro* (i) 'to crow; to boast', (ii) 'a rooster's comb'; *man* (i) 'man', (ii) 'male of any species, young or adult'; *pleyt-pisis* (i) 'dishrag' (<*plate* + *pieces*), (ii) 'an effeminate male'; *sawa* (i) 'sour', (ii) 'purulent, festering'.

The intricacy of some Krio lexical derivations in this category may be shown by the word meaning 'scab' or 'dried mucus in the nose', which is *krawo*. The same word has as its primary meaning 'burnt food stuck to the bottom of the pot', and derives from a reference to the Kru people of Liberia, who call themselves *Krao* or *Klao* (Note 9) and who are well known for their fondness for this. The secondary gloss is a calque upon Yoruba *eekpa* meaning both a scab, and burnt food (Note 10).

The position of modern English vis-à-vis Krio has had some repercussions upon it, such as the common folk-etymologizing of African-derived items, reflecting a desire to anglicize the language or spelling pronunciations, probably resulting from the efforts of those attempting to improve their command of English from books, but never hearing the spoken English word, or else the over-correction of Krio pronunications in accordance with English phonology.

Folk etymologies include for instance *bat* 'girlfriend' and hence the further term *klob*, supposedly English 'bat' (but cf. Temne *u-baths* 'ladyfriend, favorite wife'); *kekrebu* or *kekerebu* 'dead', said to be derived from 'kick the bucket' (but cf. Gã *kekre* 'stiff' + *bu* 'become'); or *kontofili* 'misunderstanding', said to be from English 'counter feelings' (but cf. Susu *kɔntɔfili* 'embarrassed; troubles') (Note 11).

Spelling pronunciations include *drojis* 'druggist', *keytrain* 'Catherine', *listin* 'listen', *banaisi* 'Bernice', *salmon* 'salmon', *fastina* 'fastener'. Some of these may prove to be phonological retentions of earlier British forms.

Examples of overcorrection are *skola* 'to collar someone', *kwilt* 'porcupine quill', *raul* 'row, argument', *streyn* 'train (of thought)', *rimaind* 'to remand', *bait* 'bet', *flando* 'flounder (fish)', *wisko* 'whiskers'.

Changes that have taken place in English as well as Krio account for some of the negative attitudes of Krio speakers toward their language. Pronunciations such as *kyandul, gyalik, skit, jonsin*, ('candle', 'garlic,' 'skate (fish),' 'Johnson') are often regarded as resulting from laziness or sloppy speech, it being generally unknown that these were at one time also legitimate British phonological forms.

For some younger creoles, however, their language is regarded as a badge of ethnicity; with the current American-influenced assertion of Black awareness, Krio is sometimes identified in a positive way with "soul talk," a kind of English uniquely black. This is especially evident among the creole youth resident outside of Sierra Leone (e.g., in London, Toronto, Washington, D. C., or New York). But for the majority, Krio is still a way of speaking punishable in the schools, a means of expression without books or newspapers, having no official status, and apart from its use in news-readings, being used in broadcasting only for children's programs—and seldom even then. Against this stands English, fulfilling all the positive roles of communication and providing access to the outside world. It is hardly surprising that fluency in it is regarded as a highly desirable social and educational goal. While English intrusions into Krio are almost never corrected by parents, Krio intrusions into English generally are. A person will *spik* 'speak' English, but *tok* 'talk' Krio; if he makes a mistake in speaking English, he is said to *shut* 'shoot', and his mistakes are *shots* 'shots' (singular and plural). The expression *yu shut mi sai* 'you've shot me in the side' means 'you've made an error in your English while speaking to me', although one may *lok* 'lock' a person on the other hand with a Krio word or expression—that is, one that is too "deep," i.e., cryptic or unfamiliar. These are usually of African, rather than English origin.

Such attitudes have far-reaching adverse effects both upon personality and in the more long-term area of education, and it is clearly necessary to make known the history of creole languages to Creole speakers at the popular level, freed from the misconceptions of colonial brainwashing, before positive steps can start being taken to rectify the situation (Note 12).

Notes

1. This term normally applies to Portuguese settlers only, but is here used to include the British and other Europeans as well. Several such (Portuguese) groups were established in Sierra Leone, their members acting as middlemen for factories such as the one at Bence Island. Because of their constant evasion of the tax imposed by the Portuguese crown on all overseas trade, these Afro-Portuguese middlemen were liable to execution according to a law passed in 1518; but because of their remoteness, this law was seldom enforced. As English influence increased in Sierra Leone, the Portuguese moved to other areas or, especially in the case of the Lançados, became totally assimilated into the indigenous population. By 1750, the Portuguese influence in Sierra Leone was minimal (see Boxer, 1969, p. 31; Hancock, 1975, p. 216; Hair, 1966; Nolasco da Silva, 1972; and especially Rodney, 1970). There is little evidence to indicate that there was much communication between these Portuguese and English groups, one of the first of which must have been the merchants whom

Thomas Wyndham and Francisco Pinteado left behind, against their will, at Benin in 1553 (R. Hakluyt, 1599, pp. 12–13), and who included among their numbers Nicholas Lambert, son of the former Mayor of the City of London (Paul Christophersen, personal communication).

2. Jones (1962) assembles data that " . . . point to the existence . . . of two broad patterns of speech, the *talkee-talkee patois,* and the language we now call Krio, both of which seem to have flourished side by side (and still do), and which over the years may have influenced one another" (p. 26). "The talkee-talkee patois . . . was used in conversation with Europeans, and the patois [i.e., Krio] . . . was used among the local inhabitants in conversation with each other, and which [the European observer] calls unintelligible" (p. 21).

3. Compare this, for example, with an adoption from the later period having the same meaning, namely, *am-owl* < arm + hole (cf. Jamaican creole *aam-uol,* same derivation). In the Krio spelling used here, ow and ey represent the mid high and o and e the mid-low vowels, except when final, when o represents the mid-high, and oh and eh the mid-low vowels, thus *foto* 'photo' represents [fɔtó], etc. Other African languages are spelled using International Phonetic Alphabet symbols.

4. Not discussed here are African–English compounds such as *gbeyment* 'theft' (< Yoruba *gbe* 'take' + English *-ment*), *awangot* 'parsimonious' (< Yoruba *hawɔ* 'mean' + English *guts*), *flengbensish* 'smartly dressed' (< ? + English *-ish*), etc.

5. Attested by the Mende adoption from Krio (apparently no longer surviving in Krio itself) *abɔnabla* with the same meaning. The Mende final *-a* is the indefinite singular, back-formed from the definite singular: *abɔnabla* > *abɔnablɛi* (Krio *blai* = 'basket').

6. An extreme example of how widespread an interpretation may be is found in the name of the Mimosa pudica, or sensitive plant, in Krio called *set yu mami bowmbo* 'close your mother's vulva', often euphemized to *sok yu mami bobi* 'suck your mother's breasts'. Temne calls it *ya mompnɛ* 'mother cover yourself', in Mende it is *kpɛtɛ nana gbahagbɔmɛi* 'buttocks shut together', Yoruba has *kpatɔmo* 'close your thighs', Twi has *mumuankan kata w'ani na w'ɔsɛw rɛba* 'shut your eyes, your mother-in-law is coming', Nzima has *atɔfɔle mũwa lɔa* 'bride, close your lips', Ga has *ɔʃaɲɔ-mba* 'your mother-in-law is coming', Fula has *makbu rumbu* 'close the corn bin', Hausa *mata gara kafa* 'woman close the legs', Igbo *anasiɛyɛ ŋkpata voku* 'the king's first wife closed her legs', Nupe *ɛba 'ɔrɛbɛ* 'your husband is coming', and Efik *mba kikɔ* 'close the legs'. Many similar forms are found in the Bantu languages, while Caribbean versions include "Mary-shut-the-gate," "shame Mary," etc.

7. This is a widespread creole phenomenon: see the discussions by Berry (for Trinidad and Jamaica), Spears (for the Caymans) and Allsopp (for Guyana) in Craig (1976).

8. Not considered reduplicated forms are such simplex items as *titi* 'girl', *fufu* 'cassava dough', *deydey* 'dead', *ketket* 'hem-fastening clips', whose individual syllables carry no, or unrelated, meaning.

9. Cf. the Malay epithet *gĕragau* ('prawn') to describe the Malacca Creoles, or English *Frog* or *Froggie* for Frenchman, or *Kraut* (i.e., 'cabbage') for a German.

10. The geographical extent of an item's wandering may also be well shown by Krio *kreynkrey* or *kreynkreyn,* a mucilagenous vegetable species, Corchorus olitorius. The word seems to be of Twi origin, namely *kyɛrɛŋkyɛ* 'basket'. This was the source form for Jamaican Creole *kreng-kre* or *krengkreng,* also meaning 'basket', and hence the compound *kreng-*

kreng kalalu, a mucilagenous vegetable, callaloo, customarily gathered in a basket. In being brought to Sierra Leone with the Maroons, the second element was lost, leaving Krio *kreynkrey(n)* as the name of the slimy vegetable only. From Sierra Leone, the word then traveled to Trinidad with the free labor force during the 1840s, where *kleng-kleng* or *kreng-kreng* survives as a local name for red sorrel, and to Cameroon, where it has the forms *kering-kering* or *kering-keri,* meaning 'slimy', 'muddy', or 'mucilagenous', as well as being the name of a local edible plant. At least seven indigenous Sierra Leonean languages have adopted some form of the word from Krio.

11. There are several folk etymologies in Krio explaining English-derived items as well: *makleyt* 'vaccinate' (*<maculate*) is explained as < *mark* + *late,* i.e., after being vaccinated, a mark appears later. Similarly *kabaslot* 'an overall' (*<coverslut*) is explained as deriving from *Cabbah's lot,* Cabbah being a one-time merchant who sold cloth from a stall in a vacant lot.

12. Although this paper deals with lexical expansion without recourse to outside models, the same type of processes apply to the development of creole language structure. See in particular Bickerton (1975, Chapter 1).

References

Bickerton, Derek
  1975 *Dynamics of a creole system.* London: Cambridge University Press.
Boxer, C. R.
  1969 *The Portuguese seaborne empire, 1415–1825.* London: Hutchinson.
Craig, D. (ed.)
  In press *Proceedings of the Conference on Creole Languages and Educational Development.* London: New Beacon Books.
Dillard, J. (ed.)
  1975 *Perspectives on black English.* The Hague: Mouton.
Hair, Paul E. H.
  1966 The use of African languages in Afro-European contacts in Guinea, 1440–1560. *African Language Review* **5,** 5–26.
Hakluyt, R.
  1599 *Principal navigations* Vol. II.
Hancock, Ian F.
  1971 *A study of the sources and development of the lexicon of Sierra Leone Krio.* Ph. D. dissertation, University of London, School of Oriental and African Studies.
  1972 A domestic origin for the English-derived Atlantic creoles. *The Florida FL Reporter* **10** (spring/fall). Based on Hancock (1971).
  1975 Malacca Creole Portuguese: Asian, African or European? *Anthropological Linguistics* **17**(5), 211–236.
Jones, Eldred
  1962 Mid-nineteenth century evidence of a Sierra Leone patois. *Sierra Leone Language Review* **1,** 19–26.
Koefoed, Geert
  1976 Some remarks on the baby talk theory and the relexification theory. In *Readings in creole studies,* edited by M. Goodman *et al.* Antwerp: Story-Scientia Press.

Nolasco da Silva, Maria da Graça Garcia
1972 Subsidios para o estudo dos lançados na Guiné. *Boletin Cultural da Guiné Portuguesa* **105**.
Rodney, Walter
1970 *A history of the upper Guinea coast, 1545–1800*. Oxford, England: Clarendon Press.
Selinker, L.
1972 Interlanguage. *International Review of Applied Linguistics*, **10**, 209–231.

Finnish in America: A Case Study in Monogenerational Language Change

FRANCES KARTTUNEN

When pressed about the mechanics of language change, linguists generally describe the cumulative effect of small changes and imperfect learning over generations. Certain kinds of change are more likely to accumulate than others, especially in phonology, as witnessed by the similarity of historical changes in unrelated languages at different times. Often a single small change in a language will set off a series of adjustments until a whole new set of tensions and complexities results. All languages in use are constantly undergoing this sort of slow change. It is not aimless linguistic drift or a falling away from some ideal state, but principled and, to a point, predictable working out of ever present internal tensions.

When tensions arise from sudden close contact with another language, linguistic change can be massive and swift. The transformation of English after the Battle of Hastings is a most stunning documented example of this. Another is the accommodation of Spanish by Nahuatl, the language of the Aztecs, since the sixteenth century (Karttunen and Lockhart, 1976). Generally, however, one of the languages succumbs. The very Normans who brought a variety of French to England after 1066 were the offspring of Norse and Danish invaders of France not long before. After these "northmen" were ceded Normandy in 911, they maintained their West Scandinavian language only briefly. They had a practice of bearing double names, one Scandinavian and the other Frankish, and in thirty years' time, a chronicle relates that one Norman had to send his son away to be tutored in Danish.

At just the same time, other Vikings had moved east and established powerful trading colonies at Novgorod and Kiev. According to the Russian Primary Chronicle, the original ruler of the Novgorod settlement had the Scandinavian name Rurik, but a century later, despite unbroken contacts with Sweden and Gotland, leaders in Kiev were named Igor, Vladimir, and Yaroslav.

In both cases, in France and in Russia, a typical language contact situation obtained. Once a group of people came to stay and raise families in a new country with a different language, they were unable to maintain their own language more than a generation or two. The children learned the language of their country of residence and failed to master their parents' primary language (Jones, 1968, pp. 229–232, 244–266).

This, of course, has been the paradigm for almost all non-English speaking people who have settled in North America. Maintenance of a second language along with English requires tremendous pressure, and this pressure in almost every case has been one of rejection. Groups maintain their languages when they are isolated because of differences in religion (Catholics, Jews, Pietists), culture (Gypsies, any nonnorthwestern Europeans), or appearance (Africans, Indians, Asians). Only in cases of geographical isolation have home languages been maintained in a fairly neutral setting. Homogeneous settlements such as the various Scandinavian ones in the northern forests and plains of the United States and Canada have continued speaking their home countries' languages longer than immigrants in urban centers. For a while, such settlements had rather limited contact with English, and it was possible to remain monolingual in North America. Once contact began, however, English rather quickly took over (Haugen, 1969, pp. 244–260; Jalkanen, 1969, pp. 211–212; Hoglund, 1960, p. 129).

It might appear that internal language change and contact phenomena are quite different things. The following case study is presented to show the two at work, not across several generations, but in the speech of individuals. For these people, contact with English in early adulthood brought forth not novel and ad hoc devices for coping with the new language, but methods of dealing with ill-fitting material that were inherent in their native language. The immigrants who came to North America as adults neither lost their language nor spoke a deteriorated form of it, observers' claims to the contrary. Rather, they dealt with masses of new linguistic material in rational ways they had brought with them. We have evidence that suggests that some of the American-born who did not master their parents' language as a whole did, however, master the principles of morphology and pronunciation and can apply them productively in speaking English among themselves when they want to evoke the older generation and old country manners for humor or nostalgia.[1]

Finns came to North America in a wave of immigration between 1880 and 1920, when the United States imposed a rather small annual quota. They continued arriving in Canada in considerable numbers for a few years thereafter. But by then, the effects of the Bolshevik revolution, a

---

[1] Karttunen and Moore (1974) analyze a collection of stories, limericks and bilingual jokes written down and circulated among American Finns by Mr. Heino Puotinen.

civil war at home, and World War I had undercut most of the motivation for moving to North America. In 1902, the peak year of emigration from Finland, 23,000 people left. As a result, in 1920 the United States census reported somewhat over 150,000 foreign-born Finns in the United States and over 130,000 American-born children in families where both parents were born in Finland. However, Finland had been a Russian grand duchy during most of this period, and Finns carried Russian papers, so they were sometimes counted as Russians. By 1920, many were undoubtedly extremely reluctant to reveal this to census takers and did what they could to mislead them. Also this figure does not include the sizable settlements in Canada or the fact that some Finns spoke Swedish as their home language. From Finnish records, it appears that over 300,000 left during this forty-year period. Men outnumbered women up to the war years, the unmarried vastly outnumbered the married for both men and women, and the significant age group was 16–30. They commonly traveled back and forth between Finland and America, and perhaps as many as a third eventually returned to Finland permanently. According to the 1960 census, there were still about 70,000 Finnish-born residents of the United States (Hoglund, 1960, pp. 6–8, 175).

This means that as minorities in North America go, the Finns were a minuscule group. In addition, they were ideal for the melting pot. They had very few identifying characteristics. Fair-skinned, Protestant, literate, their only noticable vices were alcoholism and socialism, which sometimes made them unwelcome in company towns. All they had to overcome was the language barrier, which was formidable for the adult immigrant but not so much so, generally, for his children. As a result, in most places, the familiar pattern obtained that the oldest child remained monolingual until he reached school. Then he suffered greatly learning English and did his siblings the favor of speaking English with them at home before they went to school. The home would then become generationally bilingual, the parents speaking Finnish to the children and being understood, the children speaking English to each other and their parents and being understood, and only the eldest of the children retaining a more than passive knowledge of Finnish.

The insecurities of the foreign-born and the first American-born generation—linguistic, social, political, and emotional—make them hard to approach. Both practice a great deal of self protection. The second generation born in America is very securely American and can afford an interest in the history of their families, but they are generally monolingual speakers of English.[2] If they learn Finnish, they do so by studying it in university courses, and what they learn is modern literary Finnish, a language

[2] In a few paragraphs, Jalkanen (1969, pp. 211–212) gives a more subjective and somewhat poignant description of the sudden cultural and linguistic transition.

the American Finns never spoke. So it is to the rapidly diminishing group of immigrants and some of their children that we must turn, despite the difficulties, to learn about the product of Finnish–English language contact known among Finns as "Finglish."

This Finglish, or American Finnish, has been the object of a number of investigations, the most thorough of which was, undoubtedly, the 1965 field trip for the Helsinki University archives led by Prof. Pertti Virtaranta. The information about American Finnish to follow is based on field notes made on that trip and material in Prof. Virtaranta's description published in 1971 (Virtaranta, 1971; Karttunen, 1966). Since then, the 236 hours of interviews have been transcribed and are available for study in Helsinki. In addition, there are several other sources of information about Finnish in America, and other quite different varieties of Finglish have been reported (Karttunen and Moore, 1974; Larmouth, 1974; Lehtinen, 1966). Time is running out for further collections, because for the most part, American Finnish is monogenerational. Its speakers were monolingual adult speakers of Finnish when they encountered English, a unique situation. There has been no pressure to perpetuate the results. If there turns out to be an English-based Finglish as well, that is also likely to be monogenerational, relying as it does on at least a passive knowledge of American Finnish. Time and assimilation combine to make Finnish in America an ephemeral as was Norse in Normandy.

When interviewed in 1965, Finns who had immigrated fifty years or more before were very uncomfortable about speaking Finnish to visitors from the old country. They felt their Finnish had deteriorated badly over the years, and they were universally apologetic. But in fact it was not the gradual cumulative effect of a half century away from home that marked their speech as emigrant speech. New arrivals in the heyday of immigration and visiting clergy from Finland had complained about the shocking Americanization of their language from the very first years.[3] On the other hand, in 1965, Finnish dialectologists were interested in the Finns in America as a repository of rural dialects no longer to be found at home.

These apparently contradictory characterizations of American Finnish as (1) invaded by English to the point of unintelligibility and (2) also remarkably conservative are both valid. For the visitor from the old country, American Finnish really was bewildering. It was full of English

---

[3] The indignant letters to the editors of Helsinki newspapers and to home parishes from outraged and scornful visitors to the American Finns in the first decades of the century (mostly from visiting clergy, who often did not stay long) are not easily accessible to American readers. But Haugen (1969, pp. 54–58) has translated excerpts from very similar letters written by Norwegian observers about the state their language had fallen into in America.

vocabulary, and to intimidate the greenhorn, there were special sentences which contained only loan words such as: *Pussaa[p] peipipoki petiruumasta kitsiin.* 'Push the babybuggy out of the bedroom into the kitchen.' The dialectologist, on the other hand, would observe that all these English loan words had been fitted to Finnish morphology and that they are inflected as one would expect them to be. In this sample sentence, grammatical relations are expressed with case endings, and in pronounciation, the imperative verb causes gemination of the initial consonant of the following word.

In a sizable sample from many different speakers, variant forms of loan words show dialectal differences from Finland. Speakers of Finnish dialects that have some initial consonant clusters have the same clusters in loan words from English. Speakers of dialects that permit only single initial consonants drop all but one consonant in loans:[4]

E *train* > AF *treini, reini*

Speakers of dialects that break up medial consonant clusters in native Finnish words by repeating the vowel of the preceeding syllable do so in English loans too:

Standard F *silmä, kolme* 'eye, three' > dialect *silimä, kolome*
E *De Kalb* > AF *Käläppi* (with intrusive vowel), *Tekalppi* (without)

Dialects that have no *f* replace it with initial *v* and medial *hv:*

E *farm* > AF *farmi, varmi*
E *stuff* > AF *staffi, toffi, tovhi*

American dialects also are reflected in American Finnish; *paana* 'barn', *paanari* 'partner', and *paalameeti* 'parlor maid' appear to be from northeastern coastal *r*-less English. Likewise, *paati* 'bath' seems to be from this same regional dialect in which long [a] appears in place of the front vowel [ä] in a number of words, including *bath*. It is probably also due to American dialectal variation that American Finnish has such pairs as *staffi, toffi* 'stuff'; *japi, joppi* 'job'; *äksitentti, eksitentti* 'accident', and *haali, hooli* 'hall'. The wide geographical spread of rather restricted American dialect features among American Finns is good evidence that the

---

[4] In this section, the burden is on the reader to keep in mind the phonetics of the English words cited. Finnish orthography makes a close match with the broad phonetics of the language. For this reason, to dispense with almost total redundancy, the words are not repeated in phonetic brackets. The letter *y* represents the high front rounded vowel [ü], and *ö* and *ä* are the front vowel counterparts to *o* and *a*. Long vowels are spelled with double letters. Geminate consonants are also indicated with double letters.

speakers spread these words among themselves and did not create all their English loan vocabulary on the spot.

This fitting of new words, often preserving some markedly regional pronunciation, into Finnish by sound simplification, replacement, or deletion is just how Swedish vocabulary has been taken into Finnish for centuries and is not an innovation due to American English influence. Moreover, in the speech of the immigrants, the majority of whom were adults when they encountered English, the Finnish inflectional paradigms remained intact, the phonological rules with dialectal variation remained in force, and the whole range of grammatical structures continued in use. This is evident not only in the interviews recorded, but in the masses of American Finnish newspapers, letters, plays, and poetry preserved over the past fifty years. In sum, for this generation there was no great deterioration of the language and very little minor change. They went on speaking their home dialects, often maintaining them in their relative isolation from standard literary Finnish after they had ceased to be spoken in their old home parishes.

Almost the whole substance of the language change of the Finland-born was vocabulary addition and replacement. It is no wonder that American Finns immediately took up English words concerning work: *kuori* 'quarry', *maini* 'mine' (iron, copper, coal), *paanari* 'partner', *paasi* 'boss', *kuitata* 'to quit', *junio* 'union'; American holidays: *fortsulai* 'Fourth of July', *haloviini* 'Halloween', *tenskivi* 'Thanksgiving'; and foodstuffs that had to be bought in American stores by their English names, even if they had their own names in Finnish: *käretsi* 'carrots', *häirinki* 'herring', *käpetsi* 'cabbage'. It is rather surprising that American Finnish should also replace such basic vocabulary as *talo* 'house', *huone* 'room', *järvi* 'lake', *mäki* 'hill', *juosta* 'to run', and *keskustella* 'to talk' with *haussi, ruuma, leeki, hilli, runnata,* and *tookentaa,* respectively. Rooming houses and place names may have been behind the nouns. The rationale of the verbs is more of a challenge to the imagination.

In any case, in loan vocabulary, nouns and adjectives appear to have a great lead on other parts of speech. In a sample of 378 different vocabulary items (excluding dialectal variation in form), which almost exhaustively covers the examples in the field notes and in Prof. Virtaranta's article, 78% are nouns and adjectives and 15% are verbs. There is one preposition, and the remainder includes many unanalyzed phrases such as *enuvei* < *anyway* and *aitunnou* < *I don't know*. This sample is based on material selected from the interviews as examples in discussion of semantics and morphology. As such, it may be that verbs are underrepresented, although intuitively it seems right. [These figures agree very closely with the ones Haugen (1969, p. 406) cites for American Norwegian and American Swedish.] It remains for the percentages and the relative frequency of use to be computed directly from the transcribed interviews. The unanalyzed phrases have very high frequencies, even by informants with poor knowledge of English. Their speech was liberally punctuated with *juu nou* < *you know, mai kutnes* < *my goodness,* and *jesseri* < *yes siree* to mention but a few.

To make a Finnish noun or adjective from an English one, a stem vowel is usually necessary for attaching inflectional suffixes. Of the 252 nouns and adjectives in the sample that have stem vowels appended, 87% are *i*-stems. Although *i* is a neutral vowel with respect to Finnish vowel harmony, stem *i* dissimilates to *e* in the plural, so it is not an optimally simple stem vowel from the point of view of phonology. Yet the preference for *i*-stem loans is quite old in Finnish, although it has never been exclusive. An invariant stem vowel pair would be *u/y* ([ü]) (the back and front counterparts in vowel harmony). For any given word ending in one of these vowels, the stem vowel would remain unchanged throughout the paradigm. These vowels never drop or dissimilate. But only six items in the sample are formed with *u/y*. There are 22 *a/ä* stems, although this vowel pair undergoes both dissimilation and deletion in various environments. Apparently, American Finnish does not shy away from native phonological complexities.

Most American Finnish verbs from English are of the *-ata* form, 83% in the sample. Many are paired with agentive *-ari* nouns. Faced with English *-er*, American Finnish sometimes simply made an *i*-stem of it, especially if it was not clearly agentive: *tiitseri* < *teacher, piiveri* < *beaver, lumperi* < *lumber.* But more often the English agentive *-er* was replaced with *-ari,* which has as its ultimate source Swedish loan words in Finnish:

> Sw *läkare* 'doctor', *riddare* 'knight', *borgare* 'bourgeois' > F *lääkäri, ritari, porvari*
> E *helper, heater, peddler* > AF *helppari, hiitari, petlari,* and the associated verbs *helpata, hiitata, petlata*

Again, this is not the phonologically least complex verb derivation, since *-ata* verbs alternate long and short stem vowels before suffixes and have a potential environment for consonant gradation.

In addition to the derivational processes for nouns and verbs, there are general phonetic rules for fitting loan words into Finnish. The major ones are the following.

1. Finnish has initial stress. This generally means shifting stress in English loans: E *Califórnia* > AF *Kálifornia, Kálivornia;* E *vacátion* > AF *vákeesi.* Previously, Finnish had done the same with other foreign loans: Sw *musιk* 'music' > F *músiikki;* Russian [pirók] 'pasty, pie' > F *piírakka.* Another way of having stress fall on the initial

syllable of a loan word is to drop an unstressed initial vowel or syllable: E *garáge* > AF *kráatsi,* E *apártment* > AF *pármentti,* E *exámple* > AF *sámppeli.*

2. Finnish has no voiced obstruents except *v.* In loan words, all voiced obstruents are devoiced but this one: E *busy* > AF *pisi,* E *girl-friend* > AF *köölfrentti.*

3. Palatal fricatives are replaced with alveolar ones: E *to shovel* > AF *soveltaa,* E *shower* > AF *saueri,* E *to push* > AF *pussata.*

4. Lenition of affricates takes place where the affricate must be syllable initial: E *chance* > AF *senssi,* E *to pinch* > AF *pinssata.* Where the affricate can be treated as two segments distributed over two syllables, the stop is often retained: E *to pitch* > AF *pitsata,* E *satchel* > AF *setseli, sesseli.* Together with devoicing and the change from palatal to alveolar articulation, this merges English [tš] and [dž] as AF *s, ts* depending on the syllable structure.

5. As might be expected, interdental fricatives are replaced with stops: E *south* > AF *sautti,* E *diphtheria* > AF *tipteeri,* E *that's enough* > AF *täts inaf.*

6. The labial glide *w* is replaced with the labial obstruent *v:* E *sweater* > AF *veteri,* E *whistle* > AF *visseli,* E *to work* > AF *vorkkia.* For some dialects that lack the voiceless labial fricative *f,* this is also replaced with its voiced labial counterpart *v* initially, *hv* medially, and sometimes the voiceless labial stop *p:* E *Philadelphia* > AF *Filatelfia, Vilatelhvia;* E *freight* > AF *preitti;* E *half and half* > AF *hääpnähääp.*

7. Generally, a consonant after a nasal is geminate, especially when it immediately precedes the stem vowel: E *agent* > AF *akentti,* E *tramp* > AF *trämppi.* This also tends to be the case after other resonants: E *nurse* > AF *nörssä,* E *De Kalb* > AF *Tekalppi.* But there are many exceptions to this: E *plenty* > AF *plänti,* E *point* > AF *pointi,* E *yard* > AF *jaarti* (rarely *jaartti*), E *beans* > AF *pinsi, pinssi.* The resonant-plus-geminate cluster has the advantage of not becoming opaque in regular Finnish consonant gradation.

8. In forming words from monosyllabic English words with non-tense vowels, the vowel is generally short and the consonant following it, preceding the stem vowel, is geminate: E *dock* > AF *tokka,* E *kid* > AF *kitti,* E *shop* > AF *sappa,* E *bum* > AF *pommi.* There are exceptions to this rule too: E *block* > AF *ploki,* E *lucky* > AF *luki.* If the English word has a tense vowel or diphthong, it is borrowed with a long vowel or diphthong, and the following consonant is often short: E *lake* > AF *leeki,* E *game* > AF *keimi,* E *beer* > AF *piiri.* Here, the exceptions are of two sorts. Some long vowels and diphthongs are followed by geminates: E *house* > AF *haussi.* And some loan words with long vowel and no gemi-

nation were borrowed from English words with nontense vowels: E *boss* > AF *paasi*.

9. Consonant cluster simplification at the beginning of words is accomplished by dropping consonants from the left until the cluster (or single consonant) is acceptable to the borrowing dialect: E *street* > AF *triiti, riiti*. Finnish has handled older loans in just the same way: Sw *strand* 'shore' > F *ranta*, Sw *stol* 'chair' > F *tuoli*. Some western dialects of Finnish have Swedish loan words with initial clusters of obstruent plus resonant and admit English loans with them: *plänketti* 'blanket', *freitti* 'freight', *kliinata* 'to clean', *kriimeri* 'creamery'. Others trim English words down to one initial consonant: *länketti, reitti, liinata, riimeri*. The rule of dropping consonants from the left is not limited to loan vocabulary. It operates internally in native Finnish stems when suffixation creates unacceptable clusters: /laps/ 'child', /juoks/ 'to run'; *laps + ta* (partitive suffix) > *lasta, juoks + ta* (infinitive suffix) > *juosta*.

10. The English [ə] presents a problem in loan vocabulary that seems most generally resolved by resort to spelling pronounciation (just of the vowel in question, not of the whole word): E *chisel* > AF *sysseli*, E *bacon* > AF *peikoni*, E *idea* > AF *aitia*, E *Hungarian* > AF *hunkeri*.

11. The English postconsonantal glides [y] and [w] are realized as the vowels *i* and *u:* E *mule* > AF *miuli*, E *quit* > AF *kuitata*.

To some of these rules there are exceptions, although rather few, and there are none at all to the first two.

In stems, violation of Finnish vowel harmony is rare to the point of nonexistence when words of four syllables and longer are taken as compounds: *sosiali/kiäri* 'social security', *resto/räntti* one variant of 'restaurant'. Vowel harmony does not extend across compound juncture. Estonian, a language closely related to Finnish that has had a long history of contact with German, has front/back vowel distinction only in stressed syllables, and American Finnish might have come to the same if it were spoken by many generations in contact with English.

In contrast with the maintenance of vowel harmony, violations of Finnish consonant gradation are easy to find. The genitive of *ploki* 'block' may be either *plokin* (no gradation) or *ploin*. Informants were bothered to discover that they did not pronounce the genitives of the Finnish words *matto* 'rug' and *mato* 'worm' differently, because they weaken the geminate consonant of the first word but not the single consonant of the other. The weakened geminate and the unweakened single consonant are indistinguishable. But failure of consonant gradation is selective. It is single stops that are affected by this failure—just those for which the weak grade is opaque and subject to considerable dialectal variation. The same failure is to be found in recent loans, names, and acronyms in the old country. This is not an American development.

Upon inspection, American Finnish is found to put to productive use word formation rules that operate internally in native vocabulary (consonant cluster reduction from the left, the long–short stem vowel alternations of *-ata* verbs, dialect repetition of the vowel from the preceding syllable between adjacent consonants) and others by which loan vocabulary, especially Swedish, has been shaped in the past (obstruent devoicing, stem vowel addition, etc.). The old-country Finns who were frustrated in their ignorance of all the new vocabulary and the speakers of the literary language whose taste was offended by American Finnish disregard for conservatism (mainly lexical) have given American Finnish an undeserved reputation as chaotic and unesthetic. The speakers of American Finnish who had come upon English too late in life to speak it with anything like native fluency were caught in the middle. Unable to live up to American English standards or the puristic standards of literary Finnish, which they had never spoken, they were cruelly criticized. Scarcely anyone has appreciated the fact that they creatively extended their language by adding to it from English in an orderly way by rules inherent in Finnish.

It is unlikely that there have been monolingual American-born adult speakers of American Finnish. Finnish–English bilingualism very quickly became English-dominant bilingualism, and samples of American Finnish that has spanned more than one generation give the impression of greatly imperfect learning. Sentence structure appears rather limited, and inflection breaks down. It also seems that the principles of vowel harmony and consonant gradation are only partially mastered or not learned at all.[5] Aside from Finnish-language church services and fraternal lodge activities, there has been very little in the way of Finnish-language education to supplement what is learned at home, and the emotional overtones of the home learning situation make it hard for older children to keep on improving their knowledge of the language and becoming sophisticated, fluent speakers.

If American Finnish had continued vigorously over more generations, it would be reasonable to expect that it would have acquired more initial consonant clusters, the western dialects adding to those it had from Swedish, the eastern dialects acquiring their first. New consonants would also make their way into the language. Instead of AF *kuortti* 'quart', an

---

[5] Larmouth (personal communication) states that most of his informants are marginally fluent and restricted in the domain of their conversation. Moreover, they tend to centralize unstressed vowels, and from the samples in his article in "Language," it would appear that vowel length is no longer distinct.

American-born Finn had *kvartti* with, for Finnish, a really outlandish initial cluster. American-born informants also produced *šakletti* 'chocolate' and *šeeri* 'sherry', using initial palatal fricatives. As in old-country Finnish, voiced obstruents might have begun to appear in loan words in American Finnish as in F *bussi* 'bus', which some Finns pronounce with a voiced stop and other Finns devoice. Vowel length and frontness, except under primary stress, might have become nondistinctive. Also, the environments for weak–strong consonant alternations, which are for the most part clearly phonological in Finnish, are obscured in Estonian by loss of final consonants. Perhaps American Finnish would have changed in a similar way. With loss of case endings, alternation of weak and strong forms of the stem would become a matter of memory, and simplification to the point of nonalternation could be expected.

In syntax, where old-country Finnish has both relative clauses and participial constructions, sentential complements and infinitival clause substitutes, American Finnish might have gravitated to its relative clauses and complements, which parallel English structures, to the neglect and abandonment of its participial and infinitival constructions. Constituent order might have taken up the burden of indicating grammatical relationships in a sentence from case inflection.

Except for the very last of these, all these processes can be seen happening in Finnish dialects and related languages far from North America in contact with languages other than English. Contact phenomena seem to be not just the effect of intrusion of novel material, but also a speeding up of internal change under pressure from outside. In this aspect, the identity of the new language and its particular grammatical structure are not all-important. Russian, Swedish, and English have all had similar effects on Finnish, and these effects are comparable to that of German on Estonian.

In general, in language contact situations, it appears to be true that vocabulary replacement is pervasive and immediate. Phonology, the most obvious area of systematic linguistic change, seems to be affected next, and syntax remains most resistent to change. In light of this, it is a matter of some interest that there exists a corpus of English-based Finglish that applies many of the phonetic rules discussed above to words in English sentences.[6] This corpus has a rather simplified version of English, espe-

---

[6] Oddly enough, there is not much native Finnish vocabulary left in Puotinen's writing, but masses of the earliest loans from English. The consistency of Puotinen's vowel stems, for instance, with the examples in Virtaranta's collection, shows that much of the vocabulary has been learned from older Finns. But learning has been selective, because it is the loan words, which are obviously related to English though somewhat arbitrarily with respect to final vowels, that have been preserved. Through neologisms, Puotinen makes it clear that he has not only learned a large set vocabulary of American Finnish, but has productive use of the rules of word formation and pronounciation.

cially the verb tenses and aspect, and a modal verb of its own: *kaaru* < *got to*. Vowel length is indicated, but nonneutral front vowels are few, so vowel harmony is not much in evidence. Since it is uninflected, consonant gradation is also not in evidence. It is the surface phonetics rather than the major phonological processes of Finnish that one finds in this Finglish. If one accepts from the beginning that this is English, it is rather remarkable that the pronunciation rules of American Finnish have outlived the language they came from.

References

Haugen, Einar
  1969 *The Norwegian language in America*. Bloomington, Indiana: Indiana University Press.
Hoglund, A. William
  1960 *Finnish immigrants in America, 1880–1920*. Madison, Wisconsin: University of Wisconsin Press.
Jalkanen, Ralph J. (ed.)
  1969 *The Finns in North America, A social symposium*. Hancock, Michigan: Michigan State University Press.
Jones, Gwyn
  1968 *A history of the Vikings*. London: Oxford University Press.
Karttunen, Frances
  1970 *Problems of Finnish Phonology*. Indiana University doctoral dissertation.
  1974 Phonemes, syllables, and words. *Working Papers in Linguistics of the University of Oslo*, September, 1974.
Karttunen, Frances, and James Lockhart
  1976 *Nahuatl in the middle years: Language contact phenomena in texts of the colonial period*. Berkeley and Los Angeles, California: University of California Press.
Karttunen, Frances, and Kate Moore
  1974 *Finnish in America: two kinds of Finglish*. Presented at the winter meeting of the Linguistic Society of America, December, 1974.
Karttunen, Lauri
  1966 *American Finnish (Finglish)*. Indiana University unpublished paper.
Kolehmainen, John I.
  1947 *The Finns in America, A bibliographical guide to their history*. Hancock, Michigan: Michigan State University Press.
Larmouth, Donald Wilford
  1974 Differential Interference in American Finnish Cases. *Language*, **50**(2).
Lehtinen, Meri
  1966 *Analysis of a Finnish-English bilingual corpus*. Indiana University doctoral dissertation.
Virtaranta, Pertti
  1971 Finskan i Amerika, *Språk i Norden*, pp. 79–109.

Historical and Sociocultural Aspects of the Distribution of Linguistic Variants in Highland Chiapas, Mexico

NICHOLAS A. HOPKINS

Each speaker of a language normally interacts linguistically with a number of other speakers of the language, and these in turn interact with still others. A speech community is composed of many overlapping sets of speakers who participate in the network of oral communication. Some pairs of speakers within such a network interact with each other almost continually, other pairs infrequently or not at all. Bloomfield (1933, Chapter 3) noted that no speech community is ever entirely uniform in speech and postulated that the amount of linguistic variation within a speech community was related to the density of communication between speakers—linguistically distinct subgroups within the community being separated from others by lines of "weakness" in the net of oral communication. Hockett's (1958, Chapter 52) model of phonological change supports Bloomfield's suggestion. For each dimension of linguistic variation there is a normal value set by convention of the community of speakers (e.g., the amount of aspiration on initial voiceless stops in English). The learner infers this value from the performance of speakers to whom he is exposed and attempts to produce in his speech values close to the norm (see King, 1969). But speech production is never too precise, and each speaker in fact produces a range of values clustering around the perceived norm. Overall, the examples to which the learner is exposed will consist mostly of values close to the norm, with fewer examples toward the extremes; it is, in fact, this tendency of speakers to produce variants within a restricted range that leads the learner to infer that there is a norm. This is a circular process. Learners infer, from what they hear, a normal value for each dimension of variation for each phonological unit. They then reinforce this norm by attempting to produce it consistently. Since such norms are a matter of unwritten convention—it is nowhere inscribed just how much aspiration of initial voiceless stops is proper—chance but consistent deviations from the norm in one direction or another may lead new learners to infer new norms, shifting the normal value of a linguistic variant in the direction of the now most frequent value. Consistent deviation from the norm in one direction or another does not, of course, have to be the product of pure chance; it may also be due to functional pressures, to bilingualism and the influence of speakers of another language, etc. Over a series of generations, the norms of the speech community may change significantly, no one being the wiser.

A probable important factor in the learner's acquisition of linguistic variants, then, is the frequency with which he is exposed to the various possibilities. In terms of Bloomfield's model, as innovations arise in the various subgroups of a speech community, they spread along lines of interaction where the density of communication is greater, i.e., where speakers are exposed to the new values with greater frequency. By the same token, innovations tend not to spread past lines of weakness in the net of oral communication, so that subgroups of the speech community that are separated from one another by lines of weakness become linguistically distinct.

It would be overly simplistic to hold that the amount of exposure to an innovation is the sole factor that determines who adopts what variant as a norm. The attitude of the hearer toward the speaker who uses the innovation is certainly a factor, and where linguistic variants are ascribed social value, the attitude of the hearer toward the innovation itself may be important. On the other hand, where it can be shown that a linguistic innovation has arisen in one subgroup of a speech community and has spread to others, the clear implication is that there has been intimate contact and interaction between the subgroups. The distribution of innovative variants within a speech community reflects the lines of social interaction that have joined the subgroups of the speech community in the past.

The study of the distribution of linguistic variants has had a long and fruitful history in linguistics. The comparison of phonetic features as evidenced in standard or literary languages was the foundation of the comparative method of historical linguistics in the nineteenth century. The concept of phonetic laws that account for the regular phonological correspondences between languages believed to be related was based on these studies. Dialect surveys of nonstandard varieties of speech (Wenker, 1895; Gillieron, 1918, 1921, 1922; Gillieron and Edmont, 1902–1910) furnished the data for heated debate over the validity of the concept of immutable phonetic laws. As the methods for carrying out a dialect survey became established (see Dauzat, 1944; Pop, 1927) studies of the geographical distribution of linguistic features covered much of Europe (Wrede, 1926; Jaberg, 1908, 1937, 1943; Jaberg and Jud, 1928, 1928–1940) and the eastern parts of the United States (Kurath, 1939–1943, 1949; Kurath et al., 1939). Surveys of the literature in dialect geography and dialectology (Bottiglioni, 1954; Pop, 1950) document a wide variety of interests and methods. For the most part, earlier studies focused on the geographical distribution of linguistic variants, plotting on maps the isoglosses that separated the area of distribution of one feature from the area of distribution of another. The influence of patterns of social organization and interaction on these distributions was not overlooked. Isogloss distributions like the Rhenish fan (Bloomfield, 1933, pp. 343–344) showed the influence of political and economic ties on the distribution of variants. Italian dialect surveys (Jaberg, 1928–1940) showed the Italian speech community to be cut by bundles of isoglosses that sharply defined linguistic areas; French dialect surveys (Gillieron and Edmont, 1902–1910) showed the transitions from one geographical zone to another to be more gradual, isoglosses tending not to coincide. The different patterns of isogloss distribution in France, Italy, and Germany were related to the political and economic histories of the three areas (Jaberg, 1936). The influence of population movements on the distribution of linguistic variants was clear from surveys of the United States. Sharply defined dialect areas on the Atlantic seaboard, reflecting colonial settlement patterns, become less sharply defined to the west, where populations from the various dialect areas have mingled in westward expansion; the influence of urban centers of trade and cultural influence on the surrounding areas was likewise noted in dialect survey data (McDavid, 1958).

More recently, attention has turned to the nongeographic aspects of linguistic distribution. Where social groups are not distributed in discrete geographical units, but are coresident in the same communities, differential lines of social interactions create "social" or nongeographical dialects. Studies in India (Gumperz, 1958; Bright, 1960; Ferguson and Gumperz, 1960) show that caste lines correlate with the distribution of linguistic variants, for instance, while in rural Guatemala (Mayers, 1960) the correlations are with combinations of features of age, sex, wealth, and prestige. Labov's (1963, 1966) studies in New York City further document relations between social and linguistic variants.

A large number of empirical studies, then, support the notion that the distribution of linguistic variants tends to correlate with lines of social interaction. For the most part, these studies have been carried out in areas whose histories are well known, where the linguist who suspects his isoglosses to be artifacts of former social, political, and economic structures may check his hypotheses against historical records. The success with which such correlations have been made where historical data are available suggests the potential utility of studies of the distribution of linguistic variants to generate hypotheses about past political, social, or economic ties where historical data are not available, as in the reconstruction of prehistoric culture history in the New World.

The situation is somewhat analogous to that of the comparative method of historical linguistics, a body of theories and methods relating to the reconstruction of earlier stages of languages from data on historically attested languages. The comparative method was worked out in the context of Old World languages, many of which were attested at various stages of their development. In this context, it was possible to perfect methods of reconstruction by testing hypotheses against written records [see the famous case of Saussure's hypothesis concerning Protoindoeuropean laryngeals, supported years later by new data from Hittite. (Lehmann, 1962, p. 39)]. Once the techniques had been developed and their predictive value established, the same methods were available for work on languages whose early stages are not subject to attestation (Hass, 1966). While rigid standards of proof of hypotheses have never been established among practitioners of the art, there is nevertheless consensus among linguists concerning the validity of the approach in general (Hymes, 1959).

The same would seem to be true for studies of the distribution of linguistic variants within a speech community. The knowledge that isogloss distributions reflect social, political, and economic ties—as has been demonstrated in areas whose history is well known—should make the dialect survey a valid instrument for generating hypotheses about such ties where direct historical verification is not possible. Unfortunately, this research instrument has not often been employed in studies of New World populations, a notable exception being Gudschinsky's (1958) study of Mazatec dialects in Mexico. For the most part, a survey of contemporary work in indigenous dialectology in Latin America (Mayers, 1968) reveals the paucity of research being carried out at present.

The dialect survey of Tzeltal and Tzotzil discussed below provides ample material for a preliminary test of the utility of the dialect survey to generate hypotheses about patterns of social interaction between indigenous communities. It should be pointed out that the results of the analysis of this survey material must be regarded as preliminary rather than definitive. The major data elicitation instrument, a 200-phrase questionnaire, was intended to provide enough data to reveal the rough outlines of community relationships but not the fine details; likewise, the sample of informants interviewed was considerably more a function of who was readily available to the visiting linguist than a carefully designed statistically valid sample.

Tzeltal and Tzotzil are two Mayan languages spoken in the highlands of the State of Chiapas, Mexico. The southern boundary of the Tzeltal–Tzotzil area is the upper Grijalva River valley southeast of Chiapa de Corzo, Chiapas. The northern boundary of the area is the northern flanks of the Chiapas Highlands, which are occupied by speak-

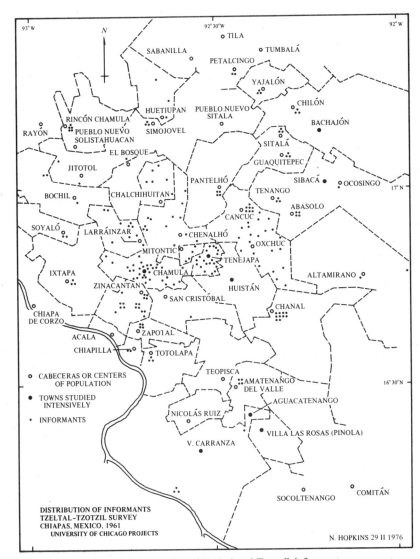

Figure 1. Distribution of Tzeltal and Tzotzil informants.

ers of Chol, another Mayan language. Tzotzil speakers occupy the western half of this region, Tzeltal speakers the eastern half, the border between the two approximating 92°30'W, a north–south line that passes just east of San Cristóbal Las Casas, the economic center of the highlands. Tzotzil communities extend westward to approximately 93°W. Tzeltal communities extend eastward to approximately 92°W (see Fig. 1).

Just northeast of San Cristobal, the peak of Volcan Tzontehuitz rises to about 9000 feet above sea level. To the south and east, the land drops 8000 feet in a series of steps to the lowlands. To the north and west, minor peaks and sharp ridges define numerous small highland valleys before a sharp drop to the lowlands is encountered. Differences in altitude define cold, temperate, and hot climatic zones with well-defined differences in vegetation. The broken nature of the terrain, with its abrupt changes in altitude, combined with differential rainfall and available moisture, create a complex mosaic of small ecological zones. Population density ranges from about 120 people per square mile in the central highlands to only 20 people per square mile in the lowland flanks. Of this population, some 60% were Tzeltal and Tzotzil Indians in the early 1960s; both the Indian and non-Indian (Spanish-speaking Ladino) populations were predominantly rural. In 1960, the Mexican census reported about 70,000 Tzotzil speakers and 50,000 Tzeltal speakers in the highlands of Chiapas (see Table I, compiled from Olivera de V. and Sanchez, 1964; Marino Flores, 1963); the IX Censo General de Población, 1970 (p. 73) reports 94,625 speakers of Tzotzil and 96,423 speakers of Tzeltal in Chiapas.

As indicated in the table, the percentages of Indian language speakers in local communities varies from close to 100% in the center of the zone (Chamula, Mitontic, Chanal) to less than 20% on the southern and western fringes (Soyalo, Teopisca, Villa Las Rosas). Bilingualism in Spanish tends to be high in areas where the percentages of Indians is low and vice versa, although there are notable exceptions to this general rule (e.g., Oxchuc).

There are some forty-five Indian communities in the Highlands of Chiapas, only a few of which have been studied extensively by anthropologists (see Vogt, 1961; Cancian, 1965, for Zinacantan; Pozas, 1947, for Chamula; Siverts, 1968, for Oxchuc; McQuown and Pitt-Rivers, 1970, for the Highlands in general). A typical community has a ceremonial center composed of a building where the community's civil officials meet, a church or chapel where the central figure is the patron saint of the community, and an open space or plaza where market is held periodically. Some few Indian communities are nuclear communities with all or most of the population residing permanently around the ceremonial center (e.g., Venustiano Carranza, Pantelhó). The population of most Indian communities, however, is scattered in small hamlets, or parajes, and the center is occupied permanently, if at all, only by Ladinos. In these latter-type communities, Indians reside temporarily in the ceremonial centers during their term of service to the community as civil or religious officers in the local variants of the Mesoamerican institutions known as cofradía systems, cargo systems, or mayordomías. The men serving in these posi-

TABLE I

Distribution and Number of Speakers of Tzeltal and Tzotzil (ca. 1950–1960)

Municipio	Number of speakers[a]			
	A	B	C	D
Tzeltal (general location, eastern parts of Chiapas highlands)				
Altamirano	2,845	74.20	1,256	32.76
Amatenango del Valle	1,773	86.32	9	–
Chanal	2,318	99.96	2,279	98.28
Chilón	9,048	95.98	7,977	84.62
Las Rosas	1,380	22.71	38	–
Nicolás Ruiz	–	–	–	–
Ocosingo	9,170	78.84	7,297	62.74
Oxchuc	4,074	87.95	91	1.96
Sitalá	5,546	95.90	2,187	37.78
Tenejapa	6,215	92.77	5,665	84.56
Yajalón	6,026	73.12	4,968	60.28
Totals	48,395		31,767	
Tzotzil (general location, western parts of Chiapas highlands)				
Amatán	362	10.14	–	–
Bochil	1,700	38.74	513	11.69
Chalchihuitán	2,222	96.69	2,176	94.69
Chamula	17,488	99.42	10,456	59.44
Chenalhó	5,787	91.36	3,332	52.60
Chiapilla	–	–	–	–
El Bosque	311	85.80	1,086	29.95
El Zapotal	202	15.12	86	6.44
Huistán	5,172	84.28	4,761	77.58
Huetiupan	2,348	64.28	1,554	42.54
Ixtapa	1,187	28.31	91	2.17
Jitotol	2,331	65.16	95	2.78
La Concordia	–	–	–	–
Larráinzar	7,127	94.91	3,885	51.74
Mitontic	3,542	99.58	3,541	99.55
Pantelhó	2,159	65.11	2,011	60.65
Pueblo Nuevo Solistahuacán	2,343	43.98	585	10.98
Sabanilla	2,995	73.82	1,201	29.60
San Cristóbal Las Casas	3,296	16.77	1,054	5.36
Simojovel de Allende	6,730	71.63	4,965	52.84
Soyaló	229	10.86	3	–
Teopisca	754	17.01	278	6.27
Totolapa	697	56.44	–	–
Venustiano Carranza	3,966	33.72	714	6.07
Zinacantan	4,466	84.77	4,116	78.13
Totals	70,415		47,503	

[a] (A) Monolingual and bilingual Indian language speakers, (B) percentage of Indian language speakers, (C) monolingual Indian language speakers, (D) percentage of monolingual Indian language speakers.

tions move into the ceremonial center with their families during their year of service and then return to their hamlets. As a year's service requires that a family be able to support itself in the center for a year, bearing the cost of ceremonial activities that pertain to the office, and as few Indians can afford to hold office for two years in a row, the Indian population of the center changes almost entirely from year to year. The stable residential units within a typical community are thus the hamlets rather than the ceremonial center. Coresidence in the ceremonial center during periods of office holding is an opportunity for the formation of friendship and "compadrazgo" bonds between residents of different parajes who otherwise may have little or no contact with one another.

The Dialect Survey

In order to determine the linguistic diversity of the Tzeltal and Tzotzil communities, the Chiapas Study Projects of the University of Chicago (McQuown and Pitt-Rivers, 1970) carried out a dialect survey in the summer of 1961. It was suspected at the beginning of this survey that there were six major zones of linguistic variation—a northern, central, and southern zone within each language area. The principal goal of the dialect survey was to test this hypothesis by collecting linguistic materials from each of the indigenous communities. A secondary goal was the collection of materials that would make possible the reconstruction of proto-Tzeltal–Tzotzil, the language ancestral to all the modern dialects of Tzeltal and Tzotzil. In addition, linguistic data were collected from a number of bilinguals (in Spanish and one of the Indian languages) to determine the manner in which bilingual speech differed, if at all, from monolingual speech.

The survey was carried out by O. Brent Berlin, Nicholas A. Hopkins, Terrence S. Kaufman, Norman A. McQuown, Andres Medina Hernandez, R. Radhakrishnan, Harvey B. Sarles, and Gerald E. Williams. Over most of the area, linguists traveled with social anthropologists, who collected census materials from the linguistic informants. Each of several teams of linguist and anthropologist covered a part of the Tzeltal–Tzotzil area in which either the linguist or the anthropologist had previous experience. Those communities that had been studied intensively by social anthropologists were surveyed in detail; fewer informants from other communities were interviewed. (For details of the composition of the survey teams and the areas covered by each, see McQuown and Pitt-Rivers 1970, pp. 9–20.)

The principal instrument employed for the elicitation of linguistic material was a list of 200 Spanish phrases designed to elicit two kinds of material. The first 100 phrases were designed to elicit the items on the Swadesh "noncultural" vocabulary list (Hymes, 1960, p. 6) so that glottochronological calculations could be made. The remaining 100 items were designed to elicit lexical and phonological material of special importance for the reconstruction of proto-Tzeltal–Tzotzil. The phrases within which the desired lexical items were elicited were designed to elicit data on the nominal and verbal morphology of the two languages. Given the difficulty of eliciting data from monolinguals, the majority of the data were collected from informants who had at least a working knowledge of Spanish [census data from the Mexican national census of 1960 cited in Marino Flores (1963) and Olivera de V. and Sanchez (1964) indicate that about 35% of the speakers of Tzeltal and about 40% of the speakers of Tzotzil are bilingual in Spanish]. In Chamula and to a certain extent in the northeastern Tzeltal zone, use was made of a series of "paraphrases" in the Indian languages to elicit the items on the survey list. These paraphrases, similar to riddles, were used to elicit material from monolinguals. Responses to the eliciting instruments were transcribed in phonetic symbols according to a standard established in training sessions prior to the beginning of the survey. Whenever possible informant responses were recorded on magnetic tape. Somewhat over 400 informants were interviewed from the parajes and ceremonial centers of 41 communities. Some additional linguistic data were collected in the form of responses to the Thematic Apperception Test, and sociocultural censuses were occasionally elicited in the Indian languages. Some information was collected on the Spanish of Indian and non-Indian (Ladino) informants (McQuown, 1970).

Analysis of Data

A preliminary analysis of the survey data was made in the field in 1961; more detailed analysis of the materials was carried out in Chicago from 1962 to 1964. The original survey materials—questionnaires, tape recordings, and other data—are kept in Chicago as part of the files of the University of Chicago's Macro-Mayan Project. The first step in the analysis of the dialect survey data was compilation of an inventory of all responses made to each item on the survey questionnaires. As this inventory was made, obvious errors were eliminated. Some of these derived from the lack of control of Spanish on the part of either the informant or the linguist—usually the latter. In one village, for instance, informants consistently responded to the item that should have elicited the word for "liver" by giving a word which elsewhere meant "godchild." A check with the taped record of this elicitation revealed that the linguist had pronounced the phrase *su hígado* 'your liver' as *su higádo,* which was interpreted by the informants as *su ahijado* 'your godchild'. Such errors were few in number and easily identified. When the inventory had been completed, cognate sets were identified, and each questionnaire was coded and later key-punched to make possible the glottochronological analysis of the survey data. Computation and analysis of the glottochronological data is still under way.

Although the quantitative analysis of the survey data is not yet complete, the qualitative differences between the Tzeltal and Tzotzil dialects have been examined in some detail. This analysis is based on the notions that linguistic change is not random but systematic; that people who are in constant contact tend to adopt the same changes in their patterns of speech; that innovations tend to spread along lines of social interaction; and that the study of the modern distribution of linguistic variants can give insights into the patterns of interaction and the barriers to interaction between discrete groups of people.

The analysis of the Tzeltal and Tzotzil dialect survey material involved the listing of all the phonological changes which had taken place in any of these dialects since the time of their common ancestor (based on Kaufman 1962), as well as the determination of the geographical areas within which these changes were regular—in so far as regularity could be judged from the survey materials. Special attention was paid to cases of apparent irregularity of phonetic change and a number of dialect loans were identified.

EXAMPLE A

An illustration of an area of regular phonological change bounded by an area of apparent irregularity—where it may be inferred that lexical items have spread from the former to the latter areas—is found in the northeastern extent of the East Central Tzotzil development of /*h/ before front and back vowels. The change of /*h/ to /y/ before front vowels and to /w/ before back vowels is regular in forms elicited from informants representing the speech of Zinacantán, Chamula, Mitontic, and Chenalhó. Materials elicited from Chalchihuitán and Pantelhó informants, to the north and northeast of Chenalhó, include some forms which show these changes and some which do not. A selection of these forms is shown in Table II.

Thus, all informants from Chalchihuitán and all but one from Pantelhó have the form /yiʔ/ 'sand', showing the development of *h to /y/ before the front vowel /i/. Some but not all of these informants have forms that show the change of *h to /w/ before back vowels, but the change is regular in all

TABLE II

Distribution of Some Variants in Northern Tzotzil[a]

	Forms			
Informants	*hiʔ 'sand'	*hVʔVn 'I'	*hAʔ 'water'	*hun 'paper'
Chalchuhuitán				
1. Chiquinxulub	yiʔ	huʔun	hoʔ	hun
2. Saclum	yiʔ	huʔun	yošoʔ	hun
3. Jolitontic	yiʔ	huʔun	hoʔ	hun
4. Sisim	yiʔ	huʔun	hoʔ	hun
5. Balunacó	yiʔ	wuʔun	hoʔ	hun
6. Pom	yiʔ	wuʔun	woʔ	hun
Pantelhó:				
Barrio Sta. Cruz				
7. No. 1	hiʔ	hoʔon	hoʔ	hun
8. No. 2	yiʔ	hoʔon	hoʔ	hun
Barrio Los Naranjos				
9. Male	yiʔ	hoʔon	yošoʔ	Hun
10. Female	yiʔ	hoʔon	yošoʔ	wun
Chenalhó				
11. Quextic	yiʔ	wuʔun	woʔ	wun
12. Polo	yiʔ	wuʔun	woʔ	wun
13. Ch'itic	yiʔ	wuʔun	woʔ	wun
14. K'anlumtic	yiʔ	wuʔun	woʔ	wun
15. La Libertad	yiʔ	wuʔun	woʔ	wun
Mitontic				
16. Holxokonk'ak'al	yiʔ	wuʔun	Hoʔ	wun

[a] /yošoʔ/ is a compound of /yoš/ 'green' and /hoʔ/ 'water'.

relevant elicited forms for none of these informants. Both changes are regular for all informants from Chenalhó and Mitontic (as well as Chamula and Zinacantán). The distribution of these forms appears to indicate that what has diffused from the east central to the northern Tzotzil communities is not a phonological rule, but lexical items. That is, the inference can be drawn that the items 'I', 'water', and 'paper', having developed in East Central Tzotzil with /w/ as their initial consonant in accordance with a regular phonological change, were later adopted into the vocabularies of some but not all northern Tzotzils. A map of the distribution of these items is shown in Fig. 2.

Regular change and the diffusion of items showing such change are not limited to phonology but equally affect morphology and lexicon. A questionnaire of 200 items, however, does not provide sufficient material to clearly demonstrate morphological changes. With 200 selected phrases, the investigator can expect to find examples of all the phonemes of a given dialect and a certain number of subphonemic variants, but can only hope

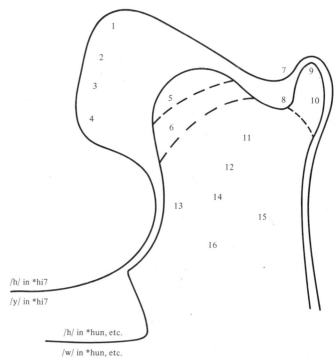

/h/ in *hi7

/y/ in *hi7

/h/ in *hun, etc.

/w/ in *hun, etc.

Figure 2. Isoglosses of developments of *h in northern Tzotzil. Numbers correspond to informant numbers in Table II.

to find a limited number of inflectional and derivational features. Lexical information is likewise limited. Consequently, lexical and morphological features were analyzed in a different manner from phonological features. The relative frequency of the occurrence of a lexical or morphological feature in the speech of informants of a given community was taken as an index of its diffusion.

If, for example, all of the informants of one community employ a given feature, some informants of a nearby community use the feature, and no informants from any other communities use the feature, it may be inferred that the homogeneous community is either the source of the innovation that had diffused to the nearby community or is a relic area in which a formerly more widespread feature is still conserved in the face of innovations from the outside.

EXAMPLE B

An example of this sort of distribution is found in the elicited material from central Tzeltal informants. The glottalization of plain consonants after internal /*h/ is regular only in Oxchuc, but forms showing this change also occur in neighboring communities where the change is not regular. These forms are illustrated by the form /naht'/ 'distant', which shows Oxchuc to be center of an area out of which lexical items have diffused. Other lexical items that are characteristic of Oxchuc informants' speech but which occur irregularly in neighboring communities may be inferred to be diffusing outward along the same lines. The distributions in Table III illustrate this pattern.

Given that in the model used in the analysis of the phonological, morphological, and lexical data diffused items are assumed to follow lines of social interaction, it was expected that the three kinds of diffused items would follow somewhat the same lines of diffusion. Since the direction of diffusion of phonological features could be determined—diffusion is from areas of greater to areas of lesser regularity—it was assumed for purposes of the present analysis that morphological and lexical items that showed the same patterns of distribution as phonological features were following the same directions of diffusion as the phonological features.

Thus, when in the following analysis statements are made about the direction of diffused linguistic features, these statements are based on a variety of indices. For phonological features, diffusion is assumed to have occurred from areas of greater regularity to areas of lesser regularity. For morphological and lexical features, the direction of diffusion was deter-

TABLE III

Oxchuc Diffusion Patterns[a]

	Guaquitepec	Tenango	Sibacá	Ocosingo	Altamirano	Oxchuc	La Plaizada	Chanal	Abasolo	Cancuc	Tenejapa	Amatenango	Aguacatenango	Pinola
/naht'/ 'distant'						+	+	+						
/naht'/ 'long'						−	+	−	+	−		+	+	
/k'aal/ 'day'	−					−	+	+		+	−	−		
/tumut/ 'egg'	−					+	+	+	−					
/k'ešen/ 'left'					+	+	+	+	+	·				
/sakil 'ool/ 'white squash'						+		−	−					
/lah/ 'die'						+	−	+		+	+			
/simal/ 'nose mucus'				−	−	+	+	+	+	+	+	+	+	
/ʔakan/ 'foot'	−	−	−			+	−			+	+	+		

[a] + = all informants, − = some informants.

mined by the frequency of occurrence of the features in the given dialects and the patterns of diffused phonological features between the various dialects.

Historical Development of Tzeltal and Tzotzil

In a series of publications, Kaufman (1961, 1962, 1964, 1970) has clarified the position of Tzeltal and Tzotzil within the Mayan family of languages. Kaufman (1962, pp. 126–127) states that Tzeltal and Tzotzil are very closely related to languages of the Chol group (Chol, Chontal, and Chorti), on the one hand, and to languages of the Tojolabal group (Tojolabal and Chuj), on the other hand. Together, Tzeltal and Tzotzil constitute a single linguistic area. Speakers of both languages inhabit the same geographical area, share a common culture, and appear to consider Tzeltals and Tzotzils as a single kind of Indians, distinct from Chols, Tojolabals, Zoques, Zapotecs, and other nearby Indian groups of whose existence they are aware. Any speaker of Tzeltal or Tzotzil will indiscriminately refer to the speech of any other Tzeltal or Tzotzil community with the same term: *baȼ'il k'op* 'true (proper) speech'.

Kaufman has carried out a reconstruction of proto-Tzeltal–Tzotzil based on data from the Tzeltal communities of Bachajon, Tenejapa, Oxchuc, Aguacatenango, and Pinola and the Tzotzil communities of Chamula, Huistan, San Bartolo (Venustiano Carranza), and Zinacantan. The word lists collected in the 1961 Chicago Chiapas Project survey were examined by Kaufman and incorporated into his reconstruction (Kaufman, 1962, pp. 130–131).

The model of proto-Tzeltal–Tzotzil proposed by Kaufman has been adopted here, since it is strongly supported by the data of the present study. Although the present study analyzes data from several Tzotzil communities from which Kaufman had no data, the additional Tzotzil material motivates no significant changes in his reconstruction. The phonemes of proto-Tzeltal–Tzotzil have been reconstructed as follows (Kaufman 1962, p. 150):

Simple stops and affricates	p	t	ȼ	č	k	ʔ
Glottalized stops and affricates	p'	t'	ȼ'	č'	k'	
Voiced glottalized stop	b'					
Fricatives			s	š	x	h
Nasals	m	n				
Semivowels	w	y				
Lateral		l				

The columns represent labial, dental, dental, alveopalatal, velar, and glottal points of articulation, respectively; and six vowels: i, e, a, A, o, u, with high front, low front, low central, high central, low back, and high back points of articulation, respectively.

Some important phonological developments separate Tzeltal from Tzotzil. The principal isogloss involves developments of /*A/ as /a/ in Tzeltal and as /o/ in Tzotzil. The development of /*h/ is also diagnostic: in roots of the shape *CVhC, the internal /*h/ has been lost completely in all varieties of Tzotzil. In the community of San Bartolo, the loss of internal /*h/ has been compensated by the development in that community of a bitonal contrast in which the vowels that were followed by internal /*h/ have low tone in the modern dialect. Elsewhere in Tzotzil, the loss of internal /*h/ is complete and without compensation. In two varieties of Tzeltal, /*h/ internal to the root has also been lost, in Teopisca without compensation and in Sitalá with compensatory length on the preceding vowel in some forms. Elsewhere in Tzeltal, internal /*h/ has been lost only before certain consonants.

The principal morphological feature that separates Tzeltal from Tzotzil involves a group of verbal prefixes in Tzotzil that correspond to a group of verbal suffixes in Tzeltal. Tzeltal has a series of personal suffixes that function as subjects of intransitive verbs and objects of transitive verbs. The corresponding affixes in Tzotzil are noncognate prefixes, although Tzotzil also has a set of cognate suffixes that can be used in place of or in addition to the Tzotzil personal prefixes as objects of transitive verbs. The set of Tzotzil prefixes are not unique in the Mayan family (Kaufman, 1962, pp. 142–144), but between Tzeltal and Tzotzil they are an unambiguous diagnostic for Tzotzil dialects.

In addition to the phonological and morphological features, there are a number of lexical items that unambiguously distinguish between Tzeltal and Tzotzil dialects. Kaufman (1962, p. 236) lists the following in their reconstructed forms:

Tzeltal only	Tzotzil only	English gloss
pahč'	pašak'	pineapple
paxel	ʔohk'ob'	tomorrow
tumin	tuš-nok'	cotton
tuhl	woʔ, waʔ	numeral classifier for persons
tulan	¢o¢, ¢a¢	strong
čuš	k'ab'	urine
ʔit	čak	buttocks
ʔihnam	ʔaxnil	wife

Continues on following page

Tzeltal only	Tzotzil only	English gloss
ʔeč'ex	ʔek'el	axe
ʔač'iš	ȼayob', ȼayub'	girl
č'ah	ʔič̌	bile
č'uhul-čan	winahel	sky
k'aš, nel	ʔeč'	to pass by
k'ayob', k'ayub'	wAhb'	drum, guitar
b'ehen	šanaw	to walk
xoy	či ʔil	companion
mamalal	malal	husband
namey	wo ʔney	long ago
waš	wet	fox
wayib'	tem	bed
-leh	-sa ʔ	to look for
iš̌	ša	already

The dialect survey confirms all these diagnostic pairs except one; the pair *wayib* 'bed' versus *tem* 'bed' is not without ambiguity, since the term *wayeb'* 'bed' occurs in the Tzotzil of San Pablo Chalchihuitán, a community for which Kaufman had no data. In addition, two more diagnostic pairs have been revealed by the dialect survey; Tzeltal *k'al* and Tzotzil *čob'* 'cornfield' (milpa), and Tzeltal *ʔek'* and Tzotzil *k'anal* 'star'.

In addition to these, there is a second type of lexical distinction between Tzeltal and Tzotzil revealed by the dialect survey. These are sets of lexical items, one of which will occur in any Tzeltal dialect but none of which occurs in any Tzotzil dialect (and vice versa):

Tzeltal only	Tzotzil only	English gloss
b'i, b'in(ti), b'e(luk), tut, tu ʔti, tut ʔ	k'u	what
b'ayel, b'ayal, b'ayil, ȼob'ol	ʔep	much, many
b'a(ti), b'an(ti)	b'u	where
k'ešan, k'ešen, k'ešam, šin	ȼ'et	left side
hos, humen, ȼa ʔlos	woskon, tanhol, lo ʔȼo ʔ	buzzard (black head)
šut, šuht, tut, č'in, ȼael, ȼail	čut, b'ik'it	small

From Kaufman's list of oblique or nonrecurring phonological correspondences, more diagnostic items emerge. They are presented in their reconstructed forms on page 201.

Limiting the establishment of such diagnostic pairs of lexical items that unambiguously distinguish between Tzeltal and Tzotzil dialects is the large number of lexical items that are cognate for all informants, for all Tzeltal informants, or for all Tzotzil informants. Of the first 100 items on

Tzeltal only	Tzotzil only	English gloss
pay	pan	to boil
tik-un	tak	to send
toh(y)ib', toh(y)iw	tahiw	frost
¢ukum	ȼukut	belly
čum, čun	ȼan	to set afire
čuhyel	kuhel	smallpox
ʔip(al)	ʔep(al)	much
ʔištaʔ, ʔištab'	ʔištAl	toy
ʔahtay	ʔaht	count
ʔo(h)b'ol	ʔab'ol	cough
ʔulaʔ, ʔulab'	hulAʔ	visitor
p'ahl	p'el	numeral classifier for words
č'iwič	č'iwit	market
b'ak'	b'ek'	seed, pit
b'ahal	bel	contents
sit	sat	fruit
šuhk	šohkon	side
hič	heč	thus
nehkel	nehk'eb'	shoulder
nap	map	coyol palm

the dialect survey list, the Swadesh glottochronological list, some 60% of the responses are cognates between all dialects; among Tzeltal informants, an additional 20% of these responses are cognate between all dialects; and among Tzotzil informants, an additional 10% are cognate for all dialects. That is, the maximum time depth for any two dialects of Tzeltal or Tzotzil is approximately 1108 years (60% cognates), for any two Tzeltal dialects approximately 514 years (80% cognates), and for any two Tzotzil dialects 823 years (70% cognates).

An examination of the distribution of the various phonological, morphological and lexical variants reveals certain relationships between dialects. In the following sections, these relationships are discussed, some of the evidence for the establishment of the relationships is presented, and the contributions of these analyses to the reconstruction of the cultural history of the Tzeltal and Tzotzil communities is discussed.

Dialects of Tzotzil

Dialect survey questionnaires were taken in the Tzotzil communities of Bochil (3 informants), Chalchihuitán (6), Chamula (38), Chenalhó (5), Chiapilla (2), Hueitiupan (1), Huistán (15), Ixtapa (3), Jitotol (3), Magdalenas (3), Mitontic (4), Pantelhó (4), Santiago (3), San Andrés Larráinzar

(7), San Bartolomé de Los Llanos (Venustiano Carranza) (24), San Juan El Bosque (1), Santa Marta (2), Simojovel (3), Soyaló (2), Totolapa (3), Zinacantán (19), and Zapotal (5). Agricultural colonies of some of these communities were also studied; questionnaires were taken in the Huetiupan colonies of Azufrc (1) and Santa Catarina (1); the Chamula colonies of Rincón Chamula (5) and Flores Magón (1); and the San Andrés Larráinzar colony Yuquim (1). In each community, an effort was made to interview informants from various hamlets or residential subdivisions of the community.

Three groups of regular phonological developments are of interest in the study of Tzotzil dialects:

1. Developments of /*x/ and /*h/ in word-initial position. (a) In Huistán, /*x/ becomes /h/; /*h/ becomes /H/, manifested phonetically as a voiced nonsyllabic vocoidal onset with local friction that varies from pharyngeal to velar. (b) In Zinacantan, Chamula, Mitontic, and Chenalhó, /*x/ becomes /h/; /*h/ becomes /y/ before the front vowels /i/ and /e/, becomes /h/ before /a/, and becomes /w/ before /o/ and /u/. For some speakers of these dialects, developments of /*h/ are sometimes voiced and accompanied by local friction, i.e., /*h/ becomes /y h w/ varying with /H/. (c) In the remaining Tzotzil dialects, /*x/ and /*h/ merge as /h/.

2. Developments of /*h/ in roots of the type *CVhC. (a) In San Bartolo, *CVhC becomes CVC with low tone. (b) Elsewhere in Tzotzil, there is no tonal system, and *CVhC becomes CVC.

3. Developments of /*p'/ and /*b'/. (a) In Chamula, /*p'/ and /*b'/ merge as /p'/. (b) Elsewhere, /*p'/ and /*b'/ remain distinct, as /p'/ and /b'/, respectively.

Morphological variants of interest are:

1. Verbal prefixes meaning 'nonpast': all dialects have the prefix /ta-/, but some have an additional prefix that may occur in place of or in addition to /ta-/. (a) Simojovel, Huetiupan, and their colonies have /ipa; (ta)/ as the nonpast prefix. (b) Bochil, Soyaló, and western parajes (hamlets) of San Andrés Larrainzar have /yak (ta)/. (c) Ixtapa has /yot (te)/. Note that all these communities are located on the western fringes of the Tzotzil area.

2. Intransitive verb prefixes meaning 'past'; there are variations on the forms of the first, second, and third person singular prefixes. (a) San Bartolo, Zapotal, Totolapa, and Huistán have /ni-, na-, ?i-/ for first, second, and third person, respectively. (b) Elsewhere, the prefixes are /li-, la-, ?i-/.

Items that illustrate Tzotzil lexical distributions are:

'sand' proto-Tzeltal–Tzotzil /*hiʔ/:
  (a) Chalchihuitán, Chenalhó, Mitontic, Zinacantan, most Chamula, Santa Marta, some Pantelhó, some Zapotal, Chiapilla, Magdalenas: /yiʔ/.
  (b) Huistán, the remaining Chamula: /Hiʔ/.
  (c) Elsewhere: /hiʔ/.

'year' /*haʔb'il/
  (a) Huistán, most Chamula: Haʔwil/.
  (b) Elsewhere: /hab'il, haʔwil/.

'I' /*hAʔon/
  (a) Chenalhó, most Chamula, most Mitontic, eastern parajes of Chalchihuitán: /wuʔun/.
  (b) Remainder Mitontic, remainder Chamula, Zinacantan, Chiapilla, most Zapotal: /woʔon/.
  (c) Huistán: /Hoʔon/.
  (d) Santa Marta, north and west parajes of Chalchihuitán: /huʔun/.
  (e) Elsewhere: /hoʔon/.

'you' /*hAʔAt/
  (a) Chenalhó, Mitontic, Chamula, Zinacantan, Chiapilla, some Zapotal: /woʔot/.
  (b) Huistán: /Hoʔot/.
  (c) Elsewhere: /hoʔot/.

'paper' /*hun/
  (a) Chenalhó, some Mitontic, some Chamula, Zinacantan, some Chalchihuitán, some Magdalenas, Santiago, Chiapilla, some Zapotal: /wun/.
  (b) Remainder Mitontic, remainder Chamula, Huistán: /Hun/.
  (c) Elsewhere: /hun/.

'one' /*xun/
  (a) All dialects: /hun/.

'head' /*xol/
  (a) All dialects: /hol/.

'black' /*ʔihk'/
  (a) San Bartolomé: /ʔik'/ (low tone).
  (b) Elsewhere: /ʔik'/.

'wind' /*ʔik'/
  (a) San Bartolomé: /ʔik'/ (high tone).
  (b) Elsewhere: /ʔik'/.

'intelligent' /*p'ix/
  (a) Chamula, Mitontic, Chenalhó: /b'ih/.
  (b) San Bartolomé, scattered informants from Bochil, Soyaló, and Jitotol: /wiwo/ (from Spanish).
  (c) Elsewhere: /p'i, p'ih/.

'name' /*b'ih/
  (a) All dialects: /b'i, b'ih/.

'buzzard'
  (a) Huetiupan, Azufre, Santa Catarina, Simojovel, northern paraje of Chalchihuitan: /woskon/.
  (b) Totolapa, some Huistan: /tanhol/.
  (c) San Bartolo: /loʔ¢oʔ/.
  (d) Elsewhere: /šulem/.

'small'
  (a) Heutiupan, Azufre, Santa Catarina, Simojovel, northern paraje of Chalchihuitán: /čut/.
  (b) Elsewhere: /b'ik'it/.

'eggs'
  (a) Huetiupan, Azufre, Santa Catarina, Simojovel, northern and western parajes Chalchihuitán, Pantelhó, some Chamula, some Chenalhó, some Mitontic, San Bartolo: /ton mut/.
  (b) Magdalenas, some Chamula, one San Andrés, one Huistán: /ton ʔalak'/.
  (c) Totolapa: /ton kašan/.
  (d) Elsewhere: /ton kašlan/.

'meat of the pig'
  (a) Pantelhó: /tiʔb'ol čitom/.
  (b) Elsewhere: /b'ak'etal čitom/, b'ek'tal čitom/.

'who'
  (a) Huetiupan, Santa Catarina, some Chalchihuitán, some Pantelhó, some Chemalhó: /b'oč'o/.
  (b) San Bartolo, Zapotal, Totolapa, some Huistán, southern parajes Zinacantan: /muč'u/.
  (c) Elsewhere: /b'uč'u/.

'girl'
  (a)   Santiago, Bochil, Soyaló, western parajes San Andrés: /¢eub'/.
  (b)   Ixtapa: /¢iob'/.
  (c)   San Bartolo: /¢eob'/.
  (d)   Elsewhere: /¢eb'/.

'mountain'
  (a)   Bochil, Soyaló: /¢el/varying with/č'en/.
  (b)   Elsewhere: /wi¢/.

'rainbow'
  (a)   San Bartolo: /me?k'inab'al/.
  (b)   Zinacantan, Huistán, Zapotal, Totolapa: /ma?k'inub'al/.
  (c)   Ixtapa: /b'aknab'al/.
  (d)   Most Chamula: /waknak'ob'al/.
  (e)   Western San Andrés, Jitotol, Yuquim: /wakneb'al/.
  (f)   Some Santiago: /wakb'alnab'/.
  (g)   Elsewhere: /waknab'al/.

'heart'
  (a)   Bochil, Soyaló, Jitotol, San Andrés, Santiago, San Juan El Bosque, Santa Marta, Zinacantan, some Chenalhó, some Zapotal, some Chiapilla: /?o?on(ton)/.
  (b)   San Bartolo: /?o?n/.
  (c)   Ixtapa: /?o?non/.
  (d)   Elsewhere: /?o?nton/.

'bat'
  (a)   Santiago and western paraje Chalchihuitán: /nukul čak/.
  (b)   Elsewhere: /so¢'/.

'navel'
  (a)   Southern parajes Chalchihuitán, Chenalhó: /mišak'/.
  (b)   Totolapa, San Bartolo, Huetiupan: /mikiš/.
  (c)   Elsewhere: /mišik'/.

'guava'
  (a)   Northern and western parajes Chalchihuitán, some Huistán: /poto?/.
  (b)   Most Chenalhó, Totolapa, San Bartolo: /potoh/.
  (c)   Elsewhere: /potow/.

'ant'
  (a)   Chamula: /hinič'/.
  (b)   Elsewhere: /šinič/ (scattered /šinič'/).

'all, everyone'
  (a)   Chamula, San Bartolo: /tekel/ varying with /kotol/.
  (b)   Elsewhere: /kotol/.

'prickly pear'
  (a)   Ixtapa: /č'u/.
  (b)   Eastern paraje Chalchihuitán (Pom):   /petek/.
  (c)   Northern and western parajes Chalchihuitán, most Chenalhó:
         /petak/.
  (d)   Eastern paraje Chalchihuitán (Balunacó), Mitontic: /petuk/.
  (e)   Simojovel, Santa Catarina, Pantelhó, Soyaló, five scattered in-
         formants: /tuna/ (from Spanish).
  (f)   Elsewhere: /petok/.

'claw'
  (a)   Azufre, Santa Catarina: /ʔič'ak'/.
  (b)   San Bartolo, one Huistán: /ʔik'ač/.
  (c)   Elsewhere: /(sniʔ) ʔič'ak/.

'moon'
  (a)   Huetiupan, Santa Catarina, Ixtapa, most Huistán, one Zapotal:
         /ʔu/.
  (b)   Elsewhere: /(č'ul) meʔtik/.

'sun'
  (a)   Huetiupan, Azufre, Santa Catarina, most Simojovel, some Ji-
         totol, some Bochil, some Soyaló, most Ixtapa, most Zinacantan,
         most Totolapa, Zapotal, some Chamula, Huistán: /k'ak'al/.
  (b)   Remainder Simojovel, remainder Ixtapa: /totik k'ak'al/.
  (c)   Remainder Totolapa, San Bartolo: /č'ul k'ak'al/.
  (d)   Remainder Jitotol, remainder Bochil, remainder Zinacantan,
         some Chamula, some Santiago, one Pantelhó, one San Andrés:
         /č'ul totik/.
  (e)   Elsewhere: /totik/.

'night'
  (a)   Santa Catarina, some Simojovel, Magdalenas, some Santa
         Marta, some Mitontic, Ixtapa, Totolapa: /ʔak'ab'al/.
  (b)   North and west parajes Chalchihuitán, remainder Mitontic,
         most Santiago, most Huistán, Chamula: /ʔak'ob'al/.
  (c)   Some Chenalhó, some Huistán: /ʔak'b'al/.
  (d)   Elsewhere: /ʔak'ub'al/.

'round'
(a) Huetiupan, Azufre, some Simojovel, most Chalchihuitán, some Pantelhó, some Chenalhó, Ixtapa, Huistán, southern Zinacantan, San Bartolo: /sep (sep)/.
(b) Elsewhere: /set (set)/.

The distribution of lexical items reveals several groups of Tzotzil dialects that tend to share lexical items of limited distribution. One of these groups includes the northern communities of Huetiupan (with its colonies Azufre and Santa Catarina), Simojovel, and Chalchihuitán. A second group includes San Andrés Larrainzar, Santiago, Santa Marta, Magdalenas, Bochil, Soyaló, and Jitotol. The third group includes Huistán, San Bartolo, Zapotal, and Totolapa. Some affinities between the first two groups and between the second two groups are evident. The distribution of morphological variants tends to agree with the lexical groupings.

Phonological developments identify a group of dialects composed of Mitontic, San Pedro Chenalhó, Chamula, and Zinacantan, where /*h/ regularly becomes /y h w/. Some forms showing this development, regular within these communities, also occur in neighboring communities, but the area in which the phonological development is regular is clearly limited to these four communities. Forms showing these phonological developments, which occur outside these four communities, can be taken to be loans from these dialects to others.

Sociocultural data collected along with the linguistic data shed some light on these distributions. A great part of the western Tzotzil area—Bochil, Jitotol, Pueblo Nuevo Solistahuacán, and possibly also Soyaló—have been colonized since the eighteenth century by Indians moving out of the densely populated highland communities, particularly Chamula and San Andrés Larráinzar. At least some parts of the western Tzotzil area were recently populated by speakers of Zoque and Nahuatl, and it is possible that recent immigrants are the first Tzotzil speakers to reside in these communities. Linguistically, the speech of these new colonies cannot be distinguished from the speech of the communities from which these immigrants were drawn; Bochil, Jitotol and Soyaló agree linguistically with the western parajes of San Andrés Larráinzar; the speech of Rincón Chamula, a colony of Chamulas in the municipio of Pueblo Nuevo Solistahuacán, agrees in virtually all features with the speech of Chamula proper.

The Indian population of Chiapilla is likewise composed of relatively recent immigrants who were plantation workers prior to receiving ejido lands after the Mexican revolution. Their speech is like that of the southern parajes of Zinacantán, and it is possible that they were originally recruited for the plantations from the southern parts of Zinacantán.

Considering phonological, morphological, and lexical distributions together, the dialects of Tzotzil can be subgrouped into four groups. The first group includes Simojovel, Huetiupan, and Chalchihuitán. The second includes San Andrés Larráinzar, Santiago, Santa Marta, Magdalenas, and perhaps San Juan El Bosque. The third group is composed of Chenalhó, Mitontic, Chamula, and Zinacantán. Huistán, Totolapa, and San Bartolo make up the fourth group. The dialect of Pantelhó appears to be closely related to none of these subgroups; it is phonologically distinct from the latter two groups, but is not particularly affiliated with the first two either, although it is geographically adjacent to the first two dialect groups. It is probably best thought of as a fourth "group" formed by a single dialect. Similarly, Ixtapa, which is phonologically allied to the first two dialect groups, is separated from these by a number of lexical peculiarities and at least one morphological feature; it is perhaps best thought of as a sixth dialect "group."

Within the first group of dialects, Chalchihuitán is peculiar in that its western parajes show greater lexical similarity to Simojovel and Huetiupan than do its southern parajes, which share lexical items with Chenalhó. These distributions probably reflect trade patterns, since the western parajes attend markets in Simojovel, while the southern parajes market in Chenalhó.

The single informant from El Azufre, colony of Huetiupan, where there are also Chol speakers, was unique phonologically in producing retroflex /š/ instead of the normal laminal articulations. It is not known if this pronunciation was an individual characteristic or a characteristic pronunciation of his community.

Within the second group of dialects, the western parajes of San Andrés Larráinzar and its colonies differ from the rest of the community of San Andres Larráinzar in a few features. Chamula, in the third group of dialects, shows phonological and lexical features not shared by the other three communities in that group. The fourth dialect group is unique in that the dialects that are allied on morphological and lexical grounds have different phonological systems. Huistán has the /H/ developments of /*h/, San Bartolo has a tonal system and unrounded central allophones of /u/, and Totolapa has labialized voiced velar stops as the principal allophones of /w/.

An interesting feature of Tzotzil dialects, which is repeated in the Tzeltal dialects, is the occurrence of a large number of lexical items that are universal in the speech of a single community but absent in the speech of other communities. Examples are San Bartolo /loʔȼoʔ/ 'buzzard', /ʔoʔn/ 'heart', /meʔk'inabal/ 'rainbow', /ȼeob'/ 'girl'; Ixtapa /ȼioh'/ 'girl', /ʔoʔnon/ 'heart', /b'aknab'al/ 'rainbow', /ču/ 'prickly pear'; Totolapa /ton kašan/ 'egg'; Chamula /hinič/ 'ant'; Pantelhó /tiʔb'ol/ 'meat'.

Dialects of Tzeltal

Dialect survey questionnaires were taken from the Tzeltal communities of Abasolo (4 informants), Aguacatenango (9), Altamirano (2), Amatenango (4), Bachajón (15), Cancuc (7), Chilón (3), Chanal (3), Guaquitepec (3), Ocosingo (7), Oxchuc (23), Petalcingo (2), Pinola (Villa Las Rosas) (20), Sibacá (13), Sitalá (3), Tenejapa (24), and Yajalón (3). Colonies of these communities that we studied are El Puerto (2), a colony of Aguacatenango, and La Palizada (2), a colony of Oxchuc. Efforts were made to obtain informants from various subdivisions of each community.

Phonological developments that are of interest in the study of Tzeltal dialects are the following:

1. Developments of /*x/ and /*h/: (a) in Bachajón and Petalcingo, /*x/ becomes /x/ and /*h/ becomes /h/. (b) In Sitalá and Yajalón, noninitial, nonfinal /*h/ becomes /H/, manifested phonetically as vowel length. (c) In the remaining communities, /*x/ and /*h/ in initial position become /h/, and a variety of changes affect /*x/ and /*h/ in other positions, but they do not remain distinct.

2. Developments of C_2 in roots of the shape C_1VhC_2, where C_2 is one of the consonants /p t ȼ č k/. (a) In Oxchuc, C_2 becomes glottalized. (b) Elsewhere, C_2 remains a plain stop or affricate.

3. Developments of /*p'/ and /*b'/. (a) In Oxchuc, /*p'/ and /*b'/ merge as /b'/. (b) Elsewhere, /*p'/ and /*b'/ remain /p'/ and /b'/.

Kaufman (1962, p. 141) distinguishes two groups of dialects on the basis of the developments of allophones of /b'/; one of these groups includes Cancuc, Tenejapa, Oxchuc, Teopisca, and Pinola. Kaufman discusses other phonological developments of importance for the study of Tzeltal dialects that are of little importance for the present study.

Although there are no doubt morphological variants between the Tzeltal dialects, none have been used here to identify dialects of Tzeltal. It is interesting to note that the verbal prefix /yak (ta-)/, mentioned in reference to western Tzotzil dialects, is common in the majority of Tzeltal dialects.

Examples that illustrate the Tzeltal phonological developments and the patterns of distribution of lexical variants in the Tzeltal area follow.

'tomorrow' /*paxel/
(a) Bachajón, Petalcingo: /paxel/.
(b) Elsewhere: /pahel/.

'thin' /*xay/
(a) Bachajón, Petalcingo: /xay/.
(b) Elsewhere: /hay/.

'butterfly' /*pehpen/
(a) Sitalá, Yajalón: /pe:pen/.
(b) Oxchuc, some Abasolo, one Sibacá, one Tenango, one Chanal: /pehb'en/.
(c) Some Pinola: /tultuš/.
(d) Elsewhere: /pehpen/.

'duck'
(a) Petalcingo, Chilón, Sitalá, Yajalón, one Bachajón: /peš/.
(b) Tenejapa, Cancuc: /peč'/.
(c) Elsewhere: /peč/. (No data from Amatenango.)

'horse' (all from Spanish *caballo*)
(a) Petalcingo, Chilón, Sitalá, Yajalón, Bachajón, some Ocosingo, one Amatenango: /kawu/.
(b) Aguacatenango, one El Puerto, Pinola: /kah/
(c) Elsewhere: /kabayo, kabayu, kawayo, kawayu/.

'distant'
(a) Petalcingo, Sitalá, Yajalón, Chilón, Tenango, Guaquitepec, Bachajón, one Sibacá, one Ocosingo: /namal/.
(b) Remainder of Ocosingo, some Sibacá, most Abasolo, some Altamirano: /šač'al/.
(c) Remainder of Sibacá, Aguacatenango, El Puerto, Amatenango: /hakal/.
(d) Remainder of Abasolo, most Cancuc, most Tenejapa: /k'ub'ul/.
(e) Remainder of Cancuc, remainder of Tenejapa: /naht/.
(f) Chanal, Oxchuc, La Palizada: /naht'/.

'lake'
(a) Petalcingo, Sitalá, Chilón, Guaquitepec, most Bachajón, most Sibacá, most Ocosingo, some Abasolo, some Yajalón, one El Puerto: /pam (pam) haʔ/.
(b) Remainder Abasolo: /čamel haʔ/.
(c) Altamirano, some Sibacá: /čamen haʔ/.
(d) Chanal, Tenejapa, remainder Tenango, some Yajalón, some Bachajón, most Oxchuc, some Pinola, some Amatenango, one La Palizada, one El Puerto: /nab'il/.
(e) Remainder of Amatenango: /tiʔ haʔ/.
(f) Aguacatenango, some Oxchuc, one La Palizada: /haʔ/.
(g) Elsewhere: /ʔalaguna/ (from Spanish).

'lungs'
  (a) Petalcingo, Bachajón, Sitalá, some Yajalón, some Guaquitepec, some Abasolo, some Oxchuc, some Tenejapa: /sot'ot'/.
  (b) Aguacatenango, El Puerto, some Amatenango, some Pinola: /puhpu(ʔ)/.
  (c) Remainder of Amatenango: /pum/.
  (d) Elsewhere: /puȼ(uȼ)/.

'left (hand)'
  (a) Petalcingo, Sitalá, Yajalón, Chilón, Sibacá, Ocosingo, Cancuc, some Altamirano, some Aguacatenango, some Bachajón: /k'ešan (k'ab')/.
  (b) Remainder Altamirano, Oxchuc, La Palizada, Chanal, Abasolo: /k'ešen (k'ab')/.
  (c) Guaquitepec, Tenango, remainder Bachajón, some Aguacatenango, some Pinola: /k'ešam (k'ab')/.
  (d) Remainder Aguacatenango, El Puerto, remainder (most of) Pinola: /k'ešem (k'ab')/.
  (e) Tenejapa: /šin/.
  (f) Amatenango: /k'ešom/.

'armadillo'
  (a) Petalcingo, Sitalá, Yajalón, Chilón, Bachajón, Sibacá, Ocosingo, Altamirano, Abasolo, Tenango, Guaquitepec, Amatenango: /ʔib'/.
  (b) Cancuc, some Oxchuc, some Tenejapa: /mayil tiʔb'al, ȼ'ol tiʔb'al/.
  (c) Aguacatenango, El Puerto: /tuluk' čan/.
  (d) Pinola: /meʔmut/.
  (e) Elsewhere: /mail čan/.

'where'
  (a) Petalcingo, Chilón, Tenango, Guaquitepec, most Bachajón, most Sitalá, some Sibacá, Cancuc, most Oxchuc, most Tenejapa, most Abasolo: /b'anti (ʔay)/.
  (b) Yajalón, Altamirano, Ocosingo, remainder Abasolo, remainder Sibacá, remainder Bachajón, remainder Oxchuc: /b'an (ʔay)/.
  (c) Chanal, La Palizada: /b'ati (ʔay), b'ate (ʔay)/.
  (d) Pinola, Aguacatenango, Amatenango, El Puerto, remainder Tenejapa: /b'a(ʔ)/.

'ant'
  (a) Tenango, Guaquitepec, most Bachajón, most Chilón, some Sibacá, some Ocosingo: /šanič'/.

(b)   Abasolo: /sanʔič'/.
(c)   La Palizada, most Amatenango: /šanʔič/.
(d)   Elsewhere: /šanič/. (No data from Oxchuc, Chanal, Altamirano, Cancuc.)

'many'
(a)   Some Bachajón, some Petalcingo, one Ocosingo, one Chanal: /¢ob'olik/.
(b)   Tenango, Sibacá, Altamirano, remainder Chanal, Abasolo, Oxchuc, Aguacatenango, Amatenango, Pinola, some Ocosingo, La Palizada: /b'ayal/.
(c)   Guaquitepec, Sitalá, Yajalón, Chilón, remainder Petalcingo, remainder Bachajón, remainder Ocosingo, Cancuc, Tenejapa: /b'ayel/.
(d)   El Puerto: /b'ayil/.

'small'
(a)   Petalcingo, one Oxchuc: /šuht/.
(b)   Yajalón, two Oxchuc: /šut/.
(c)   Tenango, Guaquitepec, Chilón, Bachajón, Sibacá, Ocosingo, some Cancuc, one Abasolo, one Sitalá, one Tenejapa: /tut/.
(d)   Remainder Sitalá: /b'ik'it/.
(e)   Remainder Cancuc, two Tenejapa, most Oxchuc: /¢ael, ¢ail/.
(f)   Chanal, Altamirano, Amatenango, Aguacatenango, El Puerto, La Palizada, Pinola, remainder Oxchuc, remainder Tenejapa, remainder Abasolo: /č'in/.

'seated'
(a)   Tenango, Sibaca, Ocosingo, Altamirano, some Abasolo, one Aguacatenango: /hu¢(ul)/.
(b)   Bachajón, one Chilón: /huk(ul)/.
(c)   Chanal, remainder Aguacatenango, some Oxchuc, La Palizada, El Puerto, some Abasolo: /čot(ol)/.
(d)   Elsewhere: /nak(al)/.

'claw'
(a)   Tenango, Guaquitepec, Sitalá, Yajalón, Chilón, some Ocosingo, one Bachajón, one Sibacá: /ʔek'ač/.
(b)   Oxchuc, Tenejapa, Chanal, Abasolo, Amatenango, La Palizada: /ʔehk'ač/.
(c)   Cancuc, Altamirano, Aguacatenango, El Puerto: /ʔehk'ač/.
(d)   Elsewhere: /ʔeč'ak/.

'oranges' (all from Spanish *naranja, naranjas*)
(a) Petalcingo, Yajalón, Sitalá, Chilón, Bachajón; loans replacing /n-/ by /ʔ-/: /ʔalašaš/, /ʔalešaš/.
(b) Tenejapa: /ʔalčaš, ʔalšaš/.
(c) Tenango, Sibacá, Ocosingo, Abasolo, Altamirano, some Guaquitepec; loans retaining /n-/: /naranšaš, narašaš, narišaš, nalašaš, naranka, naranha/.
(d) Most Oxchuc, some Cancuc: /naraš/.
(e) Remainder Oxchuc, remainder Cancuc, Chanal, La Palizada, some Abasolo: /naršaš/.
(f) Pinola, Aguacatenango, Amatenango, El Puerto, Remainder Guaquitepec: /nalaš/.

'white squash'
(a) Tenango, Sibacá, Ocosingo, Altamirano, most Bachajón, some Abasolo, some Guaquitepec, most Cancuc, some Pinola: /sakil č'um/.
(b) Oxchuc, some Tenejapa, some Chanal: /sakil ¢'ool/.
(c) Elsewhere: /(sakil) mayil, mail/.

'nose mucus'
(a) Bachajón, Yajalón, Chilón, Petalcingo, Tenango, Guaquitepec, Sitalá, most Sibacá, some Ocosingo, Aguacatenango, El Puerto, Pinola: /¢aʔ(il/al/ul) niʔ/.
(b) Elsewhere: /simal/.

'above'
(a) Petalcingo, Yajalón, Tenango, most Sitalá, most Bachajón, some Sibacá, some Guaquitepec, some Aguacatenango, some Amatenango, most Pinola, one Tenejapa, one Ocosingo: /toyol/.
(b) Oxchuc, most Abasolo, most Guaquitepec, most Chanal, some Tenejapa, some Amatenango (remainder), La Palizada: /kahal/.
(c) Elsewhere: /ʔahk'ol/.

'what'
(a) Petalcingo, Yajalón, Bachajón, Tenango, most Sibacá, some Ocosingo, some Abasolo, Altamirano, some Guaquitepec, some Sitalá, some Chilón: /b'in/.
(b) Cancuc, Tenejapa, remainder Abasolo, remainder Sitalá, remainder Guaquitepec, remainder Sibacá, remainder Ocosingo, remainder Chilón, some Oxchuc, one Chanal, one La Palizada: /b'i/.
(c) Remainder Chanal, remainder La Palizada: /b'eti(1)/.
(d) Remainder (most) Oxchuc: /b'eluk/.
(e) Some Aguacatenango: /tu/.

(f)   Remainder Aguacatenango: /tut/.

(g)   Pinola: /tuʔti/.

(h)   Amatenango: /tut'/.

'root'

(a)   Chilón, Bachajón, Ocosingo, some Tenango, some Guaquitepec, some Sitalá, some Altamirano: /lohp/.

(b)   Some Sibacá: /ʔismal/.

(c)   Aguacatenango, El Puerto: /ʔehk'ač/.

(d)   Elsewhere: /ʔisim/.

'day'

(a)   Petalcingo, Guaquitepec, Bachajón, Sibacá, Ocosingo, Altamirano, Abasolo, some Tenango, some Chilón, most Yajalón, some
Amatenango, some Oxchuc, some Aguacatenango: /k'ahk'al/.

(b)   Remainder Yajalón, one Sitalá, one Ocosingo: /k'ak'al/.

(c)   Remainder Sitalá, remainder Chilón, most Tenejapa: /k'al/.

(d)   Remainder Tenejapa, remainder Tanango, Chanal, Cancuc, remainder Oxchuc, La Palizada, some Amatenango: /k'aal/.

(e)   Remainder Aguacatenango, El Puerto, some Pinola: /k'ahal/.

(f)   Remainder Pinola: /k'aʔal/.

'sun'

(a)   Petalcingo, Altamirano, some Abasolo, most Guaquitepec,
most Yajalón, one Chilón, most Bachajón, Sibacá, Ocosingo, some
Amatenango, one Aguacatenango: /k'ahk'al/.

(b)   Remainder Yajalón, most Sitalá, one Chilón: /k'ak'al/.

(c)   Remainder Sitalá, one Chilón, one Bachajón, one Tenejapa:
/k'al/.

(d)   Remainder Abasolo, Tenango, remainder Guaquitepec, Chanal,
Cancuc, Oxchuc, La Palizada, some Tenejapa: /k'aal/.

(e)   Some Aguacatenango: /k'ahal/.

(f)   Some Pinola: /k'aʔal/.

(g)   Remainder Bachajón, one Aguacatenango: /tati k'ahk'al/.

(h)   Remainder (most) Aguacatenango, El Puerto, some Pinola:
/tati k'ahal/.

(i)   Remainder (most) Pinola, some Amatenango: /tati k'aʔal/.

(j)   Remainder (most) Tenejapa: /č'ul tatik/.

(k)   Remainder Amatenango: /č'ul k'ahk'al/.

'fox'

(a)   Petalcingo, Bachajón, most Yajalón, most Chilón, some Guaquitepec, Pinola: /pahay/.

(b)   Tenango, most Sitalá, remainder Yajalón, remainder Chilón,
some Sibacá: /pahy/.

(c)   Remainder Sibacá, remainder Sitalá, some Abasolo, Chanal, Cancuc, La Palizada, Aguacatenango, Tenejapa, some Amatenango: /pay/.
(d)   Elsewhere: /soro/ (from Spanish *zorro*.)

'near'
(a)   Aguacatenango, El Puerto, Tenejapa, Amatenango, one La Palizada, two Oxchuc: /tihil/.
(b)   Remainder Oxchuc, some Cancuc: /kom/.
(c)   Elsewhere: /nopol/.

'tree trunk'
(a)   Aguacatenango, El Puerto: /kohteʔ/.
(b)   Some Bachajón: /stomalteʔ/.
(c)   Most Sibacá: /slohpteʔ/.
(d)   Some Oxchuc, one Petalcingo, one La Palizada: /čuminteʔ/.
(e)   Some Tenejapa: /čomanteʔ/.
(f)   Chanal, most Oxchuc, one Abasolo, one Tenango: /čumunteʔ/.
(g)   Some Amatenango: /yeʔtalteʔ/.
(h)   Elsewhere: /čumanteʔ/.

'to work'
(a)   Aguacatenango, Amatenango, Tenejapa, La Palizada, El Puerto: /ʔaʔtel/.
(b)   Pinola, some Bachajón, most Sibacá, Ocosingo, Cancuc, some Oxchuc: /ʔatel/.
(c)   Elsewhere: /ʔat'el/.

'dead'
(a)   Oxchuc, Chanal, Cancuc, most Tenejapa, one La Palizada: /lah/.
(b)   Elsewhere: /čam/.

'long'
(a)   Oxchuc, Chanal, Aguacatenango, Amatenango, El Puerto, some Abasolo, some Altamirano, one La Palizada: /naht'/.
(b)   Elsewhere: /naht/.

'stone'
(a)   Most Oxchuc: /č'en/.
(b)   Elsewhere: /ton/.

'foot'
(a)   Oxchuc, Cancuc, Tenejapa, Abasolo, most Tenango, most Guaquitepec, some Sibacá, one La Palizada: /ʔakan/.
(b)   Elsewhere: /ʔok/.

'egg'
(a)   Oxchuc, Chanal, La Palizada, some Abasolo, some Tenango: /tumut/.
(b)   Some Bachajón: /ton/.
(c)   Some Tenejapa, some Pinola: /tonmut/.
(d)   Elsewhere: /tomut/.

'bat'
(a)   Oxchuc: /nuhk'ul?it/ varying with /soȼ'/.
(b)   Elsewhere: /soȼ'/.

'cotton'
(a)   Oxchuc, Chanal, Abasolo, Tenejapa, Aguacatenango, El Puerto, La Palizada, some Amatenango, one Petalcingo: /tunim/.
(b)   Elsewhere: /tumin/.

'hog trough, wash trough'
(a)   Oxchuc, Cancuc, Chanal, some Abasolo, some Sibacá, some Tenejapa: /hob'inte?/.
(b)   Most Pinola: /hukute?/.
(c)   Abasolo, Tenango, Guaquitepec, Sitalá, Yajalón, Chilón, Petalcingo, Bachajón, remainder Sibacá, one Ocosingo: loans from Spanish *batea*.
(d)   Altamirano, Aguacatenango, El Puerto, Amatenango, La Palizada, remainder Tenejapa, remainder Ocosingo, remaining Pinola: loans from Spanish *canoa*.

'right (hand)'
(a)   Aguacatenango, Pinola, Amatenango, La Palizada, El Puerto, some Oxchuc: /b'aȼ'il (k'ab')/.
(b)   Some Tenejapa: /wo?el/.
(c)   Elsewhere: /wa?el/.

'horn(s)'
(a)   Aguacatenango, one El Puerto, Pinola, Amatenango: /šulb'al/.
(b)   Elsewhere: /šulub'/.

'face'
(a)   Most Pinola, some Tenejapa, one Petalcingo, one Bachajón, two Ocosingo, Amatenango, one La Palizada: /sit/.
(b)   Elsewhere: /?elaw/.

'there'
(a)   Aguacatenango, El Puerto, one La Palizada: /nun/.
(b)   Most Oxchuc: /le?/.
(c)   Some Bachajón, some Sibacá, some Cancuc, some Pinola, some

Tenejapa, some Amatenango: /tey/.
(d)   Elsewhere: /lum/.

'sweet potato' (*camote*)
(a)   Aguacatenango, El Puerto: /ʔisʔak'/.
(b)   Elsewhere: /čiʔin/.

'buzzard'
(a)   Pinola, Amatenango, most Tenejapa: /ȼaʔlos/.
(b)   Remainder Tenejapa: /ʔihk'al šulem/.
(c)   Most Oxchuc: /homen–humen/ varying with /hos/.
(d)   Elsewhere: /hos/.

'heart'
(a)   Cancuc, Aguacatenanto, Pinola, Tenejapa, Amatenango, one El Puerto, one La Palizada: /ʔoʔtan/.
(b)   One El Puerto: /ʔoʔton/.
(c)   Elsewhere: /ʔot'an/.

'frost'
(a)   Petalcingo: /b'atil haʔal/.
(b)   Ocosingo: /b'at/.
(c)   Sibacá, some Bachajón: /sik/.
(d)   Chilón, remainder Bachajón: /meʔsik/.
(e)   Amatenango: /hom/.
(f)   Elsewhere: forms from /*toh(y)ib'–*toh(y)iw/: /toyib', tuew, toiw/.

On the basis of the phonological and lexical evidence, a number of Tzeltal dialect groups can be identified. The first of these includes the northern and eastern communities of Petalcingo, Yajalón, Chilón, Sitalá, Bachajón, Guaquitepec, Tenango, Sibacá, Ocosingo, and Altamirano. The second group is formed by the central Tzeltal communities of Oxchuc, Abasolo, Cancuc, and Tenejapa. The third group is composed of the southern Tzeltal communities of Aguacatenango, Amatenango, and Pinola.

Within the first group, a subgroup is formed by Petalcingo, Bachajón, Sitalá, Yajalón, and Chilón. Oxchuc, Chanal, and Abasolo form a subgroup within the central area. The three southern communities are grouped alternately in pairs by a number of features.

Abasolo shows affinities to Tenango and Sibacá on the one hand and to Aguacatenango on the other hand. Cancuc shares features with Ocosingo and Sibacá; Tenejapa shares features with Sitalá and Guaquitepec to the north and with Amatenango to the south.

As in the Tzotzil dialects, agricultural colonies of the Tzeltal communities are very similar linguistically to their communities of origin. The speech of El Puerto agrees with that of Aguacatenango in almost all details. La Palizada, a colony of Oxchuc located in the neighborhood of Aguacatenango, maintains a basic similarity to Oxchuc but has begun to acquire features characteristic of Aguacatenango.

Tzeltal lexical items which are universal within a community but limited in distribution to that community are: Petalcingo /b'atil haʔal/ 'hail'; Oxchuc /nuhk'ul ʔit/ 'bat ; Abasolo /san ʔič) ant; Tenejapa /šin/ 'left side'; Amatenango /k'ešom/ 'left side', /hom/ hail, /tut'/ 'what'; Aguacatenango /nun/ 'there', /kohteʔ/ 'trunk of tree', /ʔisʔak'/ 'camote', /tuluk' čan/ 'armadillo'; Pinola /tuʔti/ 'what', /meʔmut/ 'armadillo'; El Puerto /b'ayil/ 'many'. In addition to these lexical peculiarities, there are a number of phonological developments that are limited in distribution to single Tzeltal communities (Kaufman, 1962, pp. 168–218).

Patterns of Distribution

There are two patterns of distribution of linguistic variants that are of interest in the study of Tzeltal and Tzotzil dialects. The first is the formation of dialect areas—groups of adjacent communities that share a large number of linguistic features but that can be subdivided on other criteria. The second is the occurrence of lexical items and phonological developments that are limited to single communities—features that occur in the speech of all informants from a given community but that are absent from the speech of all other communities.

Dialect Groups

Since the linguistic unity of Tzeltal and Tzotzil has been firmly established, all dialects of Tzeltal and Tzotzil are the descendants of a single language, proto-Tzeltal–Tzotzil. Phonological developments, morphological distributions, and the number of lexical items that can be reconstructed only for proto-Tzeltal or proto-Tzotzil indicate that this language developed two major varieties, one the ancestor of Tzeltal, the other the ancestor of Tzotzil. Glottochronological figures indicate this diversification had begun by the middle of the ninth century A.D. The internal diversification of Tzotzil had begun by the first parts of the twelfth century A.D., while Tzeltal had begun to diversify by the middle of the fifteenth century A.D. Since it is possible that continued contact between the developing dialects has retarded independent lexical innovation, these dates should be conservative; i.e., the population movements and formation of political and economic subgroups that gave rise to the dialect diversification may have in fact taken place somewhat earlier than the indicated dates. At any rate, it seems probable that the diversification of proto-Tzeltal–Tzotzil is, in terms of Mayan archaeology, a Late Classic and Postclassic phenomenon. The archaeological investigations of Adams (1961, 1970) in the highlands of Chiapas support this contention. Pre-classic sites were small and scattered. In the latter parts of the Early Classic there was a considerable increase in population. In the Late Classic, ceremonial and residential centers were widely distributed and relatively independent of one another rather than grouped into regional coalitions. In the Postclassic, there are changes in the locations of settlements (from easily defended ridgetop locations to greater utilization of strategically located valleys) and there are indications that developing regional groupings of interdependent communities may reflect new patterns of political and religious control (Adams, 1970, p. 43).

A detailed correlation of the archaeological and linguistic data on the Chiapas highlands must await more detailed archaeological and linguistic studies. Available evidence suggests that a proto-Tzeltal–Tzotzil population moved into the highlands in the latter part of the Early Classic and began to diversify throughout the Late Classic into relatively independent communities. From the linguistic evidence, it appears that a major east–west division of the communities into proto-Tzotzil and proto-Tzeltal communities began during the Late Classic. In the Post-Classic, smaller regional groupings appear to emerge, and it is possible that these latter regional alliances are reflected in the linguistic evidence as the major dialect groups of Tzeltal and Tzotzil. A strong note of caution should be attached to any such speculations—the archaeological data are slim, and these communities were subjected to some relocation and reorganization during the colonial period, as ethnohistorical investigations (Calnek, 1970) are beginning to show.

Calnek's investigation of Mexican archives reveals, for instance, that in the northern Tzotzil area both Hueitiupan and Chalchihuitán received population from Pantelhó in 1605; Pantelhó belonged to Magdalenas in 1560. Simojovel was populated by former subjects of Zinacantan, the Amaitic, in 1549–1580, and in 1604–1605 these were joined by other Amaitics who had previously settled near Plátanos. In the central Tzotzil area, Bochil and Soyaló were reported as Mexican (Nahuatl) in speech in the eighteenth century. (During the dialect survey, an aged Soyaló Nahuatl speaker recalled that during his youth most of the village spoke that language.) Magdalenas was, with Santa Marta, the head of nine pueblos in 1560, from near Jitotol in the west to Pantelhó in the northeast. Chamula, conquered in 1524, later formed a rebellious alliance with Huistán, but became part of Bernal Diaz' encomienda and was moved to its present location from a location slightly to the east. Zinacantan had been conquered by Montezuma II, was visited by Aztec traders, and was a center of trade and the richest Tzotzil town in the conquest period. Ixtapa belonged to Zinacantan before the conquest, and in 1549 five unidentified pueblos were added to Ixtapa. In the southern Tzotzil area, Totolapa was Nahuatl-speaking in 1528. San Bartolomé, reported as early as 1598, received a large influx of population from the surrounding area during seventeenth century plagues.

In the northern Tzeltal area, Petalcingo, while Tzeltal-speaking, was subject to Chol-speaking Tila in 1535, and after an insurrection, it was placed administratively with Tila, Tumbalá, and Palenque, all Chol-speaking towns. Bachajón was founded in 1564 with population from the area north of Ocosingo. Guaquitepec was formed in 1558 from formerly independent communities. Tenango and Cancuc were part of the same encomienda in the early 1700s; after insurgence, some of the population were relocated. Oxchuc was Tzeltal-speaking in 1535 and underwent considerable growth in the sixteenth and seventeenth centuries; some groups were resettled there. Oxchuc included Abasolo until late in the seventeenth century. In the south, Amatenango was under Teopisca through the sixteenth century, and Aguacatenango was lumped with a community named Quetzaltepec. Pinola, mentioned by Bernal Diaz, was reduced by drought in 1770–1773, and its population was moved.

All these disturbances in the colonial and postcolonial periods, to say nothing of disruptions that occurred during later insurrections and the Mexican revolution, argue against any facile attempt to view the present linguistic distributions as the simple result of precontact community relations. In this regard, it would perhaps be interesting to carry out a detailed study of the distributions of the variants of loan words from Spanish. Some of these show by their phonology that they are relatively early (e.g., those that have /š/ for Spanish /j/) while some are clearly late. In general, the distributions of these loans, where there are variant forms, seem to follow roughly the same patterns as native forms (cf. Tzeltal 'horse', 'oranges', 'horse trough' above). A comparison of native and nonnative variants, together with a more detailed investigation of archival evidence, could contribute greatly to our understanding of the history of these communities.

Whatever their connection with prehistoric archaeological cultures, it is clear that there are a number of ill-defined subgroups of Tzeltal and Tzotzil dialects, and each group occupies a contiguous geographical zone, with the exception of the relatively recent agricultural colonies that have carried the speech patterns of their homelands to distant locations.

On the other hand, very few isoglosses cut across the area in exactly the same way. The lack of strong isogloss bundles, with the exception of those that separate Tzeltal from Tzotzil, indicates that there is considerable linguistic interchange between neighboring communities and no long-standing barriers to the spread of innovations. While each community tends to share features with certain neighboring communities, each community has a unique set of dialect features. Two communities that are identical in some respects, reflecting their mutual interaction, also differ in other respects, reflecting their differential interaction with still other communities. The overall pattern is one of relative independence of each community within a network of regional affiliations.

COMMUNITY-BOUND FORMS

The pattern of strictly limited distribution of some lexical items and phonological developments—features universal to a single community but absent elsewhere—seems to be a direct reflection of the closed nature of the Tzeltal and Tzotzil communities, which are for the most part endogamous. Although each community or municipio is composed of a number of hamlets and subdivisions, these are closely linked by social, economic, political, and ceremonial ties. The parajes of a municipio may be widely scattered, but their populations interact regularly in ceremonial activities regardless of their geographical separation. There are clear barriers to social interaction between communities manifested in the land tenure system and marriage customs as well as ceremonial obligations, which also express the corporate nature of each Indian community. The linguistic reflection of these social patterns is found in the relative homogeneity of speech within the municipio and the isogloss boundaries that separate the different communities.

The various agricultural colonies reflect in their speech the influence of their new neighbors; the speech of El Puerto, for instance, while still very similar to the speech of its parent community Aguacatenango, has begun to take on a quality of its own due in part to contact with an immigrant population from Huistán. La Palizada is still linguistically similar to Oxchuc, but has acquired new lexical items from the southern Tzeltal communities with which it is in contact.

Some phonological innovations make it possible to trace loans from one dialect to another. The Oxchuc dialect of Tzeltal, for instance, has glottalized some stops and affricates after preconsonantal /*h/. This change is regular in the vocabulary of Oxchuc; neighboring Tzeltal dialects, however, often have one or two words that show this change; these are no doubt loans from Oxchuc and show the influence of Oxchuc on its neighbors. The east central Tzotzil phonological innovation in which /*h/

222 Nicholas A. Hopkins

becomes /y h w/ allows the identification of words loaned from this area into the dialects that are commercially linked to the markets in the east central Tzotzil area; a number of such loans occur in the southern parajes of Chalchihuitán. Tzotzil speakers in Pantelhó, whose market serves the majority of the Tzeltal population located on nearby plantations and the communities of Cancuc and Tenejapa, have adopted the Tzeltalism /tiʔb'ol/ 'meat'. Cancuc and Tenejapa, on the other hand, use the term /peč/ 'duck', apparently a loan from Tzotzil.

There is at least one indication of Chol influence, or mutual Chol–Tzeltal–Tzotzil influence, in the northernmost Tzeltal and Tzotzil dialects. Huetiupan and its colonies Azufre and Santa Catarina, Simojovel, and the northern Chalchihuitán parajes Chiquinxulub and Saclum have the variant /čut/ 'small'. Elsewhere in Tzotzil the variant /b'ik'it/ 'small' is standard. In the northern Tzeltal area, Petalcingo, Yajaón, and some Oxchuc informants have the variant /šut/ or /šuht/ 'small'. Elsewhere in Tzeltal, the forms /tut, b'ik'it, ȼael, ȼail, č'in/ 'small' occur. Whittaker and Warkentin (1965, p. 170) list /xut (šut)/ as 'tip of a wing, part, piece', and it is possible that this Tumbalá Chol form is related to the northern Tzeltal and Tzotzil forms.

A notable exception to the general rule of community homogeneity is the Northern Tzotzil community of Chalchihuitán (Hopkins 1967). Chalchihuitán has no large regular market, and as a consequence its population regularly attends outside markets. The northern parajes regularly attend market in Simojovel, and their speech shares a number of features with the speech of Simojovel. The southern parajes market regularly in Chenalhó, and their speech reflects this contact in dialect loans from the east central Tzotzil area.

A more detailed dialect survey designed to collect the kinds of information that would reveal these patterns could no doubt furnish more definitive statements of the relationships between the speakers of the Tzeltal and Tzotzil dialects. The present study can do no more than demonstrate that given detailed linguistic analysis of local dialects, patterns of interaction and influence between indigenous communities can easily be identified. The linguistic homogeneity of each community in the Tzeltal–Tzotzil area is clear from the present investigation. Not only is each community relatively homogeneous, but a large number of the communities (and perhaps all, if more data were available) can be shown to have undergone phonological, morphological or lexical innovations independent of all other communities. These patterns reflect the social and political organization of the indigenous communities in the Chiapas highlands. On the other hand, contact between the populations of the various communities does take place, and this contact is reflected in the small number of dialect loans that have been definitely identified; in general, these seem to follow lines of interaction related to economic exchange.

References

Adams, Robert M.
 1961 Changing patterns of territorial organization in the Central Highlands of Chiapas, Mexico. *American Antiquity* **26**(3), 341–360.
 1970 Patrones de cambio de la organización territorial. In McQuown and Pitt-Rivers, pp. 43–76. *Ensayos de antropologia en la zona central de Chiapas* edited by Mexico: Instituto Nacional Indigenista.
Bloomfield, Leonard
 1933 *Language*. New York: Holt.
Bottiglioni, Gino
 1954 Linguistic geography: achievements, methods and orientations. *Word* **10**, 375–387.
Bright, William
 1960 Social dialect and language history. *Current Anthropology* **1**, 424–425.
Calnek, Edward E.
 1970 Los pueblos indigenas de las tierras altas. In *Ensayos de antropología en la zona central de Chiapas* edited by McQuown and Pitt-Rivers, pp. 105–133. Mexico: Instituto Nacional Indigenista.
Cancian, Frank
 1965 *Economics and Prestige in a Maya Village*. Stanford: Stanford University Press.
IX Censo General de Población: Mexico
 1970 *Dirección general de estadística*, México, D. F.
Dauzat, A.
 1944 *La géographie linguistique*, Paris. (First edition, 1922.)
Ferguson, Charles A., and John J. Gumperz
 1960 Linguistic diversity in South Asia. Supplement to *International Journal of American Linguistics*, Vol. 26.
Gilliéron, Jules
 1918 *Généalogie des mots qui désignent l'abeille d'après l'atlas linguistique de la France*. Paris.
 1921 *Pathologie et thérapeutique verbales*. Paris.
 1922 *Ménagiana du XXe siècle*. Paris.
Gilliéron, Jules, and E. Edmont
 1902–1910 *Atlas linguistique de la France*. Paris.
Gudschinsky, Sarah C.
 1958 Mazatec dialect history. *Language* **34**, 469–481.
Gumperz, John J.
 1958 Dialect differences and social stratification in a North Indian village. *American Anthropologist* **60**, 688–692.
Haas, Mary
 1966 Historical linguistics and the genetic relationship of languages. *Current Trends in Linguistics*, vol. III. The Hague: Mouton.
Hockett, Charles F.
 1958 *A Course in Modern Linguistics*. New York: Macmillan.
Hopkins, Nicholas
 1967 A short sketch of Chalchihuitán Tzotzil. *Anthropological Linguistics* **9**(4),9–25.

Hymes, Dell
1959   Genetic relationship: retrospect and prospect. *Anthropological Linguistics* 1(2),50–66.
1960   Lexicostatistics so far. *Current Anthropology* 1(1),3–44.
Jaberg, Karl
1908   Sprachgeographie. *Beigrag zur Verständniss des Atlas Linguistique de la France.* Aarau.
1936   Aspects géographiques du language. Paris: Droz.
1937   *Sprachwissenschaftliche Forschungen und Erlebnisse, Romanica Helvetica VI.* Paris.
1943   *Schweitzerische Sprachforschung.* Bern.
Jaberg, Karl, and J. Jud
1928   *Der sprachatlas als forschungsinstrument.* Halle.
1928–1940   *Sprach- und Sachatlas Italiens und der Südschweiz.* Zofingen.
Kaufman, Terrence S.
1961   The position of Tzeltal–Tzotzil in the Mayan family of languages. Paper presented to the AAA, Philadelphia.
1962   Tzeltal–Tzotzil comparative grammar, Part I: Phonology. *Microfilm Collection of Manuscripts on American Indian Cultural Anthropology,* Series IX, No. 55, pp. 125–310. Chicago: University of Chicago Libraries.
1964   Materiales lingüísticos para el estudio de las relaciones internas y externas de la familia de idiomas mayanos. In *Desarrollo Cultural de los Mayas* edited by E. Z. Vogt and Alberto Ruz. Mexico: Seminario de Cultura Maya, pp. 81–136.
1970   Posición del Tzeltal y del Tzotzil en la familia lingüística Mayance. In *Ensayos de antropología en la zona central de Chiapas* edited by McQuown and Pitt-Rivers, pp. 171–183.
King, Robert
1969   *Historical linguistics and generative grammar.* New York: Prentice-Hall.
Kurath, Hans
1939–1943   *Linguistic atlas of New England.* Providence: Brown University.
1949   *A word geography of the Eastern United States.* Ann Arbor: University of Michigan Press.
Kurath, Hans, Marcus L. Hansen, Julia Bloch, and Bernard Bloch
1939   *Handbook of the linguistic atlas of New England.* Providence: Brown University.
Labov, William
1963   The social motivation of a sound change. *Word* **19,** 273–309.
1966   Hypercorrection by the lower middle class as a factor in linguistic change. In *Sociolinguistics* edited by William Bright. The Hague: Mouton.
Lehmann, Winfred P.
1962   *Historical Linguistics.* New York: Holt.
Marino Flores, Anselmo
1963   *Distribución municipal de los hablantes de lenguas indígenas en la República Mexicana.* Mexico: Instituto Nacional de Antropología e Historia, Pub. 12.
Mayers, Marvin
1960   *The Pokomchi: A sociolinguistic study.* Chicago: Department of Anthropology, University of Chicago.
1968   Indigenous dialectology. *Current trends in linguistics,* Vol. IV. The Hague: Mouton.
McDavid, Raven
1958   The dialects of American English. In *The structure of American English* edited by W. Nelson Francis. New York: Ronald.

McQuown, Norman A.
1970 Bilingüismo indígena y ladino: contrastes socioculturales. In *Ensayos de antropología en la zona central de Chiapas* edited by McQuown and Pitt-Rivers, pp. 263–288.
McQuown, Norman A., and Julian Pitt-Rivers (eds.)
1970 *Ensayos de antropolgía en la zona central de Chiapas.* Mexico: Instituto Nacional Indigenista.
Olivera de V., Mercedes, and Blanca Sánchez
1964 *Distribución actual de las lenguas indígenas de México.* Mexico: Instituto Nacional de Antropología e Historia, Depto. de Investigaciones Antropológicas, Pub. 15.
Pop, Sever
1927 *Buts et méthodes des enquetes dialectales.* Paris.
1950 *La dialectologie.* Louvain.
Pozas, Ricardo
1947 *Monografía de Chamula.* Mexico: Instituto Nacional Indigenista.
Siverts, Henning
1968 *Oxchuc.* Mexico: Instituto Nacional Indigenista.
Vogt, Evon Z.
1969 *Zinacantan.* Harvard. Harvard University Press.
Wenker, Georg
1895 *Der Sprachatlas des Deutschen Reichs. Dichtung and Warheit.* Marburg.
Wrede, Ferdinand
1926 *Deutscher Sprachatlas.* Marburg: Lahn.

A Western Apache Writing System:
The Symbols of Silas John

KEITH H. BASSO
NED ANDERSON

In a lengthy essay published in 1886, Garrick Mallery, a retired military officer employed as anthropologist by the Bureau of American Ethnology, invited explorers, missionaries, and ethnographers to provide him with information pertaining to systems of graphic communication then in use among the Indian tribes of North America. Expressing his conviction that these " . . . primitive forms of writing provide direct and significant evidence upon the evolution of an important aspect of human culture," Mallery also warned that they were rapidly disappearing, and that unless those in existence were studied immediately the opportunity would be lost forever. Unfortunately for anthropology, Mallery's invitation went largely unheeded and his prophesy came true. In the closing decades of the nineteenth century, a number of native graphic systems went out of existence and a fledgling social science, occupied with more urgent concerns, scarcely took note of their passing.

The lack of enthusiasm that greeted Mallery's early call for research set a precedent that was destined to continue, for to this day the ethnographic study of so-called "primitive" writing systems—including those stimulated by contact with Europeans—has failed to engage the sustained interest of either linguists or cultural anthropologists. The result, I. J. Gelb (1963, p. 210) has observed, is that "Some of these writings are known very inadequately, others are known only from hearsay, and still others must exist in obscure corners of the globe as yet unnoticed by scholars." (See Note 1 at end of chapter.)

Under these circumstances, it is with marked enthusiasm that we greet the opportunity to report upon a previously undescribed writing system that is in active use today among Western Apache Indians living on the Fort Apache and San Carlos Reservations in east-central Arizona. This system has persisted essentially unchanged since its invention in 1904 by Silas John Edwards, a pre-eminent Western Apache shaman who was also the founder and leader of a nativistic religious movement which established itself on both Western Apache reservations in the early 1920s and subsequently spread to the Mescalero Apache in New Mexico. (See Basso, 1970, p. 92; Goodwin and Kaut, 1954; La Barre, 1971; Opler, 1969, p. 191; Spicer, 1962, pp. 259–260, 532, 534; Note 2 at end of chapter.)

Mr. Edwards is ninety-three years old, almost blind, but still very much alive. Known to Apaches and Anglo-Americans alike simply as Silas John, he created a writing system so that an extensive set of prayers expressing the ideological core of his religious doctrine could be recorded in permanent form and disseminated among his followers. Although the content of these prayers is deeply influenced by Christian symbolism—a result of Silas John's early association with Lutheran missionaries on the Fort Apache Reservation—the written script was entirely his own invention, initially conceived in a "dream from God" and later developed without assistance from Anglo-Americans or Apaches. An ability to read and write English, acquired by Silas John as a young man, undoubtedly accounts for his exposure to the idea of writing. However, it does not account for the graphic form of his script or its underlying structural principles, which depart radically from those of the English alphabet. Like the Cherokee syllabary invented by Sequoyah around 1820, the writing system of Silas John represents a classic case of stimulus diffusion that resulted in the creation of a totally unique cultural form (Kroeber, 1948, pp. 369–370). As such, we believe, it ranks among the significant intellectual achievements by an American Indian during the twentieth century.

Methodological Problems

Since Garrick Mallery's day and before, American Indian writing systems have been described with a set of time-honoured concepts that were originally devised by European epigraphers to classify distinct types of graphic symbols and, by extension, to classify whole systems (Cleator, 1959; Cohen, 1958; Diringer, 1949, 1962; Février, 1948; Gelb, 1963; Kroeber, 1948; Mallery, 1886, 1893; Moorehouse, 1953; Voegelin and Voegelin, 1961). For example, if all the symbols in a particular system were identified as pictographs, the system itself was classified "pictographic"; on the other hand, if stylized ideographs existed side by side with pictographs the system was termed "pictographic–ideographic." In this way, different systems were compared on the basis of what types of symbols composed them and, in conjunction with historical data, arranged sequentially in order of their presumed chronological appearance.

The typologies constructed for these purposes, almost all of which classify graphs according to attributes of external form, are strictly etic in character—the products of a long tradition of western scholarship that often lacked access to native informants and was chiefly concerned with the formulation of broad-scale comparative strategies (Note 3). Although no one would dispute the importance of such strategies nor deny the fact that adequate typologies are basic to their development, it is essential to point out that serious problems may arise when etic concepts are applied a priori to the description of individual writing systems. Unless it is first established that the distinctions and contrasts imposed by these concepts coincide with those considered meaningful by users of the system—and in the great majority of American Indian studies no such evidence is adduced—the resulting description is almost certain to suffer from bias and distortion. (See Note 4.)

The fact that the symbols in a writing system may be submitted to classification by some existing etic scheme should not be taken to mean that the classification is automatically, or even necessarily, relevant to an understanding of how the system works. It would be a simple task, for example, to classify every symbol in the Silas John script according to whether it is pictographic or ideographic. Yet, as we shall see, this distinction has no significance for the Western Apache, who classify these symbols on the basis of very different criteria. An account of the Silas John script that ignored these native (or emic) distinctions and proceeded in terms of the pictographic–ideographic contrast instead would fail to reveal the basic principles that impart structure to the system as a whole. Simultaneously, and equally damaging, such an account would suggest that the system's operation was predicated on rules that, in fact, are irrelevant to it and altogether absent from Western Apache culture.

Methodological problems of this kind cannot be dismissed as inconsequential, nor can they be ignored on the supposition that their occurrence has been infrequent. To the contrary, a recent survey of the literature on American Indian graphic systems reveals the use of unverified etic concepts to be so pervasive that in all but a few cases it is impossible to determine the kinds of conceptual skills that were actually required to produce and interpret intelligible written messages (Basso, 1971).

The adequacy of an ethnographic description of a writing system should be judged by its ability to permit someone who is unfamiliar with the system—but who has a knowledge of the language on which it is based—to read and write. It should provide him, in other words, with an explicit formulation of the knowledge necessary to become literate. Among other things, this requires that the basic units in the system be identified and defined in accordance with criteria that persons already literate recognize as valid, necessary, and appropriate. If these criteria are not disclosed, or if they are arbitrarily replaced with criteria derived from the investigator's own culture, the knowledge necessary to use the system correctly will remain hidden.

Ward Goodenough (1970, p. 129) has observed that an adequate etic typology must be sufficiently sensitive " . . . to describe all the emic distinctions people actually make in all the world's cultures in relation to the subject matter for which the etic concepts are designed." This requirement applies as much to typologies of writing as it does to those for any other cultural phenomenon. Goodenough (1970) also emphasizes that the emic and etic enterprises are not mutually exclusive, but complementary and logically interrelated. Emic concepts provide us with what we need to know to construct valid etic concepts, while the latter, besides determining the form and content of comparative propositions, assist in the discovery and description of the former.

Studies of American Indian writing systems contain so few emic analyses that the basic materials needed to construct adequate etic typologies are all but absent. Consequently, the few etic concepts that have been proposed are open to serious question. On the one hand, it has not been shown that these categories describe "all the emic distinctions people actually make" and, on the other, they are so all-encompassing that their utility for comparative purposes is seriously impaired (Voegelin and Voegelin, 1961). Obviously, these difficulties cannot be overcome through the creation of more arbitrary categories. The surest solution lies in the continued investigation of individual writing systems, which, if properly described, will contribute to an inventory of demonstrably relevant emic distinctions and thus assure that subsequent etic typologies have a more secure grounding in cultural fact. Our account of the Silas John writing system is intended as a contribution in this direction.

Development of the Writing System

In 1904, when Silas John Edwards was twenty-one years old and living in the community of East Fork on the Fort Apache Indian Reservation, he experienced a vision in which he was presented with a set of sixty-two prayers and an accompanying set of graphic symbols with which to write them. Silas John recalls his vision as follows:

> There were sixty-two prayers. They came to me in rays from above. At the same time I was instructed. He [God] was advising me and telling me what to do, at the same time teaching me chants. They were presented to me—one by one. All of these and the writing were given to me at one time in one dream . . .

> God made it [the writing], but it came down to our earth. I liken this to what has happened in the religions we have now. In the center of the earth, when it first began, when the earth was first made, there was absolutely nothing on this world. There was no written language. So it was in 1904 that I became aware of the writing; it was then that I heard about it from God.

Silas John used his writing system for the sole purpose of recording the sixty-two prayers he received in his vision. The script was never applied to the large body of traditional Apache prayers already in existence by 1904, nor was it ever employed as a vehicle for secular speech. This is important to keep in mind, because the merits of the script, as well as its limitations, stem directly from the fact that it was purposely designed to communicate information relevant to the performance of ritual and not to write the infinitude of messages capable of expression in spoken Western Apache.

In 1916, a full twelve years after Silas John experienced his vision, he publicly proclaimed himself a messiah and began to preach. At the same time, he wrote down each of his prayers on separate pieces of tanned buckskin, using paints made from a mixture of pulverized minerals and the sap of yucca plants. This technique of writing soon gave way, however, and by 1925, prayer texts rendered in ink were appearing on squares of cardboard. Today, many (and possibly all) of the original painted buckskins have been lost or disposed of, and Silas John's script is preserved in paper 'prayer books' (*sailiš jąąn bi'okąąhi*) belonging to Apaches living on the San Carlos and Fort Apache Reservations.

By 1920, when it was apparent to Silas John that his acceptance as a religious prophet was assured, he selected twelve 'assistants' (*sailiš jaan yiɬnaناɬse'hi*) to circulate among the Apache people, pray for them, and encourage them to congregate. The assistants were given instruction in how to read and write, and, after demonstrating these skills, went through an initiation ritual in which they were presented with painted buckskins of their own. Thus equipped, they were placed in charge of carefully prepared sites known as "holy grounds" and urged to perform ceremonials on a regular basis, using their buckskins as mnemonic aids. As time passed and members of the original group of assistants began to die, Silas John appointed new ones who in turn were taught the script, formally initiated, and given the texts of prayers. This process, which has continued unmodified up to the present, accounts for the fact that even among Apaches knowledge of Silas John's writing system is not widespread. From the very beginning, access to the system was tightly controlled by Silas John himself, and competence in it was intentionally restricted to a small band of elite ritual specialists. Commenting on this point, one of our informants observed:

> Silas John just let a few people know what the writing meant. He once told my father that it had to be kept just like it was when he heard about it from God. If some person ever tried to change it, he said, God would stop listening to the people when they prayed. He knew that if he let it out for all the people to know, some wouldn't know about this, some wouldn't take it seriously. Maybe some would try to change it. So he

just gave it to a few people, men and women who would learn it right—just the way he taught them—and leave it alone. It has been that way for a long time, and it [the writing] is still the way it was when it came to this earth from God.

Description of the Writing System

The following account of Silas John's writing system is based on an analysis of six texts that were copied from a prayer book belonging to one of his youngest assistants on the San Carlos Reservation. This was the only prayer book we were permitted to see, and although it contained several additional texts, instruction in these was prevented by the sudden and unexpected hospitalization of our chief informant, a much older assistant whom Silas John had recommended as a particularly well-qualified teacher. The fact that we were unable to enlarge our sample hindered our analysis at certain points (for example, we were unable to record the full inventory of symbols used by Silas John to write his sixty-two original prayers). However, it did not prevent us from discovering the underlying principles according to which the system operates, the kinds of information it conveys, or the concepts Apaches must learn to become literate. Our description should enable anyone with a knowledge of spoken Apache to read fully and correctly the six prayer texts that constitute our corpus. No more can honestly be claimed, since these were the only texts in which we ourselves received adequate training and developed an acceptable measure of competence by Western Apache standards.

A 'Silas John prayer-text' (*sailiš ǰąąn bi'okaąhi*) may be defined as a set of graphic 'symbols' (*ke'ěšcin*) written on buckskin or paper arranged in horizontal lines to be read from left to right in descending order (Fig. 1). Each symbol is separated from the one that follows it by an empty space and corresponds to a single line of prayer, which may consist of a word, a phrase, or one or more sentences.

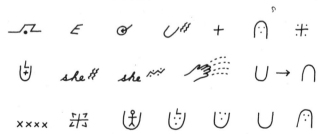

Figure 1. Text of "Prayer for Life" in correct reading form from left to right in descending order.

The sixty-two prayers authored by Silas John are partitioned into three major categories:

1. 'Prayers for life' (*'indee bi' okąąhi*), which promote health, longevity, and the maintenance of tension-free social relations.
2. 'Prayers for man and woman' (*'indee ke'istsane bi' okaahi*), which are invoked to combat and resolve marital discord.
3. 'Prayers for sickness' (*'ida'an bi'okąąhi*), which are employed to relieve physiological and mental illnesses caused by witchcraft, snakebite, or supernatural forces that have been antagonized by disrespectful behavior.

Prayers belonging to the same category are virtually identical in linguistic structure, with the result that the number and sequential arrangement of their written symbols exhibit very little variation. Consider, for example, the three prayers for life whose texts are presented in Fig. 2; note that each text contains the same number of symbols (20) and that their serial order is disturbed at only two points (4 and 8). Because this kind of uniformity is typical, the texts in each prayer category manifest a characteristic pattern. Two of these patterns can be readily discerned by comparing the prayers for life in Fig. 2 with the three texts of prayers for sickness that appear in Fig. 3.

Western Apaches assert that symbols in the Silas John script are composed of isolable 'symbol elements' (also termed *ke'eščin*), and they emphasize that to write and read a prayer text properly, it is essential to discriminate among symbols that consist of two or more elements and those that consist of only one. The former class, whose members we shall refer to as "compound symbols," is labeled by the Western Apache expression *ke'eščin łeedidilgoh* ('symbol elements put together'), while the latter, whose members we shall refer to as "noncompound symbols," is termed *ke'eščin doleedidildaahi* ('symbol elements standing alone'). Figure 4 presents the Apache classification of the symbols in our corpus into these two categories.

Symbol elements are not to be equated with discrete graphic components, for as a glance at Fig. 4 will show, noncompound symbols may consist of more than one component. For example, the symbol ⊖⟋, which might suggest itself to an outsider as having two graphic components, a circle and an arrow, is not construed as such by Apaches, who consider it a noncompound symbol that cannot be dissected. The reason, our informants explained, is that by themselves neither the circle nor the arrow has meaning and, as a result, must always occur in association with each other. In other words, they become semantically viable only as a unit, and in this respect contrast sharply with the components of compound

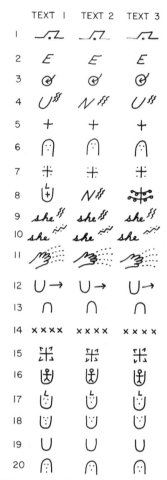

Figure 2. Three texts of "Prayer for Life" arranged in vertical order for ease of comparison.

symbols that, besides having meaning in combination, also have meaning in isolation. Thus, we arrive at an important insight; the classification of compound and noncompound symbols is based upon other than visual criteria and cannot be deduced solely from the inspection of a symbol's outer form.

When requested to identify and define the individual symbol elements in our corpus, our informants sorted them into three classes. One class is made up of elements that only occur in isolation and function exclusively in the capacity of noncompound symbols. Elements in the second class

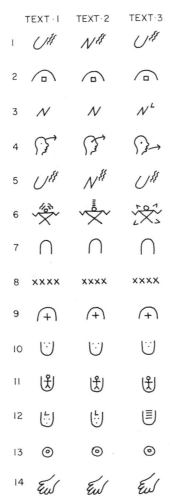

Figure 3. Three texts of "Prayer for Sickness" arranged in vertical order for ease of comparison.

also occur alone but, in addition, can be combined with other elements to form compound symbols. The third class consists of elements that occur only in compound symbols and never in isolation. In Fig. 5, each of the twenty-eight symbol elements that appear in our corpus has been assigned to one of these three classes, labeled A, B, and C, respectively.

Compound symbols may be divided into five structural types according to the number of elements they contain (two or three) and the classes (B and/or C) to which these elements belong. For the sake of convenience

Figure 4. Noncompound and compound symbols.

and economy, the members of each type are expressed in Fig. 6 as the outcome of simple formulas that operate on individual elements and specify the manner in which they are combined. We make no claim for the psychological reality of either the typology or the formulas; they are employed here simply as descriptive devices that allow us to make for-

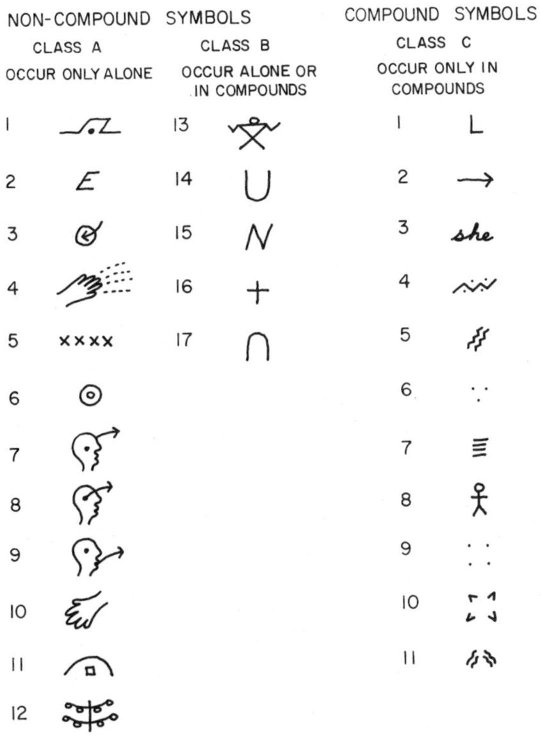

Figure 5. Symbols grouped into Classes A, B, and C.

mally explicit the knowledge an Apache must possess in order to form the compound symbols that appear in the prayer texts at our disposal.

Compound Symbol Type 1:   1 element from Class B is combined with 1 element from Class C.

Compound Symbol Type 2:   1 element from Class B is combined with 1 other element from Class B.

Compound Symbol Type 3:   1 element from Class C is combined with 1 other element from Class C.

Compound Symbol Type 4:   2 elements from Class B are combined with 1 element from Class C.

Compound Symbol Type 5:   1 element from Class B is combined with 2 elements from Class C.

A striking feature of the Silas John script is that it encodes information relevant to the production of nonverbal behavior as well as speech. This is made explicit in a distinction Apaches draw between 'symbols that tell what to say' (*ke'escin hant'e ndii*) and 'symbols that tell what to do' (*ke'eščin hant'e 'anle'*). All symbols "tell what to say" in the sense that each one signals the vocalization of some particular prayer line. However, a few symbols—those that "tell what to do"—function simultaneously to signal the performance of key ritual actions without which the prayer, no matter how correct in its linguistic details, is considered incomplete. In essence, then, a prayer text consists of a set of highly detailed instructions that specify what an individual must say and do to perform ceremonials in a manner that satisfies the standards held by Silas John and the members of his religion. So fundamental is the knowledge necessary to read these instructions, Apaches claim, that any attempt to execute the role of 'ceremonial leader' (*diiyin*) without it is certain to be flawed and unacceptable. One of our informants commented along these lines as follows:

> It's all in here [pointing to a prayer-text], how to pray in just the right way. That's why he Silas John made them like this, so the ones who pray can be sure they know how to do it right. Only the ones who can read can pray. . . . I heard of a man at Whiteriver who wanted to be a ceremonial leader like the ones who work for Silas John. So he went to many ceremonials and tried to watch everything they did. After a long time he thought he knew what to do and got ready to try it out. . . . The people came to where he was and he started up. But pretty soon they knew he didn't really know it. . . . This was because no one had taught him to read buckskins; he couldn't do it without them. When he [Silas John] chooses you to be a ceremonial leader, first you learn what the symbols say, then, after that, what the symbols mean for you to do. You must know both because if you don't you will make mistakes like that Whiteriver man I was telling you about before.

Meaning of the Symbols

The process of learning what the symbols in a prayer text represent may be considered complete when the linguistic referent of each symbol—that is, the prayer line it serves to recall in the performance of a ceremonial—has been committed to memory. The process begins, however, with the memorization of expressions that define the meaning of symbol elements. These expressions are termed 'symbol elements names' (*ke'eščin biži'*) and are held by Apaches to constitute the basic semantic units of the Silas John writing system.

The "names" of elements that function as noncompound symbols are identical to the prayer lines these symbols elicit in ritual contexts. Consequently, the linguistic referent of a noncompound symbol is always isomorphic with the meaning of the element that forms it and can be learned in a single operation. The linguistic referents of the noncompound symbols that appear in our corpus (those symbols formed by elements in Class A and, when occurring in isolation, elements in Class B) are presented below. The numbers refer to the symbols in Fig. 5.

NONCOMPOUND SYMBOLS

Class A Elements (Occur only alone)

1. *ni' 'aγolząąną'* 'earth, when it was made'
2. *'iiyaa' 'aγolząąną'* 'sky, when it was made'
3. *daitsee dagoyąąną' ni''iťdįįžę'* 'first, when it all began in the center of the earth'
4. *šilagan hadaažę' dįįgo bihadaa'istįįgo* 'my fingers, from their tips, like four rays, power emanates'
   šilagan hadaažę' biha'dit'įįgo 'my fingers, from their tips, power illuminates all' ("Power" is the power God confers upon those who truly believe in him.)
5. *naγowaahi nagoščǫǫdi nagoťdiihi behegozini* 'sinful things occurring, bad things occurring, sickness and evil occurring, together with harmful knowledge' ["Harmful knowledge" refers to the body of techniques employed by 'witches' (*iťkašn*) to cause sickness and misfortune (see Basso, 1969).]
6. *bįjii hadndin* 'his heart, sacred pollen'
7. *ya'itsii košyo* 'from where his thoughts dwell'
8. *ya' 'odišyo* 'from where he looks out'
9. *ya' 'iiyaťtii'yo* 'from where he speaks out'
10. *yoosn bihidaahi yoosn binadidzooť behe'ndzili yedaaholdi tsiyaago daadoldi nikạ'žę'* 'with his life, his breath, his power, God extends his hand and blesses you'
11. *yoosn bi goγaa* 'God, his dwelling'
12. *hadndin ťa'ašniidn* 'he who is decorated with and enriched by pollen' (This is the ritual name of Silas John; it is spoken only during the performance of ceremonials.)

Class B Elements (Occur alone or in compounds)

13. *hadndin 'iškįįn* 'sacred pollen boy' (In all rituals associated with the Silas John religion, this phrase refers metaphorically to male ceremonial patients; for female patients the phrase is modified to *hadndin naailin* 'sacred pollen maiden.')
14. *yoosn* 'God'
15. *naalezgạne* 'Jesus' [In traditional Western Apache myths and prayers, this term is the name of a prominent male figure who with a twin brother rid the earth of much that was evil and made it a suit-

able dwelling place for man (see Goodwin, 1939). Silas John uses the term in an extended sense to refer to Jesus.]

16. *hadndin 'iłna'aahi* 'sacred pollen, that which is crossed'
17. *·nagostan biɣalataže* 'world, on the surface of it'

Combining Symbols

The "names" of elements in Class C must also be memorized, since a knowledge of these constructions, together with those that label Class B elements, is basic to the interpretation of compound symbols. The numbers refer to the symbols in Fig. 5.

Class C Elements (Occur only in compounds)

1. *hidaa* 'life'
2. *'intin* 'path', 'trail', 'road'
3. *šii* 'I', 'me', 'mine'
4. *'okąąhi* 'prayer, that which is'
5. *hadndin* 'sacred pollen'
6. *hadndin* 'sacred pollen'
7. *hadndin* 'sacred pollen'
8. *'indee* 'man', 'men' (In all the prayers we collected, this term is used in the more general sense of 'all men' or 'mankind'.)
9. *dįįyo* 'four places'
10. *dįįže* 'in' or 'from four directions'
11. *dįį'įį* 'four times'

When an Apache learns the expressions that label elements in a compound symbol, he does not simultaneously learn that symbol's associated prayer line. This is because the linguistic referents of compound symbols are never isomorphic with the "names" of the Class B and/or C elements that form them. Consider, for example, Compound Symbol 2 (Fig. 6). The meaning of Class B Element 14 is *yoosn* ('God') and the meaning of Class C Element 5 (Fig. 5) is *hadndin* ('sacred pollen'). The prayer line evoked by Compound Symbol 2 is *yoosn bihadndin* ('God, his sacred pollen'), which, while replicating exactly the meanings of its elements, is not identical to either one because of the addition of the possessive pronound *bi* ('his'). It should be emphasized that the degree of correspondence between the referent of a compound symbol and the expressions that define its elements is not always this high. In the case of Compound Symbol 5 (Fig. 6), for example, whose referent is *dasižǫ' beišgaałč'idii* ('it is said that I alone go forth with this power'), the meaning of Class B Element 14 (Fig. 5) is *yoosn* ('God') and that of Class C Element 2 *'intin* ('path', 'trail', 'road').

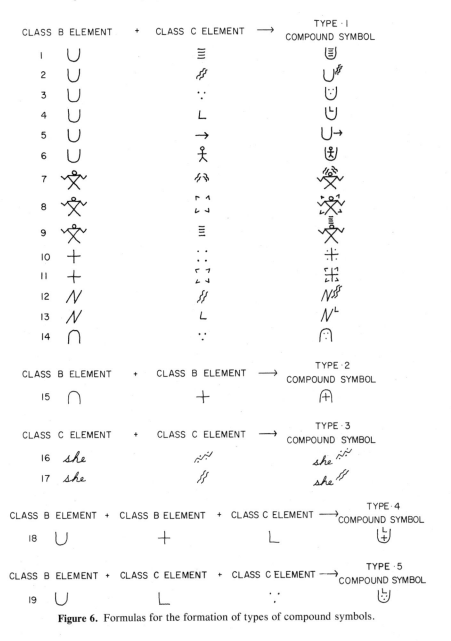

Figure 6. Formulas for the formation of types of compound symbols.

Because the prayer line associated with a compound symbol is structurally and semantically more complex than the "names" of its elements, it cannot be inferred from them and, as a consequence, must be memorized separately. However since the "names" either form some part of the prayer line or allude metaphorically to key concepts embedded within it, the elements serve as indispensable aids for bringing the prayer line to mind.

The linguistics referents of the compound symbols in our corpus are as follows. The numbers refer to the symbols in Figs. 5 and 6.

Compound Symbol Type 1

1. Class B Element 14 (*yoosn* 'God') plus Class C Element 7 (*hadndin* 'pollen') produces Compound Symbol 1 (*yoosn bihadndin* 'God, his sacred pollen'). Cattail pollen is the foremost cultural symbol of God and Jesus and their spiritual presence on this earth.

2. Class B Element 14 (*yoosn* 'God') plus Class C Element 5 (*hadndin* 'pollen') produces Compound Symbol 2 (*yoosn bihadndin* 'God, his sacred pollen').

3. Class B Element 14 (*yoosn* 'God') plus Class C Element 6 (*hadndin* 'pollen') produces Compound Symbol 3 (*yoosn bihadndin* 'God, his sacred pollen').

4. Class B Element 14 (*yoosn* 'God') plus Class C Element 1 (*hidaa* 'life') produces Compound Symbol 4 (*yoosn bihidaa* 'God, his life').

5. Class B Element 14 (*yoosn* 'God') plus Class C Element 2 ('*intin* 'path', 'trail', 'road') produces Compound Symbol 5 (*dašižǫ' beišgaał č'idii* 'it is known that I alone go forth with this power').

6. Class B Element 14 (*yoosn* 'God') plus Class C Element 8 ('*indee* 'man', 'men') produces Compound Symbol 6 (*bit'la nabąąžę' yoosn biyi' sizįįhi* 'following this, God entered into man').

7. Class B Element 13 (*hadndin 'iškįįn* 'sacred pollen boy') plus Class C Element 11 (*dįį'įį* 'four times') produces Compound Symbol 7 (*dįį'įį hadndin 'iškįįnihi* 'four times, that which is sacred pollen boy').

8. Class B Element 13 (*hadndin 'iškįįn* 'sacred pollen boy') plus Class C Element 10 (*dįįžę'* 'from four directions') produces Compound Symbol 8 (*hadndin 'iškįįn dįįžę' nadiyoołhi* 'sacred pollen boy, he who breathes in four directions').

9. Class B Element 13 (*hadndin 'iškįįn* 'sacred pollen boy') plus Class C Element 7 (*hadndin* 'sacred pollen') produces Compound Symbol 9 ('*izidadasdil hadndin 'iškįįn* 'from above it cures, pollen boy').

10. Class B Element 16 (*hadndin 'iłn'aahi* 'sacred pollen, that which is crossed') plus Class C Element 9 (*dįįyo* 'four places') produces Com-

pound Symbol 10 (*hadndin 'itna'aahi djiyo nadiyoot* 'sacred pollen, that which is crossed, breathing in four places').

11. Class B Element 16 (*hadndin 'itna'aahi* 'sacred pollen, that which is crossed') plus Class C Element 10 (*djižę'* 'in four directions') produces Compound Symbol 11 (*djižę' bithadaagoyaa* 'these things dispersed in four directions').

12. Class B Element 15 (*naalezgąne* 'Jesus') plus Class C Element 5 (*hadndin* 'sacred pollen') produces Compound Symbol 12 (*naalezgąne bihadndin* 'Jesus, his sacred pollen').

13. Class B Element 15 (*naalezgąne* 'Jesus') plus Class C Element 1 produces Compound Symbol 13 (*naalezgąne bihidaa* 'Jesus, his life').

14. Class B Element 17 (*nagostsan* 'world') plus Class C Element 6 (*hadndin* 'sacred pollen') produces Compound Symbol 14 (*hadndin hidaahi* 'sacred pollen, that which is alive'). Like God and Jesus, pollen is construed as having life.

Compound Symbol Type 2

15. Class B Element 17 (*nagostsan* 'world') plus Class B Element 16 (*hadndin 'ilna'aahi* 'sacred pollen, that which is crossed') produces Compound Symbol 15 (*hadndin 'itna'aahi nagostsan bik'ažę'* 'pollen, that which is crossed, on the surface of the world').

Compound Symbol Type 3

16. Class C Element 3 (*šii* 'I', 'me', 'mine') plus Class C Element 4 (*'okąahi* 'prayer') produces Compound Symbol 16 (*šii si'okąahi* 'mine, that which is my prayer').

17. Class C Element 3 (*šii* 'I', 'me', 'mine') plus Class C Element 5 (*hadndin* 'sacred pollen') produces Compound Symbol 17 (*šii šihadndinihi* 'mine, that which is my sacred pollen').

Compound Symbol Type 4

18. Class B Element 14 (*yoosn* 'God') plus Class B Element 16 (*hadndin itna'aahi* 'sacred pollen, that which is crossed) plus Class C Element 1 (*hidaa* 'life') produces Compound Symbol 18 (*yoosn bihadndin 'itna' 'aahi hidaahi* 'God, his sacred pollen, that which is crossed, that which is alive').

Compound Symbol Type 5

19. Class B Element 14 (*yoosn* 'God') plus Class C Element 6 (*hadndin* 'sacred pollen') plus Class C Element 1 (*hidaa* 'life') produces Compound Symbol 19 (*yoosn binadidzoothi* 'God, that which is his breath'). Pollen, a symbol of God, has life; to live is to breathe; hence the equation of pollen with the breath of God.

Coding of Nonverbal Behavior

We have already drawn attention to the fact that certain symbols in the Silas John script call for the performance of specific types of nonverbal behavior as well as the utterance of a prayer line. To cite an example, Compound Symbol 2 (Fig. 6) requires that simultaneous with the vocalization of its linguistic referent, which is *yoosn bihadndin* ('God, his sacred pollen'), the speaker bless the ritual paraphernalia that identify him as a ceremonial leader by sprinkling each item with a pinch of cattail pollen. Actions of this kind, which constitute what we shall henceforth describe as a symbol's "kinesic" referent, consistently involve the manipulation of material culture, and for this reason a brief description of the physical settings in which ceremonials take place is essential.

All rituals connected with the Silas John religion are conducted within the perimeters of what both monolingual and bilingual Apaches call "holy grounds." These are small areas of land, usually about 15 feet square, whose corners correspond to the four cardinal directions and are marked by upright wooden crosses (*'iłna'aahi 'indeez* 'long crosses'). Each cross is approximately 7 feet tall, painted a different color—east, black; north, yellow; west, green; south, white—and decorated with the breastfeathers of eagles. Other objects of material culture that assume importance in ceremonial activities include:

1. 'Wooden hoops' (*baase*). Used only in rituals held for the purpose of curing the sick, hoops are made in sets of four and suspended on the crosses that define the corners of holy grounds. Each hoop is roughly a yard in diameter, painted to match the color of the cross on which it hangs, and adorned with eagle feathers or strips of colored ribbon.

2. 'Painted buckskins' (*'epan ke'ešč̣in*). Every ceremonial leader is the owner of one or more buckskins, which he spreads on the ground before the start of a ceremonial. Roughly square or rectangular in shape, these buckskins are inscribed with nonorthographic symbols that represent 'sand paintings' (*ni'kegošči'*), and unless the ceremonial is of a particular type that requires the creation of these designs, the buckskins serve no mnemonic purpose.

3. 'Personal crosses' (*indee bi iłna'aahi*). Every ceremonial leader also owns a personal cross, which he displays at ritual gatherings by placing it on top of his buckskins. Between 10 and 14 inches long and 6 to 10 inches wide, these objects are fashioned from wood and are sometimes enclosed in an outer covering of buckskin. An eagle feather and at least one turquoise bead are attached to the center of personal crosses with a strand of sinew, and it is not unusual to see specimens whose arms have been painted yellow.

4. 'Sacred pollen' (*hadndin*). All ceremonials involve the use of cattail pollen, which is kept in an open container (usually a shallow basket) that is placed on the ground near the ceremonial leader's buckskins and personal cross.

We may now return to our prayer texts and discuss in greater detail 'symbols that tell what to do'. Ten symbols of this type occur in our corpus. Each is a compound symbol and is listed below with a description of the actions that collectively comprise its kinesic referent. In keeping with the verbal style of our Apache informants, these descriptions are phrased as instructions to be followed by ceremonial leaders.

1. Compound symbol 17—Face toward the east. Extend fully the right arm, fold the left arm across the chest, and bow the head. After remaining in this position for a few moments, drop the left arm and trace the sign of a cross on one's chest.
2. Compound symbol 1—Face toward the east. Take a pinch of sacred pollen in the right hand and hold it directly over the ritual paraphernalia, which are lying on the ground.
3. Compound Symbol 3—Take a pinch of sacred pollen in the right hand and trace four circles in the air directly over the ritual paraphernalia.
4. Compound Symbol 2—Take a pinch of sacred pollen in the right hand and place a small amount on each item of ritual paraphernalia.
5. Compound Symbol 12—Same as no. 4.
6. Compound Symbol 10—Take a pinch of sacred pollen in the right hand and place a small amount on each arm of the ceremonial cross that marks the eastern corner of the holy ground.
7. Compound Symbol 11—Same as no. 6.
8. Compound Symbol 9—Take a pinch of sacred pollen in the right hand and place a small amount on the head of the person (seated on the ground) for whom the ceremonial is being given.
9. Compound Symbol 8—Take a pinch of sacred pollen in the right hand and with the same hand trace the sign of a cross on the chest of the person for whom the ceremonial is being given.
10. Compound Symbol 7—Remove the wooden hoop from the cross that defines the eastern corner of the holy ground and pass it four times over the head and shoulders of the person for whom the ceremonial is being given.

"Symbols that tell what to do" appear to be the only ones in the Silas John script that sometimes lack unique linguistic referents. We have seen, for example, that the referent of Compound Symbol 1 (*yoosn bihadndin* 'God, his sacred pollen') is identical to that of Compound Symbols 2 and 3. Neither is it the case that all symbols of this type possess unique kinesic referents; the actions associated with Compound Symbol 10 are exactly the same as those associated with Compound Symbol 11. It should be noted, however, that symbols with identical linguistic referents never possess the same kinesic referents, and vice versa. In other words, two symbols may be kinesic allographs or they may be linguistic allographs, but they are never both at once, and consequently, complete redundancy is avoided.

According to one of our informants, the kinesic values of "symbols that tell what to do" are indirectly expressed by their linguistic referents. In some instances, this seems plausible, as when Compound Symbol 17 (*šii šihadndinihi* 'mine, that which is my sacred pollen') calls for the ceremonial leader to bless himself with cattail pollen. However, in other cases, the relationship is more obscure, as with Compound Symbol 2 (*yoosn bihadndin* 'God, his sacred pollen'), which requires the ceremonial leader to perform a blessing on his ritual paraphernalia.

What is significant is not that symbols vary to the extent to which their kinesic values can be inferred from their linguistic referents, but rather that they encode both types of information. Silas John might easily have chosen to convey kinesic instructions with one set of symbols and linguistic instructions with another. Instead, he created a script in which single symbols function in both capacities, thereby reducing the total number of symbols in the system and endowing it with added economy.

It should now be possible for the reader of this essay to translate into speech and action any and all of the prayer texts in our corpus. At this stage, of course, he will not have memorized the referent(s) of every symbol element and therefore will not be able to read spontaneously. However, he has been provided with a complete inventory of these referents as well as an explicit formulation of the rules that govern their combination and interpretation.

In general terms, the reader of a prayer text must be able to distinguish compound symbols from noncompound symbols, associate each with a particular linguistic construction, and pronounce that construction in Western Apache. In addition, he must be able to recognize symbols that call for nonverbal behavior, assign to each of these a particular kinesic referent, and transform that referent into the appropriate set of ritual gestures. With these skills and an ability to apply them swiftly and flawlessly in the physical context of a holy ground, our newly literate reader should be able to give a total performance that comes satisfactorily close to those expected of experienced Apache ceremonial leaders.

TRANSLATION OF "PRAYER FOR LIFE"

As an illustration of what these performances consist of, we now present a detailed account of the prayer for life that appears in Fig. 1. The

Apache text is accompanied by full kinesic instructions and a free translation of the linguistic material that attempts to capture some of the drama and dignity of Silas John's ritual poetry. Numbers refer to symbols in Text 1, Fig. 2.

1. *ni'ʼayolzą̖ą̖ną̖'* 'when the earth was first created'
2. *'iiyaa' 'ayolzą̖ą̖ną̖'* 'when the sky was first created'
3. *daitsee dagoyą̖ą̖ną̖' ni''iłdįįžę̖'* 'in the beginning, when all was started in the center of the earth'
4. *yoosn bihadndin* 'God's sacred pollen' (Take a pinch of sacred pollen in the right hand and place a small amount on each item of ritual paraphernalia.)
5. *hadndin 'iłna'aahi* 'a cross of sacred pollen'
6. *hadndin hidaahi* 'living sacred pollen'
7. *hadndin 'iłna'aahi dįįyo nadiyooł* 'a cross of sacred pollen breathing in four directions' (Take a pinch of sacred pollen in the right hand and place a small amount on each arm of the ceremonial cross that marks the eastern corner of the holy ground.)
8. *yoosn bihadndin 'iłna'aahi hidaahi* 'God's cross of living sacred pollen'
9. *šii šihadndinihi* 'my own, my sacred pollen' (Face toward the east, extend fully the right arm, fold the left arm across the chest, and bow the head. After remaining in this position for a few moments, drop the left arm and trace the sign of a cross on the chest.)
10. *šii ši' oką̖ą̖hi* 'my own, my prayer'
11. *šilagan hadą̖ą̖žę̖' dįįgo bihadaa'istįįgo* 'like four rays, power is flowing forth from the tips of my fingers' *šilagan hadą̖ą̖žę̖' biha'dit'įįgo* 'power from the tips of my fingers brings forth light'
12. *dašižǫ' beišgaał č'idii* 'now it is known that I go forth with power'
13. *nagostsan biyaltažę̖'* 'on the surface of the world'
14. *nagowaahi nagoščoodi nagoldiihi behe'gozini* 'sinful things are occurring, bad things are occurring, sickness and evil are occurring, together with harmful knowledge'
15. *dįįžę̖' biłhadaagoyaa* 'in four directions, these things are dispersed and fade away' (Take a pinch of sacred pollen in the right hand and place a small amount on each arm of the cross that marks the eastern corner of the holy ground.)
16. *bitl'anabą̖ą̖žę̖ yoosn biyi' sizįįhi* 'following this, God came to live with man'
17. *yoosn binadidzoołhi* 'the breath of God'
18. *yoosn bihadndin* 'God's sacred pollen' (Take a pinch of sacred pollen in the right hand and trace four circles in the air directly over the ritual paraphernalia.)

19. *yoosn* 'God Himself'
20. *hadndin hidaahi* 'living sacred pollen'

Summary and Conclusion

At the outset of this essay, it was observed that the adequacy of an etic typology of written symbols could be judged by its ability to describe all the emic distinctions in all the writing systems of the world. In conclusion, we should like to return to this point and briefly examine the extent to which presently available etic concepts can be used to describe the distinctions made by Western Apaches in relation to the writing system of Silas John.

Every symbol in the Silas John script may be classified as a phonetic semantic sign. Symbols of this type denote linguistic expressions that consist of one or more words and contrast as a class with phonetic nonsemantic signs, which denote phonemes (or phoneme clusters), syllables (or syllable clusters), and various prosodic phenomena (Gelb, 1963, pp. 2, 248).

Phonetic semantic signs are commonly partitioned into two subclasses—logographs (which denote single lexemes) and phraseographs (which denote multilexemic constructions). Although every symbol in the Silas John script can be assigned to one or the other of these categories, such an exercise is without justification (Note 5). We have no evidence to suggest that Apaches classify symbols according to the length or complexity of their linguistic referents, and therefore, the imposition of distinctions based on these criteria would be inappropriate, irrelevant, and misleading.

A far more useful contrast, and one we have already employed, is presented in most etic typologies as an opposition between compound (or composite) and noncompound (or noncomposite) symbols. Used to partition the category of phonetic semantic signs, these two comcepts enable us to describe more or less exactly the distinction Apaches draw between 'symbol elements put together' (*ke'eščin łedidilgoh*) and 'symbol elements standing alone' (*ke'eščin dołedidildaahi*). The former may now be defined as consisting of compound phonetic semantic signs, while the latter is composed of noncompound phonetic semantic signs.

Up to this point etic concepts have served us well. However, a deficiency appears when we search for a terminology that allows us to describe the distinction between 'symbols that tell what to say' (*ke'eščin hant'e ndii*) and 'symbols that tell what to do' (*ke'eščin hant'e 'anle'*). As far as we have been able to determine, standard typologies make no provision for this kind of contrast, apparently because their creators have tacitly assumed that systems composed of phonetic semantic signs serve exclusively to communicate linguistic information. Consequently, the possibility that these systems might also convey nonlinguistic information seems to have been consistently ignored. This oversight may be a product of Western ethnocentrism; after all, it is we who use alphabets who most frequently associate writing with language (Note 6). On the other hand, it may simply stem from the fact that systems incorporating symbols with kinesic referents are exceedingly rare and have not yet been reported. In any case, it is important to recognize that the etic inventory is not complete.

Retaining the term "phonetic sign" as a label for written symbols that denote linguistic phenomena, we propose that the term "kinetic sign" be introduced to label symbols that denote sequences of nonverbal behavior. Symbols of the latter type that simultaneously denote some unit of language may be classified as "phonetic–kinetic" signs. With these concepts, the contrast between 'symbols that tell what to say' and 'symbols that tell what to do' can be rephrased as one that distinguishes phonetic signs (by definition nonkinetic) from phonetic–kinetic signs. Pure kinetic signs—symbols that refer solely to physical gestures—are absent from the Silas John script.

The utility of kinetic sign and phonetic–kinetic sign as comparative concepts must ultimately be judged on the basis of their capacity to clarify and describe emic distinctions in other systems of writing. However, as we have previously pointed out, ethnographic studies of American Indian systems that address themselves to the identification of these distinctions—and thus provide the information necessary to evaluate the relevance and applicability of etic concepts—are in very short supply. As a result, meaningful comparisons cannot be made. At this point, we simply lack the data with which to determine whether the kinetic component so prominent in the Silas John script is unique or whether it had counterparts elsewhere in North America.

The view is still prevalent among anthropologists and linguists that the great majority of American Indian writing systems conform to one or two global "primitive" types. Our study of the Silas John script casts doubt upon this position, for it demonstrates that fundamental emic distinctions remain to be discovered and that existing etic frameworks are less than adequately equipped to describe them. The implications of these findings are clear. On the one hand, we must acknowledge the possibility that several structurally distinct forms of writing were developed by North America's Indian cultures. Concomitantly, we must be prepared to abandon traditional ideas of typological similarity and simplicity among these systems in favor of those that take variation and complexity into fuller account.

Notes

1. We have adapted Gelb's (p. 12) broad definition of writing as "a system of human inter-communication by means of conventional visible marks." The Silas John system is a script because it contains phonetic signs.

2. References to the impact of the Silas John movement on Western Apache and Mescalero Apache religion are not infrequent, but a systematic appraisal of the cultural and historical factors that precipitated its appearance and acceptance has yet to be made. The earliest example of the Silas John script consists of two prayer texts recorded by Harry Hoijer on the Mescalero Reservation in New Mexico during the summer of 1931. A number of symbols that occur in Hoijer's Mescalero texts are absent from those we collected at San Carlos (and vice versa), but at present we do not know whether these symbols represent innovations by the Mescalero or whether they originally appeared in Western Apache texts not included in our sample.

3. The terms "etic" and "emic" are used in this paper to refer to contrasting types of anthropological description. A description of a linguistic or cultural system is emic to the extent that it is based on distinctions that are demonstrably meaningful and functionally significant for competent users of the system. A description is etic to the extent that it rests upon distinctions (typically drawn from cross-cultural typologies) whose meaningfulness for users of a particular system has not been demonstrated and whose functional significance within the system is therefore open to question. For an extended treatment of the etic–emic distinction and its implications, see W. H. Goodenough (1970). Other general discussions of this topic include Goodenough (1971), Hymes (1970), Pike (1967), and Sturtevant (1964).

4. As a general methodological premise in cultural anthropology, this point has been made repeatedly in recent years. However, its relevance to the study of writing systems has not been explicitly noted. We are inclined to attribute this to two major factors. On the one hand, cultural anthropologists have not been accustomed to view the description of writing systems as an exercise in ethnographic theory construction. On the other, students of writing seem only rarely to look to modern anthropology for theories and methods that might enhance their own investigations.

5. Written symbols that denote single phonemes (alphabetic graphs) and single syllables (syllabic graphs) are absent from the Silas John script. Four symbols in our corpus (Class A-2; Class B-14, 15; Class C-3; all in Fig. 5) represent clear borrowings from the English alphabet, but all of these denote specific words or sentences, and, as such, would have to be classified as logographs or phraseographs.

6. In this connection, it is interesting to note that etic concepts for the classification of alphabetic and syllabic systems have received far more attention—and have proven far for adequate—than those used to classify simpler forms of writing. See, for example, the classification of alphabetic systems by C. F. and F. M. Voegelin (1961).

Acknowledgments

We thank the following Western Apaches, whose understanding, cooperation, and friendship made this study possible: Silas John Edwards, for permission to undertake the study, to publish the results, and for providing us with essential information about the origin and history of his writing system; Marshall Miller, for gifted instruction in how to read; John Nolene, for his generous loan; Mr. and Mrs. Marion Zahgotah who allowed us to disrupt the daily routine of their household and never once complained; and Mrs. Maggie Anderson, who opened her home to us as a base of operations and whose advice, warmth, and sheer good will made everything that much better. We also thank David Schneider who brought the Silas John script to our attention by pointing out the presence of Harry Hoijer's Mescalero texts in an unpublished manuscript by the late Jules Henry. Henry had given Schneider access to the manuscript, and the latter supposed, quite correctly, that it would be of singular interest to us. We are grateful to Harry Hoijer for allowing us to examine his original field-notes. Finally, we thank Bernard Fontana, Dell Hymes, William Sturtevant, and Sol Tax, who urged us not to delay our investigation and took steps that enabled us to begin.

Our field research was sponsored by the Center for the Study of Man, Smithsonian Institution, Washington, D.C., and the Doris Duke American Indian Oral History Project, Arizona State Museum, University of Arizona. Finally, we thank the following scholars whose comments on an earlier draft of this paper were especially helpful: Ellen Basso, Roy D'Andrade, Harold Conklin, Regna Darnell, Bernard L. Fontana, I. J. Gelb, Erving Goffman, McGuire Gibson, Philip Greenfeld, Kenneth Hale, Harry Hoijer, Dell Hymes, Morris Opler, Alfonso Ortiz, Joel Sherzer, William Sturtevant, and Richard Thompson.

References

Basso, K. H.
    1969   *Western Apache witchcraft*. Tucson: University of Arizona Press.
    1970   *The Cibecue Apache*. New York: Holt.
    1971   *An annotated bibliography of American Indian writing systems*. Manuscript.
         Tucson: Arizona State Museum Library, University of Arizona.
Cleator, P. E.
    1959   *Lost languages*. London: R. Hale.
Cohen, M.
    1958   *La grande invention de l'écriture et son évolution*. Paris: Imprimeur National.
Diringer, D.
    1949   *The alphabet*. London: Hutchinson's.
    1962   *Writing*. New York: Praeger.
Février, J.
    1948   *Histoire de l'écriture*. Paris: Payot.
Gelb, I. J.
    1963   *A study of writing*. Chicago: University of Chicago Press.
Goodenough, W. H.
    1970   *Description and comparison in cultural anthropology*. Chicago: Aldine.
    1971   *Culture, language and society*. Reading, Massachusetts: Addison-Wesley.
Goodwin, G.
    1939   *Myths and tales of the White Mountain Apache*. American Folklore Society, Mem.
         33.
Goodwin, G. and Kaut, C. R.
    1954   A native religious movement among the White Mountain and Cibecue Apache.
         Southwestern Journal of Anthropology **10**, 385–404.
Hymes, D. H.
    1970   Linguistic method in ethnography: Its development in the United States. In
         Method and theory in linguistics edited by P. L. Garvin. The Hague: Mouton.

Kroeber, A. L.
  1948   *Anthropology.* New York: Harcourt.
La Barre, W.
  1971   Materials for a history of studies of crisis cults: A bibliographic essay. *Current Anthropology* **12**(1), 3–44.
Mallery, G.
  1886   On the pictographs of the North American Indians. *United States Bureau of American Ethnology, Annual Report* (4).
  1893   Picture-writing of the American Indians. *United States Bureau of American Ethnology, Annual Report* (10).
Moorehouse, A. C.
  1953   *The triumph of the alphabet.* New York: Schuman.
Opler, M.
  1969   *An Apache odyssey.* New York: Holt.
Pike, K.
  1967   *Language in relation to a unified theory of the structure of human behavior.* The Hague: Mouton.
Spicer, E. H.
  1962   *Cycles of conquest.* Tucson: University of Arizona Press.
Sturtevant, W. C.
  1964   Studies in ethnoscience. *American Anthropologist* **66**(3), 99–131.
Voegelin, C. F. and Voegelin, F. M.
  1961   Typological classification systems with included, excluded and self-sufficient alphabets. *Anthropological Linguistics* **3**, 55–96.

New Insights into the Nature of Language Change Offered by Language Planning

JOAN RUBIN

Sociolinguistic theory has raised serious questions about the long-standing view that it is useful to operate as though linguistic units were all categorical. Further, sociolinguists have demonstrated that variation in performance must be included in any theory of a language code. Without such an inclusion, neither the abilities that all speakers have to manipulate and understand variation as a regular phenomenon nor the fact that language change is an on-going process that can be observed can be explained.[1]

A major tenet of homogeneous monolithic linguistic theory that has been attacked with considerable success holds that language is an organism that is independent of and prior to social values, attitudes, and change. This position is exemplified by a quote from Kurylowicz (1948): "One must explain linguistic facts by other linguistic facts, not by heterogeneous facts . . . Explanation by means of social facts is a methodological derailment." As is widely recognized, the social facts of performance were also uninteresting for Chomsky (1965) who proposed that the proper object of linguistic study was ". . . an ideal speaker–listener, in a completely homogeneous speech-community, who knows its language perfectly and is unaffected by such grammatically irrelevant conditions as memory limitations, distractions, shifts of attention and interest, and errors in applying his knowledge of the language in actual performance" (p. 3). It is clear that for Chomsky language is independent of or prior to social variation.

William Labov and others have demonstrated clearly that linguistic and social factors are closely interrelated in the process of language change. Weinreich, Labov, and Herzog (1968) make the by now well-sub-

---

[1] That variation is an important consideration in linguistic analysis was obvious at the 1972 SECOL/NWAVE meeting in Washington, D.C., where even transformational–generative grammarians began to admit the usefulness of the variation model.

stantiated claim that to explain language change by merely focusing on linguistic or social factors ". . . will fail to account for the rich body of regularities that can be observed in empirical studies of language behavior" (p. 188). The theory Weinreich, Labov, and Herzog espouse states that language variation is a regular on-going phenomenon that is a constant in any speech community. The most frequent reading I can give to these writers is that linguistic change is most often prior to social evaluation. It follows that the task of the linguist should be to focus first on linguistic variation and then to examine the extent to which such variation has acquired social meaning. "In the development of language change, we find linguistic structures embedded unevenly in the social structure; and in the earliest and latest stages of a change, there may be very little correlation with social factors. Thus, it is not so much the task of the linguist to demonstrate the social motivation of a change as to determine the degree of social correlation which exists and show how it bears on the abstract linguistic system" (Weinreich, Labov, and Herzog, 1968). We might conclude, as does Labov, that social change is parasitic on linguistic change. "We may think of social meaning as **parasitic** [boldface mine] upon language. Given a uniform set of linguistic rules used to express certain meanings, language may be considered as a neutral instrument. But in the course of change, there are inevitably variable rules, and these areas of variability tend to travel through the system in a wave-like motion" (Labov, 1971, p. 205).

The theory as presented gives priority to language change, even though the causes of language variability are never properly explicated. In general, Labov tends to deal with cases in which people are unaware of their own usage of language. He has dealt brilliantly with trying to get at the unconscious values that are assigned to linguistic variants by a series of subjective reaction tests.

However, while it seems that in theory and in practice, Labov and other linguists of sociolinguistic persuasion give priority to language change, they do in fact suggest that social values are sometimes a causal factor in language change. According to them, not only are such values seen to retard language change, but indeed, social values may affect the course of change. Labov (1965, p. 206) sees "oscillation between the internal process of structural generalization, and interaction with the external social system, which provides the impetus for continuous linguistic evolution." He notes that "New groups enter the speech community and reinterpret the on-going linguistic change in such a way that one of the secondary changes becomes primary." Thus, Labov does recognize that social values affect language change, although it still seems that the linguistic variation must be prior to the social evaluation.

However, we might ask whether there are cases where linguistic variation is created by social groups for their own purposes. We agree with Labov and his colleagues that many language changes do indeed occur at the subconscious level and that indeed the relationship between perception of speech differences and social valuation of the speakers may be very complex. Yet there are some important examples where we can observe conscious manipulation of language that leads to changes in the language code. We would like to look at some of these in this paper, since we feel that they will tell us a great deal about the influence of social factors on what becomes variant and on what will acquire social meaning. They will also tell us a great deal more about the extent to which language structure is indeed a consistent and independent system.

Hymes (1972) pointed out that too often social components are viewed as secondary, as acting upon the potential output of a grammar. There is a hidden assumption in this view that the theory that the linguist proposes (whether variable or not) of what the linguistic structure is like is the one that in fact most clearly predicts the direction of change. As Hymes points out in his note, "When linguists decide to 'let the grammar decide' they are ruling out the voice of the people." Hymes's (personal communication) meaning is that the theory of grammar that a group of speakers have may be as important, if not more important, in predicting or affecting language change than that proposed by any particular linguist at any one point in time. Hymes pointed out (personal communication) that the "systematic potential" of a language as it would be analyzed by a grammarian would make possible sentences that are excluded by a cultural–stylistic norm. When Newman violates this norm among the Yokuts, they tell him he speaks like a child. Thus, Hymes observes, effective competence includes the knowledge that a form, while possible, is not used/acceptable. Hymes feels that only a knowledge of the "grammar of the people" can tell us what the actualizable forms are at any one point in time.

This view corresponds closely to a view which Jernudd (1971a) also proposes, namely, that we take seriously the causal nature of social interpretation of communication settings. "I claim also that the social interpretation of language use influences the system of language so that the speech community develops distinct language rule systems to correspond more easily to the social norms of communicative appropriateness, given a period of social stability after social change." Thus, language rules may be shaped by social values. Jernudd claims also that "Appropriate features of the language system are restructured according to the needs to express social meaning." In the pidgin–creole situation examined by Jernudd, social meaning is seen to be prior to the language system.

To elaborate a bit more, what sociolinguists are claiming is that in order to understand the meaning of an utterance, we need to know more about the purpose–use–function of an utterance. The participants in a speech community share more than the rules for sentence construction or the basic meanings of a word or phrase, they share rules of speaking. There may be persons whose English I can grammatically decipher but whose message escapes me. In acquiring language, which is done in a social setting, we learn how to communicate our intent, how to identify ourselves, how to effect social control, how to achieve effectiveness regarding some communicative task.

A nice example of how interpretation varies depending on social norms for interpretation is given by Paulston in her 1974 TESOL paper:

> In Sweden, we celebrated Thanksgiving by having my immediate family and friends for a traditional turkey dinner. I was busy in the kitchen and came belatedly into the living room where my sister-in-law had just arrived. [Paulston who has been living in the United States for the last ten years asked] in impeccable Swedish, "Do you know everyone?" Any native American would correctly interpret that to mean that I wanted to know if she had been introduced to those guests she had not previously met. She looked at me sourly and said, "I don't know everyone, but if you are asking me if I have greeted everyone, I have." [Paulston goes on to explain the problem.] Proper manners demand that Swedes do not wait to be properly introduced by a third party, but go around the room shake hands with everyone and say their name aloud to those they have not previously met. Any child knows that, and my sister-in-law felt I had reprimanded her for bad manners.

Knowing the grammer didn't prevent Paulston from being misunderstood. Her purpose was quite different from that interpreted by her sister-in-law.

But even within the same speech community, communication is always an approximation. In any social interaction, there is room for the interpretation of the speaker's intention. We always guess at the speaker's intention by all the other things we know about the rules of speaking, the social situation, the individual, his self image. If we're wrong in our interpretation, the speaker corrects us. Or if we don't understand, we may ask for clarification.

The fact that communication is always being interpreted and reinterpreted leads to a considerable flexibility in language manipulation. A sentence or phrase can be assigned or acquire new meanings all the time. Children and advertisement specialists know this very well.

One anecdote was told me about a couple of nine-year-olds who passed a note in school with the words "Fuck you." The note was intercepted by the teacher, passed on to the principles and the parents called in. Obscenity was not allowed in this school. Later, the perceptive parent asked the child what she had really meant and she said "drop dead." An example from the commercial world is the attempt to change the meaning of the term "butter" to include the product "margarine." For a while, butter became a generic term through the manipulative efforts of advertisers to convince the public of the value of margarine. Now, this is illegal in the United States.

This discussion is intended to show that not only is the realization of a structure defined by social values but also (1) that the structure is only understandable when the function is understood and (2) that the structure may be changed to suit communicative purposes.

To learn a lot more about the claims of Hymes and Jernudd we need to find situations in which we can show (1) that the language user was conscious of the change he was bringing about and (2) that he was actively using the linguistic system for his own ends. Where can we find such situations?

First of all, we must pay serious attention to a point made by Hymes (1961) that people do differ in their conscious interest in the resources of their language and in their exploitation of them. We might like to use a term coined by Minderhout (1971) and speak of some people as language entrepreneurs. That is, we might find that some people are more innovative, risk-taking, and maximizing of their returns than others in regard to their use of language. This would certainly be one set of people that we could focus on.

Examples of such exploitation may be found among young Tagalog speakers who consciously change the rules of the speech disguise language in order to prevent nonmembers of one's own small social group from understanding one's conversation (Conklin, 1959). A more serious consequence of manipulation can be found in India where in pre-Western times, "Individuals wishing to enter linguistically marked occupations found their wishes made more difficult by the fact that they had to learn not only the relevant technical skills and the appropriate terminologies but also a whole new set of grammatical rules and the stylistic norms associated with them." Like a trade union that has a vested interest in limiting its membership in order to keep the demand high, each group ". . . could by manipulation of standards of correctness erect almost insurmountable access barriers to the technical skills it controlled" (Das Gupta and Gumperz, 1968, p. 156).

There are two other examples familiar to use of language entrepreneurs—poets and politicians. We are all familiar with the language manipulation game of newspeak in "1984" or the changing usage among minorities—"Black Power," not colored or nigger, and Ms., not Mrs/Miss. A more recent example is found in Cambodia, where under Communist influence the new word for "reprimand" means literally "reconstruction," ("Washington Post," November 24, 1974). There are reported fresh coverages for the concepts of "hard work," "giving orders," reprimanding," "punishment," and "secrecy."

The language of poetry consists in part of communicating by consciously breaking the rules just enough to be different to get a new message across or by the creation of new rules of syntax to get a point across or obscure the message.

Second, we need to notice, as have Neustupný (1970) and Jernudd (1973), that language treatment is a common phenomenon. Language treatment as defined by Jernudd is "native, conscious (deliberate) concern with the speech community's language resources." Looked at in this way, we can expect such concern to occur at many levels of sociocultural integration—individual, community, regional, national. When such concerns reach the national level, they may in fact be subject to planning. Language planning is thus but a special case of the more pervasive phenomenon of language treatment.

As defined by Rubin and Jernudd (1971a), "language planning is *deliberate* language change; that is changes in the systems of language code or speaking or both that are planned by organizations that are established for such purposes or given a mandate to fulfill such purposes. As such, language planning is focused on problem-solving and is characterized by the formulation and evaluation of alternatives for solving language problems to find the best (or optimal, most efficient) decision."

Since language planning meets our criterion for conscious exploitation of language resources, it is a fruitful area in which to examine the effects of social values upon the nature of the linguistic system. However, we should not forget that language treatment is a common phenomenon in all speech communities, though not always observed by scholars. We suggest that such actions do influence the course of language change and should be looked at. Thus, we cannot agree with Weinreich, Labov, and Herzog (1968), who throw out language planning as being too limited or too recent to indicate much about the general nature of linguistic evolution. "Investigations of the long-range effects of language-planning, of mass literacy and mass media, have therefore a special relevance to the over-all study of linguistic evolution, though these factors, whose effect is recent at best, may be set aside for certain limited studies of language change" (p. 103). I claim that although language planning at the national level may be a recent phenomenon, language treatment is as old as man's speaking itself and must be given serious attention in any study of language evolution.

For this reason, I consider it extremely productive to study those documented cases of language planning and language treatment in order to reveal the nature of conscious change. Further, if we begin to look for cases of conscious manipulation, we may be better able to assess the effect of native theories of language, attitudes, and beliefs upon language change. Although there are relatively few examples of this kind of influence, those we have are quite rewarding and encourage us to look further.

While most linguists would admit that language usage might be affected by social attitudes, beliefs, and values, they seem to set limits to the effects of social variables on at least some aspects of a language code, namely the resistance of grammar to social change. Thus, when one speaks of language planning, linguists will accept as possible changes in script, spelling, and even lexicon. They seem to accept these in a very blasé fashion. But then they always point to the fact that morphology and syntax have not been touched by conscious manipulation according to some social values. This viewpoint is getting more difficult to sustain in the face of Gumperz' demonstration of the syntactic merger of some varieties of strikingly different language family members through particular kinds of social interaction (Gumperz, 1972, p. 172).

It becomes even more difficult to sustain the view of the impermeability of morphology and syntax when we look at the case of changes in Standard Estonian reported on by Valter Tauli (n.d.). "In the language of many users of Standard Estonian in the 1920's the plural morpheme -te was deliberately replaced in many words by -i, which was formerly unknown in their language, e.g. *korgetes diridutes* 'in high churches' was replaced by *korgeis kirikuis;* likewise the analytic superlative expression by the particle *koige* + comparative was in many words replaced by a synthetic superlative form with the suffix *-im*, hitherto unknown in Estonian." Not only were there changes in the plural and in the superlative, but it is reported that even a new case was introduced into Estonian ". . . the introduction of new cases as is shown by the case Essiv, formed with the (na) morpheme that did not exist until 1870 neither in standard nor in popular language" (Oksaar, 1970, as reported in Aavik, 1961). Thus, we see that through language planning, deliberate changes in the morphology were successfully effected in Estonian and are in use still today. But the case of Estonian is not that unusual; similar examples can be cited for Turkey and Israel. The Turkish Language Planning Agency was instrumental in promoting the use of the regular Turkish plural *lar/ler* for almost all words where formerly Arabic broken plurals or sound plurals were used (Gallagher, 1971). As well, the Language Planning Agency was instrumental in promoting the attachment of fixed Turkish suffixes to Ara-

bic or Persian words. Such suffixes were of long standing in spoken Turkish but were looked down upon in Ottoman times (Gallagher, 1971). The
need for a modern lexicon in the development of Hebrew also had its effect on Hebrew morphology. Morag (1959) pointed out that in the process
of creating new verbs from extant nouns, a change in morphology was effected; most Hebrew roots have three phonemes, but the process of
deriving verbs from nouns led to the introduction of a large number of
four- and five-consonant roots. Although this particular process would
best be seen as language treatment, since the words were not all decided
on by the language planning agency, it was a conscious adjustment to the
needs of a modern society of the western type. Other examples of language treatment and language planning could be offered, but it seems
quite obvious that all aspects of language have been affected by conscious
manipulation in response to particular language problems. On the basis of
the already reported cases, it seems reasonable to presume that any aspect of the language code or language usage is susceptible to conscious
change, provided that the necessary motivation and proper field for im-
plementation exists.

Given the premise that all aspects of language are subject to change, we
can then ask what the necessary motivations might be for effecting such
change. It seems useful to divide such motivations into three
types—linguistic, semilinguistic, and extralinguistic.[2] As linguistic motivations, we would include changes in a language whose primary aim is to
improve communicative efficiency. These would be the sort of changes in
which the objective is stated as the achievement of greater precision, clar-
ity, understanding, or communicative efficiency. Such changes might be
effected by editors when setting up style regulations or by broadcasters
when deciding on pronunciation norms for their stations or by chemists
when agreeing on the rules for compound derivations. Although personal
values always enter into this sort of motivation, the communication goal
seems primary. We might note that this is the kind of change that Valter
Tauli (1968) feels should be the only goal of language planning.

A second type of motivation would be that which I call semilinguistic.
Here, the focus on language change seems to be based both on a desire to
improve communication as on social, political, or economic motivations.

---

[2] Adapted from Rabin (1971). A number of persons have objected to this terminology, but
I have as yet been unable to come up with a satisfactory set of alternatives. My intention is
to focus on motivations to change language in order to improve it for communicative purposes, motivations to change language that are partly based on improving the communicative function but fulfilling also social–political purposes, or motivations to change
language that are based merely on fulfilling social–political purposes without having communicative improvement as a goal.

Changes in language may consciously be related to social or political goals. Some examples are the following:

1. A recent Russian decision that ethnic languages be written in Cyrillic rather than in roman characters as they had previously been, has distinct advantages in that speakers of ethnic languages will not have to learn two systems. However, it also has political implications in that since Russian is written in Cyrillic, the Russian language will be more accessible than those written in Roman script.

2. The major motivation behind the Turkish language reform was modernization and the mobilization of the masses (Gallagher, 1971). Language differences had become so great that the masses and the elite were unable to communicate. Ataturk saw that changes in communication patterns were essential to mobilizing the masses in his modernization and westernization plans. He made language modernization one of his first priorities and effected many changes in the language code.

A third type of motivation behind language treatment–planning is what I call extralinguistic. In this case, no real language or communication problem seems to exist. Instead, social–political causes are furthered by focusing on language problems. Some examples are the following:

1. Baskakov (1960) criticized existing alphabets and orthographies for various Turkic languages for their shortcomings, inconsistencies, and unnecessary complications. Wurm (1960) felt that Baskakov had indeed put his finger on something very important; that these differences had been consciously created and established for the political purpose of making the various Turkic languages appear as different from each other as possible. Further, Wurm observed that the function of such systematic differentiation was "to hinder and prevent any possible tendencies toward unification on grounds of the great similarities of their regional forms of language." In other words, language problems were used for political purposes.

2. Das Gupta (1971) has shown how leaders of religious groups deliberately exaggerated differences between Hindi and Urdu in order to promote cohesion and mobilize their followers. "The linguistic similarity of Hinki and Urdu was gradually overshadowed by the deliberate exaggeration of the difference between these languages by leaders of religious groups for mobilizational purposes" (Das Gupta, 1971, p. 56).

3. Jernudd (1971b) raises the question of whether the current public discussion of language issues in Norway is "not because of felt difficulties of communication, but because of the possibility of using readily available language differences to demonstrate and rally support for socioeconomic and political interests."

From the above examples, we can see that language structure has been deliberately molded to serve a number of different motivations, ranging from purely communicative to purely sociopolitical. Recognizing the important fact that language definition and change are susceptible to sociopolitical pressures, we might then ask, following good culture change theory, whether the character of the language innovator or entrepreneur has any effect upon the success of the change. And as might be expected, this is indeed the case. That is, we can look at all the factors that are known to enhance the possibility of change and expect them to also affect successful management of language changes. Thus, the social standing of the innovator is often important; that is, does he have the right to affect the change, would people expect that the change would come from this source? In the case of Russia and Turkey, the changes were supported by the sanctions of the absolute ruler and were to a large extent successful and acceptable within the structure of that society. Stalin is known to have been very much interested in language planning and to have made it an integral part of his political policies (Stalin, 1950; Springer, 1956). Ataturk made language modernization an important feature of his westernization policies (Gallagher, 1971). Another example of the importance of the agent of change is the recent attempt to effect a spelling change in Indonesia after 1965. When promoted only by the Spelling Committee of the Language Planning Agency, which consisted of linguists, the change was not forthcoming, since these scholars were not in a powerful enough position to effect the change. However, in 1972, President Suharto of Indonesia approved and promoted the spelling reform, and the chances for its acceptance seem high. In many societies, when the national leader promotes such a change, we can expect that it will be more readily accepted. An entrepreneur or innovator must be aware of the social milieu in which he is attempting to affect language changes and must be skillful in bringing about the proper attitudes for acceptance of the changes he wishes to institute. As in all planned change, he must know which groups are most likely to accept language changes first, which most likely to resist. He must know a great deal about the attitudes people hold toward kinds of language change. Sometimes innovators or entrepreneurs manage to affect such changes without conscious knowledge of the social setting, yet I am sure that with more extensive investigation, we would find that some language entrepreneurs or innovators subconsciously do know the proper conditions for the introduction of change.

I have been trying to demonstrate in the last several pages that language treatment and language planning are indeed subject to the same kind of constraints as other social changes; that the social setting, the characteristics of the entrepreneur or innovator, and the kinds of motivation may affect the success of attempts at change.

We need to know more about how people feel about language in order to understand the conditions under which language treatment and especially planning can be successful. Further, I think it is extremely important to consider how native theories of language, attitudes toward language, and myths about language are determining factors in causing as well as preventing changes.

It is well known that linguists vary in their description of specific languages based in part on their own value system. We can get a hint of how values affect linguistic descriptions in Lunt (1959). "Still, it comes as a surprise [to Lunt] to find supposedly scholarly spokesmen from the Serbian and Bulgarian camps making diametrically opposed claims about one and the same local type of speech. One blandly classifies all Slavic spoken in southern Yugoslavia as South Serbian; the other with equally calm conviction calls them Western Bulgarian." If the boundaries between languages are affected by the values held even by linguists, surely the theories of natives may also affect the structure and may serve as appropriate models for predicting change.

In fact, there are probably at least two kinds of theories of language that affect change, neither of which is universal, but both of which have influenced the direction of change: (1) National traditions of language that are quite sophisticated, developed, and systematized, that are well known and propagated through writing and formal schooling. An example might be the Arabic or Bengali national language tradition. These have affected not only the language for which they were elaborated, but also have been applied to other languages. It is well known that in many African countries the theories about language are strongly influenced by the Arabic tradition. (2) Native traditions of language that are not highly elaborated, developed, or systematized and are not broadcast over a wide population but that nonetheless are influential in language change and use.

It seems reasonably clear that attitudes toward languages may affect changes in language structures. Kloss (1967) noted that if you feel that language is malleable and have the proper motivation to affect the change, that we can find many examples of what he had called "ausbau" or language by development, i.e., languages that "having been shaped or reshaped, molded or remolded—as the case may be—in order to become a standardized tool of literary expression." Not only do such attitudes about the possibilities of language change help promote changes, but attitudes toward the kinds of changes that are appropriate may affect language changes. Thus, ideas of purism may prevent the introduction of international words. Or the view that language may serve as a window on the world may enhance the acceptance of international words. The acceptance or rejection of items that are foreign often depends not on what the linguist may identify as foreign, but rather on the evaluation that the speakers may give to particular items. Indeed, the whole question of "foreign markedness" is subject to evaluation by native speakers. One of the ways in which this gets expressed in writing is through the italicization of foreign words, especially those coming from Latin or French. Once a word has been accepted as "native," it no longer is italicized and seems to be perceived as an integral part of the language.[3]

Labov (1963) has provided us with a splendid example of how social values eventually affected language change on Martha's Vineyard. He reports that residents associated a close-mouthed way of speaking with Island values and Island belongingness. As resistance to incursions of summer visitors increased, so did the features of centralization of /ai/ and /au/. This feature (and others) were exaggerated as a sign of social identity. Although the speakers were unaware of the linguistic details of the change they were effecting, they did seem aware that those who spoke in this close-mouthed fashion represented certain values, which did seem to serve as a source for imitation, though the chain between social values and language change was complex. The social values did lead speakers to hypercorrection and exaggeration of particular language features.

Although examples of how native language theories have been a causative factor in language change are hard to come by, I have been able to find several that are suggestive of the kind of material we should be looking for. Further, I think that if we begin to look for them, we might find that they are as important, if not more important, in language change than the model the linguist might propose.

In the area of vocabulary, Samarin (1966) called our attention to the fact that nonnative users of the Creole language Sango in Central Africa seem to differ considerably in the words that they use for the same item when speaking Sango. Samarin suggests that the reason for the increasing variation may be explained by the fact that "wanting to speak proper Sango, people reject whatever they think is local; proper Sango is simply that form of the language which does not betray their origin" (p. 196). The reason for this rejection of what are perceived to be mother tongue words (although in some cases they may be perfectly good standard Sango) is that the speaker is making a "conscious adjustment of one's speech to an

---

[3] A recent amusing case of native theory operating is the 1973 ordinance of the French government to eliminate certain words of English derivation in French. The ordinance listed these words and prohibited civil servants from using them in written public documents. It is interesting to consider why certain English words in French were selected and not others. Art Buchwald, in a spoof on this elimination of Franglais, described how this would be done in English in order to eliminate French words. Again, the words Buchwald missed were as fascinating as those he noted. Equally amusing was the spoof by the Englishman Auberon Waugh in "Express," February 15, 1973.

assumed prestige model of Sango." Here we have a good example of how that native view of foreignness is creating more variation than necessary, since Sango has standard terms.

Another creole example of native language systems was given by Orjala at the 1975 Pidgin–Creole conference. He says that there is a style mechanism, calling gallicizing, available to the creole monolingual that consists of "moving from wherever one is linguistically towards what one **conceives to be** (boldface mine) the Standard French Form." Orjala says it is a device for modifying creole so that its similarity to French models is increased or decreased according to the ability and purpose of the speaker. We should note that Orjala says that this is not "borrowing" from French in the usual sense, but simply dipping into a reserve inventory labeled "French," that is part of the individual's hypersystem. It may involve a shift in phonology, grammar, or lexicon.

Another example in the area of morphology has been called to my attention by Dorice Zilsel. Zilsel (personal communication), working with two basic varieties of French in Southwest Louisiana—Cajun and Creole (called Parler Negre locally)—has encountered several fine examples of where native theory about "Good French" seems to result in striking variation and potentially new pronominal forms in the language. Both Cajun and Creole are spoken in the same region, with Cajun serving as the model for Good French (although all speakers recognize that their French is not really the "Good French"). One example shows an attempt by white Creole speakers to approximate the standard French third person possessive plural person. Instead of using the Creole form *ye* or the Cajun or Standard French form *leur* for 'their', what some White Creole speakers do, trying to be formal, is use something between the two, namely, *yeur* /yör/ in the phrase *yör sar* 'their car'. A similar attempt to approximate the standard pronoun occurs in the phrase *sa se pu le dö dyö*, literally, 'This is for the two of them', where the phrase *dyö* 'of them', constitutes a loan translation from English and is, in fact, not really standard French. The Cajun–Standard French object pronoun form would be *eux*, whereas the Creole form is *ye*. What comes out when White Creole speakers are trying to impress the addressee is a mixture of the two, namely /dyö/. What seems to be happening in these two cases when White Creole speakers are approximating Cajun French is that they are developing or have developed a native theory of what the pronominal system of Cajun or the Good French consists of.

An example that shows the influence of native theories of the sound system was noted by Victoria Bricker. Bricker (personal communication) found a case where native theory about the sound system seems to have brought about a change in spelling. The source for her observations are two Mayan versions of "The Sermon of the Talking Cross." One manuscript dates to 1850 (called the Juan de la Cruz version), and the other dates to 1903 (called the Tixcacal version). The first was very much influenced by Spanish conventions for writing Mayan. It appears that the Spanish writers did not really recognize the glottal stop in two ways: (1) after /a/ and /e/ it was represented as /t/ and (2) after /o/ it was represented as /k/. But /k/ was also used to represent the phoneme [glottalized k] in Mayan. The 1903 version, which is probably several copyings removed from the 1850 version, appears to reflect the fact that the Mayans had some recognition that the glottal stop did constitute a single phoneme. In this version, the glottal stop is often either represented by a space or ignored after /a/ or /o/ or by /k/ after /o/. The glottalized k continued to be represented by a /k/. In the 1850 version, /yoʔolal/ 'therefore' is written *yoklal,* whereas in the 1903 version, it is not only written *yoklal,* but also *yolal.* The 1850 version represented /maʔ(a) ceen/ 'not only . . .' as *mat chen,* whereas the 1903 version represented it as *ma chen.* What this example seems to show is how native theory, while not explicitly stated about the sound system, is reflected in the changing spelling of these texts.

While the cases that show a direct relationship between native theories of language and language change are not reported very frequently in the literature, we can get a glimpse of their impact by the examples cited above where perceptions of sound systems, morphology, lexicon, and syntax are shown to be influenced by native interpretations. It appears that the clue to discovering such influences would be to look for variation and to look at those odd cases that appear to be anomalies at the time of investigation but that very well might reflect the direction of changes to come based on an underlying understanding of the system.

What I have attempted to do here is to demonstrate that language is more malleable than linguists heretofore have led us to believe and that changes in language code can be affected by native theories of language, attitudes and beliefs about language, and evaluation of language. Jernudd and Das Gupta (1971) have suggested that language is a societal resource much as any other resource man possesses. As such, it is subject to planned change that will depend upon the identification of language problems that require organized attention. When such attention is to be given will depend in large part on social changes. I have also suggested that individual and group attention to language problems is a continuing process, so that variations both within and between languages are to a large part contingent on motivational, biographical, and social setting factors. It is time that linguists pay more than token attention to the causal effect of social factors on language change. Realizing the importance of such factors, we should seriously consider the conscious efforts at effecting change in order to understand the conditions under which language changes are most readily effected. Language planning and language treatment offer a fertile field for looking for such insights. Instead of always asking what the social concomitants of linguistic variation are, we need to see how social meaning operates to effect real language creativity and change.

Acknowledgments

I am pleased to acknowledge the help of Robert Cooper, Roger Shuy, Dell Hymes, Björn Jernudd, and Albert Marckwardt who gave me many comments and editorial suggestions. I am indebted to Dorice Zilsel, Case Western Reserve, for sharing data with me from her ongoing field research, and to Victoria Bricker, Tulane University, for allowing me to use her observations of two Mayan documents.

References

Aavik, J.
1961   Language Reform. In *Aspects of Estonian culture*. London.
Baskakov, N. A.
1952   *The Turkic peoples of the USSR: The development of their languages and writing*. Oxford: Central Asian Research Centre.
Chomsky, Noam
1965   *Aspects of a theory of syntax*. Boston: MIT Press.
Conklin, Harold
1959   Linguistic play in its cultural context, *Language* 35, 631–36.
Das Gupta, Jyotirindra
1971   Religion, language, and political mobilization. In *Can language be planned?* edited by J. Rubin and B. Jernudd, pp. 53–62. Honolulu: East-West Center Press.
Das Gupta, Jyotirindra, and John J. Gumperz
1968   Language, communication and control in North India. In *Language problems of developing nations* edited by J. Fishman, and C. Ferguson and J. Das Gupta. New York: Wiley.
Gallagher, Charles
1971   Language reform and social modernization in Turkey. In *Can language be planned?* edited by J. Rubin and B. Jernudd, pp. 159–178. Honolulu: East-West Center Press.
Gumperz, John
1972   Communication in multilingual societies. *Language in social groups*. Stanford: Stanford University Press.
Hymes, Dell
1961   Linguistic aspects of cross-cultural personality study. In *Studying personality cross-culturally* edited by Bert Kaplan. New York: Harper and Row.
1972   Note in *Lectological Newsletter*, no. 3. Washington, D.C.: Georgetown University.

Jernudd, Björn
  1971a   Social change and aboriginal speech variation in Australia, *Anthropological Linguistics* 13(1),16–32.
  1971b   Review of Hangen, *Language conflict and language planning. The case of modern Norwegian. Language* **47**, 490–493.
  1972   Language planning as a type of language treatment. In *Language planning: Current issues and trends* edited by J. Rubin and Roger Shuy. Washington, D.C.: Georgetown University Press.
Jernudd, Björn and Jyotirindra Das Gupta
  1971   Towards a theory of language planning. In *Can language be planned?* edited by Rubin and Jernudd, pp. 195–215. Honolulu: East-West Center Press.
Kloss, Heinz
  1967   'Abstand' languages and 'ausbau' languages. *Anthropological Linguistics* **9**(7), 29–41.
Kurylowicz, J.
  1949   *Lingua,* January 1948. Quoted by Weinreich, Labov, and Herzog (1948).
Labov, William
  1963   The social motivation of a sound change, *Word* **19**, 273–309.
  1965   On the mechanism of linguistic change, *Georgetown University Monographs on Languages and Linguistics* **18**, 91–114.
  1971   The study of language in its social context. In *Advances in the Sociology of Language* edited by J. Fishman. The Hague: Mouton.
Lunt, Horace
  1959   The creation of standard Macedonian: some facts and attitudes, *Anthropological Linguistics* **1**(5), 19–26.
Minderhout, David
  1971   *The entrepreneur's use of language.* Unpublished paper presented to the 1971 American Anthropological Association Meetings.
Morag, Shelomo
  1959   Planned and unplanned development in modern Hebrew, *Lingua* **8**(3), 247–263.
Neustupný, Jiří
  1970   Basic types of treatment of language problems, *Linguistic Communications* **1**, 77–98. Monash University.
Oksaar, Els
  1970   The concept of norm and modern linguistics, *Proceedings of the XIth AULLA Conference in Sydney 1967.*
Orjala, Paul R.
  1975   *Interacting variation systems in Haitian Creole.* Presented to the International Conference in Pidgins and Creoles, January 6–10.
Paulston, Christina B.
  1974   *Linguistic and communicative competence.* Presented to TESOL, March 5–10.
Rabin, Chaim
  1971   A tentative classification of language planning aims. In *Can language be planned?* Rubin and Jernudd, eds., pp. 277–280. Honolulu: East-West Center Press.
Rubin, Joan and Björn Jernudd
  1971a   Introduction: Language Planning as an Element in Modernization, in Rubin and Jernudd, eds. pp. xii–xxiv.
  1971b   *Can language by planned?* Honolulu: East-West Center Press.
Samarin, William J.
  1966   Self-annulling prestige factors among speakers of a creole language. In *Sociolinguistics,* edited by William Bright. The Hague: Mouton.

Springer, George P.
  1956   *Early Soviet theories in communication.* Cambridge, Massachusetts: Center for International Studies, M.I.T.
Stalin, Joseph
  1950   On Marxism in Linguistics, *Pravda,* June 20. Translated in *The Current Digest of the Soviet Press* **2**(21), 3–9.
Tauli, Valter
  1968   *Introduction to a theory of language planning,* Uppsala: Acta Universitatis Upsaliensis.
  n.d.   *Language as a Means.* Hungarian Academy of Sciences.
Weinreich, Uriel, William Labov, and Marvin I. Herzog
  1968   Empirical Foundations for a Theory of Language Change. In *Directions for historical linguistics: A symposium.* Austin: University of Texas Press.
Wurm, Stephan
  1960   Comments on N. A. Baskakov, *Turkic peoples of the USSR: The development of their languages and writing.* Oxford: Central Asian Research Centre.

Language Creativity and the Psychotherapy Relationship[1]

LILYAN A. BRUDNER

Bernstein (1972) noted that language plays an important part in human socialization, particularly in education preparatory to appropriate role performance. Language enculturation is a process that requires an individual to learn to manipulate linguistic and paralinguistic channels in order to move from individual personal message sending to more widely shared selection and elaboration of conventionalized verbal messages that are appropriate to a situation defined by the context of interaction. Language enculturation has as its objective teaching an individual to select carefully among a range of linguistic alternatives to go beyond individualized message encoding to the construction of messages that are more universalistic in character and that are defined by the given social type of transaction. An important dimension of the creative use of language is its shared and conventionalized character and appropriateness to a specific genre of social behavior. If an individual is to function in a variety of roles he must learn to mark the significance of his messages in terms of priorities that are socially appropriate. By marking, here I refer to a "conventionalized stylistic device which is defined by its contrastive nature to normal morphophonemic forms used in other portions of the speech event" (Gumperz and Hymes 1972, p. 499). Appropriate linguistic behavior thus requires that an individual constantly elaborate personal meaning by various stylistic alternations so that his motives and intentions become clearer to the audience with whom he is dealing, and to behave in particular so that his behavior conforms to the expectations of his social alter to the extent that it can be correctly interpreted.

In language communities of large industrial societies, there is a wide range and variety of speech systems. Bernstein (1964, 1972) in his work on British English has suggested that some are less well adapted than others to convey highly abstract messages. His basic theory requires a

---

[1] Data for this discussion was collected in 1965 from a series of taped interviews of therapy sessions made by a physician in a California state mental hospital.

great deal of refinement and cross-community testing; nevertheless, it is quite clear that there is a wide range of variability in the speech used by members of different segments of the society. Where people have been limited to a particular kind of restricted code because of a variety of social and economic factors, certain difficulties in communication may emerge. Thus, we can expect, broadly speaking, to find that some limitations in human interaction may be related directly to problems in how individuals express their feelings, motivations, and intentions—often it is not what people intend that leads to difficulties in interaction, but rather their failure to appropriately manipulate communicative codes.

This paper is an analysis of some linguistic devices used by psychotherapists to enculturate new patients into appropriate communicative behavior. As such, this paper has a dual purpose; the first is to describe some of the aspects of linguistic enculturation in psychotherapy relationships, and the second is to suggest that in a fundamental way, the linguistic learning that occurs in the psychotherapy relationship is highly significant in assisting the individual in subordinating his expressive behavior to the linguistic code. By encouraging the subordination of expressive behavior to the linguistic code, the therapy relationship can also provide the patient with a clearer understanding of alternatives in verbal and nonverbal patterns of communication generally. Focus on the code itself is often a very important factor in changing behavior. As the patient begins to understand that in the past his own style of communication has often not been intelligible to many other speakers, he may also learn that he himself cannot take for granted that in the past he has always correctly perceived the meaning or intention of the messages sent by others.

While psychologists have not been unaware of the significance of the linguistic dynamics in psychotherapy, the particularly pedagogical aspect of the language learning process has received little attention as such. It is the assymmetrical aspect of the psychotherapy relationship that plays the most important part in setting the stage for the language learning process. In the therapy situation, the dyad is composed initially of a role player who by his ascribed status embodies the norms of a system (the psychotherapist) and a second individual who by his ascribed status embodies the neophyte (the patient). The individual identified with the norms of the system controls the nature of the interactive process, while the second participant serves merely as a "coerced link in the play of such forces" (Blumer 1962, p. 186).

Acceptance of the therapy situation implies for the patient an overt acceptance of the norms of the group and the authority of the therapist in defining these norms. Traditional psychotherapy relationships involve several major phases. In the first phase, the patient accepts membership and is enculturated into the ground rules of the interactive situation. In the second phase of therapy, the relationship becomes increasingly structured; both therapist and patient function as trained role players. The patient, at least in the ideal, internalizes his role, including the appropriate linguistic aspects of the communicative relationship. At the termination of therapy, the patient has learned to assume not only the role of patient, but to some extent the role of self-therapist as well. Implicit in the therapy relationship, then, is a dialectic process in which the patient moves from a self-defined role, to a therapy-oriented role, to a self-therapy role.

The explicit purpose of therapy may be defined as the shared expectation that the patient will learn to understand his feelings and also learn to express and channel them effectively. Thus, there are two notable dimensions involved—the cognitive and the sociolinguistic. A great deal of emphasis has traditionally been placed on the first, but too little attention has been devoted to the examination of the second.

The approach described here articulates more directly with the studies of social encounters than traditional studies in social or cognitive psychology on patient–therapy relationships, attitude change, or behavioral change. The social encounter approach uses real-life situations as a research universe and focuses on studies of real social groups. It is rarely formulated as a hypothesis testing controlled laboratory experiment; rather, the function of such studies is to view verbal and nonverbal behavior as it occurs in natural situations as a totally integrated unit of meaning, and to derive from a study of natural interaction new insights into rules of social communication. The particular research orientation has been developed to counteract typical experimental methods design utilized in more classic social and psychological experiments. As Argyle (1973, p. 11) noted:

> Recent research on social interaction has taken a different approach to theory and explanation from that now fashionable in social psychology. Dissonance theory, exchange theory, and similar formulations put forward very general and abstract hypotheses about social performance, which are applicable to a wide range of situations. These theories do not, however, appear to cast much light on the processes of social interaction. Furthermore, the experiments stemming from these theories are usually of the "stripped down" kind, and thus omit many of the essential ingredients of social behavior (speech, situational rules, etc.); it follows that something must be missing from these theories.

Most studies of cognition and social psychology related to language behavior in a patient–therapist relationship do not take into account the fact that the study of such interaction would require an information translation model based on an explication of the processual aspects of skill learning, of role theory, and of lack of sharedness in language behavior.

Such a model would have to account for the fact that patients are engaged in a process of language skill training and that in some way they are learning new semantic rules; this fact, among others, influences the messages sent by the patient far more than it might influence messages sent by the therapist. In addition, such a model would have to relax the assumption that there is only one conventionalized manner for messages to be encoded and decoded by both patient and therapist and would require the development of more sophisticated notions about language as a sociological weapon in communicative transactions.

Much of the basic research on minimal social reinforcement in behavioral exchange theory has been based on the work of Verplanck (1955), who studied the control of a conversation by paralinguistic as well as linguistic signals. Later investigators, following Verplanck, saw the parallel between the psychotherapy situation and other language learning events (e.g., Matarrazo, Saslow, Wiens, Weitman, and Allen, 1964) and noted the effects of an interviewer on a respondent. While various explanations for this kind of controlling behavior have been offered, perhaps the most satisfactory view is that offered by Garfinkel (1972). Garfinkel noted that much of the language interaction of a small group can only be interpreted in terms of the various respondents' perceptions of the total communicative event. While various studies have attempted to deal with the feedback aspect of the communicative relationship through the use of statistical measurements and controlled experimental design, it is quite clear that models from traditional psychological approaches such as operant conditioning are probably not directly applicable for the description of any real dyadic language situation involving highly complex sociolinguistic rules as well as complex and changing definitions of the situation. We are probably not ready for the development of formal and general theories about social interaction in language skill learning situations; what is needed first is to describe the social processes involved and to identify some of the stages in the learning processes; once this is done, it is possible to examine the goals being pursued by people in different situations and to examine the way different sociolinguistic patterns are related to the competence and strategies of individuals.

In the study of encounters, there has been an increasing amount of attention in the literature paid to how skills are acquired by adults in various formal situations (Bradford, Gibbs, and Benné, 1964; Corsini, Shaw, and Blake, 1961; Schein and Bennis, 1965; Wight, 1969) that focus on the dynamic and continuous process of learning in natural situations. However, even these studies do not focus sufficiently on the stages by which new sociolinguistic rules are acquired. It is quite clear that the learning of new language skills is a processual series of events that are interlinked. How does the nature of the communicative event influence the ways in which a speaker learns new sociolinguistic rules? To answer this question it is necessary to examine the constraints placed on a given speaker by his past state of competence in the particular genre used and also the function that language learning serves in the particular communicative event.

In certain kinds of real social situations, people learn to make new use of older language skills, as well as to learn how to incorporate new elements of language or cognition into their existing repertoire. We may define such situations of language learning as highly formal situations where social constraints are placed on language choice by particular status-related elements in the language contact situation—where, for example, formal, polite, or technical language is required; where titles are used by at least one party in addressing the other; and where the speech event is highly purposive and related to specific goals and tasks.

The therapy relationship is one kind of constrained language learning situation, the classroom is another, the job interviewing or training situation may be another. Since in all situations, except in the classroom situation, the occasion for the transaction is determined by some kind of business other than language learning, it is often the case that the language enculturation process is implicit rather than explicit. Similarly, the situation is defined as one in which at least one party has a demonstrating or teaching function and the other a learning function. The task of channeling verbal behavior that is task related is thus unequally divided between the parties involved; there are notable differences of kind in the verbal interaction that follows.

However, in most cases even in such situations, a two or n-party situation consists of conversational sequences that are alternating. A new meaning is identified as significant, or marked, by the fact that one speaker because of his status can define it as significant or appropriate to a particular aspect of the task of the group. Where the person who is effectively engaged in teaching a new skill defines a linguistic element as significant in some way, he is marking that element as appropriate to the specific task-oriented context. The signaling that such an element is appropriate is generally accompanied by some changes in the pattern of morphophonemic alternation in the speech of the dominant speaker. Changes in voice tone, speed, or a variety of other highly contrastive usage of supersegmental phonemes or of paralinguistic elements may be utilized to signal that a given element is highly significant in a given context; often it is up to the message encoder to determine how and in what ways it is significant.

With regard to the dynamic relationship established between patient and therapist, some but not all of the therapist's cues are derived from the way in which he conceives of his special role as therapist: some therapists are less good than others in marking behavior as significant in a clear and nonarbitrary manner; some patients are less receptive than others to the verbal cues for sociolinguistic as well as motivational factors. In addition, some ad hoc marking behavior does occur; that is, some messages are marked inadvertently or for reasons that are not related to the task at hand.

There is, however, a large body of cues that are highly regularized and used across patients by a therapist and that are standardized in some therapist subcultures. The majority of these are related to the therapists' notion of curing and may be related to a ritual or dramaturgical process. By ritual or dramaturgical, process I refer to what Nadel (1951, p. 138) has called "the demonstration of desired modes of action in the context of ceremonial and aesthetic performances" in which "the desired modes of behaving are exemplified only in formal features of the performance, that is, in the manner in which persons or situations are employed." These signals are viewed by the therapist as highly effacacious and as critically important in serving as a vehicle for reinforcing specific notions about self control and control over the behavior of others. They form part of a system that is designed to bring about some deep emotional transformation in the patient and are derived from held notions of the therapist about the causality and amelioration of psychological problems. The therapist attempts through his dramaturgical performance to cultivate a purposive attitude in the patient. These dramatic cues are therefore utilized with great care in a very rigid and prescriptive manner. I have termed verbal and nonverbal cues that are viewed as critical to the dramatic performance and to the cultivation of a purposive attitude in the patient as ritualized responses on the part of the therapist. I have used the term "ritualized" also to indicate the fact that many therapists believe that failure to perform such behavior appropriately may lead to some undoing in the performance of curing.

The recognition of the importance of these cues by the patient poses a problem. Many therapists give little explicit attention to informal and formal explanation of the dramatic process involved. The expressive component of such models may not be immediately clear to patients who come from a different subcultural environment than the therapist. It is not always clear where the responsibility for their clarification as part of the curing process lies. When their function is not explicitly clarified by the therapist, which is often the case, responsibility is interwoven with the patient's ability to intuit their meaning from his understanding of what the entire communicative relationship is all about. Such intuitions may be derived from the patient's understanding of (1) the authority relationship between himself and the therapist, (2) the oral mode of questioning used by the therapist, (3) other linguistic and nonlinguistic features in the dyadic relationship, or (4) from the entire ritual setting.

Given the traditional objectives of psychotherapy, restructuring the communicative behavior of the patient becomes of central importance. But structured sociolinguistic change is intimately related to the high degree of structure imposed on the psychotherapy relationship. The therapy relationship prescribes that the time and place of the meeting be rigidly maintained. Economic sanctions are used often to prevent any alteration in a fixed pattern. Given the highly structured nature of the interview situation, cues given by the therapist are highly significant and function as marked messages. The notable rigidity of the interactive background and setting relationships thus reinforce the signifying function of language. Language, by its very nature, can be used to "mark out what is relevant, affectively, cognitively, and socially" (Bernstein 1964, p. 254).

In a successful therapy situation, the therapist's use of language structures the situation primarily at the lexical level. After reviewing a number of taped interviews by different therapist and patient dyads, it becomes clear that the types of linguistic responses made by the therapist are highly ritualized. If we compare two interviews, one during the first phase of therapy, where the rules of the game are being transmitted, and one at the last phase, where the patient has taken on the role of the other, significant differences in the patient's verbal behavior may be noted. The patient's responses often become more stylistically varied and vocabulary, particularly that related to the expression of personal feelings, more differentiated:

1. The patient begins to limit his monologue to particular topics. Both choice of topic and choice of terms become more focused and constrained. The greater use of an elaborated code that often is characteristic of later phases of therapy is likely to be constituted by patient messages in which intentions, emotional reactions, and perceptions of specific situations are more clearly distinguished by choice of lexical and syntactic alternatives that show greater logical continuity in their organization in speech. In contrast, the early phase of psychotherapy may be characterized by unclear referential use of language, rigid and limited use of syntactic alternatives, and by extensive use of nonverbal signals. During this period, the patient tries to establish phatic communion with the therapist. This may be done through emphasis on specific details of situations where through the use of detail the patient attempts to transmit the affective quality of his situation to the therapist. Emphasis on phatic communion

decreases as sessions progress. The patient moves from what Bernstein has called "public language" to an elaborated code, with greater message encoding being placed on verbal rather than nonverbal communication.

2.   The patient begins to adopt the technical language of the therapist, relating particularly to the description of emotions and states of being that the therapist believes to be more adequate to describe fairly abstract ideas than the patient's use of ordinary language has been. As they begin to share larger portions of the technical language, the therapist is able to telescope verbal cues more quickly and efficiently to the patient. Thus, for example, if the patient fails to follow an idea in a consistent manner, the therapist may bring him back to the core of the topic through the use of a shared single technical word or phrase. The patient gradually learns to encode the paralinguistic cues of the therapist as well and to be held accountable for his own paralinguistic message sending. The sharing of a common technical language is crucial to the relationship, since it allows for more effective and parsimonious message encoding and decoding by members of the dyad. As Hammel points out, the failure to communicate efficiently can at the extreme simply result in "noise" in the system (Hammel, 1963, p. 84). The great deal of attention paid to the integration of paralinguistic and verbal communication tends to lead to the weeding out of noise in the system as the rules of the game become shared and highly conventionalized.

3.   The patient begins to recognize that he is held accountable when he sends messages through nonverbal channels. In addition, he is taught that in evading sending a specific message, the lack of talk does in fact have high communicative significance. Just as the patient accepts the therapist's belief that all signals that are pertinent to the topic at hand are not coded verbally, the failure to talk becomes in itself a highly important message that is interpreted in terms of the entire communicative event. The patient learns that only certain topics have high value content for the therapy situation. The patient is discouraged from using phatic communion. Nonverbal signals, such as crying, or gestures, failure to talk, are interpreted by the therapist as equivalent to verbal messages in their signifying function, but as less useful than more carefully coded verbal messages to communicate ideas, motives, and desires.

4.   The patient learns to examine the message form more closely and to interpret it not simply for its overt content, but in terms of the entire communicative event. The patient is encouraged to enlarge his referential concepts of message forms and to scan the behavior of others in terms of how a single message fits with other aspects of the larger communicative event.

5.   The patient learns that his verbal and nonverbal messages have a certain concrete quality for others; e.g., that words can serve as things for

others. The patient learns, for example, that certain verbal statements may have equal cognitive saliency with acts such as verbally attacking or actually hitting another interlocutor. Often, some implicit distinction is taught to the patient by the therapist between language as metaphor, language as phatic communion, informative language, etc.

6. The patient learns to account for uniformity and diversity in the message forms he decodes and encodes. The therapist teaches the patient that he must learn to translate the messages of others in terms of their communicative intent and virtuosity. The patient is encouraged to decode and encode messages in terms of a wide variety of factors, including audience, topic, speaker, message form, channel of communication, and setting.

To illustrate some of the points that we have covered let us examine two conversations between the same patient and therapist. The first conversation is a segment taken from an early therapy session. The second conversation is taken several months later after over a dozen therapy sessions. It is important to note how much of the content of the patient is discarded in the first session by the therapist and how the attention of the patient is channeled toward affective topics. In the second interview presented, it can be seen that the patient channels his own verbal behavior toward a constricted set of topics and that he has also internalized the technical language of the therapist.

INTERVIEW I

THERAPIST: Well, I understand from our conversation the other day that there are some things bothering you?
PATIENT: You know how it is. You work hard. You're tired. You don't feel good. Everybody gets in a lousy mood now and then. You can't always be smiling. [This content discarded by therapist.]
THERAPIST: [No response—several minutes pass]
PATIENT: You know how it is. I'm mostly just plain tired. [hesitation] **I don't know if I need to see you especially or not.**
THERAPIST: You must be feeling something that makes you feel you need help. [Introduces marked term "feeling"]
PATIENT: I have a lot on my mind. I can't sleep well at night. During the day I'm tired. People get on my nerves. My wife's sister and her husband don't come to visit much anymore. I'm not much of a family man. I'm not much of anything. I'm grouchy. You know what I mean. Sometimes everything you try to do goes wrong.
THERAPIST: How do you **feel** most of the time? [Repetition]
PATIENT: Like I said, I can't sleep. I'm grouchy. I can't do anything

right. Yesterday everything went wrong. [Gives detailed sequence about a series of small accidents involving the loss of his wallet. This content was disregarded by therapist.]
THERAPIST: [No response for several minutes—negative sanction]
PATIENT: Sometimes I think life isn't worth living.
THERAPIST: Do you **feel** that way often? [repetition and refocusing]
PATIENT: Seems to me I **feel** like that a lot of the time.
THERAPIST: What are your **feelings,** then? [extension]
PATIENT: I feel like there's no point in anything.
THERAPIST: Sounds like you're depressed.
PATIENT: I guess you could say that. My wife says I'm nervous.
THERAPIST: Don't let me talk you into anything. Do you actually feel it?
PATIENT: I guess I really do **feel** depressed.
THERAPIST: What does depression **feel** like to you? [extension]
PATIENT: Sort of a heavy **feeling** in my chest. When I try to breathe, it's as though I can't get enough air in. When I wake up at night, I feel like I can't breathe. When I tell my wife about it, she says I'm nervous. She says I shouldn't stay up so late. I guess I have been depressed for a long time.
THERAPIST: How do you **feel** when your wife says you're nervous?
PATIENT: I feel lousier. She's no help. She makes things worse.
THERAPIST: How do you mean she makes things worse?
PATIENT: She's harping about money. Phones her mother three times a day.
THERAPIST: You sound **angry** at your wife. [Introduction of marked form]
PATIENT: I'm not **angry,** just annoyed.
THERAPIST: Why wouldn't you be **angry?**
PATIENT: When I think of being **angry,** I think of hitting someone.
THERAPIST: [No response]
PATIENT: Being angry is like really losing your temper, and I never get like that.
THERAPIST: You say you're anoyed. I wonder if you don't mean **angry?**

INTERVIEW II

[Patient has not spoken for several minutes since being admitted into the therapy room]

THERAPIST: What are you here for?
PATIENT: I don't know what I'm doing here.
THERAPIST: Are you telling me your thoughts or your **feelings?**
PATIENT: You know I don't want to talk about my feelings.

THERAPIST: [No response]
PATIENT: I've been **feeling** lousy all day . . . really **angry.**
THERAPIST: You have been **feeling** angry all day?
PATIENT: Hell, yes, I had a big fight with my wife today.
THERAPIST: You sound pretty angry.
PATIENT: I told her I felt depressed today and she ignored me.
THERAPIST: How did you **feel** when your wife wouldn't pay attention when you tried to tell her that you were depressed?
PATIENT: I think next time she complains I won't pay any attention to her.
THERAPIST: That's not telling me how you feel.
PATIENT: It reminds me of the way my father always ignored it when I would talk about my knee.
THERAPIST: What **feeling** is that?
PATIENT: I'm yelling and nobody hears it.
THERAPIST: Can you find a word for that feeling?
PATIENT: I **feel** helpless. I can't make them **feel** what I'm telling them.
THERAPIST: What did you tell your wife?
PATIENT: I told her not to harrangue at me.
THERAPIST: You didn't tell her you were **depressed.**
PATIENT: We get along okay most of the time, but sometimes she doesn't listen to what I'm saying.
THERAPIST: You didn't tell her you were depressed?
PATIENT: No, I told her to stop harranguing me.
THERAPIST: She didn't understand that you were **depressed?**
PATIENT: It seemed clear to me.
THERAPIST: What else could she have thought you meant?
PATIENT: I guess she thought I was **angry** at her over the money.
THERAPIST: Were you **angry?**
PATIENT: Yes, I stayed out all night . . . came home around ten thirty.
THERAPIST: You were so **angry** you couldn't tell her you were depressed?
PATIENT: No, but I showed her something was wrong. I didn't talk to her all night either. She finally knew something was wrong.
THERAPIST: You were **angry** because she didn't care about your **feelings.**
PATIENT: I let her know it, too.

It can be seen that the therapist attempts to restructure the patient's cognitive patterns through the restructuring and repatterning of his language perceptions. In the therapy relationship, the processes of decoding and encoding are particularly emphasized. The patient begins to become enculturated into the norms of the group when he starts to restructure and restrict his perceptions through high-level alteration in his language patterns. However, in the therapy relationship, the problem is not defined overtly as a linguistic one. The therapist overtly emphasizes emotion, affect, and behavior, while covertly enculturating the patient into new linguistic perception patterns. In effect, however, it appears that the therapist is concerned with many of the same phenomena that are central concerns to sociolinguistics. The difference is partially the difference in levels of abstraction, in pragmatic usage, and in the development of different technical languages.

If language usage as such is not the overt focus of the therapist, what, then, are his methods of communicating its significance? The enculturation process appears to be structured in four primary ways: (1) restriction, (2) repetition, (3) refocusing, and (4) extension.

By "restriction," I mean that the therapist attempts to limit not only the topic emphasis of the patient, but to restrict his pattern and use of language. Even in the seemingly open structure of the process of free association, the patient is encouraged finally to focus his attention rather narrowly. Nonaffective language and content is deemphasized by the analyst. That is, after the patient has finished a monologue, the therapist will emphasize, and in fact, often only reply to a limited portion of the content presented by the speaker. Often, the therapist will allow the patient to finish a monologue and proceed to another before he actively responds to some portion of it. Much of the therapist's language may be viewed simply as a gloss for "continue." The therapist scans the content for particular phrases. These phrases usually relate to different aspects of affect.

The language the therapist uses contains technical terms and phrases that are often foreign to the patient. The patient is encouraged to use these selected words and phrases to express portions of his monologue which the therapist deems significant. The patient is not encouraged to use all portions of the technical language. In reference particularly to significant portions, however, the patient is discouraged from using "public" language.

This restructuring is amplified by the factor of repetition. The therapist generally uses key technical words and phrases to express significant ideas. Although there is individual variation in technique, the consistency of usage of particular words and phrases is apparent. Their number in a given context is pronouncedly finite. Eventually, through imitation, they find their way into the patient's vocabulary.

This is further reinforced by the process of refocusing. While refocusing is generally rather subtle, it may occur in two primary ways. The first has to do with the circumscribing aspect of language itself. The very fact that a question is asked limits the potential responses to some degree.[2] The very factor of asking a question limits the area of focus. In a sense, each time the therapist asks a question, he is structuring the range of the patients reply but cutting off other detail and content. One of the major functions of the therapist is to phrase messages in terms of questions.

A second type of refocusing structures the patient's response more overtly. The therapist, after a patient's monologue, will often restructure the patient's meaning through the process of substituting other words and phrases in the crucial slot. Technical words and phrases are substituted often in crucial portions for public language. For example, the patient will give a long monologue. The therapist will focus on the phrase "He was annoying me [description of the situation]." The therapist will then emphasize, "He was annoying you?" "Yes." "I was angry because [description of the situation]" "You felt hostile because [description of situation highly capsulized]."

It can be seen that this refocusing and selective playback both restricts and subtly restructures the topic and message content. It also introduces the technical language for the crucial sequences. In this way, the patient is being covertly enculturated both into the new language and continued language perception shifts, which effects pronounced change in the patient's language habits at the lexical level. In the above, the therapist has changed the implication of the patient's statement through extension. The patient, by accepting the playback sequence, must now cope with the implications of "hostile" as opposed to "annoyed [plus description of the situation]."

In addition to selective repetition, restriction, and refocusing, the patient is learning new cognitive categories through the selective intrusion of extension. The technical language is crucial for these sequences. The introduction of the technical word in the frame allows acceptance of the slot sequence substitution.

A major factor in the therapy relationship is the parsimonious use of language by the therapist. The therapist does not reply to all statements made by the patient. The stricture on language usage of the therapist is crucial, most overtly because it emphasizes the value to his signals by limiting them.

This data reinforces the idea that the therapy relationship is not constructed on a true dialogue. It is a highly structured situation consisting of

[2] The importance of the way in which questions are formulated, constraining the logical structure of a reply, has been the subject of a longer work by Langer (1942) and has also been widely discussed in relationship to ethnographic studies by Frake (1964a,b), among others.

a number of covertly directive messages from the therapist and a series of monologues by the patient; however, on this point, the paucity of this data is significant, since it is possible that this sample may be too restricted to account for differences in therapy technique. However, it would seem that a one-to-one relationship with respect to the frequency of message interchange would be less effective than the procedure followed in the sample.

This paper has presented only the gross outline of the linguistic enculturation process in the therapy relationship; however, it seems clear that the therapy relationship has as a major function the enculturation of the new patient into new linguistic perceptions and patterns.

If indeed one function of language is to circumscribe the significant and relevant, this aspect is graphically presented in the therapy relationship. Many of the linguistic processes implicit in therapy involve correcting not only faulty behavior patterns, but reconstituting old linguistic patterns and perceptions. As Hymes suggests, language may be a barrier to understanding as well as make thought possible (Hymes 1964, p. xxvii).

The psychotherapy relationship at this level involves the enculturation of the patient into the linguistic as well as behavior norms of the group and, by extension, attempts to make the patient more efficient as a member in other groups.

The therapy situation is a very highly structured and condensed learning situation. The enculturation process of role learning in therapy deals overtly with linguistic reformulations, since the overt purpose of the group is to deal with behavior by reconstituting the communication patterns of one group member. Roles are the basic component units of groups. By "role," I mean simply that "The expectations shared by group members about the behavior associated with some position in a group, no matter who fills the position, are called 'roles'" (Hare, 1962, p. 9). Since the basic function of groups involves communication, it would seem that the enculturation process in small group role learning has a significant linguistic as well as behavioral referent. The therapy relationship is pertinent as a heuristic example of the enculturation linguistic aspect of role learning. In this analysis, this aspect of role behavior was heightened by the formed function of the group and the high degree and type of structuring it evinced as an acting unit.

The therapist uses restriction, repetition, refocusing, and other devices in order to assist the patient in learning to control and direct his use of language. In order to communicate effectively, the patient must develop a theory about what functions particular styles of language usage serve in communication. Where the patient has become sensitized to the subtleties of language usage in one kind of speech act, the task of the therapist is then to convey to him the congruent or incongruent sociolinguistic rules appropriate to another speech act. To a large extent, the process of enculturation requires that the individual learn to use an elaborated code and to extend his use of this code to new domains, or that, in general, he becomes more oriented toward the verbal channel. But at the same time, he must learn to transform information from other channels into verbal messages, or at least to be able to understand the verbal equivalence of a nonverbal message. The development of a linguistic metatheoretical orientation in the patient is particularly important in bridging a cultural discontinuity that exists in certain patients who tend to utilize a restricted code and to ignore a whole range of diverse signals about motivation and intentions sent by speakers of a different cultural orientation.

In a variety of ways, the patient is taught to extend his categorization of speech. The patient is taught to observe the stream of activities that occur around him and to learn to make abstractions about different kinds of speech events, such as discussions, quarrels, negotiations, and persuasive and apologetic behaviors, and to identify the characteristics of each and to interpret social meaning in terms of the communicative relationship.

The patient is shown that certain kinds of feelings (anger, annoyance, helplessness, etc.) have particular kinds of behavioral concommitants both with respect to himself and others. He learns that being angry or being annoyed are two different states that may for some purposes be viewed as constituting members of the same set in virtue of being instances of a category of negative feelings that tend to lead to particular behavior outcomes. Thus, the patient is taught to develop new analytical categories for interpreting the behavior of himself and others and to associate them with behavioral outputs. Meaning is thus extended outward from the individual's own categories of emotion to link up with new analytical categories introduced by the therapist. It is also extended across events and actors to provide a unified system of belief for why different events occur and what they imply about the social relationships among participants. In effect, the patient is taught to manipulate various analytical categories about states of feeling and to generalize them across actors, objects, and events.

In a variety of ways the patient learns to elaborate emotional expressiveness, to extend his ability to make logical abstractions about behavior, and to utilize with greater frequency in dialogue the meaning system that he has or has acquired. The general orientation should also lead to encouraging the speaker to select with greater care among syntactic and stylistic alternatives at his disposal and encourage some differentiation in vocabulary related to the expression of emotion.

A covert goal of the therapy situation is to encourage greater use of an elaborated code in the patient with respect to the sending of messages about emotion and intention. Some of the processes involved in the linguistic transformation of the patient have been described here. The study attempted to explore some of these processes. The result suggests that linguistic variables are related in an important way to the success of therapy. One would expect that sociolinguistic variables are important determinants in the modification of behavior. It is only at some time in the future, when we have taken all relevant sociolinguistic variables into account and applied appropriate measures of them, that we can assess their actual importance. In order to accomplish this in the examination of psychotherapy, it would be necessary to isolate very specifically what sociolinguistic tasks are involved and how and under what conditions they are best mastered by persons from diverse sociocultural backgrounds. The examination of such variables in a natural small group situation primarily serves a heuristic rather than an explanatory or measurement function. However, it is important to isolate the processes that commonly do actually occur in real dyadic relationships.

References

Argyle, Michael
    1973   Introduction, Social Encounters. In *Readings in social interaction* edited by M. Argyle, pp. 9–15. Middlesex, England: Penguin.
Bernstein, Basil
    1961   Aspects of language and learning in the genesis of social process. *Journal of Child Psychology and Psychiatry* **1**, 313–324.
Blumer, Herbert
    1962   Society as symbolic interaction. In *Human Behavior and Social Process*. Boston: Houghton.
Bradford, L. P., J. R. Gibbs and K. D. Benne
    1964   *T-group theory and laboratory method.* New York: Wiley.
Corsini, R. J., M. F. Shaw and R. R. Blake
    1961   *Role playing in business and industry.* Free Press.
Frake, Charles O.
    1964a   How to ask for a drink in Subanun. In *The ethnography of communication* edited by John Gumperz and Dell Hymes. *American Anthropologist* **66**(6), pt. II, 127–132.
    1964b   Notes on queries in ethnography. In *Transcultural studies in cognition* edited by A. Kimball Romney and R. G. D'Andrade. *American Anthropologist* (special publication), **66**(3), pt. II.
Garfinkel, H.
    1972   Remarks on Ethnomethodology. In *Directions in sociolinguistics: the ethnography of communication* edited by John J. Gumperz and Dell Hymes, pp. 301–324. New York: Holt.

Gumperz, John J. and Dell Hymes
   1972   Introduction to The Stylistic Significance of Consonantal Sandhi in Trukese and
          Ponapean. In *Directions in sociolinguistics: The ethnography of communication*
          edited by Gumperz and Hymes. New York: Holt.
Hammel, E. A.
   1964   Culture as an information system. *Kroeber Anthropological Society Papers,*
          No. 31.
Hare, A. Paul
   1962   *Handbook of small group research.* New York: The Free Press of Glencoe.
Hymes, Dell
   1964   General Introduction. In *Language in culture and society.* New York: Harper and
          Row.
Langer, Susanne K.
   1942   *Philosophy in a new key.* New York: Pelican.
Matarazzo, J. D., G. Saslow, A. N. Wiens, M. Weitman, and B. V. Allen
   1964   Interviewer head-nodding and interviewer speech deviations. *Psychotherapy* **1,**
          54–63.
Nadel, S. F.
   1951   *The foundations of social anthropology.* London: Cohen and West.
Schein, E. H. and W. G. Bennis (eds.)
   1965   *Personal and organizational change through group methods.* New York: Wiley.
Verplanck, W. S.
   1955   The Control of the Content of Conversation: Reinforcement of Statements of
          Opinion. *Journal of Abnormal and Social Psychology* **51,** 668–676.
Wight, A. R.
   1969   *Cross-cultural training: a draft handbook.* Center for Research and Education.

Index